Geography
and the
Urban Environment

GEOGRAPHY AND THE URBAN ENVIRONMENT
Progress in Research and Applications

Editors

D. T. HERBERT
Department of Geography, University College of Wales, Swansea

and

R. J. JOHNSTON
Department of Geography, University of Sheffield

Geography
and the
Urban Environment

Progress in Research and Applications

Volume II

Edited by

D. T. HERBERT
Reader in Geography
University College of Wales, Swansea

and

R. J. JOHNSTON
Professor of Geography
University of Sheffield

JOHN WILEY & SONS
Chichester · New York · Brisbane · Toronto

Copyright © 1979, by John Wiley & Sons, Ltd.

Library of Congress Cataloging in Publication Data: (Revised)

Main entry under title:

Geography and the urban environment.

   Includes index.
   1. Cities and towns—Addresses, essays, lectures.
2. Anthropo-geography—Addresses, essays, lectures.
3. City planning—Addresses, essays, lectures.
4. Herbert, David T. II. Johnston, Ronald John.
GF125.G46   301.36   77–13555

ISBN 0 471 99575 4 (v. 1)
ISBN 0 471 99725 0 (v. 2)

Photosetting by Thomson Press (India) Limited, New Delhi and printed and bound in Great Britain by The Pitman Press, Bath.

For
David Aled and Nia Wyn Herbert
and
Chris and Lucy Johnston

List of Contributors

ROBERT J. BENNETT

Department of Geography, University of Cambridge, Downing Place, Cambridge CBZ 3EN, U.K.

MIRIAM J. BOYLE

Department of Geography, de la Salle College of Higher Education, Middleton, North Manchester, U.K.

J. G. BROWETT

Department of Geography, Flinders University, Bedford Park 5042, South Australia.

T. J. D. FAIR

Urban and Regional Studies Unit, University of Witwatersrand, 1 Jan Smuts Avenue, Johannesburg 2001, South Africa

ALAN M. HAY

Department of Geography, The University, Sheffield S10 2TN, U.K.

JOHN R. LAMBERT

Department of Social Administration, University College, Cardiff, P.O. Box 78, Cardiff CF1 1XL, U.K.

RISA PALM

Department of Geography, University of Colorado, Boulder, Colorado 80309, U.S.A.

CHRIS T. PARIS

Centre for Environmental Studies, 62 Chandos Place, London, WC2 4HH, U.K.

MICHAEL E. ROBINSON

School of Geography, The University, Manchester, M13 9PL, U.K.

NIGEL THRIFT

Department of Human Geography, Australian National University, Canberra, ACT 2600, Australia.

Contents

Preface

In this, the second volume in our series, we have been able to collect a range of contributions which reflects our initial aims and objectives. The first three essays fall within a category of contribution which we have previously described as reflecting contemporary changes in the orientation of geographical work and a concern for debate on key ideological, philosophical, and methodological issues. At a time when much recent research is characterized as a reaction against logical positivism and its links with a more 'scientific' human geography, it is important to guard against over-reaction and to consider the merits as well as the disadvantages. Alan Hay argues this brief in a measured and responsible way; his contribution does much to clarify the key philosophical issues in the context of geographical analysis and to suggest some bases for reconciliation among the various viewpoints. This wide-ranging discussion of the philosophical bases of geographical enquiry is followed by a more narrowly focused essay by Bob Bennett on the role of space–time models in research. While geographers have always recognized the importance of incorporating a temporal dimension into their studies, recent work has examined the time–space relationship in an increasingly systematic way. Bob Bennett offers a review of the range of models that have been used to represent urban dynamics and spatial structures, relates these to the effects of policy determination, and discusses research priorities. In the final contribution of this set of three chapters, Miriam Boyle and Mike Robinson provide a sharp contrast in terms of 'style' with Bob Bennett's essay and focus upon some of the key issues surrounding cognitive mapping. They consider ways in which people 'think about the world' using both the separate experiences of perception and memory and their innate and acquired skills. Ways in which geographers have used cognitive maps are critically examined.

The next three contributions in this volume have some common strands which include the mechanisms of the housing market in American and British cities and the polarization of key urban problems, particularly within inner city areas. Risa Palm reviews two of the most influential sets of models which have been used to describe and explain residential land values: the first that households behave in such a way that they maximize their utility, the second that in an American urban context racially defined submarkets distort relationships between price and quality of dwelling space. In an empirical study of the San Francisco Bay Area, these two models are found to provide only a partial explanation, and the roles of institutions—particularly the mortgage lenders and real estate agents—are identified as key additional variables. Nigel Thrift directs our attention to the problems of the inner city, particularly those of unemployment, and provides an example of our policy of publishing lengthy—almost 'monograph-type' —contributions on key issues or pieces of empirical research. This is essentially a review article upon the recent British experience of inner city decline, but central questions of policy and conceptualization are kept to the forefront in a discussion which has general relevance to urban problems. A close link with inner city problems is maintained by the essay by Chris Paris and John Lambert on Birmingham, England. Here the focus upon one city as a case study allows much more detail on local decision-making and its societal contexts to be elaborated. The main thrust of the essay is a concern with housing and housing policy and its impact both in the inner city and in the wider 'metropolitan' area.

The final essay in this volume provides a shift in a scale and in cultural context as Denis Fair and John Browett provide a scholarly and objective account of the emergence of the South African urban system. In particular, the extent to which the evolution of urbanization in South Africa has been the history of the 'development' of some elements of the social system and the 'under-development' of others, is discussed.

Our task in producing this second volume of the series has been made easier by our contributors who have met our deadlines and responded to our requests in an amicable and professional manner. Our back-up services have been excellent and we might in this volume particularly mention Guy Lewis and Alan Cutliffe at Swansea, through whose capable cartographic and photographic services all our illustrative material is processed. We would also thank our secretaries, and Ann Barham for an excellent index. Our editorial board has continued to respond in a positive way—to all, our thanks. Two apologies for Volume I are appropriate. First, to Leonard Guelke for placing him at the wrong institution; he is, of course, at the University of Waterloo, Ontario. Second, to Alan Gilbert and Peter Ward for leaving their chapter with a disproportionate share of typographical errors—we shall increase our vigilance.

D. T. Herbert
R. J. Johnston

Chapter 1

Positivism in Human Geography: Response to Critics

Alan M. Hay

The adoption of the epistemology and methodologies of the natural sciences as a model for the development of the social sciences has a long, not always honourable, history. The episode with which this essay is concerned occurred in geography in the 1950s and 1960s. Geographers reacted against descriptive accounts of the social and natural world, claiming that such analyses were too 'subjective'; at a later stage it became in some cases a rejection also of the inductive method (let the facts speak) in favour of the deductive method. In the deductive method there was a tendency to adopt formal languages (especially mathematics) to develop argument and to adopt statistical methods in the testing of conclusions. Neither of these was the only tool logically appropriate.

It was also hoped that the adoption of these methods would allow the subject to become more useful and thus to attract greater esteem in the corridors of power and in the market place. The success of this programme can be gauged from the enormous volume of published work which explicitly reflected the new epistemology (in contrast to much geographic methodology, including those alternatives discussed below, which attracts more expositors than practitioners). The success, however, stimulated a counter-critique in the later 1960s and 1970s, and it is with the issues raised by that critique that this essay is concerned.

In this essay, therefore, an attempt is made to evaluate the 'scientific' position adopted by many geographers in the 1960s in the light of a number of critiques which have been launched both from the stance of structuralism (especially the structuralism of Levi-Strauss and Piaget) and from the stance of subjectivism (whether stemming from the phenomenology of Husserl or from the idealism of Collingwood). The chapter falls into three main sections. In the first an attempt is made to clarify certain issues which have been confused both by the quantitative–theoretical school and by their critics. In the second section the main thrust of subjectivist thought is identified and its relevance assessed; the third section is focused upon structuralism. In the conclusion the extent to which these viewpoints may be reconciled in geographic studies is suggested, with specific reference to the work of Habermas.

The essay is written from the viewpoint of a mild Popperian, but one who has

1

recently felt an increasing sympathy for the arguments put forward by the Frankfurt school of social criticism. These loyalties undoubtedly affect the author's judgement of some work referred to below, but perhaps a knowledge of the author's bias will enable some readers to discount that bias and may encourage them to investigate their own.

THE CRITIQUE OF 'POSITIVISM' EXAMINED

It must first be noted that there is a tendency to brand all 'scientific' epistemologies as 'positivist'. This tendency clearly fails to recognize the wide variety of views held in scientific epistemology. Nevertheless, the corrupt usage of 'positivism' is accepted as a convenient and widely accepted umbrella term to describe the philosophies and methodologies of normal science (Kuhn, 1962), especially as they have been applied to social science (Hempel, 1962; Rudner, 1966). To use the term in this way is not to accept the confusion between positivism as derived from Comte, the logical positivism associated with the Vienna circle, and the other realist–scientific epistemologies (e.g. that of Popper) which have been seriously proposed and retain substantial support. It may also be noted that some authors use a slightly different umbrella term; for example, Eliot Hurst (1973) speaks of 'logical empiricism' and Guelke (1971) writes of 'neo-positivism', but investigation of the context makes it clear that their target is the same—the paradigms of normal science.

The main lines of the anti-positivist critique in geography vary according to the loyalties of the critic, but they may be summarized as follows:

1. That positivism has resulted in the abandonment by human geography of important intuitive concepts because these concepts fail to meet the positivist criteria of meaning. Alternatively, attempts to bring such concepts within a positivist operational definition have resulted in their devaluation and trivialization.
2. As a rider to (1), that positivism promotes the reification of human beings. Treating them 'as if they were' things for the purpose of theory overflows into other areas of thought and becomes doubly dangerous when used in application of the theory (for example in urban planning).
3. That positivism is 'reductionist' and/or 'atomistic': reductionist in that it assumes that the whole system is no more than the aggregate of individual elements, atomistic in the sense that attempts are made to explain elements without reference to the system itself.
4. As a corollary to (1) and (3), that positivism wrongly believes that its methods, and hence its conclusions, are free of ideological bias, whereas in reality its methods, assumptions, and findings reflect the assumptions of society (some would say the assumptions of the individual research worker, but that is a weaker case to argue). For this reason its conclusions are uncritical of the *status quo* and its findings lend themselves to the preservation of the injustice and suffering present in the *status quo*.

Each of these points will be elaborated in later sections under the main headings of *subjectivism* and *structuralism*, but before examining these schools of thought it is useful to clarify five issues which lie at the heart of the debate: the criteria of meaning, the question of normative theory, the extent to which positivists claim the existence of laws in history, the role of prediction, and incompleteness in explanation.

The criteria for meaningfulness

An important first point in any such argument is the question of demarcation. There are in fact three questions of demarcation: that between *meaningful* and *meaningless* statements, that between *scientific* and *unscientific* statements, and that between *true* and *untrue* statements. The first point is elegantly noted by Hamlyn (1970, p. 61) who quotes Wittgenstein's remark (in *Tractatus Logicus Philosophicus*) 'to understand a proposition is to know what it is like for it to be true': but,

> In that context it may be relevant to exclude certain statements from the language of science, on the grounds that they do no useful scientific work, or that they are empty of scientific content. Even so it is a further and much larger step to the view that such statements are meaningless. . . . Karl Popper did not do this, preferring to take falsifiability (the converse of verifiability) as providing a line of demarcation between scientific and non-scientific, not between meaningful and meaningless.

The same confusion may be implicit in the more dramatic claims made by enthusiasts of the quantitative revolution in geographic studies.

An example of this unjustified extension of the idea in the geographical literature is provided by Eliot Hurst (Hurst, 1973, p. 43), who characterizes all scientific approaches as follows:

> At the core of logical empiricism lies the principle of verifiability . . . thus to have any meaning a proposition must be such that either it is true by definition or that some possible sense experience would be relevant to the determination of its truth. By such a criterion propositions such as 'I exist' would be meaningless.

In this passage Eliot Hurst presents a caricature of the extreme positivist position as being the only scientific position (verification is equated with meaning) and alleges, incorrectly, that 'I exist' would not be accepted as meaningful by these criteria. In a similar manner Walmsley (1974, p. 102) argues: 'Operational definitions have been a problem to geographers for a long time [this may or may not be true]: indeed they constitute one aspect of the larger twentieth century philosophical problem of operationalism whereby a statement is either verifiable or meaningless.' Here Walmsley makes a jump from the operationalist position (associated with Bridgman) that for a statement to be *scientific* it must be specified how the relevant concepts are to be measured, to the myth that for a statement to be meaningful it must be so defined.

It is preferable to retain the Popperian distinction between *scientific* and *metaphysical* statements: a point of view supported, for example, by Robinson (1962). In such a distinction phrases like 'I exist' and 'all men are equal' are not dismissed as meaningless although they may be excluded from scientific dialogue.

Positivism and normative theory

It is clearly true that many of the geographers who supported the quantitative revolution of the 1960s drew heavily upon the concept of economic man and upon the comparatively well-developed economic theory in an attempt to derive spatial theory. For this reason many recent writers have tended to assume that positivism and economic man are necessarily parts of the same approach (e.g. Mercer and Powell, 1972, pp. 48–49). This is, however, a mistaken assumption. It is notable, for example, that Haggett (1965, pp. 161–169) introduced several of the basic location theory models as movement-minimization or least-effort models (see also Zipf, 1949) and models of agricultural location can be expressed in terms of food maximization and survival. To abandon the concept of economic man for a man who seeks to maximize votes, power, food, or *Lebensraum* is not necessarily to abandon a positivist stance, it may be merely to change the type of variables considered. Indeed it may be argued from the positivist viewpoint that the 'predictions' of location theory showed so large a margin of error (cp. Wolpert, 1964) that it was high time that quite different models of man were adopted in geographic theory. One is forced to conclude that many recent anti-positivist papers when stripped of their rhetoric do in fact fall into this neo-positivist category.

Closely linked to this is the assertion that many early quantifiers were using normative theory. This is clearly true of Losch: 'It must not, of course, be expected that we shall now consider all the factors thus far neglected in order to derive a theory that fits reality . . .' (Losch, 1954, p. 138) and in his often quoted comment that the question becomes 'whether reality is rational' (Losch, 1954, p. 363). This normative stance is echoed in some discussions of other location theorists even though the original author may have been opposed to it. Another intrusion of normative theory into geography occurred with the introduction to geography of spatial allocation models including linear programming.

The critical argument for this context is that no theory can fairly be criticized at the same time as being both normative and positive; the two approaches are mutually exclusive: 'Positive statements concern what *was, is, or will be* and normative statements concern *what ought to be*' (Lipsey, 1963, p. 5). Two glosses can be added to this distinction: first, it is not of course unknown either for the positive to masquerade as the normative or vice versa; and second, as Lipsey himself (1963, p. 5) notes, 'most apparently normative statements reveal some positive underpinning'.

Positivism and historical explanation

One of the most common characterizations of positivistic geography asserts that it attempts to establish general laws and claims that such a nomothetic approach is bound to fail. In justification of this view reference is often made to the failure of those historical methods which have sought to lay down such laws (Guelke, 1971). This claim raises three distinct questions: (1) Is it possible to have a positivistic history or geography which does not attempt to bring all phenomena under law-like statements? (2) Is prediction a necessary part of a geography which has a scientific epistemology? (3) To what extent is it permissible to use incomplete or simplified explanations in accounts of geographical phenomena? The first of these questions is addressed in this section; the second and third appear in succeeding sections.

First it must be stressed that 'positivistic philosophers' have been among the foremost to reject the belief that historical laws can be derived, and their arguments (e.g. Popper, 1959) can be extended to geographical studies. Popper argues that in historical studies the main aim is 'the hypothetical reconstruction of a historical problem situation' (Popper, 1972, p. 170). Such an explanation includes an identification of the *problem situation* (practical or political) which the individual or group was trying to solve, the identification of the *decisive* elements in that situation, and an explication of why the historical action was adequate to the situation. Such an approach is capable of falsification (further research may prove that the problem situation was incorrectly or incompletely defined). In such a way it may therefore be possible to speak of an objective and logical analysis of human behaviour which is in no sense nomological.

The role of prediction in the social sciences

The role of prediction is often used by non-scientists, and indeed by scientists themselves, as a hallmark of the scientific approach. This is based upon an alleged logical isomorphism between explanation and prediction. This point is taken up by several critics of the positivist tradition in geography (e.g. Guelke, 1971; Mercer and Powell, 1972, p. 48) and other social sciences (Smart, 1976, p. 77). There is, however, a substantial body of argument which suggests that prediction is not after all an essential part of the methodology of science, so much so that Torrance (1971, p. 8) concludes pungently, 'it is thus quite wrong headed to make prediction the hallmark of all true science'.

First, it is important to distinguish between those experiments where *prediction in time* is of the essence of an activity and those where prediction is from the *known to the unknown*, and for which prediction in time is a common and therefore useful form in which prior knowledge has been excluded. These two forms of prediction can be characterized as *prediction as prophecy* and *prediction as testing*. A confusion of the two forms has led to the assumption that to speak of the predictive power of a theory is to describe its potential use to governments and others in an attempt to foresee the future.

In scientific thought, prediction is valued as a form of testing. That it need have no element of prophecy is clear in the use of 'postdiction' by Kansky (1963) and Morrill (1965). Similarly, there is the archaeological application of geographic theory by Tobler and Wineburg (1971) and others who use theory to predict the location of sites whose existence was known (for example as place names), but whose actual locations have been lost in the intervening centuries.

Another example of *prediction as testing* is prediction from the known to the unknown, the use of a theory to explain phenomena which the theory was not originally designed to cover. This has some importance for positivist geography because many of the so-called tests of location theory are performed using cases closely similar to the phenomena which the theory was originally intended to explain (central place theory is a pre-eminent example of this). Far more demanding is the test of a theory in an entirely novel context, as for example the use of location theory to explain the existence of periodic markets in West Africa.

A similar distinction between prediction and prophecy appears in Popper (1972, p. 339). He makes two main points: first, that 'ordinary predictions in science are conditional' and only 'apply to systems which can be described as well isolated, stationary, and recurrent. These systems are very rare in nature and society is surely not one of them'. Secondly, he admits that there is an applied role for prediction in the social sciences, not as prophecy but as stating the unintended social repercussions of intentional human actions. In some cases these may allow the formulation of rules which state what, in a given system, may or may not be achieved. He gives as an example (though not he insists beyond dispute): 'You cannot have full employment without inflation.' (Clearly, in a technological rule of this kind there are unstated conditional circumstances; the whole question of such unspecified conditions will be in part the subject of the next section.)

Once again it must be noted that although the logical basis of prediction in the social sciences relates to prediction as testing, some geographers (whether as academics or as advisers to decision-makers) have adopted a role which is close to prediction as prophecy (Hall, 1969; Chisholm, 1963), although the detailed wording of their prophecies may have adopted the guise of conditional prediction by using phrases such as 'if the system continues to follow . . .'.

Incompleteness in explanation

A number of authors resist the explanations offered by geographers of the quantitative–theoretical school on the grounds that such explanations represent simplistically systems which are known to be complex, and that they represent mechanistically systems which are known to involve human beings. In some cases this is, without doubt, a legitimate complaint, a response to a culpable refusal on the part of the positivist geographers to consider all the facts in an explanation. But such simplifications or incompleteness in explanation may have a more defensible position, particularly if they represent the type of explanation which Hempel terms elliptical.

Elliptical explanation is characterized by the omission of 'certain laws or particular facts which it tacitly takes for granted, and whose explicit citation would yield a complete deductive nomological argument' (Hempel, 1962, p. 15). This type of explanation is not peculiar to the natural sciences. It is for example a recognized simplification of much historical writing: most historians admit that decapitation leads to death; they do not find it necessary to introduce medical reasoning or indeed common-sense reasoning that links the two events so closely.

In the quantitative–theoretical schools of geography elliptical arguments often appear in the form of *models*, although the fact that these are elliptical arguments may not be recognized by those who use them. In a reduced model the complete set of relationships between elements in a system is simplified by the omission of certain elements and relationships. Consider the systems described in Figure 1.1(a), where G is the event to be explained. The complete explanation involves all the elements A–F and their relationships, but in testing or investigating the system the model may be simplified to the forms shown in Figure 1.1(b). Such a reduced explanation thus involves the search for basic causes and deflects attention from certain parts of the causal chain, but in so doing it raises certain problems.

First, the complex of relationships lying between A, B, and C on the one hand and G on the other may not be really fully understood. In such a case the reduced model is in reality a black box and the reduction has been used to conceal

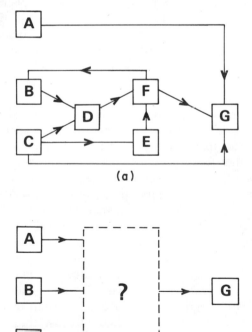

(a)

(b)

FIGURE 1.1. Systems of explanation: (a) complete explanation; (b) reduced explanation

ignorance. Secondly, the intervening relationships of the complete model may themselves reflect normative assumptions; in such a case the reduction may serve to conceal, even from the investigator, the extent to which his whole conception is normative. Thirdly, there may be elements in the reduced part of the model which are tacitly assumed by the investigator to be immutable and thus reducible when in reality he has identified only one of several possible forms. This leads to the mistaken application of the reduced model which has been tested in one context being applied to another context where it is not longer valid; it can also lead to an overlooking of fundamental or structural changes in the system (i.e. in the D, E, F area). Finally, it may lead to the assumption that a given set of inputs A, B, C can only yield one configuration of G (true if D, E, F are in a given relation, but not universally true); in this way the reduced-form model may become a fallacious demonstration of the inevitability of the *status quo*.

Another category identified by Hempel is that of partial explanation. His argument here hinges on the fact that many events can be seen as specific instances of much broader categories. For example the Longbridge (Birmingham) plant of British Leyland is a specific instance of a broader category of car manufacturing plants which is in term a subcategory of industrial plants in general. Now an explanation which fully and completely explains why the Longbridge site is in *industrial use* does not necessarily explain why it is used for car manufacture or why it is used by British Leyland: the explanation is incomplete. The question arises as to how serious such incompleteness is: in part this must be a value judgement but it also depends upon how complete the explanation claims to be.

Both these types of explanation have a tendency to ignore the human element. In elliptically reduced explanations the elements most commonly reduced are human beings in their roles as decision-makers and agents. Similarly, in a partial explanation the specific character of an event (usually its personal character) is ignored and the explanation focuses upon its general character. For some research workers, therefore, these methods will persistently fail to answer the questions which are for them of central interest.

On the other hand some authors appear not only to reject such elliptical explanation when it excludes the human element but also to insist that the human element is always of critical importance in the causal chain. Mercer and Powell (1972, p. 41) write: 'if all these [past] geographies were to a large degree the products of decisions made by living people then any reasonable account must surely attempt to reconstruct contemporary images'. In quite a different context, both Steed (1971) and Watts (1974) argue that if the industrial geographical patterns are to a large degree the products of decisions made by boardroom decision-makers then any reasonable account must elucidate these decision processes.

Incompleteness and verification

The question of incompleteness in explanation is posed in a different form by Guelke (1978), when he claims that scientific geographers have failed to accept their own criteria of falsifiability—and have persisted in pretending that theories (especially location theories with an economic basis) are true despite their manifest failure to match reality—and that the failure is thinly disguised by *ad hoc* adjustments.

Three comments are in order here. First, there is once again the internal contradiction of an anti-positivist appealing to a positivist tenet (falsification/verification) as a ground for rejecting positivist theory. On the other hand, if the critique is just, the positivist geographers are themselves perpetrators of the contradiction. Secondly, it may be noted that the history of science records many theories which in their crude original form were forced to admit exceptions and *ad hoc* adjustment but which were, nevertheless, both an advance on previous understanding and a stepping stone towards a better understanding. (Ptolemaic astronomy was clearly a scientific subject of this kind. The retention of the theory and the elucidation of its shortcomings was a step in preparation for the Copernican revolution.) The willingness to stay with a scientific geography may—one cannot say will—prove to be a similar stepping stone in geographic thought. Thirdly, and this links back to Popper's comment on prediction, the nature of the field sciences (not only in the social sciences but also in geology and botany, for example) is such that even if laws do exist (such as a plant physiologist may verify in a laboratory) they will not constitute the total explanation of the phenomena observed in the field. This is where the insistence on the geometry of location theory (as underlined by Bunge, 1966 and Haggett, 1965) is unfortunate: it may of course have been a pedagogic device, but it serves to obscure the main contributions of location theory to the types of decision-making process (e.g. land-use competition).

It is therefore argued that the question to be asked of a geographic theory is not 'does this theory *totally* explain the observed variation?' but the more modest question, 'does this theory contribute an explanation of a part of the observed variation which would otherwise remain obscure?' If the claims of location theory are couched in these terms the critique ceases to be important.

THE APPEAL TO SUBJECTIVISM

The appeal to subjectivism is probably more united in its opposition to objectivism than in its own counter-proposals. For that reason this section begins with an account of the reasons (some good, some bad) for rejecting objectivism to which most subjectivists would subscribe in whole or in part. (Whether these are the real reasons for their allegiance to subjectivism or whether the reasons lie in a deeper area of intellectual crisis (Reich, 1970; Roszak, 1971) is beyond the scope of this essay, although it can be noted that some recent geographical converts to subjectivism (e.g. Wolforth, 1976) appear to be welcoming the emergence of a philosophical *post hoc* rationalization of their own prior rejection of the quantitative–theoretical movement in human geography.) After this review of the subjectivist critique two main strands of subjectivist thought are examined under the titles 'idealism' and 'phenomenology'.

The attack on objectivism

The attack on objectivism has four components; two are neatly summarized by Marchand (1974, p. 18): 'Classical science assumed it was possible to look at things from the outside, and to study them without altering them and without letting the scientist's personality interfere. Modern physics has shown the first to be false, while modern social science does not believe that the second holds anymore.' There are, however, two additional lines of attack. The third, sometimes called *mentalism*, asserts that 'all that the objectivist can learn . . . are the external, overt features of actions. Their internal aspects, the motives, intentions and reflections, by which overt behaviour is understood as meaningful human action delude him entirely' (Brodbeck, 1963, p. 311). The fourth criticism is allied to this; it claims that to view human beings objectively is to treat them as objects, thus promoting reification and alienation. These four views may be discussed separately, although there is inevitably a degree of overlap in the discussion.

The presence of observed–observer interaction does indeed provide a challenge to the objectivist programme. Marchand is of course a little sweeping; although modern physics has asserted that such interaction is always present it does not assert that it will always determine the outcome of an experiment, but clearly in the social sciences the presence of an observer in a community may itself lead to a change in behaviour and thus mislead the observer in his interpretation of what is the usual (not observed) behaviour. It is, however, only an acute problem for the objectivist programme if the disturbance of 'usual behaviour' is unique to that individual observer—so unique and so important as to destroy any possibility that independent observers will be able to agree on what they have observed. A highly unsatisfactory version of this argument is put forward by Mercer and Powell (1972) in their discussion of interview and questionnaire surveys. They recall some clear instances of inaccuracy and bias in interview surveys and conclude that this invalidates the objectivist programme. But such an argument is itself based on objectivist reasoning (comparison of the interview data with some more 'real' evidence).

The second argument is that however value free the logics and methods of a research worker appear to him, he carries with him a social and political background which determines the problems which he seeks to solve, the type of theories with which he attempts their solution, and the interpretation of his results. In his own society this means that the objectivist is incapable of discerning the root causes (because he mistakenly takes them as given universals) and is consequently incapable of a radical critique. In an alien society his unrecognized ideological bias imposes on that society implicit conceptual frameworks which may be totally inappropriate and may lead to decisions which are destructive of the society which he seeks to study (Slater, 1975).

There are several partial answers to this element in the critique. Some authors seek to see the answer in the concept of intersubjectivity, that is to argue that objective knowledge implies the existence of a consensus: 'the objectivity of science arises not because the individual is impartial, but because many individuals are continually testing each other's theories' (Robinson, 1962, p. 23). (At this point it must be noted that the word 'intersubjectivity' is used in two senses: to cover the comparison of the subjective experiences of many observers (inter-observer subjectivity) and to describe the observer–subject relationship which is recommended by Marchand, 1974; this distinction is explored by Skjervheim, 1974.) This argument appears to have some relevance to geographic studies; if scholars from many different cultural backgrounds arrive at similar conclusions about a phenomenon and its causes it would seem reasonable to accept their consensus. What the argument totally fails to cover is the situation (which is logically possible) in which scholars from such different cultures not only radically disagree in their interpretation, they may not even agree on what conditions must be met to establish truth: 'the great difficulty in the social sciences . . . of applying scientific method is that we have not yet established an agreed standard for the disproof of an hypothesis' (Robinson, 1962, p. 22).

The mentalist position certainly dates back as far as Weber. As Brodbeck (1963) has shown, much of the argument arises from a confusion in the use of two words, 'meaning' and 'understand'. An example may help to illustrate the mentalist case: two instances of the purchase of a house will have many features in common (legal and financial arrangements, for example). But the intention or reason for purchase may be very different when we investigate the motives of the purchasers: purchase as an investment or speculation will be very different in intent to purchase for personal residence. As Harvey (1973) has so cogently argued, to treat these two purchases as identical is to confound use value and exchange value. The question which remains is: will there be no externally observable evidence by which the superficially similar actions may be distinguished? Brodbeck (1963, p. 317), in the most effective examination of the mentalist position, argues 'the investigator may of course make mistakes. But the mistakes will reveal themselves by failure of the predictions that he makes. . . .' In this example an erroneous interpretation that both purchases have the same meaning or intention will presumably be exposed by an examination of the owners' future behaviours (the one selling out as soon as the speculative gamble pays off, the second refusing to surrender his home even when threatened by compulsory eviction).

Another form of the same argument may, as Brodbeck argues, arise from the confusion over 'understand', for which it is possible to identify five common uses, and among these there is a sense in which no white middle-class, middle-aged urban geographer can claim truly to understand the situation of the black, immigrant, teenage ghetto dweller. Rudner (1966, p. 83) argues that this is a form of the 'reproductive fallacy': 'the claim that the only understanding appropriate to social science is one that consists of a reproduction of the states of affairs being studied, is logically the same as the claim that the only understanding appropriate to the investigation of tornados is that gained in the direct experience of tornados'.

The final argument seems, at least in some authors, to develop from the similarity of the word 'objective' to 'object'. This confusion is unfortunate, especially as it reinforces the tendency (already explored in earlier pages) for the human experience to be the element which is 'reduced', omitted, or bypassed in scientific approaches. It is sufficient to note here that the complete identification of objectivity with objectification is a verbal confusion, and although objectivity may often be accompanied by a culpable degree of objectification this association is not logically inevitable.

The idealist alternative

The idealist position is probably the most easily grasped of the 'new' philosophies for geography. There are three reasons for this. First, a quasi-idealist practice has probably been current in geography for many years, even when the rationale behind it was unstated or partly understood (e.g. Brown, 1938). Secondly, idealism has had cogent exponents in history (Collingwood, 1946; Dray, 1964;) and this literature was well known to *some* historical geographers. Thirdly (perhaps as a consequence of the first two), it has a longer history of explicit reference in geographic thought (e.g. Guelke, 1978; Harris, 1971; Harvey, 1969; Lowther, 1959, although not all these are sympathetic).

'The core of the idealist position is that the explanation of rational human behaviour demands a mode of understanding quite different from that which is appropriate to non-rational human and non-human phenomena', and 'The idealist maintains that a rational action is explained when the thought behind it has been understood. In the idealist view human geography derives its autonomy as a field of geographic enquiry from the fact that it is largely concerned with rational actions and products of human minds' (both quotations from Guelke, 1974, p. 193). In order to identify causes one must therefore identify 'the intention of the agent in the action to be explained' *and* identify the theoretical ideas that were employed by that agent in deciding upon his action. A first major problem in this programme for geography is that clearly geographers (unlike political historians) are more often concerned with situations resulting from a multitude of decision-makers (thousands of peasant farmers, thousands of shoppers) than with the results of a single person's decisions (Napoleon, Julius Caesar, and Christopher Columbus are popular idealist examples). This clearly forces the idealist back to the common aspirations of those individuals and the common theoretical view which they held, a revised programme with which Guelke agrees (Guelke, 1974, p. 201). Once this has been determined as a research strategy, the position appears to be approaching that of a behaviouralist (e.g. Pred, 1967) with the insistence on the goals and information of the decision-makers. Not only does it approach the position of behaviouralism, but in moving from the idealism of studying the individual to the idealism of studying the group by extrapolation there is no logical barrier to the much wider extrapolation to all human beings and the distinction between idealism and 'positivist' approaches is lost. Finally, it may be noted that Popper (1972, Chap. 4) sees the type of idealist explanation adopted by Collingwood as being no more than a special case of knowledge as problem-solving in the realm of objective knowledge, an argument which Guelke (1978) accepts.

But in addition to these ambiguities in the idealist position there are two major shortcomings in its application to geography. The first is best illustrated by Guelke's own example, 'Why did Columbus discover America?' (Answer: 'Because he was trying to reach China, which according to his theory could be achieved by sailing westward'.) What Guelke omits from his explicit account is the piece of 'objective knowledge' which completes the jigsaw 'and it is a fact that if you sail westwards from Europe you hit America before you reach China'. In a more complex problem the decision-makers similarly stumble upon aspects of objective reality, and the task of geography is to explain not only their decisions but the realities upon which their intentions become grounded. For example, a shopkeeper who seeks to set up shop with given goods for sale at a location has an intention and maybe a theory of the world, but he may stumble upon a formerly unrecognized reality that whatever pricing/sales policy he adopts he cannot make sales cover the costs of the operation.

A second argument which the idealists fail to rebut is that it appears that at least some parts of human behaviour are irrational to the extent that they reflect unconscious (or subconscious) intentions and theories about the world. It might therefore be that the behaviour of individuals (or of the groups) is not totally explained by their expressed intentions and theories. If, for example, there is a systematic but unconscious bias in the way people 'see' the city their declared intentions and decision-making criteria may yet be a false (or incomplete at best) explanation of their travel patterns. This argument becomes even more acute when the decision-makers are inaccessible to questioning or, as in historical studies, have left scanty record of their intentions and their theories. In such cases not only the unconscious but some of what to them was conscious is inaccessible to the researcher and can at best be inferred by studies of the resulting spatial pattern. (The question of 'real' but unrecognized elements in the way a system works is faced more directly by phenomenology and structuralism; see below.)

This problem can lead to another charge against idealists, that they are essentially reductionist in that they define the human individual as 'the fundamental particle' and fail to accept that communities, tribes, and societies may themselves have an ontological status which is more than the aggregation of individuals' motives and intentions. It is probably for this reason that some regional and urban geographers are strongly anti-positivist yet find the idealist alternative unacceptable.

The phenomenological alternative

Phenomenology as a subjectivist philosophy is derived mainly from the work of Husserl. The stimulus which he gave to European thought can be traced in writers as divergent as Heidegger and Sartre on the one hand and Merleau-Ponty on the other. For this essay the main focus is upon mainstream phenomenological thought developed from Husserl through Schutz (see Thevenaz, 1962, and

Paci, 1972). It is a delightful irony for geography that a main focus of phenomenological work in the English-speaking world is Northwestern University! Geographers who subscribe to subjectivist positions are extremely eclectic in their citation of phenomenologists and it is therefore difficult to place them squarely in any phenomenological tradition. Relph (1976), for example, appears to adopt an existentialist stand, quoting approvingly from Heidegger, Sartre, and Merleau-Ponty. Finally, it is worth-while to note that once again some of the phenomenologists follow Husserl by arguing that their epistemology applies to all forms of knowledge (including the natural sciences), but many of those who call themselves phenomenologists—geographers among them—are more modest in their programme and speak only of its claim in the field of human and social sciences.

Furthermore, there is a distinction between those who see phenomenology as the sole method of analysis (Merleau-Ponty, 1962, p. xix, 'Intention is the source and final test of knowledge') and those who see it as one of a number of complementary methodologies. At least part of the reason for Relph's adverse reaction to Yi-Fu Tuan appears to be due to the latter's less exclusive claims for the phenomenological method (Relph, Yi-Fu Tuan, and Buttimer, 1977).

A brief definition of phenomenology is seldom attempted by philosophical phenomenologists (see Thevenaz) but three geographical publications are indicative:

Phenomenology is descriptive and non-empirical in the sense that . . . it seeks to reveal the essences or meanings of phenomena—particularly of experiences such as thoughts, emotions, or sense perceptions—through 'pure description', in order to gain some understanding of the world as intentional or meaningful to man. (Mercer and Powell, 1972, p. 13).

Although there is a considerable disagreement about the exact nature of this philosophy most phenomenologists seem to agree on at least three basic issues: first the importance of man's 'lived world' of experience; second an opposition to the 'dictatorship and absolutism' of scientific thought over other forms of thinking; and third an attempt to formulate some alternative method of investigation to that of hypothesis testing and the development of theory. (Relph, 1970, p. 193).

The approach is phenomenological: for my purpose I take this term to mean a philosophical perspective, one which suspends, in so far as this is possible, the presuppositions and methods of official science in order to describe the world of intentionality and meaning (Yi-Fu Tuan, 1971, p. 181).

A key summary word in many phenomenological accounts is the German word '*verstehen*'.

Expressed in this way phenomenology can be seen, first, as a reaction to the shortcomings of the positivist position and only secondly as offering an alternative methodology. In contrast to idealism it appears to recognize more fully the fact that not all the springs of human action are conscious; according to

Smart (1976, p. 82), for example, the phenomenological sociologist 'attempts to make explicit to consciousness that which is latent in every day life'. In most phenomenological writing, however, it is difficult to reject a similar charge of reductionism for most phenomenological accounts of the social sciences focus upon studies of the individual without allowing for the possibility that communities, nations and indeed the whole world order have an ontological status which justifies their analysis at that level of aggregation.

Although it is difficult to rebut this charge, and some of the phenomenological geographers tend to evade it by using man in the singular-collective as the subject of their discussion, some sociologists following Schutz have attempted to argue that phenomenology does not restrict itself to micro-study (Wagner, 1973), a line of reasoning extended to geography by Mercer and Powell (1972, p. 20) when they quote Schutz:

> *Verstehen* is by no means concerned solely with seeking to understand the actions of individuals. Its aim, rather, is to construct explanations of the behaviour of ideal-typical actors in particular situations. Schutz has argued that 'it is not even necessary to reduce human acts to a more or less well known individual actor. To understand them it is sufficient to find typical motives of typical actors which explain the act as a typical one arising out of a typical situation.

If the concept of *verstehen* is extended beyond the individual or ideal individual to the community or some other grouping of individuals it immediately appears to have new geographic relevance. For the concept of man and the natural world as it has meaning to him is clearly linked to a number of classical positions in geography. On one hand there is the work of Kirk (1963) who sought to transcend the man/nature dichotomy with his concepts of phenomenal and behavioural environments. The ideas clearly find an echo, too, in the work of Yi-Fu Tuan, who also rejects the man/world dichotomy in favour of a man-in-his-world focus in which all natural phenomena (for example the hydrological cycle) and spatial relationships (front/back, core/periphery) are defined from the viewpoint of the men who are involved in that world. The most explicit attempt to synthesize 'regional personality' or the 'objectivized spirit of the cultural landscape' is an example of 'a reflexive interpretation' of the world in an 'essentialistic' manner. Such an approach may also prove convergent with Hartshorne's (1959) definition of geography as 'orderly accurate and rational description and interpretation' of 'the earth as the home of man'. Clearly, too, it finds a sympathetic chord in Harris's (1971) plea for an imaginative geographic synthesis to parallel the historical synthesis advocated by the historiographer, Mink.

The first problem which these authors fail to answer is that of verification. In such pure description of the world as meaningful to man there will inevitably be differences of interpretation. Some authors accept this:

> It is indeed questionable whether any two phenomenologists can ever have

exactly the same 'intuitions' of the same phenomenon, or indeed know whether or not they have the same intuitions. It is not possible to prove anything by the phenomenological method, and since it appeals ultimately to intuition and not to the logic of language argument is impossible. (Mercer and Powell, 1972, p. 14)

Such inability to verify or even to communicate seems to place phenomenology in opposition not only to the academic enterprise but also to the tenets of everyday life itself.

A second and similar problem is highlighted by Yi-Fu Tuan's phrase: 'a philosophical perspective which suspends, in so far as this is possible, the methods and presuppositions of official science . . .'. If the methods and presuppositions of official science are indeed wholly alien to the rest of human experience such a demand is both acceptable and capable of being met. But to claim this is an assumption; many realist philosophers argue, not without justification, that the types of knowledge-attaining process made explicit in scientific epistemology are themselves latent in much of everyday life. Similarly, many scientists who practise such an epistemological method do so instinctively and are rather surprised by the codification of their practice which the methodologists propose. If this counter-claim is true, to ask that geographers abandon the procedures of official science may be to ask that they deny their own intuitive reasoning.

A third point arises from the phrase already quoted — 'to make explicit to consciousness that which is latent in everyday life'. Some phenomenologists appear to believe that the latent content is entirely in the mind of the actors and has no reference point except in phenomenological study. Such a position has the same weakness as the idealist explanation which fails to recognize the realities upon which theory and intention become grounded. Other phenomenologists (for example, Yi-Fu Tuan, 1965) make a clear distinction between the world *as known* and the world *as experienced*, recognizing that part of what is latent in everyday life may be the subconsciously experienced but nevertheless real external world. In such moderate proponents of phenomenology as Yi-Fu Tuan, many of its doctrines appear unexceptionable and are clearly acceptable to the positivist geographer, at least as a hypothesis-generating activity; but too few geographers have really used the method for it to be possible to gauge its effectiveness as a complete methodology.

THE APPROACH FROM STRUCTURALISM

The structuralist position has been less widely expounded than subjectivism in geographic studies. Perhaps the exposition which has received widest attention is the Marxist—structuralist work on urban systems. This appears briefly in Harvey's *Social Justice and the City*, and has been developed at greater length by French urban scholars. A second area with structuralist tendencies is the study of development (Brookfield, 1972; Slater, 1975). Once again the alternative mode of thinking is not monolithic—there are many different and indeed opposing schools within the structuralist position—nor are all those sympathetic necessarily exclusively structuralist: 'The study of structure cannot be exclusive and . . . it does not suppress especially in the human sciences and biology, other dimensions of investigation' (Piaget, 1971, p. 137), but even the narrower definition of structuralism adopted by Levi-Strauss maintains, according to Robey (1973, p. 2), that 'the methods and theories of structural linguistics are directly or indirectly applicable to the analysis of all aspects of human culture, *in so far as all of these, like language may be interpreted as systems of sign* . . .' (present author's italics). In addition to those who take an explicit structuralist viewpoint there are some (chiefly because their work has a Marxist derivation) who seem to adopt substantially structuralist viewpoints. For example, Boddy, in his recent study of mortgage finance in the city (Boddy, 1976, p. 69), uses the Marxist concept of social formation and writes: 'in order to achieve an analysis of urban processes which does more than capture appearances, it is initially necessary to conceptualise the particular structure of society within which those processes are situated'.

Structuralism: some key doctrines

The key doctrines of structuralism can be summarized by two quotations: 'Structuralism is a method of inquiry based on the concepts of totality, self-regulation and transformation'. This broad definition by Robey (1973, p. 2) follows closely that of Piaget. A rather narrower concept is based by Levi-Strauss on the argument 'that arrangement alone is structured which meets two conditions: that it be a system, ruled by an internal cohesiveness, inaccessible to observation in an isolated system, be revealed in the study of transformations, through which similar properties in apparently different systems are brought to light' (Levi-Strauss, 1967, p. 31). A fuller definition of the structuralist position appears in Levi-Strauss's *Structural Anthropology* (1963, pp. 279–280):

We can say that a structure consists of a model meeting with several requirements

First the structure exhibits the characteristics of a system. It is made up of several elements none of which can undergo a change without effecting changes in all elements.

Second, for any given model there should be a possibility of ordering a series of transformations resulting in a group of models of the same type.

Third, the above properties make it possible to predict how the model will react if one or more of its elements are submitted to certain modifications.

Finally the model should be constituted so as to make immediately intelligible all the observed facts.

In the succeeding pages Levi-Strauss makes a number of additional points. He distinguishes between observational inductive methods and 'experimental' methods, by which he means 'the set of procedures aiming at ascertaining how a given model will react when subjected to change'. He also distinguishes between the conscious and unconscious structures in a society, stressing that although a culture's own conscious and explicit interpretation of its structures may be correct this is not always the case. Furthermore, although structural studies may lend themselves to measurement, their critical importance lies in the fact that they lend themselves to manipulation in terms of qualitative mathematics (e.g. set theory, group theory, topology). Finally he makes a distinction between 'mechanical models' and 'statistical models' of structure which appears to be a renaming of the common distinction between 'deterministic' and 'probabilistic' statements (in his illustration he contrasts marriage systems which determine from which clans or groups a spouse *must* be chosen with those like the class system of Western Europe which determine the *probability* of marriage outside certain social and geographical groupings). He admits the presence of hybrid models.

A number of additional points become clear in a wider reading of the structuralist position. First, a point which is implicit in Levi-Strauss's definition of an 'experimental' approach, the transformation of structures should not be thought of simply as a temporal process (Piaget, 1971, p. 11); indeed Levi-Strauss stresses that the 'opposition between synchronic (cross-section) and diachronic (dynamic) is to a large extent illusory and useful only in the preliminary stages of research' (Levi-Strauss, 1963, p. 89). This reinforces the demand for comparative studies in which contemporary societies are seen to exhibit different transformations of the same underlying structures.

Secondly, most structuralists appear to accept the existence within a major structure of minor structures and to accept that these substructures may, at least initially, be the subject of separate study. Piaget argues for the existence of substructures and notes 'in being treated as a substructure a structure does not lose its boundaries, the larger structure does not annex: if anything, we have a confederation, so that the laws of the substructure are not altered but conserved' (1971, p. 11). This is implicit in many of the empirical studies made by Levi-Strauss, explicitly introduced in his *Structural Anthropology* (1963, Chaps. XV and XVI), and has wider relevance in the work of Godelier (1970), who argues that in some cases such substructures may be in contradiction to each other (using contradiction in the Marxist dialectic sense). Clearly, this approach runs counter to the definition of structuralism in terms of totality. It is interesting to note also that such a modified structuralism is similar to the concept of 'holon' put forward by Arthur Koestler—'the concept of holon is meant to supply the missing link between atomism and holism . . . a hierarchically organised whole cannot be "reduced" to its elementary parts; but it can be "dissected" into its constituent branches of "holons"' (in Lewis, 1974. p. 63).

Finally, although this is not always recognized by structuralists, structuralism runs counter to the simpler concepts of causation espoused by scientifically inclined geographers. The argument can perhaps be best explained mathematically as follows. Consider the values of a matrix

$$\begin{array}{cc} +4 & -7 \\ -3 & 0 \\ +2 & +1 \end{array}$$

transformed by the scalar (-1) to

$$
\begin{array}{cc}
-4 & +7 \\
+3 & 0 \\
-2 & -1
\end{array}
$$

Observation of the two sets in isolation might suggest that 'because' the sign of 4 had been changed the changes in the other signs follow. In reality the whole system has been transformed and the causation cannot be identified by observing the elements in the matrices individually.

Two examples may serve to illustrate the potential of these ideas in human geography. Many studies of urban land values have treated that topic as if it were a purely economic phenomenon with its own peculiar spatial signature. It is then demonstrated that many of the proposed remedies for a housing crisis are ineffectual or even self-defeating: for example, control on land use is seen to create artificial shortages with a resultant increase in the cost of housing. It is thus concluded that the problem is incapable of solution. The structuralist, in contrast, sees the housing market as only part of a much larger social, political, and economic structure, a structure moreover which has the ability to transform itself to cope with minor political or fiscal changes without changing its basic structures of delimitation and exploitation (Boddy, 1976; Duncan, 1976).

Similarly, a structuralist view of a peasant economy underlines the interdependence of farming activities, social roles, and their geographic expressions, so that any transformation of agriculture must necessarily change also the social relations of the community. Some geographic structuralists have revived classical geographic concepts of centre–periphery interdependencies and wedded them to the Marxist theory of metropolitan capitalist domination. In such a view (Brookfield, 1972; McTaggart, 1974; Slater, 1975) any minor technical assistance or aid-giving exercise can only serve to perpetuate the established macrostructures of economic dependency and exploitation.

One consequence of the structuralist position is to challenge the classical concepts of both 'regional' and 'systematic' geography. Because the structures described are global in extent no true understanding of a region can be achieved unless it is put into that global context, and because the structures described underline the interdependence of the social, the economic, and the political any thematic study (for example, economic geography) pursued in isolation is also subject to structuralist criticism.

Structuralism and functionalism

Many geographers will react to the outline of structuralist ideas presented above with the belief that they have seen it before under the headings of 'functionalism' and 'systems analysis'. This reaction will be reinforced by the fact that the word 'structure', and indeed the title of structuralist, is used by those who are quite clearly functionalists: for example, the anthropologist Radcliffe-Brown uses the language of structure, but is clearly more closely akin to the functionalists.

The main difference between the two schools of thought appears to be that whereas the *functionalist* says we must study the behaviour and indeed the 'goal' of the whole system in order to understand the significance of various pairwise relations between elements, the *structuralist* argues that we study the pairwise relations between elements only because in so doing we begin to grasp the meaning of the underlying structures and their transformations. A second difference (although it is difficult to see that it is a logically necessary difference) is identified by Gregory when he argues that whereas functionalism is concerned with the interrelations of empirically observable elements in the system, structuralism goes beneath this surface expression: 'structure is concealed in the sense that it is not directly apparent at the empirical level . . . it is hidden from our immediate consciousness, but we can discover it . . .' (Gregory, 1976, p. 296; see also Levi-Strauss 1967, p. 28). Clearly, here Gregory is consistent with Levi-Strauss's claim that an anthropologist may have 'to construct a model from phenomena the systematic character of which has evoked no awareness on the part of the culture' (Levi-Strauss 1963, p. 282). On the other hand, as Gregory made clear in his response to Guelke, the search for deeper structures which may themselves be subconscious opposes structuralism to the idealists and phenomenologists who proceed by thinking the thoughts of the decision-makers (whether they be remote in culture, space, or time): for if the important underlying structures are indeed unconscious the empathizing process will be no more revealing. It is therefore clear that although the two schools are at one in their critique of positivism's failure to address itself to meaning, they diverge in the way in which they assert that meaning may be discovered.

Allied to this question is that of reductionism. Reductionism is the attitude to a science which claims that all its causal relationships can be explained, and completely explained, by the workings of some other science. Thus, according to this doctrine chemistry may be reduced to physics, and human behaviour may be reduced to explanations based on chemistry or physiology of the brain. In human geography (as has been argued in earlier sections) there is always present a temptation to psychological reductionism—whether this reductionism takes the form of the idealist–psychological approach or the 'rattomorphic' approach of behavioural geography.

The structuralists counter this with the argument of 'specificity', although, as Mepham makes clear, the argument of specificity is in no way uniquely structuralist in relevance. 'Specificity' says 'in the first instance that a science of a specific domain is based on the specific coherence of its object. Before any question of relationship between domains can be discussed meaningfully one must have a theory of the specific difference which marks off one domain from another' (Mepham, 1973, p. 110). This appears to suggest that if the argument is applicable to geography its specific domain and structures in that domain must be established before an appeal to (for example) psychology (or any other reductionist appeal) is attempted. This position stems from the general structuralist view that many elements of the system are only explicable in terms of the system itself and cannot be reduced to one-to-one relationships with exogenous factors. The problem which this position must raise for many individual social sciences in an acute form is whether they are distinct domains in this sense: may it not rather be true that all the social sciences together constitute such a domain? Indeed, Piaget and other structuralists repeatedly stress the interdisciplinary nature of the programme which they propose.

RECONCILIATIONS?

It is difficult for a layman in philosophy to read such a diverse literature so skilfully argued by the original authors and their supporters without feeling an instinctive sympathy for each of the views expressed in turn. This leads to tension when the protagonists assert that their methodologies are exclusive. In this conclusion two routes of reconciliation are suggested which may prove of assistance to geographers perplexed by the countervailing claims, but hoping to preserve something from each of them.

The first possible reconciliation is to distinguish sharply between the psychology, the sociology, and the logic of the social sciences. This is to assert that the way in which an *individual* 'discovers' new facts or theories in social sciences (i.e. psychological studies) should be distinguished from the manner in which a *scientific community* adopts such new ideas (i.e. sociological or historical studies), and both should in time be distinguished from the *logical (or philosophical structure)* of such developments. A number of the authors contributing to *Criticism and the Growth of Knowledge* take this view. Masterman (1970), for example, calls Kuhn's notion of a paradigm 'sociological'. Similarly, writing in 1953, Nagel (1953, p. 156) argues, 'In discussing the adequacy of *Verstehen* it is essential to distinguish between that method conceived as a way of *generating* suggestive hypotheses and that way conceived as a method of validating hypotheses.' It is clear in the context that Nagel had no objection to the former, but had a strong objection to the latter. A similar compromise is apparently advocated by Piaget (1972, p. 232).

If this distinction is accepted a question may arise as to the primacy of the three elements. It seems that Kuhn, in certain areas the original Popper (see Kuhn, 1970, p. 238), and certainly such authors as Pearce-Williams (1970) believe that historical–sociological research will resolve certain questions of logic. Similarly, Piaget (1972) seems to use the discoveries in the psychology of learning to support or demolish philosophical positions. In contrast Popper (1970) argues that such a programme embarks on an infinite regress, for the logic by which psychological (or historical or sociological) discoveries are made and validated presupposes agreed logics for acceptance. It seems that the acceptance of this position would allow the subjectivist and the structuralist to seek answers to their questions (whether in terms of explanation or hermeneutic), but it would maintain the Popperian distinction that only if the conclusions so derived met other criteria would they be truly able to claim scientific status. Until they had attained such status their acceptability would have to be a matter of judgement, based at least in part on a subjective appraisal of the skill, wisdom, and integrity of the protagonists, and could not be resolved.

The second route to reconciliation is similar but more far-reaching—it is the one for which the author feels most sympathy, but it, too, is eclectic. Habermas (1972) argues that the sciences fall into three categories:

1. empirical analytic or nomological (including 'positivist' approaches);
2. hermeneutic (including idealists, phenomenologists, and to some extent structuralists); and
3. critical (mainly structuralists, especially Marxists).

Habermas argues that each of these modes of knowledge may be related to a 'cognitive interest' in the world. He implies that they are not mutually exclusive, and appears (at least in some parts of his work) to suggest that a social science will not fall wholly within any one category:

> The systematic *sciences of social action* that is economics, sociology and political science, have the same goal as do the empirical analytical sciences of producing nomological knowledge. A critical social science . . . will go beyond this goal to determine when theoretical statements grasp invariant regularities and when they express ideologically frozen relations of dependence that can in principle be transformed. (Habermas 1972, p. 195).

There is some obscurity in this part of his argument. It will be noted that he does not say that the sciences of social action *are* empirical analytical sciences, but he does allow them the nomological goal and presumably therefore the method by which nomological knowledge is attained. In the same way it seems reasonable to assert that the cognitive interests of geography span all three categories of knowledge. This view appears to be held by Mercer and Powell (1972, p. 14) and by Bartels (1973), who not only makes explicit reference to Habermas's 'cognitive interest' but argues for critical rationality in human geography.

If this analysis is correct and applicable to geography it would allow within human geography at the same time a *nomological* geography which seeks, for example, to understand the workings of urban rent theory as positivistically observed, a *hermeneutic* geography which seeks to identify the meaning of the urban rent system for those who are participants (active or passive) within it, and a *critical* geography which points to the extent to which present urban rent systems are themselves transformations of the capitalist system, but which admits that some of its features may indeed be 'invariant regularities'. Such an urban geography (or a similarly devised economic geography) is probably an explicit philosophy for the type of approach advocated by Morrill (1973). It raises again, however, a problem of primacy which Habermas does not seem to tackle: if the same phenomena are studied in all three modes (perhaps by different scholars) there may be a conflict between the conclusions. As far as can be seen, Habermas fails to offer a method by which such contradictions might be resolved, although it appears that his basic sympathies assert the primacy of the hermeneutic and the critical over the nomological. But this is a real issue for the history of geographical thought. The main conflicts over the 'quantitative revolution' in geography occurred when nomological studies appeared to challenge established theories which had a strongly hermeneutic quality. Similarly, some of the clashes apparent today occur when the critical tradition (in the shape of radical or Marxist geographers) seeks to demonstrate the ideological content of phenomena which other empirical analytic scholars believe to be 'invariant regularities'.

A second area which it leaves unresolved is what geography 'ought' to be seeking, in Habermas's phraseology what is, or should be, the subject's cognitive interest or interests. It would probably be true to say that much geography as practised prior to 1960 assumed that the cognitive interest was given and that it included both the nomological and the hermeneutic. Many positivists could originally defend their position as being that they performed more effectively work which had always had a nomological interest, but some moved from that position to one which crudely asserted that *only* the nomological had a proper place in geography. They would presumably have rebutted Hartshorne's hermeneutical claim 'to provide accurate, orderly and rational *description and interpretation* of the variable character of the earth surface' (Hartshorne, 1959, p. 21, present author's italics). Less clear is any long-term geographical commitment to 'critical knowledge'.

Here the word 'ought' reveals an ambiguity. If a subject claims to be wanting to arrive at the deepest levels of explanation, to solve problems, and to be wanting to change the world then it is false to that claim if it refuses to accept the critical posture by which it might achieve those aims. In that sense it 'ought' to adopt a critical cognitive interest. But if it lays no claim to such exalted roles then the 'ought' becomes a judgement of personal morality and 'let he who is without sin among you cast the first stone'.

ACKNOWLEDGEMENT

I am most grateful to Malcolm Lewis for his comments on an initial draft of this paper.

REFERENCES

Bartels, D. (1973). Between theory and metatheory. In R. J. Chorley, (Ed.), *Directions in Geography*, Methuen, London, 23–42.

Boddy, M. J. (1976). The structure of mortgage finance: building societies and the British social formation. *Transactions, Institute of British Geographers*, N.S. **1**, 58–71.

Brodbeck, M. (1963). Meaning and action. *Philosophy of Science*, **30**, 309–324.

Brookfield, H. C. (1972). *Colonial Development and Interdependence*, Cambridge University Press, Cambridge.

Brown, R. H. (1938). Materials bearing upon the geography of the Atlantic seaboard, *Annals, Association of American Geographers*, **28**, 201–231.

Bunge, W. (1966). *Theoretical Geography*, Lund Studies in Geography, Series C No. 1, Gleerup, Lund.

Chisholm, M. (1963). Tendencies in agricultural specialisation and agricultural concentration. *Papers and Proceedings, Regional Science Association*, **10**, 157–162.

Collingwood, R. G. (1946). *The Idea of History*, Oxford University Press, London.

Dray, W. H. (1964). *Philosophy of History*, Prentice-Hall, Englewood Cliffs, N.J.

Duncan, S. S. (1976). Self-help: the allocation of mortgages and the formation of housing sub-markets. *Area*, **8**, 307–316.

Eliot Hurst, M. E. (1973). Establishment geography: or how to be irrelevant in three easy lessons. *Antipode*, **5**(2), 40–59.

Feyerabend, P. K. (1974). Popper's 'Objective Knowledge'. *Inquiry*, **17**, 474–507.

Giddens, A. (1976). *New Rules of Sociological Method*, Hutchinson, London.

Godelier, M. (1970). Structure, system and contradiction in *Das Kapital*. In M. Lane (Ed.), *Structuralism: A Reader*, Cape, London, pp. 340–358.

Gregory, D. J. (1976). Rethinking historical geography. *Area*, **8**, 295–299.

Guelke, L. (1971). Problems of scientific explanation in geography. *Canadian Geographer*, **15**, 38–53.

Guelke, L. (1974). An idealist alternative in human geography, *Annals, Association of American Geographers*, **64**, 193–202.

Guelke, L. (1975). On rethinking historical geography. *Area*, **7**, 135–138.

Guelke, L. (1978). Geography and logical positivism. In D. T. Herbert and R. J. Johnston (Eds.), *Geography and the Urban Environment*, Vol. 1, Wiley, New York, pp. 35–61.

Habermas, J. (1972). *Knowledge and Human Interests*, Heinemann, London.

Haggett, P. (1965). *Locational Analysis in Human Geography*, Edward Arnold, London.

Hall, P. (1969). *London 2000*, Faber, London.

Hamlyn, D. W. (1970). *The Theory of Knowledge*, Macmillan, London.

Harris, C. (1971). Theory and synthesis in historical geography. *Canadian Geographer*, **15**, 157–172.

Hartshorne, R. (1959). *Perspective on the Nature of Geography*, Rand McNally, Chicago.

Harvey, D. W. (1969). *Explanation in Geography*, Edward Arnold, London.

Harvey, D. W. (1973). *Social Justice and the City*, Edward Arnold, London.

Hempel, C. G. (1962). Explanation in science and history. In R. G. Colodny (Ed.), *Frontiers of Science and Philosophy*, Allen and Unwin, London, pp. 7–33.

Kansky, K. J. (1963). *The Structure of Transportation Networks*, University of Chicago, Department of Geography Research Paper, No. 84, Chicago.

Kirk, W. (1963). Problems of geography. *Geography*, **48**, 357–371.

Kuhn, T. (1962). *The Structure of Scientific Revolutions*, University of Chicago Press, Chicago.

Kuhn, T. (1970). Reflections on my critics. In I. Lakatos and A. Musgrave (Eds.), *Criticism and the Growth of Knowledge*, Cambridge University Press, Cambridge, pp. 231–278.

Lane, M. (Ed.) (1970). *Structuralism: a Reader*, Cape, London.

Lecourt, D. (1975). *Marxism and Epistemology*, New Left Books, London.

Levi-Strauss, C. (1963). *Structural Anthropology*, Basic Books, New York.

Levi-Strauss, C. (1966). *The Savage Mind*, Weidenfeld and Nicolson, London.

Levi-Strauss, C. (1967). *The Scope of Anthropology*, Cape, London.

Lewis, J. W. (1974). *Beyond Chance and Necessity*, Garnstone Press, London.

Lipsey, R. G. (1963). *An Introduction to Positive Economics*, Weidenfeld and Nicolson, London.

Losch, A. (1954). *The Economics of Location*, Yale University Press, New Haven.

Lowther, G. R. (1959). Idealist history and historical geography. *Canadian Geographer*, **14**, 31–36.

McTaggart, W. D. (1974). Structuralism and universalism in geography: reflections on contributions by H. C. Brookfield. *Australian Geographer*, **12**, 510–516.

Marchand, B. (1974). Quantitative geography: revolution or counter-revolution. *Geoforum*, **17**, 15–24.

Masterman, M. (1970). The nature of a paradigm. In I. Lakatos and A. Musgrave (Eds.),

Criticism and the Growth of Knowledge, Cambridge University Press, Cambridge, pp. 59–89.

Mepham, J. (1973). The structuralist sciences and philosophy, in D. Robey (Ed.), *Structuralism: an Introduction*, Clarendon Press, Oxford, pp. 109–137.

Mercer, D., Powell, J. M. (1972). *Phenomenology and Related Non-positivist Viewpoints in the Social Sciences*, Monash Publications in Geography, No. 1, Melbourne.

Merleau-Ponty, M. (1962). *The Phenomenology of Perception*, Routledge and Kegan Paul, London.

Morrill, R. L. (1965). The negro ghetto: problems and alternatives. *Geographical Review*, **55**, 339–361.

Morrill, R. L. (1973). Socialism, private property, the ghetto and geographic theory. *Antipode*, **5**(2), 84–86.

Nagel, E. (1953). On the method of *Verstehen* as the sole method of philosophy. *Journal of Philosophy*, **50**, 154–157.

Paci, E. (1972). *The Function of the Sciences and the Meaning of Man*, Northwestern University Press, Evanston.

Pearce-Williams, L. (1970). Normal science, scientific revolutions and the history of science. In I. Lakatos and A. Musgrave (Eds.), *Criticism and the Growth of Knowledge*, Cambridge University Press, Cambridge pp. 49–50.

Piaget, J. (1971). *Structuralism*, Routledge and Kegan Paul, London.

Piaget, J. (1972). *Insights and Illusions in Philosophy*, Routledge and Kegan Paul, London.

Popper, K. R. (1959). *The Logic of Scientific Discovery*, Hutchinson, London.

Popper, K. R. (1970). Normal science and its dogmas. In I. Lakatos and A. Musgrave, (Eds.), *Criticism and the Growth of Knowledge*, Cambridge University Press, Cambridge, pp. 51–58.

Popper, K. R. (1972). *Objective Knowledge*, Oxford University Press, London.

Pred, A. (1967). *Behavior and Location*, Lund Studies in Geography, Series B, No. 27, Gleerup, Lund.

Reich, C. A. (1970). *The Greening of America*, Random House, New York.

Relph, E. (1970). An enquiry into the relations between phenomenology and geography. *Canadian Geographer*, **14**, 193–201.

Relph, E. (1976). *Place and Placelessness*, Pion, London.

Relph, E., Tuan, Y.-F., and Buttimer, A. (1977). Commentary; humanism, phenomenology and geography. *Annals, Association of American Geographers*, **67**, 177–183.

Robey, D. (Ed.) (1973). *Structuralism: an Introduction*, Clarendon Press, Oxford.

Robinson, J. (1962). *Economic Philosophy*, Watts, London.

Roszak, T. (1971). *The Making of a Counter Culture*, Faber, London.

Rudner, R. S. (1966). *The Philosophy of Social Science*, Prentice-Hall, Englewood Cliffs, N.J.

Skjervheim, B. (1974). Objectivism and the study of man. *Inquiry*, **17**, 213–239, and 265–302.

Slater, D. (1975). The poverty of modern geographical inquiry. *Pacific Viewpoint*, **16**, 159–176.

Smart, B. (1976). *Sociology, Phenomenology and Marxian Analysis*, Routledge and Kegan Paul, London.

Steed, G. P. F. (1971). Internal organization, firm integration and locational change. *Economic Geography*, **47**, 371–383.

Thevenaz, P. (1962). *What is Phenomenology?* Quadrangle Books, New York.

Tobler, W., and Wineburg S. (1971). A Cappadocian speculation. *Nature*, **231**, 39–41.

Torrance, T. F. (1971). *God and Rationality*, Oxford University Press, London.

Tuan, Yi-Fu (1965). 'Environment' and 'world'. *Professional Geographer*, **17**(5), 6–8.

Tuan Yi-Fu (1971). Geography, phenomenology and the study of human nature. *Canadian Geographer*, **15**, 181–192.

Tuan, Yi-Fu (1974). Space and place: humanist perspective. *Progress in Geography*, **6**, 211–252.

Wagner, H. (1973). The scope of phenomenological sociology: considerations and suggestions. In G. Psathas, (Ed.), *Phenomenological Sociology*, Wiley, London.

Walmsley, D. J. (1974). Positivism and phenomenology in geography. *Canadian Geographer*, **18**, 95–107.

Watts, H. D. (1974). Spatial rationalisation in multi-plant enterprises. *Geoforum*, **17**, 69–76.

Wolforth, J. (1976). The new geography—and after. *Geography*, **61**, 143–149.

Wolpert, J. (1964). The decision process in a spatial context. *Annals, Association of American Geographers*, **54**, 537–558.

Zipf, G. K. (1969). *Human Behavior and the Principle of Least Effort*, Harvard University Press, Cambridge, Massachusetts.

Chapter 2

Space–Time Models and Urban Geographical Research

Robert J. Bennett

INTRODUCTION

Geographers have traditionally been concerned with long-term issues of spatial policy such as the spatial layout of transport facilities, the location of industry or service activities, and the structuring of environmental interactions. More recently, there has been a new concern with spatial policy issues which are shorter-term and more frequent and continuous in their requirements for interaction between the system of interest and the decisions about the system which must be made. In urban planning there has been a similar shift of emphasis away from the drawing up of plans as 'one-off' exercises depicting static scenarios of the future spatial, social and economic layout of a city or region. Instead a 'continuous planning' has been advocated in which goals, instruments and system evolution are kept under continuous review.

Space–time models are crucial to the development of this new continuous planning approach. It is surprising, therefore, that the interrelated topics of time, space–time and spatial models have had, as yet, relatively little impact on urban research. Most important research in this area has been carried out in other fields of geography, or in other disciplines, especially statistics, econometrics, and control engineering. The overlap between urban research and these other disciplines is a particularly fruitful area for discussion and this paper is aimed at providing an introductory overview to the range of research development on space–time models. The discussion falls into three parts. In the first section is given a review of the wide range of models that may be used to represent urban dynamics and spatial structures. In the second section an examination is made of the interrelations between these models and the effects of policy determination. In the third section is raised a number of questions which are used to define research priorities.

MODELS OF URBAN TIME AND SPACE DYNAMICS

It is convenient to approach space–time models of urban areas from a systems point of view. Any system is composed of three components: input, output, and translation operator linking the two. If we define the input as a variable X and the output as a variable Y, then the system can be represented as the single equation:

$$Y = SX + e \qquad (2.1)$$

where S is the translation operator linking input and output, usually termed the *transfer function*, and e is a stochastic error term. In urban systems the transfer function represents the stable response characteristics of social and economic interaction: otherwise known as stimulus-response, or macro-input-output translators. In general, the system input–output character of S, and the entry of X and Y, may be time, space–time, or spatially dependent. In discrete variable notation these three cases can be described as follows:

1. *Time series case:*   A simple time series of discrete observations $\{Y_t\}$, $\{X_t\}$ for observations at $(t = \ldots -1, 0, 1, 2, \ldots)$.
2. *Space–time case:*   A time series of discrete observations $\{Y_{ti}\}$, $\{X_{ti}\}$ for observations at time points $(t = \ldots, -1, 0, 1, 2, \ldots)$, and location $(i = 1, 2, \ldots, N)$ in the urban space, where N is the number of subregions in the overall urban area of interest.
3. *Spatial case:*   The observation $\{Y_i\}$ and $\{X_i\}$ are available at the points $(i = 1, 2, \ldots, N)$ in space for one period of time only.

Depending upon the case being considered, the system transfer function S will be a time series, space–time, or purely spatial operator. For each case, the transfer function determines the way in which the system input is translated to become the system output.

In reviewing various approaches to modelling the space–time structure of urban areas, it is convenient to divide the research to date into four categories: first, comparative static models in which a separate (usually equilibrium) model is fitted to each of a series of spatial cross-sections of data; second, discrete dynamic models described by difference equations; third, continuous dynamic models described by differential equations; and finally, general models of urban dynamics with elements of comparative static, discrete, and continuous components. Each of these categories of models is reviewed below.

Models of urban comparative statics

Comparative static models of urban areas suppress the detailed dynamic elements of interzonal dynamic feedback and response such that the translation operator is poorly defined over time. The models are constrained to reproduce only equilibrium patterns of spatial structure. The steps by which equilibrium is reached, and the dynamics of possible adjustments and impacts, cannot be reproduced. Typical examples of such static models are the Garin–Lowry formulation (Lowry, 1964) and subsequent developments of spatial interaction and allocation components based on gravity models using either utility theory (Neidercorn and Bechdolt, 1969) or the entropy-maximizing procedure (Wilson, 1970, 1974). Comparative statics are achieved when equilibrium models are calibrated at a series of time periods. Comparison of the spatial structure, parameters, and locational activities in each temporal cross-section then yields an indication of the directions of temporal change. It is then possible to use the models *ex post* to allocate past increments in urban variables, which are known, within the new equilibrium model at the next time period. Alternatively the models may be used *ex ante* to determine the impact of expected future increases or decreases in levels of urban variables on overall spatial structure. Indeed Reif (1973, Chap. 5) suggests that comparative static models are of most use in this latter case, to test the feasibility of future sketch plans of urban configurations and to determine special impact effects.

Examples of comparative static models abound in the urban modelling literature. Most practical studies to date have used a 'one-shot' spatial model (usually based on the Lowry–Wilson approach) calibrated to a base year which is then used, sometimes with adjustments to calibrated parameters, to allocate expected increases in population, economic activity, or other variables. The expected increases in such indicators are usually generated external to the spatial allocation model. In the case of population, cohort-survival models are normally used, while in the case of economic activity, economic growth indicators or multipliers linked to econometric models (see next section) have been adopted. The EMPIRIC model (Hill, 1965) is one of the earliest examples of this approach in which the rate of change of each of Lowry's variables over the previous time period is used to generate changes in the shares of economic activity and population of each zone in the next time period. Changes to the transport network or other predicted changes can also be incorporated. Later models by N.B.E.R. (Ingram, Kain, and Ginn, 1972), the Bay Area Simulation Study (C.R.E.U.E., 1968), the Penn–Jersey approach (Seidman, 1969), the SELNEC Transportation Study (Wilson *et al.*, 1969), and Mackett's (1976) stock allocation models have all adopted similar approaches with various methods of including the time linkages between spatial cross-sections.

Comparative statics is open to a number of obvious criticisms. Most important of these is the fact that none of the dynamic adjustment mechanisms can be simulated: we have no knowledge of the time paths or response times to changes in external factors, or internal locational adjustments. In addition, the validity of the gravity assumption can be questioned as to its interpretability in terms of understood processes of urban behaviour. Moreover, the comparative statics cannot allow for the effects of new elements or changes in behaviour. It is assumed that all behaviour patterns are equilibrating within a structure which is trapped within a straitjacket of the calibration period. Such models can therefore be of only limited value to the planner or to the model-builder interested in capturing as closely as possible the mechanisms of reality. Despite these drawbacks, however, comparative static models can be a very useful approach in limited studies conducted with care. Such models make relatively small demands on temporal data which are frequently not available. Also, lack of capacity to reproduce adjustment mechanisms may be relatively unimportant when the planner is concerned mainly with long-term impact effects. In addition, the Wilson entropy-maximizing procedure represents a useful methodological approach to location and interaction modelling which, as will be shown later, makes it possible to combine comparative static models with more truly dynamic models in order to satisfy accounting identities and achieve a consistent spatial allocation at each time period.

Models of discrete urban dynamics

Discrete models for urban dynamics are most highly developed for the time series case and draw heavily upon the considerable literature available in statistics and econometrics (see, for example, Kendall and Stuart, 1966; Box and Jenkins, 1970; Chatfield, 1975; Jenkins and Watts, 1968; Johnston, 1972; Kendall, 1973). The traditional approach to time series analysis (see, for example, Kendall and Stuart, 1966) is to split the components of the variables $\{Y_t\}$ and $\{X_t\}$ under study into three parts: trend, seasonal, and stochastic. A more recent approach, popularized by Box and Jenkins, is to model discrete dynamics as either transfer function processes in the bivariate case, where both $\{Y_t\}$ and $\{X_t\}$ are available, or as autoregressive moving-average processes in the univariate case when only a single variable $\{Y_t\}$ is available. This set of models gives a range of possible difference equations which can be summarized as follows:

1. *Distributed lag process:* TF $(0, q)$

$$Y_t = b_0 X_t + b_1 X_{t-1} + \ldots + b_q X_{t-q} + e_t \qquad (2.2)$$

2. *Autoregressive, transfer function process:* TF $(p, 1)$

$$Y_t = b_0 X_t + a_1 Y_{t-1} + \ldots + a_p Y_{t-p} + e_t \qquad (2.3)$$

3. *General transfer function process:* TF (p, q)

$$Y_t = b_0 X_t + b_1 X_{t-1} + \ldots + b_q X_{t-q} + a_1 Y_{t-1} + \ldots + a_p Y_{t-p} + e_t \quad (2.4)$$

4. *Autoregressive process:* AR (p)

$$Y_t = c_1 Y_{t-1} + c_2 Y_{t-2} + \ldots + c_p Y_{t-p} + e_t \qquad (2.5)$$

5. *Moving-average process:* MA (q)

$$Y_t = d_1 e_{t-1} + d_2 e_{t-2} + \ldots + d_q e_{t-q} + e_t \qquad (2.6)$$

6. *Autoregressive, moving-average process:* ARMA (p, q)

$$Y_t = c_1 Y_{t-1} + c_2 Y_{t-2} + \ldots + c_p Y_{t-p} + d_1 e_{t-1} + d_2 e_{t-2} + \ldots + d_q e_{t-q} + e_t \qquad (2.7)$$

In each case the terms $\{a_i\}$, $\{b_i\}$, $\{c_i\}$, and $\{d_i\}$ are the parameters of the equation and e_t is a stochastic error sequence (a normal independent random variable). Each equation can be seen as analogous to a multiple regression equation in which the independent variables are replaced by lag terms representing the dependence of the urban outputs on past values of urban system inputs, on past values of the outputs, and upon past values of the stochastic error component.

In most practical geographical applications of these models a series of stages of analysis is followed, as shown in Figure 2.1. Whatever prior knowledge is available can be used to pre-specify the important variables and directions of linkage in the overall model which it is desired to create. Stage 2 of the analysis of space–time processes is concerned with specifying and identifying the nature of the equation for the transfer function governing the system input–output relations. Stage 3 is a calibration stage which develops estimates, for example by least-squares regression, of the magnitude of the parameters making up the transfer function structure specified in Stage 2. Stage 4 of the analysis is a 'checking' stage in which the efficiency and fit properties of the resulting

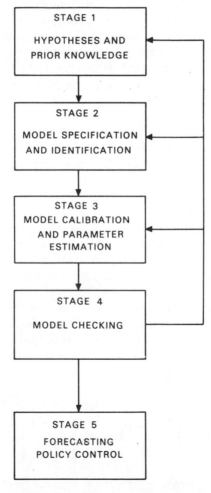

FIGURE 2.1. Stages in the analysis of
spatial and temporal systems

parameter estimates of the transfer function structure are tested in order to determine if the model is indeed a useful and successful explanatory device. If it is found that the parameter estimates are inefficient, or suboptimal in some fashion (for example, low significance levels, poor simulation properties, and residual autocorrelation), then recourse must be made to previous stages of analysis to determine if the initial hypotheses, and the resulting model specifications and parameter estimates, were correct. If the model is acceptable, then the final stage of analysis is to use the estimated model to generate forecasts, simulations, or explanations of the geographical system under study. This approach has been popularized by Box and Jenkins (1970) for time series models, and is akin to the Blalock (1964) causal-analysis procedure.

A number of examples of the use of these time series models is now available. Bell (1967) considers the specification of such models and relates them to neo-classical economic growth theory. Early applications by Czmanski (1965, 1969) to the Nova Scotia regional economy are based largely on distributed lag structure. Paelinck (1970) has extended the economic basis and has made links with comparative static models, while Glickman (1972, 1977) has given a simple two-zone disaggregation (city and suburbs) for Philadelphia which links closely to input–output formulations. Bennett (1974) has applied Box–Jenkins specification techniques to determination of local labour markets and migration components, extending the work of Smith (1942) on the possibility of modelling urban population and labour movements in the U.K., using the Registrar-General's population estimates. Most attention in urban research, however, has been directed towards the interregional dynamics of time series processes.

Space–time models of discrete dynamics have met with less attention in statistics, and most developments rely on the work of geographers (see especially Cliff and Ord, 1975; Bennett, 1975a, 1978a; Haggett, Cliff, and Frey, 1977; Martin and Oeppen, 1975). The most useful approach in most instances has been to consider the urban area of interest partitioned into N zones. Associated with each zone are the time series of urban inputs and outputs, given respectively by $\{X_{1i}, X_{2i}, \ldots, X_{Ti}\}$ and $\{Y_{1i}, Y_{2i}, \ldots, Y_{Ti}\}$, $(i = 1, 2, \ldots, N)$. In exactly analogous fashion to the time series case, the dynamics of the lead-lag dependencies between zones within an urban area can be represented by a form of transfer function model which is now a $N \times N$ transfer function in which each component is the single input–output transfer function resembling the time series translation operator. This is given by the following matrix difference equation:

$$
\begin{bmatrix} Y_{t1} \\ Y_{t2} \\ \vdots \\ Y_{tN} \end{bmatrix} = \begin{bmatrix} S_{11} & S_{12} & \ldots & S_{1N} \\ S_{21} & S_{22} & \ldots & S_{2N} \\ & & \ldots & \\ S_{N1} & S_{N2} & \ldots & S_{NN} \end{bmatrix} \begin{bmatrix} X_{t1} \\ X_{t2} \\ \vdots \\ X_{tN} \end{bmatrix} + \begin{bmatrix} e_{t1} \\ e_{t2} \\ \vdots \\ e_{tN} \end{bmatrix} \tag{2.8}
$$

In this equation the S_{ij} terms represent the transfer function relations between inputs from the jth zone into the ith zone of the urban area. The general transfer function structure of each S_{ij} element can be expanded as a set of distributed lag and autoregressive terms using the notation of Bennett (1978a, Chapter 2) such that

$$S_{ij} = \frac{b_{0(ij)}X_{tj} + b_{1(ij)}X_{t-ij} + \ldots + b_{q(ij)}X_{t-q(ij)j}}{a_{1(ij)}Y_{t-1i} + a_{2(ij)}Y_{t-2i} + \ldots + a_{p(ij)}Y_{t-p(ij)i}} \qquad (2.9)$$

The subscripts on the parameters are intepreted as follows: $b_{k(ij)}$ is the distributed lag parameter at lag k for interactions between inputs into zone j and outputs into zone i; $a_{k(ij)}$ is similarly defined for the kth time lag for autoregressive effects between outputs in zone i and zone j. The $q(ij)$ and $p(ij)$ terms are the respective distributed lag and autoregressive parameter orders for interaction between the ith and jth zones.

Once again the sequential procedure of identification, estimation, and checking can be used to determine the structure of these models and a number of examples has now been developed for categorizing spatial interactions using a model such as equation (2.8). Most of these examples have been undertaken with regional systems of cities rather than urban areas as such. King, Casetti, and Jeffrey (1969), Jeffrey, Casetti, and King (1969) and King, Casetti, and Jeffrey (1972) have applied such methods to defining interrelations between unemployment levels in a set of North American cities. This has been combined with a factor analysis of the time series components by Casetti, King, and Jeffrey (1971) in order to determine spatial and non-spatial groups of U.S. cities based on similarities in unemployment dynamics. Unemployment data have also been analysed by Bassett and Tinline (1970), Bassett and Haggett (1971), and Haggett (1971) for determining the feedback structure of labour-market areas in Southwest England and by Sant (1973) in East Anglia. Spectral and cross-spectral techniques have been applied to unemployment data by Hepple (1975) in Northeast England, and by Bartels (1977) in eleven Netherlands provinces. The interaction between unemployment and wage inflation has been examined by King and Foster (1973) and Weissbrod (1976) in the United States. Bennett (1975b, 1975c, 1975d, 1975e) has constructed a five-equation model describing interzonal transfer function relations of unemployment, migration, employment, industrial movement, and population in North-west England. Other such studies, outside an urban context, are reviewed by Cliff *et al.* (1975), Haggett, Cliff, and Frey (1977), Bennett (1978a), and Bennett and Chorley (1978).

These studies of space–time processes represent fairly simple extensions of the methods of time series analysis, using either time domain techniques based on correlation functions or frequency domain techniques based on spectral density functions. In each case, where parameters have been estimated, it has been suggested that multivariate parameter estimators should be adopted. Thus the N-zonal system of equation (2.8) is represented as N-variate estimation problem. This approach has a number of advantages. First, the application is extremely simply accomplished. Secondly, the N-variate sampling theory, significance test, and other properties of the multivariate estimators can be assumed to apply to the $N \times N$ transfer function input–output matrix on the N-regional system (see Bennett, 1975a; Cliff and Ord, 1975). Hence, urban and other geographical applications can go forward using these estimators as a simple basis. However, as pointed out by a number of discussants to the Cliff and Ord (1975) paper, a considerable degree of collinearity and correlation between error terms will usually be present, and there will be a marked loss of degrees of freedom. Considerable simplification can be achieved in some cases if *a priori* restrictions are introduced, such as contiguity constraints, distance-decay effects, and so forth. But most progress will be made by the derivation of practical small-sample estimators specifically designed for space–time problems, so there is at present a considerable research need in this area.

A special species of discrete dynamic models is given by Markov-chain models. In this case the rather restrictive assumption is made that the changes in urban state from one time instant to the next satisfies the Markov property. For a time series, this can be stated as

$$\text{prob}(Y_t/Y_0, Y_1, \ldots, Y_{t-1}) = \text{prob}(Y_t/Y_{t-1}) \tag{2.10}$$

The probability of the event Y_t at time t given the value of $\{Y_t\}$ at all other time points is conditional *only* upon the value at $Y_{t=1}$. The importance of this property is that the entire realization of the process up to time t can be defined by

$$\text{prob}(Y_1, Y_2, \ldots, Y_t/Y_0) = \prod_{\tau=1}^{t} \text{prob}(Y_\tau/Y_{\tau-1}) \tag{2.11}$$

which can be reproduced by a single parameter or a set of parameters to represent $\text{prob}(Y_t/Y_{t-1})$ (Feller, 1950). Using this type of definition, it has been usual to reduce urban systems to the first-order process implicit in equation (2.10). Land-use conversion has been modelled as Markov chains by Harris (1968) for the Sacramento area, and by Bourne (1969) and Drewett (1969) for the rural–urban land conversion process. Conversion of existing urban sites has been modelled using Markov chains by Cowan (1969) for office-floor-space creation in central London, and for relocation of industrial plants by Lever (1972) in Glasgow and by Collins (1972) in Ontario. A special form of Markov model is the cohort-survival model used in population analysis. In this case a complex matrix of interzonal birth–death and migration terms reduces population dynamics to a Markov process. The incorporation of the spatial components of migration into such models is due to Rogers (1966), but the recent volume *Spatial Population Analysis* by Rees and Wilson (1977) puts this procedure on a sound, accounts-based footing. An extension of this approach to general urban models is given by Echenique (1969) and Wilson (1974, Chap. 11).

Models of continuous urban dynamics

The use of continuous variables to represent urban dynamics results in a considerable degree of overlap with discrete urban models. The urban input and output variables are now represented by $X(t)$ and $Y(t)$ respectively, for continuously differentiable functions indexed on time t. Occasionally, continuous models may be extended also to space variables, giving input and output sequences respectively as $X(t,x_1,x_2)$ and $Y(t,x_1,x_2)$ for spatial coordinates (x_1, x_2). In the discrete case we are able to describe urban dynamics by difference equations, but in the continuous case the describing equations are replaced by differential equations. For the purely time series case these are represented by

$$Y(t) + \alpha_1 \frac{\mathrm{d}\,Y(t)}{\mathrm{d}t} + \ldots + \alpha_p \frac{\mathrm{d}^p\,Y(t)}{\mathrm{d}t^p} = \beta_0 X(t) + \beta_1 \frac{\mathrm{d}X(t)}{\mathrm{d}t} + \ldots + \beta_2 \frac{\mathrm{d}^q X(t)}{\mathrm{d}t^q} \qquad (2.12)$$

Continuous definitions of the transfer function or autoregressive moving-average equations described in the previous section can also be developed. It can be shown by a series of simple manipulations that the continuous system equation (2.12) is equivalent to the transfer function difference equation (2.4) on passing to the limit as the lag term tends to zero,

i.e. $$\lim_{\varepsilon \to 0} (Y_t - Y_{t-\varepsilon}) = \frac{\mathrm{d}\,Y(t)}{\mathrm{d}t}.$$

Hence, there is a high degree of formal equivalence between discrete and continuous models of urban dynamics. For computational purposes the discrete form is almost always to be preferred, but models with continuous dynamics are more amenable to analytical manipulation and are thus favoured in the development of deductive theories and in simulation studies. Discussion will be confined here to two sets of examples, those based on the systems-dynamics approach and those based on mathematical topology.

   The systems-dynamics approach derives largely from the work of Forrester (see especially Forrester, 1968, 1971). The current state of each variable is defined as its *level*, and adjustments to levels are made continuously as time passes by a series of *rate* equations. The rates, which represent parameter terms, are themselves subject to change and evolution which is expressed as a non-linear function of levels, or as feedback elements deriving from desired policy levels. In almost all cases there has been little attempt to estimate the structure of either the level or rate equations, and these models must be seen more as explanatory devices rather than empirically derived models. Major examples of this approach are the Susquehanna River Basin Study by Hamilton *et al.* (1969), the Kent County model of population and employment (Swanson and Waldman, 1970), and the interaction model of the northern region of England with the rest of the U.K. in the regional income and employment model of Telford, Yule, and Burdekin (1974). Other studies are those by Burdekin and Marshall (1972), Chen (1972), IEEE (1972), Lianos (1972), Mass (1972) and Constable (1973). Although these models require *a priori* definition of the structure of the system equation, the parameter terms and the rates of change of the parameters do present a useful simulation philosophy which has stimulated a great deal of research on urban dynamic structures. Thus, the systems-dynamics approach has been in the vanguard of attempts to improve the overwhelmingly static approach to urban modelling characteristic of the 1960s.

Mathematical topology provides a persuasive example of the usefulness of the analytical properties which differential equations possess and which give them considerable advantages in the formulation of deductive theory over difference equations. Most urban models, in common with a large number of other models in both the physical and social sciences, have assumed that a continuous pattern of changes results from changes in system structures, policies, or equations. More recently, however, the results of mathematical topology have opened the way for the development of models which can incorporate complex non-linear and non-stationary dynamics, and which can also encompass discontinuities, jumps, or 'flips' in the pattern of urban behaviour. The stimulus to the development of models incorporating such elements has come from two directions, one statistical and one mathematical.

In the statistical theory of state space dynamics, developments derive largely from Kalman (1960) and are often termed the Kalman filter. This approach leads to the disaggregation of urban models into two components—a system dynamic (a state equation) and a parameter dynamic (a parameter equation). The system dynamic is identical to the system equations defined in equations (2.2)–(2.7) in discrete form, or equation (2.12) in continuous form. The parameter dynamic, however, represents a new submodel which adjusts the system equation from one point in time or space to the next. These two submodels can be represented by the following two equations:

System equation:

$$\mathbf{Y}(t) = \mathbf{X}(t)\theta(t) + \mathbf{e}(t), \qquad \mathbf{e}(t) \sim N(0, \mathbf{R}) \qquad (2.13)$$

Parameter equation:

$$\theta(t) = \mathbf{F}\theta(t) + \mathbf{G}\mathbf{V}(t) + \mathbf{\Gamma}\mathbf{n}(t), \qquad \mathbf{n}(t) \sim N(0, \mathbf{Q}) \qquad (2.14)$$

In this general case shown here there is a vector of system inputs $\mathbf{X}(t)$, a vector of outputs $\mathbf{Y}(t)$, $\theta(t)$ is a vector of system parameters, and $\mathbf{e}(t)$ is a vector of system errors. The parameters evolve according to a model governed by the three matrices $\mathbf{F}$, $\mathbf{G}$, and $\mathbf{\Gamma}$ which control the entry of the respective elements of Markov evolution, exogenous variables $\mathbf{V}(t)$, and stochastic error sources $\mathbf{n}(t)$. $\mathbf{Q}$ and $\mathbf{R}$ are covariance matrices of the mutually and serially independent vector error sequences $\{\mathbf{n}_t\}$ and $\{\mathbf{e}_t\}$ respectively.

The Kalman filter is a generic term for a species of methods which make estimates of the system equation (2.13) by incorporating estimation of the changing parameters deriving from equation (2.14). A wide variety of such filters is available depending upon our degree of knowledge of each of the terms in (2.13) and (2.14) (see Bennett, 1978a, Chap. 5). The general Kalman filter structure is given in Table 2.1. This provides estimates of the system outputs and parameters at each point in time by recursive calculation of a set of extrapolation equations. The importance of this approach is that urban models need no longer be held in a straitjacket of unchanging structure; evolutionary and non-linear

TABLE 2.1 The general Kalman filter[a]

System model	$\mathbf{Y}(t) = \mathbf{X}(t)\,\theta(t) + \mathbf{e}(t)$
Parameter model	$\hat{\theta}(t) = \mathbf{F}\hat{\theta}(t) + \mathbf{G}\,\mathbf{V}(t) + \boldsymbol{\Gamma}\mathbf{n}(t)$
Parameter extrapolation	$\dfrac{d\hat{\theta}(t)}{dt} = \mathbf{F}\hat{\theta}(t) - \mathbf{K}(t)\,[\mathbf{X}(t)\,\hat{\theta}(t) - \mathbf{Y}(t) + \mathbf{G}\,\mathbf{V}(t)]$
Parameter covariance extrapolation	$\mathbf{P}(t) = \mathbf{F}\mathbf{P}(t) + \mathbf{P}(t)\mathbf{F}' - \mathbf{K}(t)\mathbf{X}'(t)\mathbf{P}(t) + \boldsymbol{\Gamma}\mathbf{Q}\boldsymbol{\Gamma}$
Kalman gain extrapolation	$\mathbf{k}(t) = \mathbf{P}(t)\mathbf{X}(t)[\mathbf{R} + \mathbf{X}'(t)\mathbf{P}(t)\mathbf{X}(t)]^{-1}$

[a] Summary of the continuous Kalman filter for stochastic systems (after Kalman, 1960). The system and parameter equations are updated continuously using extrapolation equations for the parameters. These parameter extrapolation equations give a measure of the expectation of the parameter values, and a measure of the variance envelope within which the parameters are expected with any confidence level. This covariance extrapolation equation is split into two parts for convenience, in which the Kalman gains act as a variable-memory filter governing the degree to which new information is allowed to adjust existing covariance and parameter estimates. Further discussion is given in Bennett (1978a). The prime denotes the transpose of the vectors or matrices.

dynamics can be estimated. Despite the potentialities of this approach, there has, as yet, been only a small number of applications in urban planning. The first of these appears to be Bennett (1975d) who estimated a series of models of parameter change in a distributed lag, transfer function model of the regional economy of North-west England. Shifts in parameter terms were traced over a twenty-year period and were found to affect especially the parameters controlling policy feedback. Subsequent developments by Bennett (1976, 1977, 1978e) have refined the statistical properties of the Kalman filter for the short-series cases characteristic of planning problems, and Martin (1978), Hepple (1978b), and Bennett (1978a) give some more recent examples. The Kalman filter approach allows estimation of the mechanisms of parameter change and therefore complements the Forrester system-dynamics approach in which changes to rates (i.e. parameter equations) are forced *a priori*.

The mathematical stimulus to models of discontinuity in parameter change has come from recent developments in mathematical topology often dubbed 'catastrophe theory' or 'global analysis'. Although deriving from the much earlier ideas of Lotka and Volterra, catastrophe theory encompasses many previously discontinuous structures within a new general framework which has been derived chiefly by René Thom (see Smale, 1974; Thom, 1975). Global analysis enables study of the behaviour of differential equations over the entire range of system initial conditions that can be conceived. This allows the mapping of the trajectory of system responses depending upon the form of initial conditions and the value of controlling parameters. For deterministic systems such trajectories represent smooth traces which may be interrupted by abrupt jumps of so-called bifurcations or points of singularity. For stochastic systems, the global trajectories will show a pattern of variation around smooth trajectories, again interrupted by abrupt jumps (see Bennett, 1978a, Chap. 5). The points of discontinuity relate to conditions at which the urban system becomes conditionally unstable and may move with equal likelihood in two or more different directions.

The first examples of the application of this approach to urban problems are due to Amson (1972a, 1972b, 1974). Amson (1974) constructs a series of 'urbanitic laws' which define state equations for the urban system and can be used to represent a manifold or surface in a state-space on which a trajectory represents a path of urban dynamics evolving other time. Figure 2.2 portrays Amson's four urbanitic laws and the associated morphological structures that result. The third and fourth laws are the most relevant to mathematical topology (i.e. the evanescent and saccadic cities) since these give the fold and cusp catastrophes, respectively. Amson demonstrates that discontinuous changes in urban density result from continuous changes of rentals and civic wealth in an evolving city. There are considerable criticisms of Amson's model (Liverman, 1976): first, the determinants of urban density are by no means unambiguous, and civic wealth is very difficult to define; second, the empirical evidence for discontinuous behaviour in urban systems is inconclusive; third, catastrophe theory requires instantaneous adjustments of the dependent variable to changes in the control variable, but the natural inertia in urban interactive responses results in many lag changes which will constrain the form of discontinuities which result; fourth, catastrophe theory assumes that the control variables are each mutually independent, whereas many studies of urban systems show that income values and rentals are highly correlated; fifth, the third urbanitic law yields the morphology of the fold catastrophe when the density response factor is greater than zero, but high densities are reached only if the city is very opulent and, at fixed rentals, the density will fall as poverty increases until the latter reaches a critical value where the population density becomes imaginary: this evanescent or imaginary behaviour is very difficult to interpret; and sixth, models of equilibrium growth in the city assume an underlying mechanism of economic rationality and economic man which can be very rarely justified.

Another recent study by Wilson (1978) has considered the birth and death of service and other facilities in cities over a global range of trajectories. Wilson postulates that as urban systems grow or decay, thresholds, associated with the range of retail and service goods and with economies of scale, cause unexpected results: in a growing city there is a long time lag after population thresholds have been crossed before services are provided; in a decaying city, there is a long time lag after population has dropped below a critical level before a service outlet will close. Other examples of the application of catastrophe theory to urban problems are provided by Casti and Swain (1976) and Mees (1975), both in a historical context, and by Liverman (1976). The global analysis approach is closely related to models of adaptive and non-stationary parameter dynamics. Thus Bennett (1978a, Chapter 5) demonstrates that changes in the system equation (2.13) can be mapped as topological surfaces depending upon the changes induced by the parameter equation (2.14). It is likely, therefore, that fruitful research

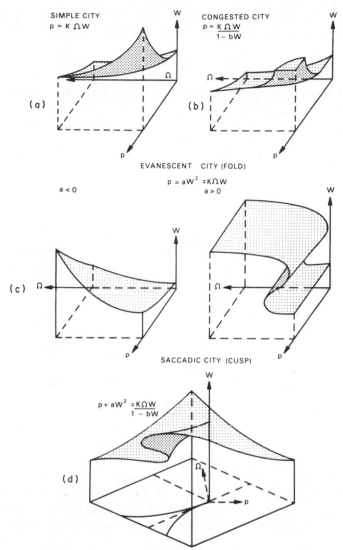

FIGURE 2.2. Four models of urban population density hypothesized by Amson (1972a, 1972b; 1974).

(a) *The simple city:* $p = K\Omega W$. Housing rental is directly proportional to density and opulence.

(b) *The congested city:* $p = (K\Omega W)/(1-bW)$. Rental is inversely related to density weighted by a parameter b which corresponds to the minimum spatial area required by a citizen. Indefinite increases in rentals in (a) lead to physically impossible densities, but (b) introduces a maximum density limitation.

(c) *The evanescent city:* $p + aW^2 = K\Omega W$. Rentals include a response to density in local area controlled by the parameter a, which reflects the willingness of citizens to pay rentals. When a is greater than zero there are two values of the density which satisfy the equation, and a fold catastrophe results.

(d) *The saccadic city:* $p + aW^2 = (K\Omega W)/(1-bW)$. This combines cases (b) and (c). The city is saccadic because densities jump discontinuously in response to changes in rentals and opulence. There is a cusp catastrophe with low values of both rentals and opulence.

Key: W = population density, p = rentals, Ω = opulence, b = personal density constraint, a = willingness to pay rentals at any density, K = constant (after Liverman, 1976)

developments will result from the closer linkage of the statistical approach of Kalman filtering and the mathematical approach of mathematical topology.

General models of urban dynamics

The description of the modelling procedures reviewed above, as comparative static, discrete, and continuous models, represents a rather artificial division when we look at most urban models that have been implemented. Inevitably, any model of the complex workings of urban systems contains elements of each of the three categories discussed, plus a number of other components. In this section, therefore, a number of attempts to combine the various approaches to urban modelling are reviewed in order to generate a more acceptable overall model structure.

Various attempts have been made at defining the requirements that may be made of the structure of a general model which is able adequately to reproduce urban spatial and temporal components. For example, Wilson (1974, Chap. 11) calls for the greater development of five steps in model building: first, better identification of system components and characteristics; second, grouping into subsystems; third, precise definition in relation to spatial, temporal and sectoral aggregation; fourth, better specification of mechanisms of causality, change, and adjustment; and fifth, better definition of the structure and interrelationships between system equations. On the basis of this call, Wilson constructs a theoretical model in difference-equation form which defines allocation and evolution components of population, land use, residence, workplace, services, and transport, in which each component can be disaggregated by socio-economic group, industry type, modal split, and so forth. It should be stated at the outset that it is rarely possible, as yet, to construct general models along the lines suggested by Wilson and others. This is due mainly to the fact that there are insufficient data, particularly on temporal evolution and disaggregated sub-categories. Hence, most practical general models have taken what Wilson (1978) terms an 'eclectic' approach to urban modelling of space–time dynamics: the elements of a general model are developed as far as possible within the context of the demands of the planning situation and the practical constraints of data availability.

One of the earliest attempts to construct a more general basis for space–time modelling was the time oriented metropolitan model (TOMM) (Crecine, 1968; Lowry, 1967). Although similar in structure to the comparative static models in that a Lowry spatial allocation procedure is used at each step, the TOMM model incorporates a number of dynamic components, the most important of which is a 'mover-pool' for both population and service employment. This allows only a portion of previously existing activities to be reallocated at each time period and thus incorporates a component of inertia or lag dynamics in the model, at least implicitly. Further refinements to dynamizing the Lowry–Wilson approach have been made by a number of workers. Sayer (1974) incorporates a series of delay components to population and service employment growth, thus explicitly recognizing lag dynamics: inspired by Forrester's urban dynamics, he uses the delays to act as feedback (autoregressive terms). Batty (1971, 1972) has developed a more general approach with distributed lag structures which, through the introduction of a geometrical time-decay factor as favoured by econometricians, includes long-term delay components. The model is calibrated for Central Berkshire and the distributed lag-delay terms control the residential and service employment-growth equations. This model is extremely useful but suffers from lack of parsimony and restrictions to modelling only of growth; decline in population or service employment cannot be allocated. Batty's approach has been developed and simplified by Rodriguez-Bachiller (1976), who combines a gravity form of location model with a linear programming relocation model for population and service employment. The gravity model component allows the typical exponential distance-decay of population from workplaces or service employment from population centres, but the linear programming model (corresponding to the case in which the exponential parameter in cost function in the gravity model tends to infinity: Evans, 1973) permits the more realistic relocation of population and service employment as near as possible to respective workplaces and population. This combined technique may offer much in future applications.

To overcome the disadvantages of the Batty approach which can only model growth, Bennett (1975b, 1975c, 1975d, 1975e) has developed a five-equation time series model of urban and regional dynamics in which many of Wilson's demands for a general model are satisfied. Equations are identified from available time series data, using characteristics of autocorrelation functions, cross-correlation structures, spectrum and cross-spectrum, and subsequent estimation is developed from least-squares, instrumental variables, and approximate maximum likelihood procedures. In addition, changes in parameter terms representing adaptive parameter or evolutionary dynamics are developed by recursive least-squares, using the Kalman filter. The whole model is calibrated for the Northwest region of England and forecasts developed over short periods of five years into the future. Spatial location and allocation identities are satisfied in Bennett's model, and growth and decline are allocated according to local and interspatial multipliers. Forecasts developed for such models may yield nonsensical results if projection is carried forward for long periods into the future. To overcome this drawback, Bennett (1975b, Appendix; 1978e) suggests combining the Kalman filtering approach with the Wilson entropy-maximizing procedure. The Kalman filter parameter estimates which are generated recursively at each time step are used to redefine the accounting identities in the Wilson singly and doubly constrained allocation models. Putnam (1975) has given a more complex approach to distributed lag modelling in a series of models INTRA-I and INTRA-II for the United States North-east Corridor Transportation Project. Again, distributed components of temporal change are combined with spatial allocation based on gravity equations. In INTRA-II, Putnam introduces a high degree of sectoral disaggregation and also introduces further components based on theories deriving from regional economics. Particularly important is the inclusion of components to model employment procurement advantage, processing advantage, the effects of agglomeration and scale economies, site cost, labour availability, distribution advantage of goods, migration equations, and a personal income sector estimating income, transfer payments, and rent, with apportionment to zone of receipt. Putnam's models are defined largely *a priori* and parameter estimates are developed by use of both single-equation least-squares and by a more complex iterative procedure. While Putnam's estimation procedures are open to some criticism, this model represents perhaps the most ambitious attempt to disaggregate urban models and construct a set of equations capable of satisfying most of Wilson's criteria. In addition, Putnam's approach allows a new set of important linkages to be forged between regional economic theory and the rather cruder hypotheses which underlie most previous urban models.

INTERRELATIONS BETWEEN SPACE–TIME MODELS AND URBAN POLICY

The preceding review should make it clear that the increasing hardware of space–time modelling is achieving a considerable degree of refinement; significant advances are being made towards the achievement of a *general* urban model of spatial and temporal dynamics. One severely neglected area of thinking, however, is how these models can aid, and should aid, the determination of appropriate urban policies. The oft-quoted adage 'models, models everywhere, but nobody stops to think' is not true, but certainly the urban modeller is open to a number of severe criticisms that his models have very largely neglected policy implications and demands. In this section, the interrelations between models and their use are explored. The role of models within a continuous planning and monitoring environment is discussed first. Second, the interrelation between policy determination and statistical calibration of models is explored and shown to lead to a number of important difficulties in model construction which have been previously ignored. Finally, the relevance of models to the creation of difficulties in legitimizing policies is explored and recent, more radical, criticisms of the scientific planner are discussed.

Space–time models, monitoring, and policy formulation

Space–time models can potentially play a very important role in urban planning and policy-making. Most crucial is the ability of dynamic models to create projections of future spatial patterns as an ongoing and continuous process of refinement over time: construction of forecasts, checking of forecasts, and reforecasting forwards. This is often termed a recursive structure within the model, for which the Kalman filter provides a number of important potentialities. In applications to policy-making a recursive structure facilitates a process of 'continuous planning'. The preparation of urban plans has traditionally been a 'one-off' exercise in which a number of possible alternatives has been evaluated and a final preferred pattern of development defined. Such plans give static scenarios of the future. Continuous planning provides an alternative approach—sometimes termed a control view of planning—in which the evolution of events and their relation to policy goals is kept under continuous review (McLoughlin, 1973). Central to this new approach to planning is the concept of monitoring and advisory systems. Monitoring is a process which detects changes which could affect the achievement of a plan, and the advisory component seeks to suggest what actions might be taken in reaction to any deviations from a plan. The general structure of such monitoring systems in regional planning has been summarized by Bennett (1978b) and is shown in Figure 2.3.

Space–time models enter into the monitoring and control structure in four ways. First, they make specific spatial and temporal data demands and serve to emphasize the dynamics of the relations between variables and indicators rather than bald statistics. Second, dynamic models allow the simulation and assessment of both natural 'free' system impacts and also induced policy changes. Third, dynamic models are essential to the development of forecasts. The dynamic models reviewed in the previous section, especially those based on statistical estimation, are especially useful for forecasting since they allow the confidence levels of forecasts to be calculated. Such conditional forecasts (as percentage chances of occurrence) are especially useful since they expose the areas of uncertainty and hence allow policy decisions to be based on choices of courses of action over the range of possible outcomes. Conditional forecasts are also particularly useful in closed-loop situations since government and political behaviour can be rarely predicted with any accuracy. A final role of space–time models in monitoring and control is that they allow the development of feed-forward controls based on forecasts (Bennett and Chorley, 1978). Thus models permit anticipatory action in response to foreseen disturbances, as well as the feedback responses emphasized by McLoughlin and other writers. This is perhaps the crucial role of dynamic models in urban planning since monitoring systems based on space–time models allow a closer approach to *optimal* planning. Each policy issue can be assessed for its likely impacts and a range of actions implemented dependent upon the need for policy changes (Dror, 1968). This approach can encompass incrementalist theories of decision-making, as developed for example by Lindblom (1965), which accept a limit of bounded rationality in making planning decisions and advocate a cautious process of policy refinement within overall goals. But the capacity also for more radical action is retained in such policy-making processes. Much of the spirit of this optimal approach derives from engineering control theory with the most eminent precursors dating from a mathematical theory of governors on steam engines (Bennett and Chorley, 1978; McLoughlin, 1973). These ideas are extremely attractive for planning since they allow continuous feedback, feed-forward, and appraisal of urban policies to determine how far pre-specified goals have been achieved. They have been propounded as part of a systems engineering approach by Jenkins and Youle (1973), Reira and Jackson (1972) and Harris and Scott

44

(1974). They are also a development of management science techniques modified for planning purposes, as for example in policy planning and budgetary systems (PPBS) and organization and management techniques. However, the technocratic structure implied by systems engineering and monitoring systems can create a number of problems in legitimizing policy decisions.

The control and monitoring approach to urban planning generates a number

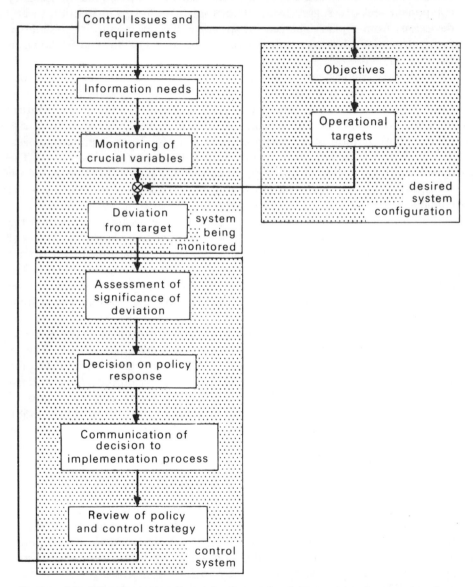

FIGURE 2.3. The elements of monitoring and advisory control systems using space–time models (after Bennett, 1978d, Figure 1)

of demands on space–time models which have not always been properly considered. First, control action requires a clear specification of urban policy goals in terms that can be operationalized and understood. In addition, the specification of goals requires the ancillary definition of tolerance levels associated with the degree to which it is possible to accommodate to non-achievement of goals, and the degree of policy change required to achieve the goals. In each case the policy goals have to enter the modelling procedure as specified conditions for assessing impacts and appropriate policy settings. This leads to a second demand on space–time models, that it is necessary clearly to identify those variables which are amenable to manipulation, i.e. can be used as policy instruments to achieve policy targets. Very few of the dynamic urban models reviewed above contain such policy instruments. Associated with the need better to define policy instruments, a third requirement underlying dynamic urban models is the need for a means of assessing the effectiveness of instruments in different situations. In particular, it is necessary to determine time and space response dynamics to policy shifts and the 'costs' associated with manipulating a given instrument. A fourth requirement of the control approach is to develop a better understanding of the interrelationships of model building (identification, estimation–calibration, and forecasting) and the effects of policy operation. This requires answers to three interrelated questions (Bennett, 1978a, Chap. 8): Can the structure of space-time models be adequately identified? Are the parameters uniquely identifiable? What is the effect of policy responses on the bias and variance properties of parameter estimators used in space–time urban models? The complexities surrounding the answers to these questions are discussed in the next section. A final requirement of a policy-oriented approach to urban planning is a deeper consideration of the implications of space–time models for legitimation (i.e. the relation of the models to participation and assent by the urban populations affected by policies implemented on the basis of these models).

Identification and estimation of space–time models in policy-controlled urban systems

Almost all approaches to urban model building (and most other developments of models in the social sciences) have ignored the fact that spatial and other patterns of urban areas result to a greater or lesser extent from policy decisions. Hence, it is usually assumed that urban systems are operating in a so-called open-loop, that the system is responding to the natural and free interplay of relationships between variables and indicators. Since, however, past policy decisions affect most social and economic systems, and especially affect urban areas, models should be developed which explicitly recognize the effects of policy determination; i.e. models must be constructed of so-called *closed-loop* struc-tures. However, closed-loop urban models cannot be constructed merely by explicit recognition of the role of policy goals and instruments. Instead, a different approach to identification and estimation of space–time models is required as discussed below.

46

Whatever form of space–time urban model is adopted it can usually be written for forecasting purposes in the simple form:

$$\hat{Y}_{t+L} = MX_t \qquad (2.15)$$

In this equation, X_t is an explanatory variable or leading indicator, Y_t is the variable it is sought to forecast, $\hat{Y}_{t+L}$ is the forecast or estimate of Y_t at lead time L, and M is used to express a general space–time model structure.

Whenever urban policy is formulated for use in a continuous planning, monitoring, or advisory system, or other feedback or feed-forward device, it will be usual to attempt to set the level of a policy instrument to achieve a given policy target. In many cases, the leading indicator used in forecasting may also be a policy instrument. Examples are the use of macro-economic variables, such as finance devoted to housing, which can act as an indicator of future population levels; investment in roads, which acts as an overall control of traffic levels; and local tax levels, which act as constraints on disposable income and local consumption. In each case policy targets can be identified as predetermined levels of the forecast variable Y_t which it is desired should be achieved. The policy question then is: At what level must we set the instrument X_t (investment in housing, roads, etc.) to achieve the goal set for Y_t (level of housing or road provision)? Let us first treat this single policy question in isolation. Our requirement is that a predetermined value of urban outcome Y_t (goals) requires the determination of an appropriate value for the policy instrument X_t. This requirement may be specified in the following form:

$$X_t = KY_{t+L} \qquad (2.16)$$

The policy problem is to determine the values of K, termed the control model, which give the appropriate settings of the instrument X_t to yield the pre-specified value of Y_t. If equations (2.15) and (2.16) are compared, it may be seen that they are identical in structure, but differ in both the form of the model and the direction of dependence specified. The use of the leading indicator as a setting for policy targets using a control model therefore gives a closed loop in which the directions of dependence are reversed, as shown in Figure 2.4. In this figure the

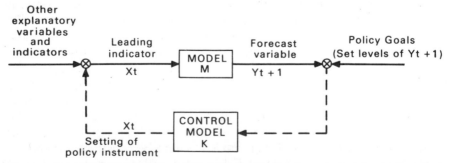

FIGURE 2.4. Closed-loop effects produce by feedback and feed-forward policy strategies. The solid line shows the pattern of free system response, and the dashed line the pattern of control effects (after Bennett, 1978b)

solid line shows the natural or free structures dependence (equation (2.15)), and the dashed line shows the control settings. We may reduce this system to a single structure by use of the feedback policy settings derived from continuous planning and monitoring as discussed in the previous section. This is given simply by substituting equation (2.15) into equation (2.16) to give

$$\hat{Y}_{t+L} = MKY_{t+L} \qquad (2.17)$$

It should be apparent that the best policy will be that which renders a minimum deviation of the forecast $\hat{Y}_{t+L}$ from the desired setting Y_{t+L}. This can be achieved by choosing the control model to have the inverse structure to the system model, i.e. $K = M^{-1}$. Substituting this result into equation (2.17) we have

$$\hat{Y}_{t+L} = MM^{-1}Y_{t+L} \qquad (2.18)$$

or

$$\hat{Y}_{t+L} = Y_{t+L} \qquad (2.19)$$

and the forecast should then equal the preset goals. A major consequence of implementation of a completely effective policy based on system forecasts of feedback is that the operation of the system becomes cancelled out, i.e. the observations of the forecast variable exactly equal the specified goals. If the desire of policy is to implement a feedback or feed-forward strategy which leads to the perfect achievement of present policy goals, in practice of course it is never possible to realize a perfect policy strategy. But even in the case of imperfect and uncertain policy effects, the consequences for statistical models of urban systems are considerable (Bennett, 1978a, 1978b). Four conditions depending upon our knowledge of the system model and the control model can be distinguished. The consequences of each of these for model building, statistical analysis, and policy determination can be summarized as follows (Bennett, 1978b):

1. *Control model (K) and system model (M) known perfectly*

In this case the substitution $K = M^{-1}$ allows the definition of the perfect policy model in equation (2.17) and we have no statistical modelling problem to determine M. This is usually a trivial case since seldom, if ever, are policies and urban systems understood with sufficient accuracy.

2. *Control model (K) known and perfect, system model (M) unknown*

This is again a fairly trivial case since K is seldom known with a high degree of accuracy, but it is important as a special case in order to show the effects of policy feedback. In this case $K = M^{-1}$ and the relation (2.18) is satisfied. Hence any attempt to determine the model M will result merely in identifying the present goals for the forecast variable Y_t. However, since K is known, M can be determined from K.

3. *Control model (K) is unknown and perfect, system model (M) unknown*

This case is similar to (2) in that the forecast variable will equal preset goals, but there is now no opportunity to determine either K or M since both are unknown. The systems operations are completely cancelled out by the policy, and future attempts to identify a forecasting relationship between Y_t and X_t will find no relation between the sample data for the two variables. No statistical method will allow this problem to be overcome. Instead, either we require additional *a priori* information, or we may estimate a 'reduced-form' equation. The reduced-form structure recognizes the stochastic nature of (2.15) i.e.

$$\hat{Y}_{t+L} = MX_t + Ce_{t+L} \tag{2.20}$$

where $\{e_t\}$ is a normally distributed independent random variable sequence. On substituting equation (2.16) and rearranging we obtain

$$\hat{Y}_{t+L} = (\mathbf{I} - MK)^{-1}Ce_{t+L} \tag{2.21}$$

Since we cannot separately determine M, K, or C, forecasts must now be generated merely from past values of the forecast variable Y_t as an extrapolation or autoprojective, autoregressive, moving-average structure.

4. *Imperfect control mode (K) and system model (M), both unknown*

This is the most frequent case to occur in practice. The policy equation is imperfect and exact achievement of goals is impossible. Moreover, policy is sufficiently intuitive and imprecise in definition that it is not possible to define as a simple mathematical structure such as equation (2.16). In addition, our knowledge of the urban system model (equation (2.15)) is also imperfect and imprecise. Thus, we have the normal statistical estimation and calibration problem of determining the structure of an unknown urban model, and an unknown policy model, in a situation in which both the policy mechanism and the urban structure are unknown. Complete cancellation of the free pattern of urban dynamics does not occur if the policy is imperfect, but the consequences are no less severe. It is only possible to obtain estimates of $M = 1/K$; i.e. from substitution of equation (2.16) into equation (2.15) with imperfect K we can determine, from data records of Y_t and X_t alone, only the rule K by which past policy has been chosen (Bohlin, 1971). Under specific conditions it is possible to identify the urban model, e.g. if the control is non-linear or non-stationary while the system is linear and stationary, or vice versa (Ljung, Gustavsson, and Söderström, 1974; Söderström, Gustavsson, and Ljung, 1975). But when these conditions do not apply, a special approach to statistical estimation and calibration of urban models must be adopted.

The statistical problem is that under feedback or feed-forward urban policies, an infinite number of space–time models can represent equation (2.15): the model is statistically under-identified. When only one of a series of leading indicators is used as an instrument of policy feedback, this element is cancelled and each independent variable affected by feedback will be collinear with each other independent variable affected by feedback. In addition, such independent variables become correlated with the errors (Bennett, 1978b, 1978c). Hence least-squares estimates are biased, and most other parameter estimators are inefficient.

Three methods for overcoming these problems are available. The first, the so-called direct method (Gustavsson, 1975), involves the use of special estimators such as maximum likelihood estimates or stochastic approximation. Secondly, the indirect method (Lindberger, 1972) reduces the model to an autoregressive moving-average or reduced-form structure as in equation (2.21). Thirdly, a joint method (Caines and Chan, 1975) applies a simultaneous equation estimation approach to estimation of a reduced-form equation for both the model and the policy elements. Each method will give the same results asymptotically, but the joint method has the advantage that it yields estimates of the policy component as well as the system model.

These various effects can be summarized very simply: if an urban system has been operating under even a fairly small degree of policy influence, statistical approaches to identification and parameter estimation of space–time models will yield unstable, inefficient, and biased results. If the urban system has been subject to a high degree of policy influence, it may not be possible to construct space–time models at all. Instead it will only be possible to model policy itself.

It is not altogether clear how far each of the models reviewed in the preceding section of this chapter are affected by the closed-loop constraint since few of these models have made clear the policy environment in which they are enmeshed. It is, however, possible to conclude that all the models reviewed must be affected to some extent by policy closed loops, and hence the validity and usefulness of their conclusions must be open to considerable criticism.

Space–time models and urban policy legitimation

The increased use of space–time models in continuous monitoring and planning leads not only to statistical problems in calibrating urban models, but also to severe difficulties in planning procedure and practice. It is a widely held view that urban planning provides a framework within which it is possible to reshape overall social well-being. As recognized by Smith (1977, p. 158):

evaluation leads directly to planning, or to the deliberate implementation of change. Planning may be regarded as applied welfare analysis; spatial planning is applied welfare geography. Any urban or regional plan has the capacity to alter the distribution of goods and bads—to change who gets what where by modifying the process of how. . . . Some conscious planning is needed in all societies, but the more complex they become the more organization and control is required to run them efficiently.

If urban policy is becoming more oriented towards the management of social well-being, an equally important trend is towards the urban planner himself becoming what Adams (1977, p. 23) terms a kind of doctor: 'They see themselves, and are seen by the general public, as doctors, as people with specialist knowledge not available to, and often not comprehensible to the lay public.' The major consequence of both the increasing interest in the management of urban well-being and the increasing skills of the urban planner are a divorce, or even an alienation, of the policy-maker from the subjects of this decision, the people living in an urban area. A major component underlying this separation is the highly developed modelling skill of the planner. Thus, Adams claims that the scientific planner and his models act almost as a kind of ameliorative drug which undermines any sense of community between people, and, most importantly, undermines the ability of individuals to participate in policy decisions in any meaningful way.

The challenge that urban models undermine the ability of the planner to legitimate decisions cannot be lightly dismissed, yet this criticism has rarely been tackled head on. How can the urban planner answer these critics of his models? The difficulties of participation in scientific planning lead few people to accept that much would be gained by abandoning scientific planning and modelling as such. Adams and other critics of scientific planning seem to hark back either to simpler societies in which decisions are not as complex, or to support a more *laissez-faire* approach to society. The latter issue, of the right mixture of planning and individual freedom in a mixed economy, is almost an irresolvable question, at least in general terms. But the first issue of a return to a simpler society discounts all the desires and aspirations of man in society as part of a syndrome of growth. Few individuals will accept the consequences of abandoning this syndrome. Certainly by abandonment of growth we are brought no closer to solution of the legitimation problem unless we accept a fundamental change to the level of well-being in urban society, and a severe reduction in the degree to which most wish to participate in the benefits of public goods. Despite this response, however, it must be firmly accepted that much more effort must be made to develop and explain the structure of the models employed in policy formulation. Related to this need is a requirement of abandoning as far as possible models based on black box devices established on statistical or mathematical criteria alone, such as parsimony. Such models reproduce the dynamics of urban areas only in a mathematical sense; their parameters can be rarely given physical meaning. For this reason, the urban planner should favour models in which economic and social processes are explicit and verifiable.

The demands of legitimation for credibility and explication form one component of desires for micro-models derived from clearly understood and verifiable urban social processes. Another component of the argument for smaller-scale models is that macro-models which ignore the real dynamics of urban processes are counter-productive to the achievement of policy goals. In the context of macro-economic stabilization theory, Ramsey (1977, p. 63) has likened macro-policy models to driving a train through the rear window: 'Macro-monitory and fiscal policy are the accelerator and brake of the engine;

micro-theory provides the link-ups between the controls and the engine and the wheels. More importantly, micro-theory, . . . provides the design of the engine in the first place.' On the basis of this view Ramsey argues, with a *laissez-faire* market approach, that much would be gained by adopting the correct micro-models and micro-policies. If this approach is utilized, the need for macro-policies and macro-models diminishes, and in some cases disappears. Taking the argument one step further, Harris (1977) argues that most of the problems of policy result from the adoption of a scientific paradigm for planning which seeks ever-larger and more general models. The search for more general models has been argued above to be an important direction of development in space–time techniques. But Harris (1977, p. 88) argues that the larger and more general the model the greater is the need for disaggregation and hence the greater is the obfuscation that the model produces: '. . . disaggregated into regions, sex, age-groups, trades. . . . However much this micro-make-believe is chopped up into sub-categories, the results are not refined substances nor necessarily even cohesive groups but still monstrous heterogenous heaps.' As in macro-economic policy, so in urban planning it can be argued that a macro-approach can lead to severe inaccuracies, with attendant policies which may work as often against as towards the goals it is desired to achieve. Hence, it can be argued that to the component of credibility of urban models should be added the demand for systems of urban space–time dynamics to be rooted in a firmly understood micro-behavioural theory. Hence, on the one hand the requirements of legitimation call for a better-understood and smaller-scale approach to model building. On the other hand, however, we have the desire for more general and larger scale models. If decisions based on black box and complex aggregates cannot be made credible to those who must suffer the adverse consequences of any policy decision, even if the model fit and forecasts are good, then the urban planner must adapt his models to the purpose in hand. While general and black box models can be made useful devices for the planner himself, if the forecasts and conclusions drawn from these models are to be used as the basis of policy then either the models themselves must be open to general debate and justification or legitimation must be sought instead in terms of small-scale models based on processes and relations that can be clearly understood and justified.

One problem in implementing this conclusion is that with the increasing use of policy, closed-loop effects become more important, and the models which must be used become more complex. In fact, the model builder is often forced to accept parsimonious, autoregressive, moving-average models or reduced-form esti-mators in closed-loop situations. In a discussion of road and air traffic forecasting models, for example, Bennett (1978b, 1978c) concludes that solving the technical issues surrounding closed loops will exacerbate the difficulties of obtaining legitimation of policies in practice. In this case the forecasts themselves should not be used to justify policy decisions as has been the case with road and air traffic forecasts where forecasting models have been the basis for decisions and arguments at public enquiries. The conclusion to be drawn from this discussion must be that the forecasts produced for road schemes, and other urban policy demands, can only be indicative (this would in any case be the view accepted by most model-builders). Hence, better understanding of local conditions, and of the policy goals themselves, will be more useful than continued use of the forecasts themselves as matters of policy. This accords to some extent with recent radical interpretations in urban geography (see, for example, Harvey, 1973) which have also questioned the value of scientific planning and have suggested instead that we need a better ability to decide on the values and choices which should underlie urban structures rather than merely to forecast likely outcomes (i.e. the policy-maker should concern himself less with forecasting urban changes and impacts, and should instead devote more attention to the critical debate and implementation of social goals). Whether we concur with the radical critics or not, it must be accepted that as dynamic models of urban spatial structures come to play an increasing role in urban planning, the planner will need to spend less time in developing and generalizing his models and more time in tailoring them to the specific policy environments within which he must act: he must become increasingly aware of the answer to the question of 'models for what?'.

CONCLUSION: FUTURE RESEARCH PRIORITIES

This chapter has reviewed a series of approaches to the construction of dynamic models of urban spatial structure and then examined the way in which these models interface with a number of issues of urban policy. It is now appropriate to ask where the research priorities should lie in future developments of space–time models in urban research. Six main areas of priority are distinguished.

First, the techniques for constructing space–time models are still very inadequate in many cases. The statistical theory of single-series problems (autoregressive, moving-average models) has been extensively researched by statisticians, but there is as yet little information on the small sample properties of many of the statistical identification and estimation techniques that must be used at the calibration stage of analysis. In particular, there is little or no information on the properties of calibration routines in closed-loop situations.

A second area of research priority is in the development of more adaptable models, especially those capable of reproducing and forecasting non-stationary and non-linear shifts in urban processes. In this context it will be important to develop the application of Kalman filter techniques for recursive calibration, and the related techniques of mathematical topology for refinements of deductive mathematical structures. Linkages with traditional urban models also need to be forged so that comparative static and entropy-maximizing models can be developed within a more adaptable framework (see Bennett, 1978e; Martin, Thrift, and Bennett, 1978). This will also permit a more thorough development of space–time models which incorporate the variety of equilibrium, quasi-dynamic, evolutionary, and emergent structures which Carlstein, Parkes, and Thrift (1978) identify. This will allow the development of models of urban systems which satisfy both equilibrium and structuralist arguments, where appropriate: Sayer (1976), for example, suggests that in this way we may encapsulate diachronic and synchronic changes within a single urban structure. This may in turn lead us to reject gravity and black box models in which the function and cause of dependence in suppressed.

The development of adaptive space–time models, whether based on structuralist arguments or not, combines with a third component of research priority concerned with development of the underpinning basis of value and meaning implicit in urban models. As models become used to a progressively greater extent for planning purposes, the need to explain and justify these models militates against models based on unknown structures and inferential assumptions such as entropy-maximizing. For the purposes of the planner these models may give good forecasts and hence justify further research development, but an important research priority exists in developing models the structure of which is transparent to both the user and those affected by policy decisions.

A fourth area requiring priority in research also relates to policy issues. This requires the better development, definition, and understanding of goals and policy instruments. Few models of urban structure at present incorporate either component so that their usefulness for simulating policy impacts is very restricted. Related to this area is a fifth research priority, to develop explicit control models in urban systems. These may adopt structures based on welfare and objective functions, as in the optimal control approach used in engineering, but more useful in many instances will be more *ad hoc* control formulations. These latter can be based on specification of monitoring structures which permit early detection and response to changing urban structures. The development of specific urban control models based on optimization approaches has been taken to an initial stage by Bennett and Tan (1978), but much research is still required in this area, especially into multi-level control problems at different spatial scales in an urban economy and into the relationships between the stages and model construction and policy determination.

Related to these control issues, and throwing more emphasis on *ad hoc* rather than optimal solutions to policy questions, a continuous approach to planning based on recursive space–time models generates a shift in emphasis in urban policy questions. Hence, a sixth priority research area is to determine how models should be constructed to deal with the effects of shorter-term policy needs. A shift of policy interest away from project appraisal and specification of urban layouts towards recurrent questions of urban planning moves the emphasis increasingly towards concern with resource allocation and public finance. This concern is greatly reinforced by periods such as the mid-1970s in which public finance is relatively scarce, but social needs are relatively great. Few of the presently available models of urban dynamics are able to tackle these important allocation questions, and it is in this area which perhaps the major priority for urban research with space–time models should lie.

REFERENCES

Adams, J. G. U. (1977). The national health. *Environment and Planning,* Series A, **9**, 23–33.

Amson, J. C. (1972a). Equilibrium models of cities: an axiomatic theory. *Environment and Planning,* Series A, **4**, 429–444.

Amson, J. C. (1972b). Equilibrium models of cities: single species cities. *Environment and Planning*, Series A, **5**, 295–338.

Amson, J. C., (1974). Equilibrium and catastrophic modes of urban growth. In A. G. Wilson (Ed.), London Papers in Regional Science, 4, *Space–time Concepts in Urban and Regional Models*, Pion, London, pp. 108–128.

Bartels, C. P. (1977). *Economic Aspects of Regional Welfare, Income Distribution and Unemployment*, Martinus Nijhoff, Amsterdam.

Bassett, K., and Tinline, R. (1970). Cross spectral analysis of time series and geographical research. *Area*, **2**, 19–24.

Bassett, K., and Haggett, P., (1971). Towards short-term forecasting for cyclic behaviour in a regional system of cities. In M. Chisholm, A. Frey, and P. Haggett (Eds.), *Regional Forecasting*, Butterworths, London, pp. 389–413.

Batty, M. (1971). Modelling cities as dynamic systems. *Nature*, **231**, 425–428.

Bell, F. W. (1967). An econometric forecasting model for a region. *Journal of Regional Science*, **7**, 109–128.

Bennett, R. J. (1974). Process identification for time series modelling in urban and regional planning. *Regional Studies*, **8**, 157–174.

Bennett, R. J. (1975a). The representation and identification of spatio-temporal systems: an example of population diffusion in North West England. *Transactions of the Institute of British Geographers*, **66**, 73–94.

Bennett, R. J. (1975b). Dynamic systems modelling of the North West Region: 1. Spatio-temporal representation and identification. *Environment and Planning*, Series A, **7**, 525–538.

Bennett, R. J. (1975c). Dynamic systems modelling of the North West Region: 2. Estimation of the spatio-temporal policy model. *Environment and Planning*, Series A, **7**, 539–566.

Bennett, R. J. (1975d). Dynamic systems modelling of the North West Region: 3. Adaptive-parameter policy model. *Environment and Planning*, Series A, **7**, 617–636.

Bennett, R. J. (1975e). Dynamic systems modelling of the North West Region: 4. Adaptive spatio-temporal forecasts. *Environment and Planning*, Series A, **7**, 887–898.

Bennett, R. J. (1976). Non-stationary parameter estimation for small sample situations: a comparison of methods. *International Journal of Systems Science*, **7**, 257–275.

Bennett, R. J. (1977). Consistent estimation of nonstationary parameters for small sample situations—a Monte Carlo Study. *International Economic Review*, **18**, 489–502.

Bennett, R. J. (1978a). *Spatial Time Series: Analysis, Forecasting and Control*, Pion, London.

Bennett, R. J. (1978b). Forecasting in urban and regional planning closed loops: the example of road and air traffic forecasts. *Environment and Planning*, Series A, **10**, 145–162.

Bennett, R. J. (1978c). Discussion of the paper by J. C. Tanner, *Journal Royal Statistical Society*, Series A, **140**, 47–48.

Bennett, R. J. (1978d). Regional monitoring in the U.K.: imperatives and implications for research. *Regional Studies*, **12**, 311–322.

Bennett, R. J. (1978e). Adaptive parameter space–time models: an entropy maximising application using the Kalman filter with unknown prior parameters. In R. L. Martin, N. Thrift, and R. J. Bennett, (Eds.), *Towards the Dynamic Analysis of Spatial Systems*, Pion, London.

Bennett, R. J. and Chorley, R. J. (1978). *Environmental Systems: Philosophy, Analysis and Control*, Methuen, London.

Bennett, R. J., and Tan, K. C. (1978). Stochastic control models of regional economies. In C. P. Bartels and R. H. Ketellapper, (Eds.), *Exploratory and Explanatory Statistical Analysis of Spatial Data*, Martinus Nijhoff, Amsterdam.

Blalock, H. M. (1964). *Causal Inference in Non-experimental Research*, North Carolina University Press, Chapel Hill.

Bohlin, T. (1971). On the problem of ambiguities in maximum likelihood estimation. *Automatica*, **7**, 199–210.

Bourne, L. S. (1969). A spatial allocation—land use conversion model of urban growth. *Journal of Regional Science*, **9**, 261–272.

Box, G. E. P. and Jenkins, G. M. (1970). *Time Series Analysis, Forecasting Analysis and Control*, Holden-Day, San Francisco.

Burdekin, R. and Marshall, S. A. (1972). The use of Forrester's systems dynamics approach in urban modelling. *Environment and Planning*, Series A, **4**, 471–485.

Caines, P. E. and Chan, C. W. (1975). Feedback between stationary stochastic processes. *I.E.E.E. Transactions on Automatic Control*, **AC-20**, 498–508.

Carlstein, T., Parkes, D. N., and Thrift, N. J. (1978). *Timing Space and Spacing Time in Socio-economic Systems*, Edward Arnold, London.

Casetti, E., King, L., and Jeffrey, D. (1971). Structural imbalance in the U.S. urban-economic system, 1960–1965. *Geographical Analysis*, **3**, 293–255.

Casti, J. and Swain, H. (1976). Catastrophe theory and urban processes (unpublished paper).

Chatfield, C. (1975). *The Analysis of Time Series: Theory and Practice*, Chapman and Hall, London.

Chen, K. (1972). *Urban Dynamics: Extensions and Reflections*, San Francisco Press, San Francisco.

Cliff, A. D. and Ord, K. (1975). Model building and the analysis of spatial pattern in human geography. *Journal of the Royal Statistical Society*, Series B, **37**, 297–384.

Cliff, A. D., Haggett, P., Ord, K., Bassett, K., and Davies, R. (1975). *Elements of Spatial Structure*, Cambridge University Press, Cambridge.

Collins, L. D. (1972). *Industrial Migration in Ontario: Forecasting Aspects of Industrial Activity Through Markov Chain Analysis*, Statistics Canada, Ottawa.

Cowan, P., Fine, D., Ireland, J., Jordan, C., Mercer, D., and Sears, A. (1969). *The Office—A Facet of Urban Growth*, Heinemann, London.

Constable, D. (1973). *Urban Growth Processes: The Forrester Model*, Department of Geography, University of Reading, GP-21.

Crecine, J. P. (1968). *A Dynamic Model of Urban Structure*, Rand Corporation, Santa Monica.

C.R.E.U.E. (1968). *Jobs, People and Land*, Center of Real Estate and Urban Economics, Bay Area Simulation Study, Berkeley.

Czmanski, S. (1965). A method of forecasting metropolitan growth by means of distributed lags analysis. *Journal of Regional Science*, **6**, 33–49.

Czmanski, S. (1969). Regional econometric models: A case study of Nova Scotia, in London Papers in Regional Science 1. In A. J. Scott (Ed.), *Studies in Regional Science*, Pion, London, pp. 143–180.

Drewett, R. (1969). A stochastic model of the land conversion process: interim report. *Regional Studies*, **3**, 269–280.

Dror, Y. (1968). *Public Policy Making Re-examined*, Chandler, San Francisco.

Echenique, M. (1969). *Urban Systems: Towards an Explorative Model*, University of Cambridge, Centre for Land Use and Built Form Studies, WP 2.

Evans, S. (1973). A relationship between the gravity model for trip distribution and the transportation problem in linear programming. *Transportation Research*, **7**, 39–62.

Feller, W. (1950). *An Introduction to Probability Theory and its Applications*, Wiley, New York.

Forrester, J. W. (1968). *Urban Dynamics*, M.I.T. Press, Cambridge, Massachusetts.

Forrester, J. W. (1971). Systems analysis as a tool for urban planning, *I.E.E.E. Spectrum*, **8**, 48–54.

Glickman, N. J. (1972). *An Area-stratified Regional Econometric Model*, Regional Science Research Institute, University of Pennsylvania Discussion Paper No. 58.

Glickman, N. J. (1977). *Econometric Analysis of Regional Systems: Explorations in Model*

Building and Policy Analysis, Academic Press, New York.

Gustavsson, I. (1975). Survey of applications of identification in chemical and physical processes. *Automatica*, **11**, 3–24.

Haggett, P. (1971). Leads and lags in inter-regional systems: A study of cyclic fluctuations in the south-west economy. In M. Chisholm, and G. Manners, (Eds.), *Spatial Policy Problems of the British Economy*, Cambridge University Press, Cambridge.

Haggett, P., Cliff, A. D., and Frey, A. (1977). *Locational Analysis in Human Geography*, 2nd edn., Edward Arnold, London.

Hamilton, H. R., Goldstone, S. E., Milliman, J. W., Pugh, H. C., Roberts, E. R., and Zellner, J. (1969). *Spatial Simulation for Regional Analysis: An Application to River Basin Planning*, M.I.T. Press, Cambridge, Massachusetts.

Harris, C. C. (1968). A stochastic process model of residential development. *Journal of Regional Science*, **8**, 29–39.

Harris, R. (1977). *A Sceotical Note on Forecasting in Britain, Economic Forecasting — Models or Markets*, Institute of Economic Affairs, London.

Harris, R. and Scott, D. (1974). The role of monitoring and review in planning. *Planning, Journal of the Royal Town Planning Institute*, **60** 720–732.

Harvey, D. (1973). *Social Justice and the City*, Arnold, London.

Hepple, L. W. (1975). Spectral techniques and the study of interregional economic cycles. In R. Peel, M. Chisholm, and P. Haggett, (Eds.), *Processes in Physical and Human Geography, Bristol Essays*, Heinemann, London.

Hepple, L. W. (1978a). Forecasting the economic recession in Britain's depressed regions. In R. L. Martin, N. Thrift, and R. J. Bennett, *Towards the Dynamic Analysis of Spatial Systems*, Pion, London.

Hepple, L. W. (1978b). Regional dynamics in UK unemployment and the effects of the economic recession. In N. Wrigley (Ed.), *Geography and Statistics*, Pion, London.

Hill, D. (1965). A growth allocation model for the Boston region. *Journal of the American Institute of Planners*, **31** 111–120.

I.E.E.E. (1972). *I.E.E.E. Transactions on Systems, Man and Cybernetics*, special issue, SMC-2.

Ingram, G. K., Kain, J. F., and Ginn, J. R. (1972). *The Detroit Prototype of the N.B.E.R. Urban Simulation Model*, National Bureau of Economic Research, New York.

Jeffrey, D., Casetti, E., and King, L. (1969). Economic fluctuations in a multiregion setting: a bifactor analytic approach. *Journal of Regional Science*, **9**, 397–404.

Jenkins, G. M., and Watts, D. G. (1968). *Spectral Analysis and its Application*, Holden-Day, New York.

Jenkins, G. M., and Youle, P. V. (1973). *Systems Engineering*, Pitman, London.

Johnston, J. (1972). *Econometric Methods*, 2nd edn., McGraw-Hill, New York.

Kalman, R. E. (1960). A new approach to linear filtering and prediction problems. *Transactions A.S.M.E., Journal of Basic Engineering*, D, **82** 35–45.

Kendall, M. G. (1973). *Time Series*, Charles Griffen, London.

Kendall, M.G., and Stuart, A. (1966). *The Advanced Theory of Statistics*, Charles Griffen, London.

King, L. Casetti, E., and Jeffrey, D. (1969). Economic impulses in a regional system of cities: a study of spatial interactions. *Regional Studies*, **3**, 213–218.

King, L., Casetti, E., and Jeffrey, D. (1972). Cyclical fluctuations in unemployment levels in U.S. metropolitan areas. *Tijdschrift voor Economische and Sociale Geographie*, **63** 345–352.

King, L. J., and Forster, J. (1973). Wage-rate change in urban labor markets and intermarket linkages. *Papers of the Regional Science Association*, **30**, 183–196.

Lever, W. F. (1972). The inter-urban movement of manufacturing: a Markov approach. *Transactions of the Institute of British Geographers*, **56**, 21–38.

Lianos, T. P. (1972). The migration process and time lags. *Journal of Regional Science*, **12** 425–433.

Lindberger, N. A. (1972). Stochastic modelling of computer-regulated linear plants in noisy environments. *International Journal of Control*, **16**, 1009–1019.

Lindblom, C. E. (1965). *The Intelligence of Democracy: Decision Making Through Partisan Mutual Adjustment*, Free Press, New York.

Liverman, D. (1976). *The Application of Catastrophe Theory to Geographical Systems*, Department of Geography, University College London, B.A. thesis, 61 pp.

Ljung, L., Gustavsson, I., and Söderström, T. (1974). Identification of linear multivariable systems operating under linear feedback control. *I.E.E.E. Transactions on Automatic Control*, **AC-19**, 836–840.

Lowry, I. S. (1964). *A Model of Metropolis*, Rand Corporation, Santa Monica.

Lowry, I. S. (1967). *Seven Models of Urban Development: A Structural Comparison*, Rand Corporation, Santa Monica.

Mackett, R. L. (1976). *The Theoretical Structure of a Dynamic Urban Activity and Stock Allocation Model*, Institute for Transport Studies, University of Leeds, WO-68.

McLouglin, J. B. (1973). *Control and Urban Planning*, Faber, London.

Martin, R. L. (1978). Kalman filter modelling of time varying processes in urban and regional planning. In R. L. Martin, N. Thrift, and R. J. Bennett (Eds.), *Towards the Dynamic Analysis of Spatial Systems*, Pion, London.

Martin, R. L. and Oeppen, J. E. (1975). The identification of regional forecasting models using space-time correlation functions. *Transactions of the Institute of British Geographers*, **66**, 95–118.

Martin, R. L., Thrift, N., and Bennett, R. J. (1978). *Towards the Dynamic Analysis of Spatial Systems*, Pion, London.

Mass, N. J. (Ed.) (1972). *Reading in Urban Dynamics*, Vol. 1, Write-Allen, New York.

Mees, A. I. (1975). The revival of the city in medieval Europe. *Regional Science and Urban Economics*, **5**, 403–425.

Neidercorn, J. H. and Bechdolt, B. V. (1969). An economic derivation of the gravity law of spatial interaction, *Journal of the Regional Science Association*, **9**, 273–282.

Paelinck, J. (1970). Dynamic urban models. *Papers of the Regional Science Association*, **14**, 25–37.

Putnam, S. H. (1975). *An Empirical Model of Metropolitan Growth with an Application to the Northeast Megalopolis*, Regional Science Research Institute, Philadelphia.

Ramsey, J. B. (1977). *Economic Forecasting—Models or Markets*, Institute of Economic Affairs, London.

Rees, P., and Wilson, A. G. (1977). *Spatial Population Analysis*, Edward Arnold, London, 240 pp.

Reif, B. (1973). *Models in Urban and Regional Planning*, Leonard Hill, Aylesbury.

Reira, B. and Jackson, M. (1973). *The Design of a Monitoring and Advisory System for Sub-regional Planning*, I.S.C.O.L. Ltd, Lancaster University.

Rodriguez-Bachiller, A. (1976). *Gravity Models in a Dynamic Framework*, Department of Geography, University of Reading, GP-40, 56 pp.

Rogers, A. (1966). Matrix methods of population analysis. *Journal of the American Institute of Planners*, **32**, 40–44.

Sant, M. (1973). *The Geography of Business Cycles: A Case Study of Economic Fluctuations in East Anglia*, London School of Economics Geography Papers, No. 5.

Sayer, R. A. (1974). A dynamic Lowry model. In M. H. Whithed and R. M. Sarly, (Eds.), *Urban Simulation Models for Public Policy Analysis*, Sijthoff, Amsterdam.

Sayer, R. A. (1976). A critique of urban modelling: from regional science to urban and regional political economy. *Progress in Planning* **6**, 187–254.

Seidman, D. R. (1969). *The Construction of an Urban Growth Model*, Delaware Valley Regional Planning Commission, Plan Report 1, Technical Supplement.

Smale, S. (1974). Global analysis and economics. *Journal of Mathematical Economics*, **1**, 1–14, 107–118, 119–127, 213–222.

Smith, D. M. (1977). *Human Geography: A Welfare Approach*, Edward Arnold, London.

Smith, W. (1942). *The Distribution of Population and the Location of Industry on Merseyside*, Liverpool University Press, Liverpool.

Söderström, T., Gustavsson, I., and Ljung, L. (1975). Identifiability conditions for linear systems operating in closed loop. *International Journal of Control*, **21**, 243–255.

Swanson, C. V., and Waldman, R. J. (1970). Simulation model of economic growth dynamics. *Journal of the American Institute of Planners*, **36**, 314–322.

Telford, K., Yule, A., and Burdekin, R. (1974). *A Dynamic Macroeconomic Model of the Northern Economic Planning Region*, IBM Scientific Centre, Peterlee, UKSC 0059.

Thom, R. (1975). *Structural Stability and Morphogenesis: An Outline of a General Theory of Models*, Benjamin, London.

Weissbrod, R. S. P. (1976). *Spatial Diffusion of Relative Wage Inflation*, Northwestern University Studies in Geography, Evanston, Illinois.

Wilson, A. G. (1970). *Entropy in Urban and Regional Modelling*, Pion, London.

Wilson, A. G. (1974). *Urban and Regional Models in Geography and Planning*, Wiley, London.

Wilson, A. G. (1978). Towards models of the evolution and genesis of urban structure. In R. L. Martin, N. Thrift, and R. J. Bennett, (Eds.), *Towards the Dynamic Analysis of Spatial Systems*, Pion, London.

Wilson, A. G., Hawkins, A. F., Hill, G. J., and Wagon, D. J. (1969). Calibrating and testing the SELNEC transport model. *Regional Studies*, **2**, 337–350.

Chapter 3

Cognitive Mapping and Understanding

Miriam J. Boyle and M. E. Robinson

Knowing about the world involves some very complex processes. The most basic depend upon the stimulation of our senses by the things, the people, and the events that are around us. We see them; in life, on film, or represented pictorially and symbolically in the pages of books and newspapers. We also *hear* them; in life, through recordings and on telephones. Particular stimuli are sometimes close enough for us to touch, or taste, or smell. In the immediacy and intimacy of these perceptions we begin to acquire the raw materials of our experience and our learning. Other processes are different because they do not depend on the sensory awareness of an immediate stimulus. Putting the matter plainly, we *think* about things that are not there. Occasionally we simply attempt to recall direct experiences from the past, because to do so would be useful to us, or pleasant for us, or whatever. At other times the way in which we think has a distinctly creative aspect, as when we attempt to anticipate things which might happen in the future, or even things which we know will never happen to us at all. These action replays and these mental rehearsals also have a positive and complex relationship with the direct perceptual activities that fill our waking life. For much of the time our thoughts and our perceptions mesh together as we categorize and cogitate on the things around us and the activities of the moment. By employing our past experiences and the things that we have learned we are able to organize and stabilize the constant stream of discriminably different things with which we come into contact as a matter of routine. Occasionally, and without great effort, we suspend our perceptual attention and focus our thoughts deliberately and purposefully on things that are outside our immediate sensory scope. But in both these situations, one perceptually active and one contemplative, we assimilate our sensory experiences into the stable structures of knowing and understanding.

In doing this we employ two remarkable innate capacities. First, we display an enormous ability to discriminate between things: we can effortlessly identify the unique properties of countless numbers of separate things and separate events when it suits us to do so. We seldom mistake one thing for another or one event for another, even when those things and those events share many common attributes. We have, in Bruner, Goodnow, and Austin's (1956, p. 1) words, 'an exquisite capacity for making distinctions'. The seeming paradox to this is that with an equal facility we are able to disregard the uniqueness of individual things and to identify instead the equivalences of similar things. Moreover, this ability to categorize things is really very sophisticated. We can usually classify objects, people, places, events, and so on in a variety of different ways, depending on the criteria we choose to employ, each one of which has a particular contextual utility which facilitates efficient thought and relevant communication. It is interesting, however, that although the ability to discriminate and to categorize is common to all of us, the precise structures that we employ are decidedly not. Many studies have shown how the influence of particular cultures colours our interpretation of the world to the extent that even the identification of a unique event may vary from one society to another (Saarinen, 1976). To the Australian, for example, snow may be an irreducible phenomenon. To the Eskimo, on the other hand, it is a category that is readily reducible on the basis of different snow attributes, each type of which has an appropriate name and a particular contextual relevance. The way in which we discriminate or categorize, therefore, depends upon previous experience of appropriate discriminating and classifying behaviour within our own culture and even within our own social and family groups. The particular structures through which we organize our understanding of the world are learned rather than innate.

Thinking about the world, we fuse together these varied sources of information and organization. We employ not only the separate experiences of perception and memory, and the separate ends of recall and anticipation, but also our innate organismic capacities and the acquired learning and skills that attend our socialization. In this chapter we want to consider some of the ways in which people think about the world and in particular those activities which have been called 'cognitive mapping' and those products of constructed reality which have been called 'cognitive maps'.

COGNITIVE MAPPING AND COGNITIVE MAPS

Thinking is an easy thing to do, but it is a very difficult thing to explain or to describe. The few observations that we have made so far are no more than a very colloquial skimming on the surface of a difficult scientific concept. Perhaps because the concept is so elastic we tend to shy away from discussing issues in terms of the comprehensive activity of thought and to refer instead to some more restricted allied or constituent process like perception, imagery, and so on. This tendency sometimes creates the impression of a greater degree of precision in meaning than our intentions actually warrant. On some occasions, as Tuan (1975) has observed, our use of psychological vocabulary is decidedly metaphorical.

Cognitive mapping is one of these difficult and ambiguous terms. It seems to imply the evocation of visual images which possess the kinds of structural properties that we are familiar with in 'real' cartographic maps. This is certainly the sense in which it is interpreted by Hart and Moore (1973, p. 248) who regard cognitive mapping as 'only one form of cognitive representation of large scale environments' and therefore falling within the more inclusive concept of spatial cognition which they define as 'the internalized reflection and reconstruction of space in thought'. This restricted view of cognitive mapping is also clearly synonymous with Tuan's (1975) use of that flexible and frustrating term 'mental map' and with Canter's (1977) 'cognitive cartography', and it is at least very close to Piaget's concept of 'topographical schema' (Piaget, Inhelder, and Szeminska, 1960).

Other writers regard cognitive mapping in quite a different light. Tolman (1948, p. 206), who coined the term in the context of the behaviour of rats in mazes, used it in a much more general sense in his 'brief, cavalier and dogmatic' foray into the realms of human social and individual maladjustment. Kaplan (1973, p. 74) also uses the term very broadly to convey something of the essence of adaptive decision-making in the internalization of 'possible situations and the relations between them'. It would make little difference to the arguments of either Tolman or Kaplan if their cognitive maps were called cognitive programmes, or cognitive diagrams, or whatever. For both of them the map is merely an analogy for the logical structures of constructive thought. Another very broad definition of cognitive mapping is the one employed by Downs and Stea (1973, p. 11), but here the mapping analogy and the role of place has a much more literal influence. Although they are careful to emphasise the *function* rather than the *form* of cognitive maps, many of the functions which they discuss are those which might be achieved through a cartographic representation. Following Blaut, McCleary, and Blaut (1970) they assert that 'the focus of attention is on a cognitive representation which has the *functions* of the familiar *cartographic* map but not necessarily the physical properties of such a pictorial graphic model'. In addition, they also emphasize the importance of assessments of choice and value, liking and disliking, wanting and not-wanting, that are inextricably bound up with the way in which we think about places. They define cognitive maps, therefore, not only in terms of the processing of physical and locational information about the geographical environment but also in the context of those features of places which lead us to think affectively about them. They call these attributes 'evaluative or connotative' and they embody the kinds of properties that formed the inferential basis of the many preference studies inspired by Gould's (1966) early paper. More directly they are the kinds of attributes that have been studied by Jackson and Johnston (1972), Harrison and Sarre (1975), Palmer, Robinson, and Thomas (1977), and many others. It appears, in effect, that Downs and Stea view cognitive mapping as a reduction of Kaplan's more general concept to a particular case defined by the properties of geographical space but not necessarily internalized in a map-like form. To use Austin's (1962, p. 68) term, it is a view of cognitive mapping that is 'substantive hungry': it is defined by the properties of rather arbitrary physical referents, but it is otherwise indistinguishable from the comprehensive activity that is known more commonly as 'thinking'.

In view of these very different interpretations of the same term it is not surprising that a good deal of confusion surrounds the topic of cognitive mapping. The difficulties certainly lie in the persistent use of the words 'mapping' and 'maps'. They are words which have a direct and particular appeal for geographers and which have probably been popularized in cognitive research for two rather simple reasons. First, they have served to convey something of the essence of relatively unfamiliar ideas in the form of an analogy with a tangible and highly familiar object: they are part of the fundamental vocabulary of geography and in an impressionistic way they set the seal of geographical respectability on research into mental phenomena. The second reason is closely allied to this and it has something to do with the awkward business of geographical *scale*. Geographers often experience some difficulty in conveying succinctly the scale of their discipline. It extends from the spatial dispositions of shops, streets, and neighbourhoods to those of countries and continents. But it does not usually extend to the disposition of furniture in a room, for example, or to the location of stars in the cosmos. An old and useful way of getting around the difficulty of defining geographical scale, as well as implying much about the content of geographical enquiry, was to say that it was 'about maps', since in a colloquial sense everyone understood the kinds of things that were portrayed on maps. Similarly, a new and useful way of getting around the difficulties of describing geographical interest in cognition is to say that it is about 'cognitive maps': it conveys, comfortably but loosely, some idea of the scale of the cognitive products which geographers find relevant and interesting.

Other geographers have used different terms to convey the same very general idea, the idea that we characterize here as simply 'thinking about the environment'. Not very long ago the most popular of these terms was 'environmental perception' (Bordessa, 1969; Goodey, 1971; Saarinen, 1969; Wood, 1970). In many cases it was inappropriate. In both psychology and philosophy, for example, 'perception' is used to describe the receipt of information that occurs in the process of becoming aware of an external stimulus through the medium of the senses. Sometimes the stimulus may be an indirect one, like the contents of a newspaper, but its immediate presence remains critical to the act of perceiving. Many geographers, however, interpreted perception more loosely and more colloquially, probably to give a contemporary flavour to situations which might earlier have been described by the use of more appropriate concepts like 'knowledge', 'belief', or 'choice'. These are all clearly states of mind that can exist independently of immediate sensory excitation. Thus, Goodey (1971, p. 54), for example, followed Gould's (1966) earlier lead in writing of 'preferential perception' rather than merely of 'preference' or 'choice', and Bowden (1969) considered nineteenth-century *perceptions* of the U.S. interior rather than nineteenth-century *beliefs* about the place. The list of examples could go on and on. Fortunately, this tendency is rapidly dying, and even in the cases cited it detracted little from the general themes that were studied. With the spread of a larger and more relevant vocabulary 'perception' is normally used now to refer to more immediate responses to sensory stimulation (Board and Taylor, 1977). This does not mean, however, that the role of perception is unimportant in the kinds of situations with which geographers concern themselves. On the contrary, it is critical not only in its own right as a factor influencing immediate understanding and activity but also in so far as it contributes to subsequent cognitive processes which depend upon the recall of previous experiences.

Unfortunately, the same cannot be said about the way in which geographers use the term 'image'. There has been a persistent tendency to follow the lead of Boulding (1956) and to conceive of the image as synonymous with 'subjective knowledge' or with 'what we believe to be true'. This seems to be the implication behind Pocock's (1976) use of the term, for example, and it is certainly the sense in which it has been used by Lynch (1960) and by those, like Francescato and Mebane (1973), who have built upon Lynch's original study. The difficulty again is that other people would define images much more narrowly. To the psychologist, in particular, the image is generally interpreted as an internalized reconstruction of some previous sensory experience or the construction of anticipated sensory responses in either a deliberate or a spontaneous way. In this sense the role of the image in thought is 'a kind of cognitive luxury, like an illustration in a novel' (Neisser, 1967, p. 157). Also in this sense the cognitive map is simply a special kind of mental construct possessing some of the features of a real map. It is an internalized, predominantly visual, structure and it is dissociated conceptually from any affective connotations. It is this view of cognitive mapping and the cognitive map that we want to examine in the remainder of this chapter.

COGNITIVE MAPS AS FIGURAL IMAGES

To define cognitive maps as figural images with a cartographic form at least sharpens the scope of our immediate discussion to one which ought to be manageable. But even this limited view presents problems. We may argue, indeed we *do* argue, that in some circumstances many of us find ourselves at least partially influenced by what we believe to be the *quality* of these images; that is to say, by the degree to which we believe our images to be congruent with reality. Where our confidence is high we may literally depend upon them; where our confidence is low we are more likely to look for alternative or supplementary information from sources which are inherently more reliable. We may, for example, consult a real map! Even when we do rely upon cognitive maps, though, the kinds of situations in which we do so are not only predictable but are often, some might say, rather trivial. Tuan (1975) has illustrated some situations of this kind. In essence they involve using mental constructs to give directions to other people, to rehearse or anticipate some occasional aspects of our own spatial behaviour, to store information about where things are in relation to other things, and finally to create imaginary worlds that may, or may not, find expression in goal-oriented behaviour. Any cynic worth his salt will point out that with the exception of the latter case all these activities can be carried out more certainly, if not more rapidly, by consulting real maps. Sometimes, of course, real maps are not readily available and it is probably true that in relying on our own inferior mental constructs we may occasionally make mistakes, travel further than we need, give directions which are wrong, and so on. In the last analysis, however, this is not a matter of life and death very often to very many of us.

We believe then that it is not very profitable to lay great stress on the utility of cognitive maps as we have defined them, at least as arbiters of our spatial behaviour. Most of our activities are routine and most of our routine activities are certainly independent of artificial constructions that look like 'maps in the head'. As Gould and White (1974, p. 49) point out with a simplicity that is rather humbling, 'people drive to places just using signposts and national route numbers or fly to them with complete faith in the airlines'. Bruner has said somewhere that in many of our daily activities we employ enactive representation, relying not on models in the mind but on representational responses 'in our muscles, so to speak'. (see Bruner, Goodnow and Austin, 1956; Bruner, 1966) We do not need, as a matter of survival, anything more than a rather crudely integrated framework of spatial relationships. Occasionally this framework may be recalled in the form of a map, but usually it is not. This kind of reasoning, we suspect, lies at the core of Graham's (1976, p. 261) recent attack on mental mapping research. 'In the explanation of human behaviour', she observes, 'it appears to be no help at all to appeal to mental maps.' Unfortunately, by casting her net very widely, and by failing to resolve the awkward questions of meaning which we discussed above, she throws out not only the baby and the bath water, but the bath and its associated plumbing system as well! In fact, it is precisely in *explaining* human behaviour that cognitive maps may have some use.

Our argument is really rather simple. We accept that cognitive maps play only a minor and intermittent role in effective thinking and that it is misleading to impute to them any great significance in the coordination of our spatial activities. At the same time no one would deny that this behaviour is governed by *some* kind of cognitive structure that in remarkably successful ways combines our organismic capacities and our large learning skills. It is a structure that allows us to perform habitual or commonplace acts without resort to careful deliberation and that also allows us to recall and manipulate information in several different modes in ways over which we do exercise some conscious control. It consists not only of cognitive characteristics but also of dispositional ones which we 'tease apart' quite artificially for the purposes of simplicity. It is not only extremely complex and very dynamic but it is probably also highly individual. We cannot, in any total sense, expose the cognitive structures which inform our spatial behaviour; we can merely acknowledge their existence and attempt to uncover some of their properties in a reliable and orderly way.

One method which we can use is to encourage people to evoke images of maps which will structure some particular aspects of their own experience in a controlled form. By doing this we may render some limited segments of highly idiosyncratic minds at least partially comparable. The form, however, is one which is imposed by the investigator rather than one which is inevitably assumed by the respondent in the course of normal thought. In this sense the cognitive map serves as a vehicle for the examination of material which often may not adopt a cartographic style at all. It is, therefore, analogous in conception to many other *methods* of psychological research in that it persuades people to schematize, order, or generally tidy-up some aspects of their stored experience within a framework that is determined primarily by its usefulness to the researcher rather than its familiarity to the respondent. In the case of semantic scaling tests, for example, people are encouraged to respond within an artificially structured linguistic framework; in the case of cognitive maps they are persuaded into an initial mode of rather specialized and often unfamiliar visual imaging. For this reason, and from the point of view of subsequent inference, it is important that we recognize the artificiality of our demands and that we are aware of the probable lack of congruence between the narrow, corseted response which we require and the less formal, more flexible, and complex structures which people actually use. Some of the sense of this view is recognized by Beck and Wood (1976, p. 205) who note that 'the very calling for the map brings cognitive operations into play that would not otherwise have been necessary for the subject'. We think of cognitive mapping, therefore, as one of a range of strategies open to the researcher who is interested in the relationship between mental phenomena and physical activity. If it is possible to develop some reliable methods for representing them, then they may be used to help *explain* some features of behaviour with which we readily admit they do not *govern*.

SOME PROBLEMS OF METHOD

Bruner (1966) has suggested that we can usefully distinguish three systems by which people process information that is incorporated in their understanding of the world. They are systems of action, imagery, and language. In part they are innate and in part they are learned and they are certainly systems which develop with increasing maturity through childhood to the adult state. Of the three we probably know least about imagery and this is also the most difficult to investigate. Actions, after all, are observable and language is not only our primary mode of thought but also our principal means of communicating with each other. Researchers can look, ask, and listen, albeit that this looking, asking, and listening may be a very sophisticated business these days. With imagery it is not so easy. Most of us can experience images readily enough, but only in a few simple or special cases can we communicate them accurately to others. The reasons are simple enough. Images are internalized reconstructions of sensory experience or sensory anticipation, and the precise details of sensory information are very difficult to communicate. It is quite impossible, for example, to tell a man who has never seen it exactly what the *Mona Lisa* looks like so that he could subsequently evoke a veridical image of it. It is equally impossible to describe in words the smell of a lemon, the taste of a curry, or the tactile sensation of a peach skin. The nearest we can come is to use analogies which depend equally heavily on common sensory experience for their effect. Language, despite its massive generality, its fluency in the communication of countless abstract concepts, and its subtle power to convey fine shades of meaning, is singularly ill-equipped to cope with the idiosyncrasy of sensory data. While we may look to language to explore the questions of meaning and disposition that are an integral part of our cognitive processes we cannot expect it to reveal very much of the sensory activities around which our feelings are constructed. Some people may argue that this matters little anyway, and that it is precisely in the examination of dispositions that we are likely to find the answers to the behavioural problems which we set ourselves to solve. It is a defensible but rather conservative point of view. It is similar to the attitude of those information theorists who believe that neuro-psychological concern with the relationship between brain morphology and cognitive functioning is irrelevant to the study of intellectual ability (McFie, 1972). We prefer to think otherwise and to see in the long chain of interests from neuro-psychology to the mass observation of behaviour our great strength as 'ordinarily curious human beings', curious about our extraordinary capacities (Tuan, 1975).

Even so, the problem remains. How do we communicate the figural details of visual images? By discounting language, or by asserting that verbal or literary contributions can only be relatively limited, we are led to a consideration of other modes of expression: one is graphic and the other is kinaesthetic. In other words we are led to examine the drawings that people construct or complete and the actions that people perform. In general, geographers have relied heavily on graphic techniques while psychologists have been more concerned with the performance of specified actions in controlled experimental situations. In both cases, though, it is apparent that we can do no more than infer from an external product backwards to an unseeable internal image. In the remainder of this chapter we shall focus our attention on two graphic methods, partly out of considerations of space and our own limited experience, but also because they are likely to be more familiar to a geographical audience.

Sketch maps

The publication of Lynch's (1960) work on urban images was something of an event because his *methods* caught the imagination of many people interested in questions that were loosely similar. In particular his use of sketch maps had a great influence on the design of many subsequent studies. It is no exaggeration to say that their use is now commonplace and familiar and that their value as an inferential source has been adequately demonstrated. Little point would be served, we think, by reviewing the considerable body of literature that demonstrates the use of sketch maps at scales ranging from the college campus, through the small neighbourhood (Ladd, 1970), to urban environments throughout the world (Appleyard, 1969; Gulick, 1963; Pocock, 1975), to individual countries (Pacione, 1976) and to the entire global land surface (Saarinen, 1973a, 1973b). They are already well reviewed elsewhere (Saarinen, 1976). It is enough to make one straightforward observation about the general character of inferences made from sketch maps. These inferences fall fairly readily into one or other of two principal categories. They are either inferences made about the physical information present in cartographic images, or they are inferences about the structural character of the images. Together they go some way towards answering the question: What is contained in our cognitive maps and how is it organized? There are, however, one or two niggling problems associated with the interpretation of sketch maps. Many people might feel them to be trivial, and we would not deny that they are certainly peripheral to the examination of aggregated responses. At the same time, with a method that has such widespread appeal and that seems to have so much common sense behind its adoption, it is perhaps permissible to snipe around the edges a little.

The production of freehand sketch maps is a task approached with ribald humour by some and with injured resentment by others. On being asked to draw a freehand world outline one of our own colleagues, a professional geographer and therefore probably familiar with the subject, with maps, and with many other graphic display devices, felt compelled to assert that the end product proved 'more that I can't draw than anything else'. In effect he was excusing his capacity to communicate information graphically by inferring that the motor skills on which it depended were somehow inferior to the 'higher' skills of verbal, literary, or numerical communication. To admit that one's drawing ability is poor, it seems, is perfectly acceptable even among professional people who rely heavily on several modes of visual expression in the course of their work. By contrast, we suspect that few of them would so readily confess to equivalent difficulties with writing, with numeracy, or with the awkward business of lecturing.

The readiness with which we dismiss motor skills of the kind involved in drawing sketch maps is significant but not really surprising. Despite the emphasis on creative activities among specialists in the education of young children, the typical lay view of schooling is that learning only begins properly with the development of word and number skills. It is a view that reflects individual experiences within our educational system where creative work is quickly relegated to the status of a recreational activity similar to physical education and games. Often it is assumed that one either can or cannot do these things and that in any event it does not matter very much. Our education system in effect reinforces the tacit assumption that performance in the mechanical arts lies outside the proper ambit of intellectual development and scholarship. People familiar with admission procedures at universities, for example, may sometimes be persuaded to confess that they largely discount examination performance in art or needlework when filling places for undergraduates. The universities themselves, though often teaching art criticism or history, do not teach the performance of the basic skills involved: this is left to other institutions whose status in the educational hierarchy is decidedly 'inferior'.

There is another symptom of the same disregard for mechanical skills that is certainly identifiable in many geography departments. We refer, of course, to the teaching of cartography. In recent years our own department, for example, has shifted the emphasis of teaching in its 'techniques' course away from the preparation, design, and production of graphic material, towards the elaboration of numeracy and the teaching of statistical methods. The significant feature of this change is that it has been a *shift* in teaching rather than an extension of teaching: mechanical skills, though certainly not ignored, are no longer so highly regarded. We make this point, not in criticism of an evolving pattern of priorities in teaching, but merely to outline yet another reason why people respond as they do to requests which involve some mechanical skill like drawing. To ask people to draw a map seems to elicit reactions similar to those observed when people are asked to sing: there is usually some embarrassment, plenty of reluctance, and occasional outright refusal. But paradoxically, there is also an emphatic belief among these same people that the skill in question is trivial and not really relevant to effective intellectual functioning, or socialized behaviour. Yet it is upon single forays into this rarely exercised and seldom developed skill that we depend for much of our inferential data. We do so, for the most part, in singular encounters with unsuspecting individuals whose levels of preparedness may differ widely and whose familiarity with maps as a mode of communication is probably wildly different. We are able to conclude, not altogether surprisingly, that some people produce 'better' maps than others in ways that may be developmentally connected (Moore, 1973) and that are usually related to coarsely defined socio-economic attributes (Francescato and Mebane, 1973). One is led to wonder, however, whether differences in mechanical expression necessarily imply that people conceive and conceptualize their world in such different ways. It is not a question that we can readily answer, but we can explore, a little hesitantly, one or two largely intuitive ideas about the business of drawing, drawing maps, and evoking images of maps.

The evocation of cognitive maps may be either a relatively simple or a relatively complex cognitive operation, depending very largely on the real geographical scale of the areas involved. Milgram (1973) has observed that the capacity to imagine maps of the global land surface is related to the degree of exposure to formal maps of the kind contained in atlases and the like. At a much smaller scale it seems reasonable to suppose that the ability to imagine maps of areas like one's "neighbourhood" (however that is defined) depends far more on the recall of kinetic experiences and the appropriate mental transformation of these experiences into the symbolic lineations of a 'map'. The demands imposed are very different in these two cases, and they present a rather interesting paradox. In the case of 'mapping' one's neighbourhood, for instance, the operations involved are far more numerous and complex, even though the frequency of exposure to appropriate basic information may be very much higher. According to Beck and Wood (1976, p. 225) the operations which must occur to produce a map of this kind involve 'rotation, scaling, generalization, symbolization, verbalization and representation'. On the other hand, the demands made on the individual drawing an outline map of the world are not particularly great: it is a question of remembering shapes many of which have the added clue of ready association with proper names which are heard frequently. There is, in addition, a degree of stability in the patterning of world land surfaces and even in the political units which subdivide it, whereas at a smaller scale, and a scale which is usually subjectively defined, there is perhaps a greater element of plasticity and ongoing reappraisal.

In any event, the realization of these images through shapes drawn on paper raises questions about the relationship between the memory traces on which the drawings are based and the mechanical skill which purports to represent them. Nobody, of course, believes that drawings are literal reflections of images. There is little need to add support to such a basic and negative observation, but it is worth pointing out the disparity that exists even between drawings of objects that are directly perceived and the objects themselves. We know, for example, that if one of us attempted to draw our typewriter the product would be identifiable as *a* typewriter and maybe even *our* typewriter, but it would fall far short in detail of the percept which we can elaborate and examine at our leisure. When we consider images which are quite removed from immediate sensory experience and which are therefore less easily fixed, less sharply defined, and less readily checked, it is not surprising that the relationship of the drawing which depends on them and the original objects which they are intended to reproduce should be a very imprecise one, and even perhaps a rather unstable one. If we make two consecutive drawings of our typewriter they will differ in more or less obvious ways; if we make two drawings from memory the differences will probably be greater still.

Let us consider for a moment the business of drawing an outline map of the world of the kind that Saarinen (1973a, 1973b) has explored in such interesting ways. The global land surface, represented on a map, is essentially a collection of shapes too large to have been directly perceived but sufficiently relevant to our routine social functioning to have been reproduced graphically at scales which are amenable to direct perception and which can be stored in memory for recall in suitable circumstances. The cognitive operations which are involved in the recall of such an object are no more complex than those involved in the recall of a typewriter. To draw such a map is a matter of matching mechanical skill and memory to reproduce basic shape–scale relationships. The shapes involved are static, self-contained, and clearly circumscribed and recall depends primarily upon distinguishing these static but relevant shapes from the equally static but irrelevant and homogeneous background of the sea.

Some psychologists would argue that shape perception and memory depend heavily on an internalized taxonomy of shape categories (Berlyne, 1969). These categories in turn reflect a conceptual identity which the shape possesses. Shapes which are easily categorized, because they have familiar identities, will be relatively easily recalled. In any particular case, however, as Arnheim (1970, p. 81) has argued, the memory trace of a categorical shape may be modified in two opposing directions. First, it may be subject to what he calls 'tension reduction'. Essentially, this involves the simplification of the shape in question in which 'the trace pattern will shed details and refinements and increase in symmetry and regularity'. This is the tendency to 'betterment' which Pocock (1976) has examined in the context of urban sketch maps. Second, and sometimes acting against this tendency, is the inclination to 'preserve and indeed sharpen the distinctive features of the pattern'. In sketch maps the treatment of projecting peninsulas seems to display this kind of distortion. Shapes which lack a categorical identity in past experience or through a variety of associations are more difficult to recall, except where constant exposure creates for them their own special identity. But even here the counter-tendencies to paring down and elaboration are also probably present.

In the context of sketch maps of the world it is not difficult to find examples of both categorical and idiosyncratic shapes. Africa is a 'pear drop', or is it a 'bicycle seat'? Italy is a boot. But what shape is Iraq, or Afghanistan, or Canada? Clearly, countries which do not possess shapes with associational identities acquire unique categorical status only as a result of frequent exposure and situational relevance. This is an important point and one which has been recognized in the interpretation of sketch maps. It does not follow, however, that the obverse is true and that the situational relevance of countries with familiar shapes, like Africa and Italy, is necessarily greater just because their recall is easier. Both of us know, for example, that Nepal is rectangular; it is all we do know about Nepal. In contrast, we have only a vague notion of the shape of West Germany, yet we have both travelled there, we know something of its history, society, and economy. We can name its major regions and its major settlements and we can plan a route which will take us from one end of the country to the other without ever consulting a real map. But, precisely, what shape is it? Our ideas are hazy.

We are arguing, for what it is worth, that for any individual the recall and representation of shape may be far removed from their knowledge of other features of particular places and that inferences about associational con-notations, based on drawn shapes, should be made very cautiously. We would go further and suggest that the recall of shape depends primarily on perceptual experiences which have little to do with functional associations that are not themselves inherently shape related. In other words, our ability to draw an outline of the British Isles depends far more on the frequency and the manner in which we are exposed to such an outline than it does upon the effective or emotive associations that we might have for the place itself. In the same vein we are led to wonder whether it is realistic to interpret a drawing of the U.S.A. as exhibiting a high degree of familiarity on the part of respondents who get the basic outline correct, and at the same time to interpret a map of Africa with a correct outline but with no internal differentiation as exhibiting a lack of familiarity (Saarinen, 1973a). A lack of familiarity with what? A level of familiarity with what? These are tasks of recall of quite a different order and it is likely that they tell us more of primitive figure-ground influences than they do of anything else. It is significant, for example, that even the maps of Saarinen's African respondents did not differentiate strongly within the continent. We are not suggesting, for one moment, that North American or European students are likely to be as familiar with Africa as they are with their own continent, but we do not need sketch maps to realize so basic a conclusion; a simple list of names would serve as well if not better, for then the cognitive tasks involved in the response need not become snarled up with the mechanical skills of representation.

It is easy to believe that the problems involved in drawing a map of the world, or the outline of a particular country, are the same as the problems involved in drawing maps of smaller areas such as neighbourhoods or cities. After all, the product is a *map* in both cases. On the other hand, as we have already implied, the sources and the character of the information used in the two cases may be very different. In the case of the smaller areas we rely essentially upon perceptual experiences that are far removed from a neat plan view. We see our neighbourhoods from eye-level; we walk the streets or we ride along them. Our memories of them are dominated by pictorial images which re-create our eye-level precepts. In order to produce a map or plan we have to reorganize our store of information into a form with a geometry that might be quite novel for us. We have to make judgements about distances and about angles that exist in our memory with all the familiar distortions of visual perception. We have to decide, sometimes on the basis of not-very-explicit instructions, just what to leave in and just what to leave out. It is a difficult thing to do. Nor is it made any easier by the variable impact of secondary information which inevitably supplements our active environmental experience at an urban scale. The sources of this information are numerous. Some people, for example, may be familiar with actual maps or street plans of places. If they are, and if these are remembered reasonably well, then the map-drawing task begins to resemble the world map type of exercise. But this is probably rare among most urban dwellers. More often we are exposed to indirect information of a quite different kind; some of it may be verbal, some literary, and some pictorial. It may be deliberately acquired or it may be unconsciously derived. Somehow this loose assemblage of facts and impressions must be welded to our own direct experiences in ways which are sufficiently integrated and harmonious to prevent total disorientation and confusion. The more we consider the complexities of this jumble of variously derived urban information, the more extraordinary it seems that anyone is capable of sorting out the muddle sufficiently to communicate it graphically and, as it were, 'off the cuff'. For, as we have already observed, it is unlikely that subjective urban knowledge is spontaneously structured in the organized and coherent form of a map. Some people, of course, are better able to cope with the problem than others. They are better able, for example, to reduce their visual experiences to some other form of symbolic or iconic representation, or they are better able to conceptualize larger units from the fragmentary nature of individual elements in their environment (Appleyard, 1969; Beck and Wood, 1976; Goodchild, 1974).

Despite the obvious difficulty of the task it is apparent from the work of Lynch (1960), Appleyard (1969), Pocock (1975), and many others that there are important regularities in the way in which people represent their cartographic images of cities. In some ways this is not surprising since individual ideas of what maps should look like probably condition responses to structuring styles and ensure that they will not differ very widely. In essence, maps are made up of lines or areas, or some more or less sophisticated combination of routes and places. For the most part their quality is assessed in terms of the volume and accuracy of the spatial coverage which they achieve and inferences are made back from this to the images on which the maps are based. We do not wish to repeat, or even to question, the conclusions of the many studies of urban areas that have employed sketch maps. Most of them depend on the aggregation of the products into systems of classification that have been variously devised to suit different ends and different cultures. We are led instead to wonder about another peripheral issue. For while it is relatively easy to classify most sketch maps in terms of either structure or style, our own experience suggests that there are occasional instances of usual responses that defy simple treatment. This leads us to wonder about the notion of 'creativity' and about its relevance to the apparently mundane and practical business of drawing a map from memory. One difficulty, of course, is that creativity is so difficult to define and to measure and that it is also a bandwagon theme in contemporary psychology. Clearly, we do not mean the kind of lofty creativity that characterizes 'great' work, but rather the kind of creative response that is simply unusual or different, the 'tinker shuffle' as Bruner, Goodnow, and Austin (1956) called it. To resort to rather different jargon, though retaining (we think) the same basic idea, we are concerned with the occasional product of what other psychologists might call 'divergent' thinkers.

The distinction between convergent and divergent thinkers stems largely from Guilford's (1956, 1967) work on cognition. Briefly, convergent thinkers tend to be more analytical and conventional in their approach to problem solving, while divergent thinkers are usually more flexible, open-ended, and original. The testing of these qualities is extremely difficult and there are serious differences of opinion among psychologists as to the relative merits of the various testing procedures employed (Getzels and Jackson, 1962; Wallach and Kogan, 1965). But if there is something in the basic notion of different cognitive styles, and Hudson's (1966) work in Britain convinces us that there is, then it might be expected that these differences will sometimes show themselves in responses to open-ended and unstructured tests of the sketch-mapping type.

Consider, for example, the maps in Figure 3.1. They are both maps of Sunderland. Figure 3.1(a) is a conventional sketch map. It covers the whole of Wearside and shows the river, the coast, the town boundaries, the major districts, and the major road network. It is the product of a woman who has had considerable experience in the handling of maps and it follows standard cartographic conventions. It is, in other words, a 'good' map. Compare it with Figure 3.1(b) which hardly resembles a conventional map at all. The method adopted by this respondent is simply to trace a continuous line from her home to the town centre and out again through the districts to the west and south, returning to Grangetown where she lives. The striking feature of this map is that, although the scale is occasionally distorted, the relative locations identified are essentially correct: to get to Grangetown from Herrington one does have to travel through Silksworth, and so on. We are inclined to ask of products like this whether they are simply 'bad' maps, produced perhaps by someone who can't draw, or whether they represent a genuinely exceptional and rather skilful collapsing of a complex structure into a basic and familiar concept which is easy to understand and follow. After all, if places are signposted—and places *are* signposted—what more information does one need? It hardly matters in practice that the turns that one makes are to the right or left, the north or south. As a map this funny crumpled triangle could work; as a mnemonic it almost certainly works for the respondent. It would be difficult to believe, however, that she really envisages Sunderland as a circle or that she is incapable of imagining in greater detail the geography of the town.

We should not always expect to interpret sketch maps in literal terms. They are, after all, drawings and we do not always assess drawings in terms of their isomorphism with reality. On the contrary, we look for indications of originality that usually imply a particular and what we call 'creative' interpretation of the subject. The 'best' drawings are not usually those which recapture a percept with the veracity of photographic plate. They are those which, in a variety of subtle ways, take the viewer beyond shape and light and suggest an understanding of less tangible properties. Even though sketch maps do not have to contend with the intricacies of light and depth they do lend themselves to distortions of form and shape which might reflect more than a simple lack of mechanical skill or a decayed and primitive image. Distortions of this kind may be innovative.

Our remarks about drawing serve to emphasize the strongly metaphorical nature of sketch maps. However carefully the test instructions are designed, and as Boyle (1978) has pointed out, they need to be very carefully weighed indeed, the investigator exercises little real control over the responses of his subjects. By sacrificing control for openness and flexibility, of course, he often encourages a degree of richness and depth in the output that is impossible to match through any other medium. But it is an output which is as scrambled and as multifaceted as the minds which produce it. It slips readily into 'selection, emphasis and distortion' to go beyond the narrowness of visual images and out into the fullness of life style and feeling (Milgram and Jodelet, 1977, p. 235). As far as our cognitive maps are concerned, it takes us further than we want to go.

Completion tests

At least some of the fascination of sketch maps arises from their 'lucky-dip' element and the genuine intellectual challenge of bringing order to the apparent chaos which they present. It may be academically unfashionable to say so, but sketch maps are often fun to work with and that is not a property to be despised, nor is it one that is often encountered in geographical data bases. Other graphic techniques, though, work rather differently and by comparison seem a little sober and even dull. These are the varieties of completion tests which work by presenting an incomplete cartographic stimulus to a respondent who is required to add information to the map. Clearly, tests of this kind are much more restricted than sketch maps. They are designed to examine specific elements in the image rather than to encourage the holistic reproduction of its mappable properties. In general, however, the results are much more readily comparable and potentially more reliable since the instructions are normally quite specific and the task itself is usually unambiguous and, in a motor sense, very easy. Lee's

(1963, p. 91) work is a good example of a simple and effective completion test. The cartographic stimulus was a six-inch-to-the-mile Ordnance Survey map. It was given to a sample of housewives who were asked to 'draw a line round the part which you consider acts as your neighbourhood or district'. There is no need to repeat the empirical details of Lee's results since they do not materially affect our argument. He could, however, have given his respondents a blank sheet of paper and asked them to draw sketch maps of their neighbourhood, but since his interest was in the spatial extent rather than the detailed morphology of areas,

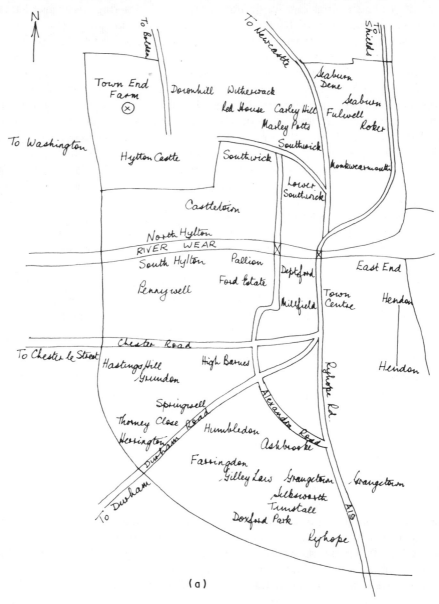

(a)

much of the content of drawings of that kind would have been redundant. It is also quite possible, as Boyle (1978) has shown, that difficulties with the motor skills involved in producing a map might have led to a short-fall in the spatial coverage that lay at the core of Lee's interest.

The most formal kind of completion test is known as *cloze procedure*. It was first developed for use with textual material but its origins go back to the *Gestalt* notion of 'closure' or 'completion' which refers to the tendency for perception to extend beyond the immediate sensory stimulation provided by an object to 'fill-in' parts that are missing or obscured. For example, we have no difficulty in 'seeing' the top of our desk even though it is blanketed by books, papers, ashtrays, and the like. It is possible to elicit a similar response to gaps in spoken or written sentences. Most English-speaking people when confronted with the sentence, 'Dogs bark but ducks——', would instinctively fill in the gap with the word 'quack'. This indicates not only a measure of linguistic competence in the selection of an appropriate word-form, but also a degree of contextual awareness showing that the message has been understood despite the missing item. Cloze procedure provides a vehicle for the expression of these abilities and is an extremely useful method of assessing the readability of textual material and the

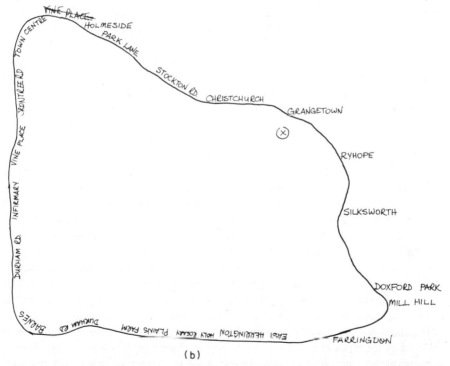

(b)

FIGURE 3.1. Sketch maps of Sunderland: (a) drawn by a respondent with cartographic experience; (b) drawn by a respondent with no cartographic experience. *N.B.* Although the content and style of the original diagrams have been maintained, some redrawing has been necessary in order to achieve legibility

level of comprehension attained by the reader (Gilliland, 1972; Osgood, 1959). It is also very sensitive to individual differences in linguistic habits and this has encouraged its use in personality and psychiatric research (Holsti, 1969).

Cloze procedure can also be used with graphic material. A grid is superimposed on the graphic base and the information contained in some of the grid squares is deleted. Subjects are then asked to identify particular elements in these blank squares with the help of the contextual information retained in the remaining open squares. Clearly, when this kind of procedure is employed with maps it demands the evocation of visual images which will enable the completion of the perceived context. By implication, the relevant segments of this image must possess properties of scale and projection that are congruent with those of the perceived stimulus. This might be achieved in at least two ways. First, it might involve the recall of an actual *map*—which is then scaled to match the stimulus by appropriate internal logico-mathematical operations. This is likely to be the case, for example, with the completion of large-scale world maps and the like. Second, it is also likely that the figural images which permit successful clozure at a smaller scale are derived from reproductive images of the kinetic kind that recall actual experiences of places and that are subsequently transformed to meet the properties dictated by the test map. In any individual case it is difficult to know which of these two processes will be dominant, but it is apparent that in both of them visual completion requires the conscious structuring of environmental information into a form which is explicitly cartographic.

Despite its conceptual simplicity, however, there are a number of technical issues which complicate the use of cloze procedure with graphic material. Some of them are fairly straightforward and relate to the characteristics of the grid that is superimposed on the base map (Robinson, 1974). The selection of suitable grid dimensions and the choice of a frequency for the deletion of particular grid squares are the most obvious ones. On the one hand, the grid size must not be too fine to prevent at least partial clozure success at a level that will usefully discriminate between respondents. At the same time too coarse a scale could reduce the test to redundancy by making replacement too simple. It is also obvious that the size of the grid will determine the upper limit of the number of possible deletions over any given area. The selection of a suitable deletion frequency is very largely a matter of guesswork (or careful judgement, depending on one's point of view). Tests with graphic material have tended to use a ratio of 1 in 5 (Dicken and Robinson, 1974; Porter, Hart, and Machin 1975; Robinson, 1974), although in the context of an urban study Boyle (1978) used a ratio of only 1 in 7. The method of selecting grid squares for deletion can also vary. Sometimes it may be appropriate to select them in a purely subjective way on grounds determined by the specific needs of the research. Alternatively, they may be selected using random numbers, or simply by deleting every *n*th square. There is some evidence, not particularly strong, that the latter strategies do not yield significantly different scores (Dicken and Robinson, 1974).

In some ways more serious problems are raised in deciding on the amount and type of information which is presented in the open squares of the grid. It is clearly difficult to avoid design-induced bias in the selection of contextual clues. Surprisingly, however, increases in the amount of contextual information do not inevitably lead to greater replacement success. Two exercises in Sunderland illustrate this point (Boyle, 1978). The first base map retained the entire range of cartographic information contained on a published street map of the town, whereas the second showed only the town boundary, the coastline, river, main railway line, and a skeletal network of named main roads. Despite the substantially reduced level of information on the second test, however, results were not noticeably different. Apparently the original, more comprehensive context, was not fully exploited. This suggests that an optimum may exist beyond which additional clues are redundant. It is even possible that a thinner spread of information may more closely resemble the highly selective and schematic form often ascribed to cognitive maps.

The remaining problems concern the nature of the responses which the tests are designed to encourage. Studies at a national level, for example, have simply required respondents to complete a base map by identifying the name of a town in each of the deleted grid squares (Dicken and Robinson, 1974; Robinson, 1974). Scoring on tests like this is very simple. At an urban scale, however, the problems may be more complex. In particular decisions must be made about whether to ask respondents for specific kinds of environmental elements, thus risking bias towards certain types of people, or whether to allow the whole unspecified range of possible responses, thus introducing complications of scoring and complications related to individual differences in response content and level of generalization (Boyle, 1978). Problems like this are not insurmountable, however, and it seems possible to adapt cloze procedure to any spatial scale providing sufficient attention is paid to relevant practical issues. The technique can measure not only the areal extent of accurate spatial cognition but also its depth and complexity. Besides this, it is possible to analyse mistaken responses and areas of non-response which allows the build-up of a relatively complete picture incorporating patterns of ignorance and error as well as those of veridical information (Boyle and Robinson, 1978).

An important practical advantage of completion exercises like cloze procedure is that they avoid the kinds of co-operation difficulties which often plague sketch-mapping research. Also, the structured response format is straightforward to operate and analyse yet it can produce quite detailed material. Moreover, the test eliminates those unmeasured individual differences caused by variable innate or acquired mechanical skills. Although active map construction is not involved, however, cloze tests do require a degree of competence in understanding cartographic form which is by no means universal. As a result, they probably still contain an element of bias towards the kinds of people who are more familiar with established map conventions. Even such basic properties as the traditional northerly orientation may be a hindrance, especially at an urban scale, if this does not match the individual's subjective conceptualization of the city. Cloze scores in Sunderland suggested that variable aptitude and experience regarding maps did exert a sizeable impact on test performance (Boyle, 1978).

The ideas about convergent and divergent thinking, mentioned earlier in connection with sketch maps, may also have some relevance with regard to completion tests. While convergent thinkers are disconcerted by an open-ended format which lacks a unique correct answer, divergers thrive on unstructured tests (Hudson, 1966). This suggests that people whose cognitive style is predominantly convergent may be at an advantage in tests like cloze procedure where the response mode is clearly defined for them, whereas divergers, who are relatively free from the tendency to see the world in preconceived patterns, enjoying ambiguity and self-expression, may feel inhibited by the more constrained style of these completion exercises. Such influences depend upon the degree of cognitive bias and, of course, their impact is merely a matter of conjecture until this has been more fully examined. Nevertheless, the idea is an interesting one and it seems to promise some contribution towards clarifying the psychological influences which affect the communication of cognitive maps.

CONCLUSIONS

Where, in the end, do our remarks fit in the broader universe of geographical questions? Wherever it is, and we shall shortly try to decide, it is evident that they occupy a very tiny niche indeed. We have tried to do two things, both rather humble and neither very original. We have defined our own limited view of cognitive mapping and we have said something about two graphic methods which are used in its exploration. In essence, we conceive of cognitive mapping as an intriguing tactic that is still in search of wholly comprehensible techniques. The ones that we have described, though not exhaustive, seem to produce information that is idiosyncratic and logically elusive, or else that is so restricted as to be empirically frustrating. However this may be, it is evident that we do not regard cognitive mapping as a central theme in human geography or even as a core issue in the rather loose jumble of postures that go under the heading of behavioural geography. We do not see it as a thread in the weave of geographical philosophy and we do not need to find a place for it anywhere in the continuum from positivist to phenomenological paradigms.

At the same time, though, there is something rather seductive about even our very limited view of cognitive maps. They are, after all, products of the mind, and products of the mind are easy to think of as elusive and 'deep'. Sometimes it makes no matter that the methods we use to tap them compare unfavourably with the subtlety of a plumber's wrench. They appeal because, in a loose way, they are redolent of the humanism that is sidling skilfully and cyclically back into geographical explanation. The tactical examination of cognitive maps swings comfortably between very different approaches to geographical questions. We can nod from them readily enough in the direction of Lowenthal's (1961) eloquence or Tuan's (1974, 1975, 1977) whimsical brilliance and yet feel that we are still close to the more firmly behavioural work of, say, Wolpert (1965) or Johnston (1972). The reason, again, is simple. It is because we are discussing *methods* of ordering information, not approaches to explanation or prediction.

They are methods, like Hudson's (1972, p. 78), that produce data 'as hard as the next man's, or nearly so'. But in addition they also leave us free, like him, to edge towards 'systems of intuitive meaning' that will lend experiential shape to our raw data.

The problems that we have identified and discussed are essentially problems of interpretation. What does a sketch map signify? How reliable are our controlled and limited cloze tests? We do not know. But if cognitive mapping is to be more than a novelty which is ageing rapidly then we must look for ways of finding out. The answers, it seems, may lie in a reductionist perspective. We must understand the products of our methods before we can confidently relate them to the questions of behaviour at a macro-scale that lie at the root of geographical enquiry. On balance, cognitive mapping has made little progress in the last decade, because in the end progress must depend on the development of suitable tools to do the job. To date, we do not really understand the tools that we use and we are making little systematic effort to learn about them. If we accept, for example, the communicative potential of graphicacy (Balchin, 1972), how far are our sketch maps simply measures of differential degrees of appropriate training? We could find out, but so far we have not bothered. We elect instead to classify the aggregated products of individual minds in ways which make subjective sense to us, the researchers, irrespective of the sense which each of these products makes to the individual who creates it. It is possible that our conclusions tell us more about ourselves and the prejudices of our training than they tell us about the minds of our subjects. Even our careful little cloze tests present problems. For example, knowing the location of a place with particular identifying characteristics does not necessarily involve knowing its name. Conversely, knowing the location of a name on an image with a cartographic form does not necessarily involve knowing anything else at all about the real location that is symbolized in the name. For reasons like this it is necessary to exercise caution and not to impute to such measurements meanings which they do not necessarily possess.

On balance our remarks may seem pessimistic and it does occur to us from time to time that many geographers may too readily have abandoned normative models of *human* behaviour in favour of approaches based on the meanderings of behaviouralists' rats. But in fact we are merely ruminating on a hiatus that seems to have affected cognitive mapping research and the understanding of spatial schemas as a whole. At an experimental level it is time that we addressed ourselves to a more rigid and systematic testing of methods and to the search for different ways of eliciting the kind of information which indisputably forms the basis of many of our behavioural dispositions. It may also be the case that there is much to learn from developmental studies, like that of Jahoda's (1963), which places more emphasis on the conceptual structures within which information is stored and rather less on the molecular fragments of data bits. At the same time we should welcome and foster the room that is given to us by the more emphatic emergence of experiential bases to explanation. Without them our cognitive maps and the patterns of behaviour that they may help us to elucidate are no more human than the activities reported by Tolman (1948) so long ago.

REFERENCES

Appleyard, D. (1969). City designers and the pluralistic city. In L. Rodwin and associates (Eds.), *Planning Urban Growth and Regional Development: The Experience of the Guyana Program in Venezuela*, M.I.T. Press, Cambridge, Massachusetts pp. 422–452.

Arnheim, R. (1970). *Visual Thinking*, Faber and Faber, London.

Austin, J. L. (1962). *Sense and Sensibilia*, Oxford University Press, London.

Balchin, W. G. V. (1972). Graphicacy, *Geography*, **57**, 185–195.

Beck, R. J. and Wood, D. (1976) Cognitive transformation of information from urban geographic fields to mental maps. *Environment and Behaviour*, **8**, 199–238.

Berlyne, D. E. (1969). Measures of aesthetic preference. In J. Hogg (Ed.), *Psychology and the Visual Arts*, Penguin, London, pp. 129–146.

Blaut, J. M., McCleary, G. S., and Blaut, A. S. (1970). Environmental mapping in young children. *Environment and Behavior*, **2**(3), 235–349.

Board, C., and Taylor, R. M. (1977). Perception and maps: human factors in map design and interpretation. *Transactions of the Institute of British Geographers* (New Series), **2**(1), 19–34.

Bordessa, R. (1969). Perception research in geography: an appraisal and contribution to urban perception. *Seminar Paper No. 8,* Department of Geography, University of Newcastle upon Tyne.

Boulding, K. (1956). *The Image: Knowledge in Life and Society*, University of Michigan, Ann Arbor.

Bowden, M. J. (1969). The perception of the western interior of the United States, 1810–1870: a problem in historical geography. *Proceedings of the Association of American Geographers*, **1**, 16–21.

Boyle, M. J. (1978). Aspects of Spatial Cognition in Sunderland. Unpublished Ph.D. Thesis, University of Manchester.

Boyle, M. J. and Robinson, M. E. (1978). Cloze procedure and cognitive mapping: an experiment in Sunderland. *Research Paper No. 4*, School of Geography, University of Manchester.

Bruner, J. S. (1966). On cognitive growth. In J. S. Bruner, R. R. Olver, and P. M. Greenfield, (Eds.), *Studies in Cognitive Growth*, Wiley, New York, pp. 154–167.

Bruner, J. S., Goodnow, J. J., and Austin, G. A. (1956). *A Study of Thinking*, New York, Wiley.

Canter, D. (1977). *The Psychology of Place*, Architectural Press, London.

Dicken, P. and Robinson, M. E. (1974). *Cognitive Mapping: An Investigation into some Aspects of Information and Preference*. Report to the Social Science Research Council, School of Geography, University of Manchester.

Downs, R. M. and Stea, D. (Eds.) (1973). *Image and Environment*, Edward Arnold, London.

Francescato, D. and Mebane, W. (1973). How citizens view two cities: Milan and Rome. In R. M. Downs and D. Stea (Eds.), *Image and Environment*. Arnold, London, pp. 131–147.

Getzels, J. W. and Jackson, P. W. (1962) *Creativity and Intelligence*, Wiley, New York.

Gilliland, J. (1972). *Readability*, University of London Press, London.

Goodchild, B. (1974). Class differences in environmental perception: an exploratory study. *Urban Studies,* **11**, 157–169.

Goodey, B. (1971). *Perception of the Environment: An Introduction to the Literature*. Occasional Paper No. 17. Birmingham Centre for Urban and Regional Studies, University of Birmingham.

Gould, P. R. (1966). *On Mental Maps*. Discussion Paper No. 9. Michigan Inter-University Community of Mathematical Geographers, Ann Arbor, Michigan.

Gould, P. R. and White, R. (1974). *Mental Maps*, Penguin, Harmondsworth, Middlesex.

Graham, E. (1976). What is a mental map?. *Area*, **8**, 259–262.

Guilford, J. P. (1956). The structure of intellect. *Psychological Bulletin*, **53**, 267–293.
Guilford, J. P. (1967). *The Nature of Human Intelligence*, McGraw-Hill, New York.
Gulick, J. (1963). Images of the Arab city. *Journal of the American Institute of Planners*, **29**, 179–197.
Harrison, J. and Sarre, P. (1975). Personal construct theory in the measurement of environmental images. *Environment and Behavior*, **7**, (1), 3–57.
Hart, R. and Moore, G. T. (1973). The development of spatial cognition: a review. In R. M. Downs and D. Stea (Eds.), *Image and Environment*. Edward Arnold, London, pp. 235–288.
Holsti, O. R. (1969). *Content Analysis for the Social Sciences and Humanities*, Addison-Wesley, Reading, Massachusetts.
Hudson, L. (1966). *Contrary Imaginations*, Methuen, London.
Hudson, L. (1972). *The Cult of the Fact*. Cape, London.
Jackson, L. E., and Johnston, R. J. (1972). Structuring the image: an investigation of the elements of mental maps. *Environment and Planning*, **4**, 415–427.
Jahoda, G. (1963). The development of children's ideas about country and nationality. *British Journal of Educational Psychology*, **33**, 47–60.
Johnston, R. J. (1972). Activity spaces and residential preferences: some tests of the hypothesis of sectoral mental maps. *Economic Geography*, **48**, 199–211.
Kaplan, S. (1973). Cognitive maps in perception and thought. In R. M. Downs and D. Stea (Eds.), *Image and Environment*, Edward Arnold, London, pp. 63–78.
Ladd, F. C. (1970). Black youths view their environment: neighborhood maps. *Environment and Behavior*, **2** (June), 74–99.
Lee, T. R. (1963). Psychology and living space. *Transactions of the Bartlett Society*, **2**, 9–36.
Lowenthal, D. (1961). Geography, experience and imagination: towards a geographical epistemology. *Annals of the Association of American Geographers*, **51**, 241–260.
Lynch, K. (1960). *The Image of the City*. M.I.T. Press, Cambridge, Massachusetts
McFie, J. (1972). Factors of the brain. *Bulletin of the British Psychology Society*, **25**, 11–14.
Milgram, S. (1973). Introduction to Chapter Two. In W. Ittleson (Ed.), *Environment and Cognition*, Seminar Press, New York, pp. 21–27.
Milgram, S., and Jodelet, D. (1977). The way Parisians see Paris. *New Society*, 3 Nov., 234–237.
Moore, G. T. (1973). Developmental differences in environmental cognition. In W. Preiser (Ed.), *E.D.R.A.*, Vol. 2, pp. 232–239.
Neisser, U. (1967). *Cognitive Psychology*, Appleton-Century-Crofts, New York.
Osgood, C. E. (1959). The representational model and relevant research methods. In I. de S. Pool (Ed.), *Trends in Content Analysis*, University of Illinois Press, Urbana, Illinois, pp. 33–88.
Pacione, M. (1976). Shape and structure in cognitive maps of Great Britain. *Regional Studies*, **10**, 275–283.
Palmer, C. J., Robinson, M. E., and Thomas, R. W. (1977). The countryside image: an investigation of structure and meaning. *Environment and Planning*, **9**, 739–749.
Piaget, J., Inhelder, B., and Szeminska, A. (1960). *The Child's Conception of Geometry*. Basic Books, New York.
Pocock, D. C. D. (1975). *Durham: Images of a Cathedral City*. Occasional Publication (New Series) 6, Department of Geography, University of Durham.
Pocock, D. C. D. (1976). Some characteristics of mental maps: an empirical study. *Transactions of the Institute of British Geographers*, (New Series), **1**, (4), 493–512.
Porter, J., Hart, T. and Machin, J. (1975). Cloze procedure tested in Hampshire. *Area*, **7**, (3), 196–198.
Robinson, M. E. (1974). Cloze procedure and spatial comprehension tests. *Area*, **6**, (2), 137–142.

Saarinen, T. F. (1969). *Perception of the Environment.* Commission on College Geography Resource Paper 5, Association of American Geographers, Washington D. C.

Saarinen, T. F. (1973a). The use of projective techniques in geographical research. In W. H. Ittleson (Ed.), *Environment and Cognition,* Seminar Press, New York, pp. 29–52.

Saarinen, T. F. (1973b). Student views of the world. In R. M. Downs and D. Stea (Eds.), *Image and Environment,* Edward Arnold, London, pp. 148–161.

Saarinen, T. F. (1976). *Environmental Planning Perception and Behaviour,* Houghton, Mifflin Co., Boston.

Tolman, E. C. (1948). Cognitive maps in rats and men. *Psychological Review,* **55,** 189–208.

Tuan, Y. F. (1974). *Topophilia,* Prentice-Hall, Englewood Cliffs, New Jersey.

Tuan, Y. F. (1975). Images and mental maps. *Annals of the Association of American Geographers,* **65**(2), 205–213.

Tuan, Y. F. (1977). *Space and Place,* Edward Arnold, London.

Wallach, M. A. and Kogan, M. (1965). *Modes of Thinking in Young Children.* Holt, Rinehart, and Winston, New York.

Wolpert, J. (1965). Behavioral aspects of the decision to migrate. *Paper and Proceedings, Regional Science Association,* **15,** 159–172.

Wood, L. J. (1970). Perception studies in geography. *Transactions of the Institute of British Geographers,* **50,** 129–142.

Chapter 4

Financial and Real Estate Institutions in the Housing Market: A Study of Recent House Price Changes in the San Francisco Bay Area

Risa Palm

INTRODUCTION

The cost of homeownership has risen markedly during the 1970s in cities throughout the United States. According to recent Congressional testimony, if present trends continue, the average price of a new house will exceed $90 000 by the end of the next decade, placing homeownership far beyond the means of the average American family.

Because of recent cost increases, households have been forced to use the earnings of two or more family members to support the costs of the purchase of their first home (Hayghe, 1976). In some cities, this has meant that entire neighbourhoods have shifted from occupancy by families with a more traditional life style (male wage-earner, female homemaker, and children) to mixtures of households including childless and even 'gay' (homosexual) couples. Since it can be demonstrated that increasing housing costs have resulted in important changes in the social fabric of neighbourhoods, the study of housing cost trends can yield important insights into contemporary urban spatial processes.

The purpose of this essay is to review and critique two of the most influential sets of models which have been developed to describe and explain residential land values. The first set of models is based on the behavioural postulate that households attempt to maximize their utility with respect to access to place of work, size of dwelling unit, and quality of dwelling unit, neighbourhood, and public services. The results of such utility maximization, within given budget constraints, are a set of household bid-rent functions and, given particular levels of supply, an equilibrium price structure for the city as a whole. The second set of models is based on the premise that racially defined submarkets distort other relationships between price and the quality and quantity of the dwelling unit and its environment. These two types of models, which one may abbreviate as 'accessibility' and segregation ('arbitrage') models respectively, are derived from theories of residential preferences. What has been omitted from such models is the explicit consideration of the role of institutional behaviour in the pricing process; the mechanisms by which mortgage lenders and real estate agents can affect the relationship between price and quality/quantity of housing. This essay will explore the relationship between institutional behaviour and price through a study of recent price change.

After a brief overview of the recent trends in house prices in the United States, a general discussion of the two types of market model is presented. Next, the historical basis for government intervention in the housing market is described, along with current government influences on the behaviour of financial and real estate institutions, and the roles of these institutions in the house valuation process. The major portion of this essay reports the findings of a study of house price trends in the San Francisco Bay Area and presents an assessment of the utility of variables derived from the accessibility and segregation models in accounting for these trends. The independent roles of mortgage investment policy and realtor evaluations are indicated. The essay concludes with the suggestion that the segregation model be broadened to include the contributions of financial and real estate institutions in the assessment of house prices.

RECENT HOUSE PRICE TRENDS

Although housing costs have increased throughout the United States, the rate of increase has varied from one metropolitan area to another. The average cost of homeownership increased by 94.4 per cent between 1967 and 1977, an increase which was 21.8 per cent higher than the general increase in the cost of living, as indexed by the Consumer Price Index (*Monthly Labor Review*, 1977). However, in some cities the percentage increase over this ten-year period exceeded 120 per cent, while in others the percentage increase was well below the average (Table 4.1). Although the pattern is not entirely clear, cities which experienced net inmigration in the first part of the 1970s also usually had higher than average price increases, while metropolitan areas which lost population between 1970 and 1974 had smaller cost changes.

At the intrametropolitan level, the spatial variation of cost change has not been systematically studied. This is partly because of the difficulty in gaining access to accurate data on housing and population characteristics more recent than the 1970 census. An important exception is the study of price change in Chicago between 1968 and 1972, using data obtained from the Society of Real Estate Appraisers (Berry, 1976). This study yielded important findings on the role of racial change in affecting house values, and also revealed the impact of property tax appraisals on house values (Berry and Bednarz, 1975). However, the termination date for the study coincided with the beginning of a period of particularly rapid price change which has continued through the present (1977), and shows no sign of abating.

The present period of rapid price change has attracted much attention and speculation, but the mechanisms and patterns of change seem to be poorly understood. Community observers, without access to academic studies of price changes in other neighbourhoods or of intrametropolitan patterns in other cities, have frequently turned to proximate conditions in their search for explanations for why their particular community has experienced price changes. The explanations put forward for local price increases include legislation restricting population growth and an increase in the number of dwelling units, such as that in effect in Boulder, Colorado, and Petaluma, California (Alonso, 1973; Exline, 1977), where restricted supply and continued high demand are said to result in price increases. Such reasoning has been justified even when the objective situation of supply and demand does not fulfil these conditions on the grounds that perceived or anticipated supply constrictions drive up prices (as is the case of Boulder, Colorado, where after the slow-growth ordinance was passed, but five months before it went into effect, house prices were reported to be rising at a rate

TABLE 4.1 Intrametropolitan variations in homeownership cost trends: September–November 1976

Metropolitan area (SMSA or SCA)	CPI for home-ownership	CPI for all goods	1970–1974 population change due to migration	
			Number	Percentage
Houston	228.8	182.0	112 600	5.6
San Diego	228.3	173.9	110 400	8.1
Baltimore	227.8	176.5	22 300	1.1
Cincinnati	201.6	172.1	− 50 000	− 3.6
Philadelphia	200.9	174.5	− 111 000	− 2.3
Minneapolis–St. Paul	200.5	173.4	− 25 600	− 1.3
Los Angeles–Long Beach	200.1	173.4	− 329 800	− 4.7
St. Louis	198.3	169.9	− 104 800	− 4.3
Dallas–Ft. Worth	198.3	169.9	10 400	0.4
New York, N.E. New Jersey	196.2	178.6	− 501 500	− 5.0
Seattle–Tacoma	195.9	167.9	− 62 100	− 4.4
Kansas City	195.3	168.7	− 15 300	− 1.2
Atlanta	194.5	171.6	102 300	6.6
National Average (cities)	194.4	172.6		
Pittsburg	193.2	170.9	− 89 400	− 3.7
Detroit	189.9	171.3	− 155 300	− 3.5
Washington, D.C	189.6	174.7	− 13 500	− 0.5
San Francisco	180.7	167.1	− 34 100	− 1.1
Boston	178.5	176.1	− 2 300	− 0.1
Chicago	176.1	167.5	− 226 200	− 3.2
Buffalo	175.0	173.8	− 41 700	− 3.1
Milwaukee	169.5	170.5	− 27 400	− 2.0
Cleveland	169.2	173.0	− 127 400	− 6.2

Consumer Price Index (CPI), 1967 = 100.
Source: CPI detailed report, and current population reports, population estimates, and projections. Bureau of Labor Statistics (1977)

of 8 per cent per month). It should be apparent, however, that before one can argue that any particular set of factors has resulted in price increases, the general intrametropolitan pattern of house price trends should be specified, so that 'control' areas can be compared with those communities in which local legislation has intervened in the 'natural' supply–demand relationships.

A REVIEW OF MARKET MODELS

The assignment of a particular price to a house is the result of a complex process. Individual perceptions, as well as some consensus as to the value of a set of site characteristics, environmental characteristics, and accessibility, are involved in assessing the value of a dwelling unit. Several models have been developed to isolate the specific characteristics which best summarize the present price of a particular dwelling. These models are often similar in form, but differ with respect to the behavioural postulates on which they are developed. For the purpose of this exposition, these models will be treated separately as accessibility and segregation models, although it should be noted that most empirical studies (hedonic studies) do not make such distinctions, but rather draw variables from either model.

Accessibility models and their variants

The general models developed by Alonso (1964), Muth (1969), and Wingo (1961) may be considered as the classic portrayals of urban land values. In them, a set of bid-rent curves portrays the utility to the household of various combinations of location, quantity of housing space, and expenditure on other goods. Household equilibrium occurs at the point at which the market price structure for the combination of location and space is tangent with the household bid-rent curve yielding the maximum household utility. Changes in transportation costs in the city affect the equilibrium solution, although not necessarily in a straightforward manner (Dewees, 1976): a reduction in transportation costs, increasing the disposable income which could be spent on housing, might be allocated either towards more space (and a more suburban location), or towards greater accessibility with the same amount of space (and a more central location) (Muth, 1969).

The general land market of the city is derived from the composite of the bid-rents of households competing in a single land market. Urban residents bid for locations to maximize locational utilities. The result of the actions of individual households is a housing market in which land values, measured on a square-footage basis, decline with distance from the central business district.

Accessibility models have been widely tested, and are effective in explaining generalized land values (Casetti, 1971; Mills, 1969; Yeates, 1965). However, they have been criticized on several grounds. First, they are usually based on assumptions which preclude the portrayal of the complexity of contemporary cities; for example, cities are frequently assumed to have but a single centre, the focus for work and shopping trips. Other non-central nodes which may be of great significance in the spatial–temporal routine of the household are ignored (Hagerstrand, 1970; Pred, 1977). Housing and neighbourhoods are also assumed to vary quantitatively but not qualitatively, and such variables as the reputation of the local school district, which can be very important in the residential location decision, are omitted (Nelson, 1972). Models extending the analysis to multi-centred cities with variable 'residential attractiveness' have been formulated, but also have as their goal the derivation of a composite land rent function which would obtain in an equilibrium market situation (Papageorgiou, 1971, 1976).

The second objection which has been raised concerning accessibility models is that they are not directed at uncovering the complex processes of decision-making which lie behind the observed patterns. Since consumers cannot specify their utility functions such that they can make purchase decisions in accord with these functions, and are typically aware of only a small portion of the housing choices potentially available to them, the trade-off principles on which accessibility models are based cannot be interpreted as descriptions of consumer behaviour (Adams, 1969; Flowerdew, 1976).

Despite these objections, a plethora of studies have attempted empirically to derive the utility surfaces of home buyers. In these studies, consumer utility functions are examined by breaking down the house price into components, and assigning a market value to each attribute (Davies, 1974; Edelstein, 1974; Hammer, Coughlin, and Horn, 1974; Wilkinson and Archer, 1973). A 'hedonic price index' (Griliches, 1967) is derived by fitting, through multiple regression analysis, a subset of those characteristics which could be used to describe and evaluate a housing unit to its sale price. Ball (1973) reviewed ten such studies done for cities in the United States and the United Kingdom, but drew no conclusions concerning the best set of variables which explain housing values because: (1) the studies all achieved high levels of variance explained with very different sets of variables; (2) there were differences in supply–demand relationships among the cities studied; (3) samples had been obtained through different research methods; and (4) there exists a possibility that the values of the regression coefficients were distorted because of spatial autocorrelation.

Elaborations of the accessibility models have included air quality and property taxation as explanatory variables. Investigations of the relationship between air quality and house price are based on the belief that households wish to avoid polluted areas, and therefore are willing to pay a premium to live in neighbourhoods of higher air quality. However, empirical findings are not consistent. In a study of sales prices of matched neighbourhoods in Chicago, Wall (1972) found that 'the effects of air pollution on this specific property type were for all purposes non-existent'. Other studies have yielded varying results:

If the sulfation levels to which any single-family dwelling unit is exposed were to drop by 0.25 mg./100 cm^2/day, the value of that property could be expected to rise by at least $83 and more likely closer to $245. Using the latter figure and assuming the sulfation levels are reduced by 0.25 mg, but in no case below 0.49

mg (taken as the background level) the total increase in property values for the St. Louis standard metropolitan statistical area could be as much as $82 790 000. (Ridker and Henning, 1967, p. 254)

Too much significance should not be attached to the magnitudes of coefficients of the individual pollution variables. Taken together, the coefficients imply an elasticity of offer price for owner-occupied housing with respect to 'composite' pollution of between 0.1 and 0.2, or at the mean, a marginal capitalised loss ranging from about $300 to $700 per property. (Anderson and Crocker, 1971, p. 177)

The effects of air pollution, as measured by the levels of suspended particulates, on property values and rents do not appear to be statistically significant. At best, one might argue for a marginally significant coefficient with the owner equation. (Smith and Deyak, 1975, p. 282).

Some of these findings have generated vigorous debate on two issues: the question of over-interpretation, or projection of a dollar value in benefits to the general population of a metropolitan area based on a regression equation which describes relationships *ceteris paribus* (Freeman, 1971); and the issue of how one specifies the relationship of any variables with house value when one cannot assume that the housing market is in equilibrium (Straszheim, 1974).

Studies of the impacts of property taxation on land values and the behaviour of investors show greater consensus. Property taxation increases seem to lead to a lessened propensity for land investment and a decline in land values (Netzer, 1968). In a study of residential investment in New York City from 1950 to 1967, Barlev and May (1976) found that an increase in 'one percentage point in the property tax will lower applications for investment by 90 million dollars', and that 'the effect of raising the tax rate by one percentage point is to raise demolitions by 4.5 times'. Similarly, Grieson (1974) established that the reduction of property taxation by one-third would 'raise property values by about 10%, increase the supply of structures by 23%, increase land values by 46%, and reduce the price of structures by 23%. . . . The above property tax implies a deadweight loss of 12% of the market value of the real estate and 25% of the tax collections thereupon'.

Several studies have pointed to systematic bias in the assessment of properties within city boundaries. Berry and Bednarz (1975) found that assessors in Chicago under-assessed areas which were increasing in price, and over-assessed areas which were relatively declining. Similar findings of high assessment/sales ratios for older, low-income, and non-white neighbourhoods were reported for Boston (Oldman and Aaron, 1965), and San Bernardino,California (T. R. Smith, 1970). One might conclude from these studies that:

(1) If assessment practices within a single municipality vary, then those areas which are consistently under-assessed for the purposes of property taxation are given a bonus with respect to property value: a lower relative property

tax in a particular neighbourhood will increase the average sales price and therefore the value of the property.

(2) Variation in property taxation rates among municipalities within a metropolitan area acts in the benefit of those properties which are taxed at a lower rate, *ceteris paribus*: if certain suburbs are providing equal levels of service to residents, but are providing those services with lower property tax rates, then property values in these suburbs should be higher than in those suburbs with higher tax rates.

In summary, accessibility models which, in their simplest form, involve the computation of elasticities for quantity of housing unit (size of dwelling unit and size of lot), distance from place of work (or other foci), and other expenditures, have been modified to include other variables in the estimation of housing value: environmental quality and property taxation. Even the most complex of these models, however, involves the computation of elasticities for the market taken as a whole.

Segregation or arbitrage models

Segregation or arbitrage models not only evaluate the characteristics of the dwelling unit and its location, but also modify the estimate of house price, partially in response to the location of the property within a submarket defined according to the racial or ethnic composition of neighbouring residents. In these models, a given set of demographic or racial preferences results in an arbitrage situation in which elasticities for particular housing and neighbourhood characteristics will vary among a set of relatively segregated populations. Although many other issues are involved, research has centred on two themes: the effect of neighbourhood racial change on individual property values, and the related question of whether or not black households pay more than white households for comparable dwelling units.

White property owners, real estate agents, and real estate appraisers have long held the belief that when a neighbourhood changes from white occupancy to non-white occupancy, property values decline. Homer Hoyt's classic study of *One Hundred Years of Land Values in Chicago* (1933) goes even further in actually ranking various nationalities and ethnic groups on the basis of their effects on property values: (1) English, Germans, Scottish, Irish, Scandinavians; (2) North Italians; (3) Bohemians or Czechoslovakian; (4) Poles; (5) Lithuanians; (6) Greeks; (7) Russian Jews; (8) South Italians; (9) Negroes; and (10) Mexicans. To protect property values, residents were urged to formulate restrictive covenants proscribing the sale of property to non-Christians and non-Caucasians, and real estate salespersons were cautioned by their code of 'ethics' against the sale of property to 'undesirable' ethnic or racial groups (Helper, 1969).

To counter such beliefs, a major research effort under the auspices of the Commission on Race and Housing produced arguments that the assertion that non-whites or non-Christians lowered property values was a self-fulfilling prophecy: if property owners believe that prices will decline with the entry of non-whites or non-Christians into the neighbourhood, and anxiously sell their houses en masse to avoid financial losses, they themselves bring about a decline in property values by glutting the market (Laurenti, 1960; McEntire, 1960; Rapkin and Grigsby, 1960). The argument concludes that if white property owners did not participate in the panic selling, such a decline in house prices could be avoided.

Despite the evidence which these studies brought to bear on the question of the effects of racial change on property values, appraisers have continued to assign lower values to property in racially mixed neighbourhoods. The fears of white property owners have thus had a basis in the behaviour of those professionals who are in the most direct position to control housing values. As a result of this complex of factors, racial transition does seem to result in a series of changes in property values (Berry, 1976, p. 418):

> Controlling for housing characteristics, income differences, etc., price levels of single-family homes in Chicago in the period 1968–1972 were highest in the peripheral white areas, dropped in 'threatened' white neighbourhoods, showed a modest increase in the zones of black expansion, and collapsed to their lowest levels within the traditional ghetto.

House prices seem to decline as the neighbourhood moves from total white occupancy to total black occupancy, although there is a temporary increase in values during the period of 'black expansion'.

Conclusions on the second major research issue, whether blacks or whites pay more for comparable housing, have varied. What is remarkable about these studies is that they have all used similar econometric models, and yet have often come to very different conclusions:

> The present study reports on the influence of segregation on housing prices in Oakland, California housing market and provides new evidence that whites, not blacks, are paying premiums for comparable quality housing. (Daniels, 1975, p. 105)

> There is no statistical difference in black–white housing costs. (Lapham, 1971, p. 1244)

> Rents and housing values fall with the neighbourhood's concentration of blacks and rise with its concentration of Italians, Puerto Ricans, and 'other Non-Whites'. (Schnare, 1976, p. 111)

> Relative to whites in the white interior, blacks in the ghetto pay 9 percent more for equivalent dwellings. (King and Miewszkowski, 1973, p. 601).

At issue in these studies are the definition of 'comparable' in the measurement of which race is paying how much for what services, the extent to which one racial group, especially white home buyers, will pay a voluntary premium for the 'benefit' of segregation, and the effect of variation in the supply of ghetto or non-ghetto housing on consumption of housing by black households. In general, empirical conclusions are probably affected by short-run supply of housing in various parts of the city, the supply–demand relationship in the study area during the study period within particular price classes, the relative numbers of black or white home buyers during the study period, variations in long-run preferences for the racial composition of the local neighbourhood, and the extent to which financial institutions are providing mortgage money within the study areas, as well as differences in data, level of aggregation, and statistical methods used. Thus, even a single and seemingly straightforward indicator of racial composition shows a highly varying relationship with price level in the several studies which have attempted to isolate its impact.

Segregation models may be summarized as giving attention to the processes through which groups—defined by race or ethnicity, or by life style or other demographic characteristics—choose to share urban space, and the translation of these preferences into relative prices. This model of the housing market still rests on an equilibrium assumption—a complete adjustment of supply and demand—but is a closer approximation to consumer behaviour, because it is based on a mapping of preference structures.

Although accessibility and segregation models are often highly successful in accounting for price levels, the behavioural principles on which they are based concentrate on only a part of the pricing process: buyer preferences for space, location, quality of the neighbourhood, and racial composition of the neigh-bourhood, and the resolution of household bid-rents for these qualities. What is omitted from this description of the housing market is an explicit consideration of the more direct influences on house price, such as government activity in the housing market through construction and mortgage insurance policies, the valuation of housing by real estate appraisers, and the role of real estate agents in accentuating or reducing local demand for housing, and thereby affecting house prices. The purpose of the next section is to review these factors, which together may be referred to as 'institutional' impacts on the housing market.

INSTITUTIONAL IMPACTS ON THE HOUSING MARKET

Government, financial, and real estate institutions have had a major influence on the housing market. Although this influence is less amenable to a quantitative assessment than simple descriptors of housing or neighbourhood quality, it is none the less vital that the role of these institutions be made more explicit. Government intervention in the housing market has evolved from a minimum of regulation and activity before 1930, to a policy which assumes an affirmative responsibility for the quality of housing, within the strictures of a capitalistic political economy. Similarly, the roles of financial and real estate institutions have changed in recent years as their activities have increasingly come under public scrutiny and regulation. Because institutional policies are still changing, it is useful to gain a perspective on present trends by reviewing the roles these institutions have played within the American housing market over the past half century.

The effect of federal government on housing values

Programmes undertaken and supported by the federal government have affected the distribution and availability of housing, both directly through such policies as housing subsidies, and indirectly through federal aid to highway construction and income taxation laws. This discussion will be limited to those policies directly affecting the financing of single family housing.

The federal government has consistently put an emphasis on providing housing through stimulating private enterprise. There were few housing programmes before the 1930s and federal legislation was limited to the provision of housing for shipyard employees and servicemen during the First World War. Before 1932, housing programmes were mainly at the state and municipal level, and were in the form of regulations (tenement codes, for example) or state loans for house construction and state tax exemptions (Wendt, 1963; Mandelker, 1973). Several Acts were passed in the 1930s which heralded an increased federal responsibility for housing. In 1932, the Federal Home Loan Bank System was created as an aid to private mortgage lending institutions. In 1932, the National Housing Act established a Federal Housing Administration (F.H.A.) to stimulate mortgage loans by insuring lenders against losses should the borrowers default on the loan. In addition, the Federal Savings and Loan Insurance Corporation provided federal insurance to individuals making deposits in savings and loan companies, increasing the amount of capital available for home loans. The 1937 Housing Act included a provision to make loans to local housing authorities for 90 per cent of the cost of public housing, which local authorities were to match with 20 per cent of the cost, or property tax abatement. In this series of Congressional acts, the principles of federal intervention in the housing market were established which were to hold through the 1950s.

Severe housing shortages accumulated during the Second World War. In response to the heightened demand for housing after the war, the federal government passed legislation which was to affect the very nature of American cities. A series of mortgage financing measures ensured a steady flow of funds, at least in support of new suburban housing. The Federal Home Loan Bank system provided reserve credit for savings and loans. The F.H.A. insured residential loans made by private lenders for Second World War veterans, providing for very low down payments, low interest rates, and longer repayment terms. The Federal National Mortgage Association, established in 1938, acted as a secondary market for F.H.A. or V.A. (Veterans' Administration) mortgage funds. In addition, the 1949 Housing Act provided for joint federal and local participation in the construction of subsidized low-rent public housing and for slum clearance. The Housing Act of 1949, with its goal of 'a decent home and suitable living environment for every American family', became the basis for the twin actions of inner-city slum clearance and public housing construction, and the stimulation of the building of suburban single-family housing through mortgage guarantees. The monumental problems which have accompanied federally sponsored public housing have been considered at length elsewhere, but it should be pointed out that the actions of the federal government provided a substantial subsidy to the middle classes, vast profits to residential developers and land speculators, and a federally guaranteed windfall to financial institutions (Glazer, 1967; Weinstein, 1974). F.H.A. financing was notably absent from inner-city areas, where speculators and financial institutions requiring extra premiums ('points') for mortgages or onerous contracts for deed were the chief sources of mortgage financing (Harvey and Chatterjee, 1974; Stone, 1975).

Legislation of the 1960s signalled a redirection in the investment policies of the F.H.A. Section 203 of the 1966 National Housing Act waived the requirement that an area be 'economically sound' in order for F.H.A. insured mortgages to be provided, and F.H.A. loans in low-income neighbourhoods increased rapidly (Kaiser, 1969; Fried, 1971). One of the most important provisions of the 1968 Housing Act with respect to homeownership was the Section 235 programme. Families with incomes low enough to qualify them for admission to public housing could purchase a home with no down payment, and a contract to pay 20 per cent of their income in monthly payments, with the federal government contributing the remainder required to complete mortgage payments at the market interest rate (8 per cent in 1976). The maximum term of the mortgage extended to forty years.

Despite the good intentions of the housing programmes passed during the 1960s, they have often failed to provide benefits for the low-income families for whom they were intended, and have even led to the abandonment of large portions of such cities as Detroit and Chicago (Boyer, 1973). New housing under these programmes was appraised by the F.H.A. for values in excess of true market values, often providing government-insured loans on housing 'of such poor quality that there is little or no possibility they can survive the life of the mortgage' (Fried, 1971, p. 109). When such abuses became well known in government circles and to the general public, the programmes were cut back and some were abandoned. However, as house prices for all income groups continue to increase, the federal government will most likely attempt to counteract these trends with new programmes and subsidies. It is apparent that the form and administration of such programmes will require even more careful consideration and scrutiny than those enacted during the 1960s, lest the taxpayers again find themselves subsidizing the mortgage bankers and speculators rather than the persons for whom the programmes are intended.

Investment policies

Since financial institutions are, to a large extent, affected by regulations of federal and state governments, investment policies cannot be considered as independent of federal and state legislation. But in comparison with governmental policy, financial institutions are more directly involved in the setting of house values for a wider spectrum of properties, and have a more immediate effect on house price trends. How do financial institutions determine their investment policies, and ultimately the values of houses? According to one current textbook (W. F. Smith, 1970, pp. 294–302), mortgage investment policies are formulated according to the current cost of funds (interest rates), liquidity and locational requirements set by state or federal regulations, and the trade-off between the yield which the loan promises and its risk.

Given the overall lending policy of a financial institution, the characteristics which are considered when a loan application is evaluated are (1) the characteristics of the borrower, including his credit rating and income stability, and (2) the characteristics of the property offered as collateral. Although in the abstract the textbook investment principles seem equitable, they can have serious deleterious effects on the financial viability of neighbourhoods as well as on the financial stability of homeowners. When lenders decide that they should not invest in certain portions of the city on the grounds that the area is threatened with decay and the lenders may not be able to recover their loan in the event of a default, they may doom by policy the entire area to decline and even abandonment.

Arguments concerning investment policies are emotionally charged and often very complex. The complexity of mortgage loan procedures, and the selling and reselling of loans among financial institutions including the Federal National Mortgage Association ('Fannie Mae') and the Government National Mortgage Association ('Ginnie Mae'), make the debate on this subject difficult to comprehend fully (perhaps a reason for the rather naïve provisions of the 1968 Housing Act, according to Boyer (1973)). Very simply, the argument of the lenders is that their assessment methods and lending policies are prudent, and that such policies are essential to their fiduciary responsibilities, in particular the protection of the savings which individuals have invested with them. An example of this type of argument was presented to the Senate Committee on Banking, Housing and Urban Affairs by a representative of the U.S. League of Savings Associations: 'We will not make loans at our risk on buildings that are falling down, to families that are unable to carry mortgages, and in neighbourhoods which are blighted or, within the limits of foresight, threatened with blight. . . . This is not unfair discrimination, but, rather, prudent underwriting policy.' In opposition to these arguments are those of proponents of inner-city investment who charge that 'a savings and loan association's determination that an area is deteriorating may be a self-fulfilling prophecy' (Greenberg, 1975, p. 74). An Indianapolis community research group has outlined a series of stages through which a healthy neighbourhood, diagnosed by savings and loan associations as 'threatened', is abandoned:

1. Proportionately smaller mortgage loans are given for property assessed at a given value (the value-to-loan ratio drops).
2. Loans are made over a shorter term (with higher monthly payments).
3. Real estate agents advise buyers to avoid the neighbourhood.

4. Conventional mortgages become more difficult to obtain.
5. Speculators begin buying up property for rental or sale through government-insured mortgages.
6. Supply of houses to be sold increases because of the above factors.
7. Rental housing becomes common with absentee landlords.
8. Tax base decreases, services provided by the city decline, taxes rise.
9. Non-institutional mortgages become common, institutional mortgages are only made through F.H.A. and V.A. insured sources. (An example of a non-institutional mortgage is the land instalment contract, described in detail by Sternlieb, Burchell, and Listokin (1975), Harvey (1974), and Stegman (1972). Under this agreement, a speculator with a satisfactory credit rating purchases a low-cost house, redecorates and repairs the house, adds finance and overhead costs, and then sells the property. The sale is financed by the speculator who takes out a conventional mortgage on the appraised value, and a separate contract on the money spent to redecorate and to cover his expenses. The buyer has immediate possession of the property, but has to pay off the second loan to the speculator before gaining title. Non-institutional mortgages were found to be most common in inner-city areas.)
10. Businesses and stable families move to other neighbourhoods.
11. Foreclosures increase and urban renewal begins.

In short, community interest groups and others have claimed that the investment policies of mortgage lenders may push an otherwise stable and sound neighbourhood into a deteriorated condition.

It is clear that the investment policies of mortgage lenders have a direct and important effect on current and future house prices, and on the stability and financial well-being of entire neighbourhoods. Regardless of the arguments in favour of a spatially or locationally differentiated investment policy, the results of such a policy can take only one form: a spatially differentiated set of house price trends.

Realtor behaviour and land values

It is the real estate agent who translates the investment policies of financial institutions to the potential buyer. Real estate agents are in an excellent position to know the characteristics of at least a portion of the housing market. In daily contact with sellers, buyers, and mortgage lenders, they gain a detailed and practical picture of the nature of housing values and neighbourhood trends.

In the past, real estate agents provided direct and rather blunt evaluations of neighbourhoods. They frequently steered buyers to neighbourhoods which they felt would be most appropriate for them. Signs and advertisements for property indicated neighbourhoods which were 'restricted', often to white Christians, and real estate agents acted in the interest of maintaining these social and ethnic distinctions. A 1953–1954 study of a New England suburban community (Thoma and Lindemann, 1961) provides an example of the way in which the real estate agents defended the character of the neighbourhood:

With detailed knowledge of the town and considerable skill in translating the prospective home buyer's outer symbols—occupation, name, behaviour—into a 'type', the agent steers his client to the 'right' house in the 'right' neighbourhood for him. Houses more attractive to the buyer or locales more in line with his aspirations may never have been shown him if the agent decides the client would not 'fit in' there.

These conclusions are corroborated by the statements of several Chicago real estate salesmen who were asked why it was their policy not to sell property to black people in a white neighbourhood or white block (Helper, 1969, pp. 118–121):

I just don't like to hurt those people that's in there. I just don't think it's fair. I'm not that hungry for money.

I wouldn't sell it to anybody, if it would make the rest of the neighborhood rightfully or wrongfully unhappy. I cannot change the world, and for a measly few dollars I certainly don't want to make people unhappy, to put people in there whom they think they don't like.

I believe in doing what's right, and I believe it would be wrong thing to do.

Can a man live up to the code of the profession and go into a neighborhood where he knows the Negro is not wanted as a neighbor or resident and sell property to them without violating the trust and respect that people have or should have for a member of the real estate profession?

The Negroes we deal with are sensitive, and I don't believe it's a good policy to put him in a place of embarrassment where his feelings are hurt, and his feelings are easily hurt.

If you want to ruin a neighborhood, just let the colored in. We wouldn't open a neighborhood. We wouldn't harm the neighborhood.

In general, real estate agents believed that they were acting ethically, in line with professional standards, and in the best interests of property owners in steering black buyers away from white neighbourhoods in Chicago in the middle of the 1950s. A decade later, despite new civil rights laws, the same set of beliefs was reported in a New Haven, Connecticut survey (Barresi, 1968). Most real estate agents stated that it is important to 'protect' the neighbourhood:

I not only try to sell the house, but I try to sell it to an individual who will pretty much fit into the neighborhood.

He [the Realtor] is needed to improve communities by upgrading residents of the neighborhood.

You have to ask yourself how they would fit into the neighborhood. You don't want to put a Catholic or Protestant into a Jewish neighborhood because they are generally unhappy there. . . . If they're unhappy with their house they blame the Realtor, and they certainly won't go back to him.

These excerpts provide evidence that in the past, real estate agents believed that it was their duty to preserve the social and ethnic composition of neighbourhoods by ensuring that buyers were similar to present residents, and by directing persons of different races, religions, or economic classes to other parts of the city. Today the influence of the real estate agent is more subtle.

Surveys have been taken to determine the influence of the real estate agent in the house purchase process. Findings are somewhat contradictory. Rossi (1955) found that in Philadelphia, real estate agents were used by 50 per cent of the movers, but were used 'effectively' by only 14 per cent. Barrett (1973) found that Toronto buyers became acquainted with the neighbourhood by driving or walking through it, and also by consulting real estate agents. Hempel (1969) found that real estate agents were the most helpful sources of information for locating a home and for advice during the purchase process. In this study, the real estate agent was 'recommended to other buyers' as an aid in the home-purchase decision by the largest proportion of respondents, in these Hartford and south-eastern Connecticut surveys. Herbert (1973) found that only 8 per cent of the low-income respondents and 17 per cent of high-income respondents used real estate agents (in Swansea), but the report did not distinguish between the use of information sources by renters as opposed to home buyers. The National Opinion Research Center (1974) asked recent movers to specify the information source which had been most important to them in finding their current residence. Real estate agents were the second most frequently cited information source, indicated as 'most important' by 20 per cent of the respondents in a nation-wide sample. This dependence on real estate agents in the N.O.R.C. survey did not vary to any great extent by income group (19.2 per cent for low income, 21.0 per cent for high income), nor did it vary across ethnic groups. In sum, a sizeable proportion of the home-buying population is influenced by real estate agents in several key decisions in the home purchase process. Although surveys vary as to the relative importance of the real estate agent, it has been estimated that well over 75 per cent of all sales involve a real estate agent in some part of the transaction. The real estate agent is therefore in a position to be a key agent in communicating information about neighbourhoods or communities which may be translated into increased or decreased local demand, and therefore relative house price levels.

In general, one can argue that the general policies set by the federal government, which are translated into investment policies by mortgage financing institutions and retranslated into counsel given by real estate agents, have an important effect on the housing market, and specifically on relative house price trends. The study reported in the following section sought to document intrametropolitan house price trends, and the extent to which the accessibility and segregation models, as well as institutional behaviour, can account for these trends.

INFLUENCES ON HOUSE PRICE CHANGE IN THE
SAN FRANCISCO BAY AREA: 1971 – 1975.

The purpose of this empirical study of house price change was to test the efficacy of accessibility and segregation variables in the explanation of price change for a metropolitan area and for its component submarkets. If the commonly used variables account for a large proportion of the non-random pattern of price change, then there is no need to consider the behaviour of financial or real estate institutions because the explanatory or predictive power of institutional behaviour would be subsumed in a simpler hedonic analysis. If the spatial variability of price change is clearly non-random, but is only partially accounted for by the variables used in cross-sectional studies of price structure, then clearly some supplement to the standard market model is called for. If this were the case, the role of financial and real estate institutional behaviour should be explored for potential improvement of the explanatory model.

The San Francisco–Oakland metropolitan area (SMSA) was selected for an investigation of house price trends. The diversity of this metropolitan area adds to the complexity of price-trend patterns, and it must be emphasized that distributions that appear to be a 'random' may, upon closer study, represent clear and consistent relationships between the physical and cultural setting and market behaviour. A brief review of the factors which add to the complexity of house price trends is therefore in order.

Residential areas of the Bay Area show great diversity in both climate and topography. Of particular significance is the climatic variation. Summer temperatures provide an example: the mean maximum temperature within the metropolitan area ranges from the high 80s (over 29°C) to the low 60s (15°C) (Fig. 4.1). Climate is important in the process of neighbourhood selection: recent intra-urban movers indicated that they consider summer temperatures and the distribution of fog in selecting one portion of the metropolitan area over another (Palm, unpublished survey). For example, some respondents replied that they chose to live in central Contra Costa County or northern Marin County because of higher temperatures and more days of sunshine; others responded that they preferred Berkeley or southern Marin County because of lower summer temperatures. Associated with summer temperatures and prevailing local winds is the distribution of smog, particularly noxious in the late summer and early autumn, also cited as a factor in residential location.

Topographic contrasts are also well defined: terrain in the urban area includes steep slopes, rolling country, and flat salt marsh, all of which contain sometimes dense residential development. Slopes rising over 100 feet within two city blocks are not unknown in the densely settled portions of San Francisco. Furthermore, 'views' of the Pacific Ocean, the lights of the city of San Francisco from the hills of Marin or Alameda counties, or the two mountain peaks, Tamalpais in Marin County and Diablo in Contra Costa County, add to the desirability of residential districts.

The metropolitan area is culturally diverse, including numerous distinct lifestyle and ethnic communities (Vance, 1976). Many residents have migrated to the Bay Area from elsewhere in the United States and from foreign countries, as reflected in the census statistic that only slightly more than half of the population of the Bay Area were born in the State of California, and 11.4 per cent were foreign-born. The largest minority populations are blacks (more than 330 000

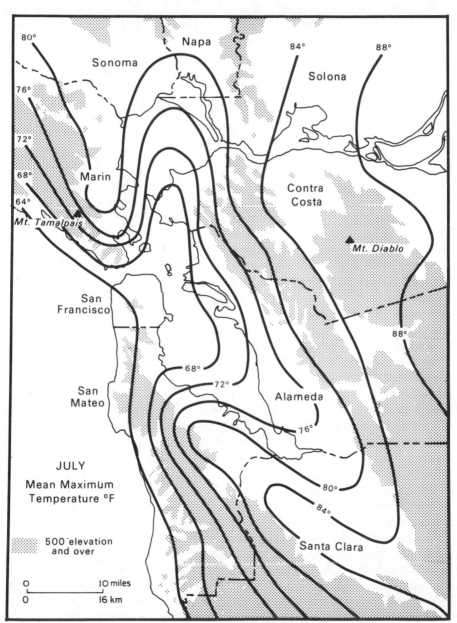

FIGURE 4.1. Climate and topography of the San Francisco Bay Area

of the 3.1 million people in 1970) and Spanish-speaking persons (especially persons of Mexican parentage), numbering nearly 283 000 in 1970. In addition there are more than 50 000 persons listed as foreign stock from each of the following countries: Italy, Germany, the Philippines, the United Kingdom, Mexico, Canada, and China. A large 'gay' (homosexual) community, estimated at exceeding 100 000 in the city of San Francisco, and other non-conformist groups add to the diversity of the Bay Area population (Loyd and Rowntree, 1978).

Because of its internal diversity, the Bay Area is not representative of any other American metropolitan area, and is not appropriately represented by an isotropic plain or distance-decay models. It is a region in which one would expect to find distinct housing submarkets and complex, though not chaotic, spatial patterns.

Data and methods

To trace the price changes of individual neighbourhoods, one might either keep track of the sales price of individual properties over a period of time, or compute an average sales price for small, homogeneous areas, and analyse changes in these averages (Wilkinson with Archer, 1976). The first strategy has the advantage of holding constant dwelling unit characteristics, although variations in owner maintenance might distort findings. Another advantage of the first strategy is the reduction of the dampening effects of dealing with aggregate data. The advantages of the second strategy are an increase in the number of observations possible at any time period, the elimination of idiosyncracies in property upkeep, and data manageability. For these reasons, the second strategy was selected for this study and average house prices, weighted by the average square footage of dwelling space, were calculated for neighbourhoods.

Data were obtained from the Society of Real Estate Appraisers (Table 4.2). Their listings include a wealth of information on houses sold with conventional and government-insured mortgages, including the address, map code, sales price, mortgage type, percentage of down payment, closing date, number of rooms, number of bathrooms, number of bedrooms, square feet of living area, lot size, zoning, year built, estimates of quality and condition, type of heating, presence of air conditioning and appliances, whether the house has been remodeled, special improvements, view lot, basement, type of floor plan, type of deed, and number of storeys. Given the history of the development of housing tracts in American cities, one can usually assume that within small areas developed since the First World War there will be a large measure of neighbourhood homogeneity with respect to dwelling-unit characteristics, and that the most important differentiating feature will be square footage of dwelling space. For this reason, the detailed housing characteristics were not considered further, and only the price, square footage of living area, type of mortgage, and whether or not the lot had a 'view' were tabulated.

TABLE 4.2 Variables and sources of information

Variables	Source from which computed
Percentage of blacks (*PBLK*) Percentage of 'other non-whites' (*POTH*) Percentage of Spanish-language population (*PSL*) Median years of school completed (*SCH*) Professional–managerial workers (*PRO*) Percentage single-family dwellings (*PONEU*) Percentage owner-occupied dwellings (*POWN*) Median age of housing (*AGE*) Percentage of commuters who drive an automobile (*PDRV*) Index of household diversity (*INDEX*) Percentage of 1970 population who lived in the same house in 1965 (non-movers) (*PNMV*)	U.S. Bureau of the Census, *Census of Population and Housing: 1970, Census Tracts, Final Report PHC (1) —189 San Francisco–Oakland, Calif. SMSA*, U.S. Government Printing Office, Washington, D.C., 1972.
Population density (*DENSE*)	U.S. Bureau of the Census and Manpower Administration *Urban Atlas, GE 80–7360, San Francisco–Oakland, Calif., SMSA*, U.S. Government Printing Office, Washington, D.C., 1974.
Standardized reading scores for local elementary schools (*READ*)	California State Board of Education
Time–distance at peak traffic hours to San Francisco central business district (*ACCSF*)	Metropolitan Transportation Commission
Air pollution (*POLLU*)	Bay Area Air Pollution Control District, Technical Services Division
Crime rates (*CRIME*)	Crime and delinquency in California
Property tax rates (*TAX*)	County tax payers' associations
Price of housing in 1971 and 1975 (*PRC71*) Square footage of dwelling space, 1971 and 1975 Percentage of houses sold with 'views' (*VIEW*) Type of mortgage (*FHA*)	Society of Real Estate Appraisers, Market Data Center

Neighbourhoods were defined on the basis of the grid (based on Thomas Brothers' atlas of Bay Area counties) in which the property was located. Grids varied in size from areas of about 10 acres (4 hectares) in densely settled San

Francisco to 40 acres (16 hectares) in the rest of the metropolitan area. If a grid had at least fifteen sales during the last six months of 1971 and fifteen sales during the last six months of 1975, it was included in the subsequent analysis. Following this procedure, those neighbourhoods or grids which were composed largely of multi-family dwellings, rental units, industrial or business sites, which were sparsely populated, were extremely stable, or where there were few sales involving mortgage financing, were omitted because there were too few sales to produce reliable neighbourhood averages. Grids were also eliminated if there was a major change in the average square footage of living space over the four-year study period. If, as is probable, the relationship between price and square footage of living space is non-linear, then one requires detailed information on the nature of this relationship to be able to assume that a change of X square feet anywhere within the distribution would be associated with a change of Y dollars. To reduce the possible distortions which major changes in square footage of living space might introduce into findings on average price change, grids were eliminated if the average living space had increased or decreased by over 200 square feet (or the equivalent of one and a half average rooms).

Grids were matched with census tracts using the Thomas Brothers' atlas of census tract boundaries. Where grids were divided among two or more tracts, the grid was assigned to that tract in which most of the housing was located, as indicated by the density of street intersections. The median price for the tract for each of the two six-month periods was then calculated. The 1975 price was weighted by the change in the general cost of homeownership between November 1971 and November 1975 to express the terminal price in 1971 dollars; if the average price in the neighbourhood increased at exactly the rate that house prices throughout the metropolitan area increased over the 1971–1975 period, its change of price would be $0.00.

Finally, in order to eliminate any residual price change in the census tract which would be accounted for by the change in dwelling space of less than 200 square feet in the two sales periods, a regression of price change in 1971 dollars on absolute change in square footage was calculated. The simple correlation was 0.35, and the scatter diagram showed a linear relationship. The residuals from this regression, representing the change in prices of dwelling units in the census tracts, holding constant the change in average size of dwelling units sold, and expressed in 1971 dollars, was the dependent variable, *PRCH*, in the subsequent analysis.

Correlates of price change

Local neighbourhoods sharply differed in the rate and direction of house price change. Because of the complexity of social and cultural areas in the Bay Area, simple spatial associations are not immediately discernible. There was no obvious increase or decrease in price change with distance from either of the major central business districts, nor were there clear sectoral patterns (Fig. 4.2). Each of the five counties included tracts which varied from high positive price changes through relative price stability to large negative price changes. The counties with the greatest overall increase were Marin ($3 426 average change) and San Mateo ($2 173 average change).

Because the spatial distribution of price change (*PRCH*) was not a simple function of distance from the central business district, and yet there was a

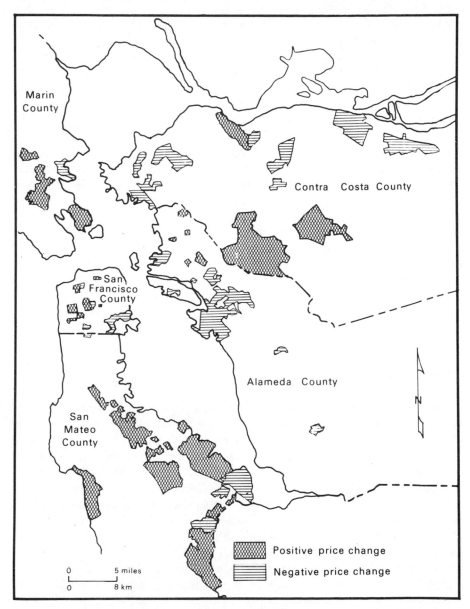

FIGURE 4.2. Price change in the San Francisco Bay Area. Tracts with price change values greater or less than $1 000 are shaded

suspicion that price change had a systematic set of associations, a statistical analysis of the ecological correlates of price change was undertaken. Twenty variables summarizing the social, demographic, and locational characteristics of the census tract were selected from those most frequently used in previous research in determining hedonic price indices for house price levels, based on both the accessibility and segration models.

Despite the difficulty of measuring accessibility as a general construct in a multi-centred metropolitan area, two indicators were used: time–distance to the two major central business districts, and the percentage of commuters who drove an automobile to work—a measure of the extent to which public transportation is available and an acceptable alternative, as well as, in some cases, family income (Table 4.2).

Neighbourhood characteristics included several variables indexing socioeconomic status, age, household composition, and racial composition. School achievement tests in reading by sixth-grade students in local elementary schools were included as an indicator of the quality of the local schools, a characteristic which home buyers are urged to consider in their choice of neighbourhoods (Porter, 1975). Ethnic groups included in the analysis were black, Chicano (Mexican-American), and Chinese-American populations ('other non-white'). Socio-economic position was estimated by using census tract data on median years of school completed, and the percentage of professional and managerial workers in the tract, as well as by the two S.R.E.A. indicators of housing costs, median price of houses sold in 1971 and percentage of mortgages requiring only a minimum down payment and supporting income (F.H.A. mortgages). Demographic character was indicated by the median age of housing, gross residential density, the extent of family composition homogeneity (an index of household diversity, Palm, 1976a), the percentage of single-family dwellings, the percentages of non-movers, and the percentage of owner-occupied dwellings. Quality of the physical environment was measured by the presence of 'view' lots, and air quality.

Two other variables which were included based on previous studies of house values were crime rates (Kain and Quigley, 1970) and property tax rate (Beckmann, 1974). Both of these statistics were available only at a municipal level. The rate of criminal offences per thousand varied from lows of zero and 85 in two of the wealthiest municipalities in southern San Mateo County, to highs of 687 (Oakland) and 650 in one of the west Contra Costa County municipalities (San Pablo). Tax rates also varied markedly. In 1975, a house assessed at a market value of $60 000 in one San Mateo County municipality (Millbrae) would have a monthly property tax bill of just under $100; a house with the same market price in Berkeley would have a monthly tax bill of $208.60.

To eliminate the distorting influence of multi-collinearity within this set of variables, the twenty were reduced to a smaller number of uncorrelated dimensions through principal component analysis (Cheng and Iglarsh, 1976; Wilkinson and Archer, 1973). Fourteen components, accounting for 99.8 per cent of the common variance, were interpretable (Table 4.3). However, the first six dimensions, accounting for 71.9 per cent of the variance, were found to perform just as well in the subsequent regression analysis.

To test whether these variables could be combined adequately to distinguish

TABLE 4.3. Principal component models

A. Twenty-component solution

Label	Variables with loadings exceeding 0.30	Percentage of variance explained
Age-accessibility	*ACCSF* (0.76), *PDRV* (0.79), *POTH* (−0.69), *AGE* (0.54), *DENSE* (0.42), *PONEU* (0.34), *FHA* (0.32), *POLLU* (0.31), *CRIME* (−0.31)	27.4
Municipal costs/disamenities	*TAX* (0.85), *CRIME* (0.77), *PBLK* (0.56), *FHA* (0.49), *READ* (−0.45)	15.9
Socio-economic status	*PRO* (0.87), *SCH* (0.84), *FHA* (−0.44), *VIEW* (0.36), *PBLK* (−0.33)	9.2
Pollution	*POLLU* (0.88)	8.8
Non-movers	*PNMV* (0.80), *PONEU* (0.40)	5.5
Age-diversity	*INDEX* (−0.65), *AGE* (0.41)	5.2
Spanish-language	*PSL* (0.75)	4.3
Price-view	*VIEW* (0.64), *PRC71* (0.61)	3.7
Density	*DENSE* (0.54)	3.3
Age of housing	*AGE* (0.38)	2.8
Single family housing	*PONEU* (0.54), *POWN* (0.46)	2.2
F.H.A. mortgages	*FHA* (0.41)	2.1
Black	*PBLK* (0.40)	1.8
Reading scores	*READ* (0.33)	1.6

B. Six-component solution

Label	Variables with loadings exceeding 0.40	Percentage of variance explained
Age-accessibility	*AGE* (0.76), *PNMV* (−0.74), *ACCSF* (0.60), *PDRV* (0.55), *POLLU* (0.54), *DENSE* (0.52)	27.4
Socio-economic status	*PRO* (0.87), *SCH* (0.84), *FHA* (−0.57), *VIEW* (0.59), *PRC71* (0.48), *READ* (0.40)	15.9
Municipal costs/disamenities	*TAX* (0.83), *CRIME* (0.76), *PBLK* (0.59), *FHA* (0.49), *READ* (−0.48)	9.2
Single-family housing	*PONEU* (0.75), *PDRV* (0.55), *PNMV* (0.51), *POTH* (−0.45)	8.8
Environmental disamenities	*POLLU* (0.65), *VIEW* (−0.45)	5.5
Spanish-speaking	*PSL* (0.67)	5.2

among those tracts which had a positive or negative value for price change (*PRCH*), a discriminant function was calculated. Tracts were classified as positive in price change if their score exceeded $1 000, and negative in price change if the value of *PRCH* was less than — $1 000. Of the 260 tracts grouped in one of these two categories, the discriminant function correctly classified 207 of them, or 79.6 per cent. The chi-square value for this classification performance was significant at 0.001, and five of the six major dimensions had univariate *F*-ratios significant at 0.001. The dimensions, in order of their contribution to the discriminant function, were: socio-economic status, municipal costs and disamenities, environmental disamenities, age-accessibility, and Spanish-language population. Because these components successfully discriminate among tracts with a positive or negative value for price change, we could proceed to the question of the *extent* to which price change is explained by cross-sectional tract characteristics.

Multiple regression equations were calculated to determine the percentage of the variance of price change (*PRCH*) that could be accounted for by the component scores. Using the component scores as independent variables, and a stepwise procedure with a minimum *F*-statistic of 2.5 and a tolerance level of 0.60 for the addition of new variables to the equation, a regression equation was calculated including three of the six components:

$$PRCH = 60.99 + 2812.2 \text{ socio-economic status}$$
$$- 1276.6 \text{ municipal costs and disamenities}$$
$$- 427.0 \text{ Spanish-language population}$$

The multiple R^2 for this equation was 0.394, as compared with an improvement of less than 1 per cent when the component scores for fourteen interpretable components were used in a second regression equation ($R^2 = 0.403$). It should be noted that cross-sectional models, using the same types of methods and variables, typically account for at least 70 and as much as 90 per cent of the variance of price *level*. Although a high coefficient of determination is obtained in the study of price *change* when the original variables are used without reduction into component scores, problems of multi-collinearity may cloud the reliability of this result. Even if this higher coefficient of determination could be accepted, one must still conclude that the variables describing housing quality, demographic characteristics of the neighbourhood, physical environment, accessibility, and race (derived from the accessibility and segregation models) do not perform as well in the prediction of price change as they do in predicting price level. This finding is in accord with a Chicago study (Berry, 1976). A set of variables was applied to both the explanation of price level and the annual inflation rate. For the first set of equations, the coefficients of determination ranged from 0.48 to 0.72, but dropped to 0.09 to 0.20 for the second set of equations.

In sum, the set of independent variables used in cross-sectional analyses of price levels provide some measure of prediction of price change. The relationships noted conform with the accessibility and arbitrage (segregation) models. As a matter of fact, the empirical relationships follow from the definition of the arbitrage model which predicts that 'household utility depend[s] positively on neighborhood income and negatively on the proportion of nonwhites' (Little, 1976). Furthermore, these results confirm earlier findings that higher property taxes are associated with lower prices. However, the coefficient of determination for the change equation is substantially lower than what one would expect for a static model, and one must conclude that the set of variables used in the cross-sectional models fails to explain price change adequately. There are two possible reasons for the limited success of the cross-sectional model: first, the existence of submarkets in the Bay Area may distort the overall relationships between cross-sectional variables and price change; and second, institutional behaviour may interfere with the supply–demand relationships to inflate prices in certain neighbourhoods and decrease them in others, regardless of the quality of dwelling unit and environmental characteristics of these neighbourhoods. The next sections of this essay will investigate both of these possibilities.

Price change within housing submarkets

It has been argued that segmentation of the urban housing market into submarkets confounds the results of multiple regression analyses of housing rents and values (Straszheim, 1974). According to this argument, multiple regression analyses must be undertaken within behaviourally meaningful submarkets, particularly if the standardized regression coefficients are to be interpreted as elasticities, reflecting household utility. A major empirical problem, however, is the delimitation of the boundaries of any given submarket (Bourne, 1976). For our purposes, we will accept Grigsby's definition that submarkets can be defined on the basis of substitutability: that housing units are likely to be within the same submarket if one could be substituted for another by the buyer, and that the price or rent of one has an effect on the price or rent of the other (Grigsby, 1963, p. 34). Housing submarkets have been classified according to several criteria: type of structure, tenure, price, location, size, or the ethnic composition of buyers. Whether these classes actually represent housing submarkets is questionable if the probability that one dwelling unit could be substituted for another is used as a defining criterion, for it is possible that there are more linkages between certain classes (for example, small apartments and suburban single-family detached dwellings) than within them. It is probably most useful to identify major submarkets on the basis of the probability that moves will take place within the submarket boundaries.

Because most home purchases (at least 75 per cent) involve a real estate agent, the districts defined by the real estate industry were used in the present study. Such a delimitation can be justified on the grounds that the action space and awareness space of real estate agents in the San Francisco Bay Area is highly limited (Palm, 1976b, 1976c), and that the geographical divisions of the Boards of Realtors sharply circumscribe the concept which member agents have of the metropolitan area and form the basis for disjunct opportunity spaces for buyers.

108

For this reason, the jurisdictions of the four groups of Boards of Realtors who share information on vacancies were considered as housing submarkets: Marin County, San Francisco County, San Mateo County (including four separate realty boards) and the East Bay (including six Boards of Realtors). Discriminant functions were computed for these four large submarkets to test the effectiveness of the components derived in the metropolitan-level analysis in describing price

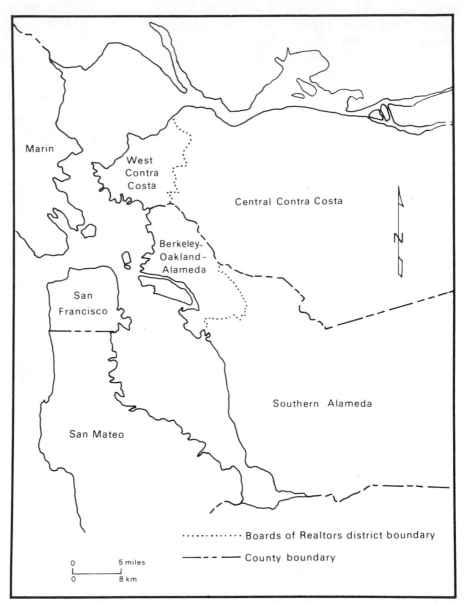

FIGURE 4.3. Boards of Realtors districts, San Francisco Bay Area

change within real estate board districts. The within-district functions proved to be effective in correctly classifying tracts by price change categories (Table 4.4).

Multiple regression equations were then calculated to determine the within-board correlates of price change (Table 4.5). Although in every case the coefficient of determination for the submarket exceeded that for the metropolitan area as a whole, in no case did the coefficient of determination reach 0.50. In addition, the four submarket equations differed significantly in variables used to explain price change. Although the socio-economic status component had a

TABLE 4.4. Discriminant analysis for metropolitan area and Boards of Realtors districts

Component label	Order of entry into discriminant function				
	East Bay	San Francisco	San Mateo	Marin	SMSA
Age-accessibility	5	1	5	1	4
Socio-economic status	1	4	4	6	1
Municipal costs and disamenities	4	3	3	4	2
Single-family housing	6	5	6	3	5
Environmental disamenities	2	2	1	2	3
Spanish-speaking	3	6	2	5	6
Eigenvalue	0.504	1.90	0.976	0.815	0.629
Canonical correlation	0.614	0.810	0.703	0.670	0.621
Percentage correctly classified	73.4	94.6	90.0	83.3	79.6

TABLE 4.5. Regression equations for the metropolitan area and Boards of Realtors districts

Component label	Standardized regression coefficients				
	East Bay	San Francisco	San Mateo	Marin	SMSA
Age-accessibility				− 0.388	
Socio-economic status	0.609	0.291	0.632	0.428	0.539
Municipal costs and disamenities	− 0.257		− 0.200		− 0.317
Single-family housing					
Environmental disamenities	− 0.211	− 0.421			
Spanish-speaking			− 0.154		− 0.192
R^2	0.422	0.461	0.446	0.405	0.394
Number of cases	181	44	89	30	344
Value of PRCH					
Mean	− $2 161.6	$1 031	$2 173.6	$3 425.8	0
Standard deviation	3 575.7	4 686.8	4 544.5	7 034.9	4 876.5

univariate F-value which was significant at 0.001 in every equation, price change was associated with different circumstances for each of the Board of Realtors districts: in San Francisco and the East Bay, the physical environment was an important explanatory factor; in San Mateo, the presence of a Spanish-speaking population was significant; in the East Bay and San Mateo, municipal costs and disamenities (and concentrations of black population) was an important factor; and in Marin, age and accessibility were primary.

The inter-submarket variations noted here corroborate the warnings which Straszheim (1974) issued concerning the effects of areal aggregation on the results of a multiple regression analysis, and place in doubt the generality of the conclusion reached by Schnare and Struyk (1976) on the similarities among submarkets. The more detailed relationships between sets of characteristics at the submarket level affect and distort relationships observed in a metropolitan-wide analysis. Since the relationships are so different at different scales of analysis, it is vital that any research project specifies the unit of study which is most comparable to the actual housing market within which consumers make decisions if one is then to proceed to describe statistical relationships within a housing market.

Even at the submarket levels, however, cross-sectional variables are less than adequate in their power to account for price change. Because the variables derived from accessibility and segregation models explain only a small portion of the variance of price change, either at the metropolitan or submarket level of analysis, one must turn to other influences on price trends to attempt improvements to the model. In this context, it is appropriate to consider the role of mortgage lenders and real estate agents. Although the influence of these institutions cannot be specified with the precision of a regression equation, particularly because of the paucity of data on their roles in the house purchase process, a survey of their general impact on the housing market may provide insight which will complement and augment the power of the accessibility and segregation models.

Institutional practices: financial institutions and urban disinvestment

'Urban disinvestment', the practice of favouring suburban areas to the disadvantage of properties in the inner city, has been widespread among Bay Area financial institutions. The institutionalized decision that loans will not be made in certain 'high-risk' neighbourhoods, regardless of the credit rating and financial stability of the prospective buyer (known as 'redlining'), has been practised since the 1930s. Smith (1975, p. 3) reported that mortgage investors actually drew red lines over 'high-risk' areas on a city map:

Back in 1936, the Home Owners Loan Corporation prepared a detailed survey and classification of mortgage credit risk areas in Oakland and Berkeley, California. Four classifications were employed and each of some seventy neighborhoods were color coded on an accompanying map. Areas deemed 'hazardous' were colored red. The purpose of this government survey was to guide mortgage lenders in the area who were beginning to get involved with the newly-introduced FHA mortgage insurance program. In the blunt language of the times, the central criterion used to classify an area as 'hazardous' for home loans was the proportion of 'undesirable population.'

The investment practices reported for the 1930s established patterns which have remained as guidelines through the present time.

Loans by conventional mortgage financing sources have been scarce in areas of black or other minority settlement. In the late 1960s, the practice of 'redlining' by Oakland savings and loan companies was documented (National Committee Against Discrimination on Housing, Inc., 1972), and reaffirmed in a study of loan activity in East Oakland during 1973 (Frej, 1975). Although recent state and federal legislation has had as its goal the restriction of the power of mortgage lending institutions to 'redline' entire neighbourhoods, this goal is far from realized. Federal legislation (the Home Mortgage Disclosure Act of 1976) requires banks, savings and loans, and other similar financial institutions to release for public scrutiny information on the sources of savings deposits and the destinations of home mortgage loans (by census tract or postal district). However, this legislation does not prohibit the many practices through which 'redlining' can be continued.

During the 1970s, efforts have been made to formulate a method by which 'redlining' can be demonstrated in a court of law. Beginning in 1977, it is possible to use data made available as a result of the Home Mortgage Disclosure Act to identify discrepancies between areas from which banks draw deposits and areas in which they invest mortgage money. Before such data were available, however, the practice of 'redlining' was identified to some extent by the presence of large numbers of F.H.A.-insured mortgages: 'F.H.A. activity appears to be taken as a signal that a neighborhood is changing racially and is hence an unsound area in which to make loans' (Daniel, 1975, p. 444).

It is important to note that assuming it were possible to choose between 'conventional' (loans not insured by the federal government) and F.H.A.-insured financing, it would be in the best interest of the buyer to obtain conventional financing. In late 1976, the interest rate on a conventional loan was 8.75 per cent. Although this is 0.25 per cent higher than the interest rate charged by the F.H.A., the difference between the rates would be balanced by 'points' or a loan charge. Each 'point' represents a cost of 1 per cent of the loan so that, for example, the payment of one 'point' on a $25 000 loan would amount to a fee of $250. Although the government requires that 'points' on F.H.A. loans be paid by the seller, they are usually passed on to the buyer in the form of an increased purchase price. In addition, the added cost of mortgage insurance on an F.H.A. loan would bring the effective interest rate to 9.0 per cent. Finally, there is usually a longer waiting period for F.H.A. mortgage loans to be approved, a period which might not be acceptable to the seller. Since conventional mortgages bring a higher return on the loan to the lending institution (8.75 per cent instead of 8.50 per cent), it is the lender's best interest to provide conventional rather than

F.H.A.-insured financing. For these reasons, conventional mortgages have all but replaced F.H.A.-insured loans in areas which lenders believe are sound investment districts.

To explore the effects of urban disinvestment in the San Francisco Bay area, the distribution of F.H.A. loans and the correlates of this distribution were studied. For each census tract which met the criteria established for the computation of price change (*PRCH*), the numbers and percentages of conventional, F.H.A., and V.A. (Veterans' Administration) loans were tabulated. Since V.A. loans made up less than 1 per cent of all the loans studied, only the F.H.A. and conventional loans were considered here.

F.H.A.-insured loans were unevenly distributed (Fig. 4.4). Of the 344 census tracts considered in this study, 190, 55.2 per cent, had *no* F.H.A.-insured mortgages. Another 39 tracts had less than 10 per cent of their mortgages insured through the F.H.A. programme, bringing the total to 66.6 per cent of the tracts with 10 per cent or less government-insured mortgages. Of the remaining tracts, 28 (8.1 per cent) had over two-thirds of their mortgages insured by the F.H.A., and three tracts had 100 per cent F.H.A. mortgages. Government-insured mortgages were concentrated in southern San Mateo County (especially in the unincorporated area of east Menlo Park, an almost totally black residential area), west Contra Costa County (particularly in Richmond, a municipality with large black concentrations, and San Pablo, a working-class white area), west Oakland (a predominantly black residential district), and southern Alameda county (a white and Spanish-speaking working-class area). There was virtually no F.H.A. activity in the upper income portions of San Mateo and Contra Costa counties, and in Marin County.

Overall, there was a strong negative relationship between the proportion of F.H.A.-insured loans and house price trends. The mean value of price change (*PRCH*) for the metropolitan area was $0.00, but the mean value of *PRCH* for the twenty-four tracts with concentrations of F.H.A. loans was − $5579. The simple correlation between *PRCH* and the percentage of F.H.A. loans was − 0.50 for the metropolitan area as a whole, and ranged from − 0.62 for central Contra Costa County to − 0.16 for Marin County (with less than two-tenths of 1 per cent of its loans insured by F.H.A.). In addition, F.H.A. mortgages were related to the component structure, loading negatively on the socioeconomic status dimension, and positively on the municipal costs and disamenities dimension (along with crime rate, property taxation rate, and percentage of black population).

The consistent negative relationship between the presence of government-insured mortgages and price increase may be interpreted in at least two ways. Community groups would charge that it is the investment policies themselves which precipitate price change, while investors would argue that the withdrawal of funds from declining neighbourhoods had nothing to do with their decline. This study has not produced detailed data spanning a sufficient period of time to separate the causes and effects. However, the absence of conventional financing is clearly associated with drastic changes in house value, a consequence which has an important effect on the distribution of wealth. Since equity in property is one of the important sources of wealth for the middle- and low-income household, those persons living in 'redlined' areas are suffering a reduction in their savings because of factors external to themselves. On the other hand, persons living in areas evaluated as stable and sound (all too often chiefly on the basis of the racial or ethnic composition of the population), receive external bonuses in the form of

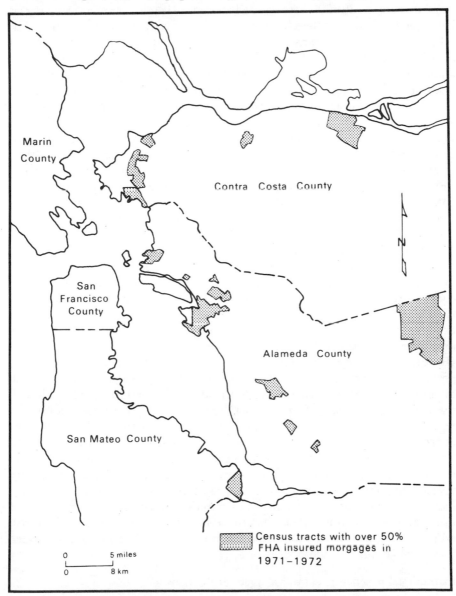

FIGURE 4.4. Concentrations of F.H.A.-insured mortgage loans. Census tracts with 50 per cent or more F.H.A.-insured loans are shaded

increased house value, and therefore household savings. The other side of this coin is that price declines permit low-income households to obtain housing they would not be able to afford if all neighbourhoods were increasing at the same rate, but this benefit is of dubious value if the house that such a family purchases actually declines in value or can never be resold.

However, the findings reported here should not be over-interpreted. One must recall that any study of the association between F.H.A. loans and price change is incomplete as a study of the effects of financial disinvestment on price trends. The presence of F.H.A. loans in an area is not an adequate indicator of disinvestment, for it provides no information on areas in which *no* institutional loans are available (and in which transactions take place for cash or with non-institutional mortgages whose interest rates and terms are not subject to usury laws), and no information on areas where conventional mortgages are obtainable, but only the payment of excess points or the acceptance of other unfavourable loan terms. Therefore, although there are simple spatial associations between government-insured mortgages and price decreases, we do not have enough evidence to assess with precision the role of institutional behaviour. Further empirical work on urban disinvestment may be assisted by the post-1976 data made available because of the Home Mortgage Disclosure Act, and it is obvious that these data will merit careful attention by those who wish to gain a better understanding of intra-urban variations in house price trends.

Although the precise impact of financial investment policies on house price trends has not been specified, there is enough evidence to conclude that the availability of mortgage financing is associated with house price trends. Of course, the average home buyer is not aware of the investment policies which mortgage-granting institutions have devised. It is only through personal experience in attempting to buy or sell a house that the individual may become aware that some parts of the city receive more favourable loan terms than other. However, the prospective buyer may (and usually does) short-circuit the painful process of loan application rejections due to 'redlining' by gaining information on financially stable neighbourhoods through a real estate agent. Although realtors consider many factors when recommending particular houses or neighbourhoods to prospective buyers, one of the factors which they must consider for practical reasons is the likelihood that the buyer will be able to obtain a satisfactory mortgage loan on the property. The recommendations of real estate agents, therefore, may be considered as translations of mortgage investment policy, as well as representations of the perceptions and biases of the individual agent. The final section of this empirical investigation of price changes in the San Francisco Bay Area undertook to study the evaluations which real estate agents communicate to prospective buyers, and the relationships between these evaluations and subsequent price change.

Institutional practices: real estate agent evaluations

A survey of over 450 real estate agents was taken to assess the overall evaluations which agents make of neighbourhoods in the San Francisco Bay

Area (Palm, 1976b, 1976c). Agents were not asked to rank neighbourhoods on the basis of general residential desirability, for such a ranking would involve such a complexity of attributes and attitudes that it would be difficult to evaluate the meaning of the responses or the dimensions along which agents appraise locations. Furthermore, agents probably do not rank all neighbourhoods, but are more likely to assess the appropriateness of particular neighbourhood sets for particular household types. Because it is likely that agents make *ad hoc* evaluations of neighbourhoods when confronted with potential home buyers of given social, economic, and ethnic characteristics, this survey was designed to elicit the neighbourhood rankings which agents would make when faced with four different kinds of families. Respondents were asked to match each of these four families with one or more of eighty-four named neighbourhoods or municipalities from the five-county metropolitan area and Sonoma County. At least three, and as many as eight agents from each of the ninety-five largest companies in the Bay Area responded to the mail questionnaire, a response rate of about 60 per cent. Each of the four hypothetical families was headed by a male, working in downtown San Francisco, whose occupation was selected from one of four positions along a standard occupation rating scale (Lasswell, 1965). The female spouse was a housewife not employed outside the home, and the family included two children, aged eight and fifteen. The children were included in the household so that the agents would be encouraged to consider the social composition of the neighbourhood and the quality of local public schools in their responses. A cover letter instructed the respondent to advise the family about neighbourhoods it should consider in its search for a house to buy. Respondents were instructed that they could recommend as many or as few neighbourhoods as they chose.

It was expected that there would be an overall correspondence between areas recommended and the present distribution of such occupation and income groups. Although in general, recommendations were in accord with actual socioeconomic patterns, two types of discrepancies occurred. First, agents had a tendency to concentrate their recommendations within the areas in which they sold property, ignoring large sections of the metropolitan area as possible destinations, and often recommending neighbourhoods which would require three or more hours of driving per day for the head of household to get to work in downtown San Francisco. A second kind of discrepancy was the recommendation that the hypothetical family move to neighbourhoods which did not, according to the 1970 census, have concentrations of that occupation type, and which were not appropriate for the household, given its income and the average sales price of housing in that area. It is this second kind of discrepancy which is of interest here, for if such recommendations are made to actual buyers with sufficient frequency, the character of neighbourhoods and the actual sales prices could be affected.

The highest income family of the four hypothetical households was headed by a physician with an annual income of $38 000. According to the general real estate principle that the purchase price should not exceed two and one-half times the annual income, such a family could afford a house priced up to about $95 000. Although respondents recommended all of the neighbourhoods including high-cost housing, they also recommended seven 'discrepancy areas', neighbourhoods with no existing concentrations of doctors or other professional workers, and with relatively moderately priced homes. One can argue that if real estate agents could convince high-income families to move to formerly moderate income areas, they would increase house prices here by boosting local demand. To ascertain whether or not such recommendations, made in 1974, were associated with a positive price change in the 1971–1975 period, the *PRCH* was tabulated for each of the seven communities (Table 4.6). In every case, although the median sales price in 1975 was well below the $95 000 which this family could afford, the value for *PRCH* was positive. The overall value of *PRCH* for this sample was $3459.60. The *Z*-score for such a sample mean is 1.877, enabling one to reject the null hypothesis that such a sample could have been randomly drawn from the metropolitan area as a whole. We may conclude that there is an

TABLE 4.6. Neighbourhoods or municipalities recommended by real estate agents, but with inappropriate income and occupational characteristics

A. Recommended to the physician, but with no concentrations of 'health workers', and median family incomes of less than $15 000 in 1970.

Community name	Median sales price, 1975	Median family income, 1970	PRCH
Novato	$52 256	$12 015	$1 431.8
Corte Madera	$50 234	$14 863	$566.5
Fairfax	$49 947	$11 607	$4 748.0
San Anselmo	$49 556	$12 573	$3 732.8
Walnut Creek	$55 444	$14 647	$2 417.5
Burlingame	$69 201	$13 250	$7 324.0
Belmont	$64 062	$14 900	$3 996.0
			Mean PRCH = $3 459.6

B. Recommended to the assembly worker, but with no concentrations of 'operatives and kindred workers', and median family incomes greater than $10 000 in 1970.

Community name	Median sales price, 1975	Median family income, 1970	PRCH
Livermore	$38 736	$12 440	− $1 474.4
Concord	$45 272	$12 614	− $1 895.8
San Leandro	$44 518	$11 938	− $1 900.0
Albany	$33 172	$10 206	− $1 163.8
Daly City	$41 120	$12 229	− $1 664.8
Parkside-S.F.	$45 609	$12 300	− $201.9
Pacifica	$49 967	$12 851	− $700.5
S. San Francisco	$49 967	$12 281	$395.9
San Burno	$47 019	$12 986	$746.0
			Mean PRCH = − $873.6

association between the recommendations of real estate agents to hypothetical high-income families and house price trends.

At the other end of the income and occupation scale in the sample survey was a hypothetical family headed by an assembly worker, with an annual income of $10 000. The assembly worker was also employed in the San Francisco central business district. With such an income, this family would be able to afford only $25 000 for a house. Although overall recommendations to this family were in accord with the distribution of 'operatives and kindred workers', several communities were recommended despite median incomes much higher than $10 000, and no existing concentrations of assembly workers. In all but two of these nine areas, price change (*PRCH*) was negative. The mean for this sample was − $873.26, but the negative value was not large enough to reject the null hypothesis that it was equal to zero. The observation that recommendations did not include those neighbourhoods which were most rapidly declining in value was to be expected, since it is likely that agents would avoid recommending such neighbourhoods to *any* type of household. It is therefore of interest and of some significance that 'discrepancy' areas recommended to low-income households experienced a relative decline in house prices.

These findings are not easily 'explained away'. One cannot argue that house prices have simply increased at a faster rate in high-income areas, and therefore the association of real estate agent recommendations to the high income family and price increases is merely a part of a more general metropolitan-wide trend. One must recall that the 'discrepancy' areas on which the statistical tests were based were not the high-income areas which we would have expected the real estate agents to recommend to high-income families, but were rather middle-income areas with no concentrations of professional workers. Similarly, it is not merely that house prices declined in low-income areas, for again the 'discrepancy' areas were neighbourhoods which one would not have expected real estate agents to recommend to low-income households based on median income in these neighbourhoods in 1970, occupational distributions, or 1975 house prices.

Several factors may account for these observations. Perhaps real estate agents were communicating trends which were well known to investors and real estate agents, but which are not disclosed from a statistical analysis of housing costs and population distributions. Perhaps these views reflect the actual changes of occupancy which are taking place in the 1970s and which will be better revealed in the 1980 census. Another possible explanation is that real estate agents are indeed steering certain groups to certain neighbourhoods, and in this way affecting average house prices.

If the latter explanation were plausible, it would be important to speculate on who would benefit from the process of real estate agents steering buyers to particular areas. In the case of induced price increases to formerly moderately priced housing, the beneficiaries would be easy to identify: former residents, who might include real estate agents and investors, selling their homes would gain increased equities; real estate agents would gain directly through increased commissions on higher priced houses; municipalities would gain from a higher tax base. Losers would be the new residents who would pay a premium to live in such neighbourhoods, and long-term residents, especially those with fixed incomes, with no intention of selling their homes who would pay higher property tax rates on houses which had increased in resale value. If there are induced price decreases, the beneficiaries are more difficult to pinpoint, but might include real estate agents and investors benefiting through speculative activity (although such activity would most likely be clandestine, and not as easily noted as straightforward gains or losses in commissions), and long-term residents would pay lower property taxes, although the prospect of less equity and a lower eventual resale value, in addition to the many other correlates of declining house prices, would make such a benefit of dubious value. But such speculation goes far beyond that which has been demonstrated in the correlations between real estate agent evaluations and house price trends.

Surveys taken in the 1960s have indicated that the real estate agent wished to protect the areas in which he worked from influences which might threaten property values (Barresi, 1968; Helper, 1969). Are the practices reported in these surveys current in the Bay Area, and if so, do they have an impact on house prices? Answers to questions concerning the causal influence of real estate agents on buyer behaviour and therefore house prices will require sensitive research, for it is unlikely that a general survey of agents in the 1970s would reveal the frank opinions which earlier surveys reported—too many lawsuits and community pressures have made the real estate industry wary of surveys and academic research. The findings reported here do suggest that such a study would be of great value, for it might shed new light on the process of neighbourhood change through house price fluctuations.

CONCLUSIONS

Accessibility and segregation models of house prices provide only a portion of the explanation of the variance in recent house price change. This is not a surprising finding, considering the nature of the behavioural postulates from which these models have been developed. The accessibility model, which has as its empirical goal the derivation of utility functions of home buyers, is based on the postulate that home buyers express their preferences by matching their desires for accessibility, and for the quantity and quality of the dwelling unit and neighbourhood, with the supply of housing. It is obvious that such a postulate reflects neither the decision-making process of the household, nor the workings of the housing market. The segregation or arbitrage models are a closer approximation to the decision-making process of home buyers, postulating that prospective buyers will pay more for a higher status neighbourhood which also meets their criteria for racial and ethnic composition. However, this model assumes that house prices result from the resolution of the supply of housing and the demand for houses and neighbourhoods with particular characteristics. It does not recognize explicitly the influence of governmental, financial, and real estate institutions in the valuation of property. What is argued in this essay is that the arbitrage model should be modified to take into account institutional behaviour.

As a first approximation of the type of model which is required, two variables might be developed and tested which have not been used in previous studies of the urban housing market. The first variable would index the perceptions and behaviours of mortgage lenders, using data which have become available as a result of the 1976 Home Mortgage Disclosure Act. This variable would be a measure of the balance between mortgage funds invested in a neighbourhood and the amount of savings which the financial institution derives from the neighbourhood. Areas of positive balance of investment funds (with more mortgage funds invested than generated in local savings) could be compared to those with negative balances. The areas with positive balances could be considered areas of investment, and those with negative balances would be disinvestment neighbourhoods. The investment/disinvestment continuum would be used as a measure of the investment behaviour of mortgage lending institutions, and could be related to subsequent house price trends.

A second variable might be developed to index the perceptions of real estate agents. Neighbourhoods vary with respect to the intensity with which real estate agents seek new listings to sell. Those areas which receive a great deal of attention from real estate agents, in the form of door-to-door solicitation, and telephone and mail contacts, might be compared to those in which real estate agents are relatively passive in obtaining listings. Areas which were intensively 'farmed' by real estate agents could then be contrasted to those which are not sought after, on the assumption that the former are perceived as highly profitable sales areas which real estate agents would be likely to recommend to buyers, while the latter are not actively recommended to newcomers to the city. It would be of interest to determine the relationship between house price trends and the sales practices of real estate agents, using such an index. Both of these statistics would be relatively straightforward, and data from which they could be derived would be fairly easy to collect. They would probably also reveal more about the behaviour of real estate and financial institutions than an opinion survey, since they would directly assess behaviour rather than opinions.

The consideration of the impact of the impact of institutional behaviour in the housing market seems essential for the development of an urban theory which comes to grips with not only settlement patterns, but also the processes from which these patterns emanate. Institutional behaviour has affected settlement patterns throughout human history, and it is not unreasonable that urban geographers should begin to give more attention to their influence.

ACKNOWLEDGEMENTS

The author would like to acknowledge the financial assistance of the Committee on Research, the Chancellor's Faculty Development Program, and the Institute for Governmental Studies of the University of California, Berkeley. Thanks are also due to Professors Brian Berry, John Britton, David Greenland, and

R. J. Johnston for their advice, and to the following students for their help in collecting and processing the S.R.E.A. data: Kim Allen, Robin Blakely, Derek Chugg, Matt Disston, Joel Michaelson, Nancy Melone, Roger Miller, and Tonia Wisman.

REFERENCES

Adams, J. S. (1969). Directional bias in intra-urban migration. *Economic Geography*, **45**, 302–323.

Alonso, W. (1964). *Location and Land Use*, Harvard University Press, Cambridge, Massachusetts.

Alonso, W. (1973). Urban zero population growth. *Daedalus*, **102**, 191–206.

Anderson, R. J., Jr., and Crocker, T. D. (1971). Air pollution and residential property values. *Urban Studies*, **8**, 171–180.

Ball, M. J. (1973). Recent empirical work on the determinants of relative house prices. *Urban Studies*, **10**, 213–223.

Barlev, G., and May, J. (1976). The effects of property taxes on the construction and demolition of houses in urban areas. *Economic Geography*, **52**, 304–310.

Barresi, C. M. (1968). The role of the real estate agent in residential location. *Sociological Focus*, **1**, 59–71.

Barrett, F. A. (1973). *Residential Search Behavior: A Study of Intra-urban Relocation in Toronto*. Geographical Monographs No. 1, York University, Atkinson College, Toronto.

Beckmann, M. J. (1974). Spatial equilibrium and the housing market. *Journal of Urban Economics*, **1**, 99–107.

Berry, B. J. L. (1976). Ghetto expansion and single-family housing prices: Chicago, 1968–72. *Journal of Urban Economics*, **3**, 397–423.

Berry, B. J. L., and Bednarz, R. S. (1975). A hedonic model of prices and assessments for single-family homes: does the assessor follow the market or the market follow the assessor? *Land Economics*, **51**, 21–40.

Bourne, L. S. (1976). Housing supply and housing market behaviour in residential development. In D. T. Herbert and R. J. Johnston (Eds.), *Social Areas in Cities*, Vol. 1, Wiley, London, pp. 111–158.

Boyer, B. D. (1973). *Cities Destroyed for Cash: The FHA Scandal at HUD*, Follett, Chicago.

Bradford, C. P., and Rubinowitz, L. S. (1975). The urban–suburban investment–disinvestment process: consequences for older neighborhoods. *Annals, American Association of Political and Social Sciences*, **422**, 77–96.

Bureau of Labor Statistics (1977). *Consumer Price Index Detailed Report* (Jan).

Casetti, E. (1971). Equilibrium land values and population densities in an urban setting. *Economic Geography*, **47**, 16–20.

Cheng, D. C., and Iglarsh, H. J. (1976). Principal component estimators in regression analysis. *Review of Economics and Statistics*, **58**, 229–234.

Coalition to End Neighborhood Deterioration (1975). Redlined! The case for disclosure in Indianapolis. *U.S. Senate Banking, Housing, and Urban Affairs Committee, Testimony on S. 1281*, U.S. Government Printing Office, Washington, D.C., pp. 345–381.

Daniel, E. C. (1975). Redlining! *Journal of Housing*, **9**, 441–444.

Daniels, C. B. (1975). The influence of racial segregation on housing prices. *Journal of Urban Economics*, **2**, 105–122.

Davies, G. (1974). An econometric analysis of residential amenity. *Urban Studies*, **11**, 217–226.

Dwees, D. N. (1976). The effect of a subway on residential property values in Toronto. *Journal of Urban Economics*, **3**, 357–369.

Doehrman, T. C. (1975). Redlining: potential civil rights and Sherman Act violations raised by lending policies. *Indiana Law Review*, **8**, 1045–1073.

Edelstein, R. (1974). The determinants of value in the Philadelphia housing market: a case study of the Main Line. *Review of Economics and Statistics*, **56**, 404–418.

Exline, C. (1977). The impacts of growth control policies on land values in Marin County, California., unpublished Ph.D. thesis, Department of Geography, University of California, Berkeley, California.

Flowerdew, R. (1976). Search strategies and stopping rules in residential mobility. *Transactions, Institute of British Geographers*, New Series, **1**, 47–57.

Freeman, A. M. (1971). Air pollution and property values: a methodological comment. *Review of Economics and Statistics*, **53**, 415–416.

Frej, W. M. (1975). Discriminatory lending practices in Oakland: a study for the Oakland Training Institute. In *Hearings Before the Committee on Banking, Housing and Urban Affairs, S. 1281*, U.S. Government Printing Office, Washington, D.C., pp. 483–506.

Fried, J. P. (1971). *Housing Crisis U.S.A.*, Praeger, New York.

Glazer, N. (1967). The bias of American housing policy. *Journal of Marriage and the Family*, **29**, 145–163.

Greenberg, F. L. (1975). Redlining—the fight against discrimination in mortgage lending. *Loyola University Law Review*, **6**(1), 71–89.

Grieson, R. (1974). The economics of property taxes and land values: the elasticity of supply of structure. *Journal of Urban Economics*, **1**, 367–381.

Grigsby, W. G. (1963). *Housing Markets and Public Policy*, University of Pennsylvania Press, Philadelphia.

Griliches, Z. (1967). Hedonic prices revisited: some notes on the state of the art. *Proceedings, Business and Economic Statistics Section, American Statistical Association*, **10**, 324–329.

Hagerstrand, T. (1970). What about people in regional science? *Papers of the Regional Science Association*, **24**, 7–21.

Harvey, D. (1974). Class-monopoly rent, finance capital and the urban revolution. *Regional Studies*, **8**, 239–255.

Harvey, D., and Chatterjee, L. (1974). Absolute rent and the structuring of space by governmental and financial institutions. *Antipode*, **6**(1), 22–36.

Hayghe, H. (1976). Families and the rise of working wives—an overview. *Monthly Labor Review*, **99**(5), 12–19.

Helper, R. (1969). *Racial Policies and Practices of Real Estate Brokers*, University of Minnesota Press, Minneapolis.

Hempel, D. (1969). *The Role of the Real Estate Broker in the Home Buying Process*, Department of Marketing, University of Connecticut, Center for Real Estate and Urban Economic Studies, Storrs, Connecticut.

Herbert, D. T. (1973). The residential mobility process: some empirical observations. *Area* **5**, 44–48.

Hoyt, H. (1933). *One Hundred Years of Land Values in Chicago*, University of Chicago Press, Chicago.

Kain, J. F. and Quigley, J. M. (1970). Measuring the quality of the residential environment. *Environment and Planning*, **2**, 23–32.

Kain, J. F. and Quigley, J. M. (1975). *Housing Markets and Racial Discrimination: A Microeconomic Analysis*, National Bureau of Economic Research, New York.

Kaiser, E. and others (1969). *A Decent Home: The Report of the President's Committee on Urban Housing*, U.S. Government Printing Office, Washington, D.C.

King, A. T. and Miewszkowski, P. (1973). Racial discrimination, segregation, and the price of housing. *Journal of Political Economy*, **81**, 590–606.

Lapham, V. (1971). Do Blacks pay more for housing? *Journal of Political Economy*, **79**, 1244–1257.

Lasswell, T. E. (1965). Occupational status. In T. E. Lasswell, (Ed.), *Class and Stratum*, Houghton Mifflin, New York, pp. 421–453.

Laurenti, L. (1960). *Property Values and Race: Studies in Seven Cities*, University of California Press, Berkeley, California.

Little, J. T. (1976). Residential preferences, neighborhood filtering and neighborhood change. *Journal of Urban Economics*, **3**, 68–81.

Loyd, B. and Rowntree, L. (1978). Radical feminists and gay men in San Francisco: social space in dispersed communities. In D. Lanegran and R. Palm (Eds.), *An Invitation to Geography*, McGraw-Hill, New York, pp. 78–98.

McEntire, D. (1960). *Residence and Race: Final and Comprehensive Report to the Commission on Race and Housing*, University of California Press, Berkeley, California.

Mandelker, D. R. (1973). *Housing Subsidies in the United States and England*, Bobbs-Merrill, Indianapolis.

Mills, E. S. (1969). The value of urban land. In H. Perloff (Ed.), *The Quality of the Urban Environment*, Johns Hopkins Press, Baltimore, pp. 231–253.

Muth, R. (1969). *Cities and Housing*, University of Chicago Press, Chicago.

National Committee Against Discrimination in Housing, Inc. (1972). *Patterns and Practices of Discrimination in Lending in Oakland, California*, The Committee, San Francisco.

National Opinion Research Center (1974). Personal communication from Elihu Gerson.

Nelson, R. H. (1972). Housing facilities, site advantages, and rent. *Journal of Regional Science*, **12**, 249–259.

Netzer, D. (1968). *Impact of the Property Tax: Effect on Housing, Urban Land Use, Local Government Finance*. Research Report No. 1 to the National Commission on Urban Problems, U.S. Government Printing Office, Washington, D.C.

Oldman, O., and Aaron, H. (1965). Assessment/sales ratio under the Boston property tax. *National Tax Journal*, **18**, 36–49.

Palm, R. I. (1976a). An index of household diversity. *Tijdschrift voor Economische en Sociale Geographie*, **57**, 194–201.

Palm, R. I. (1976b). The role of real estate agents as information mediators in two American cities. *Geografiska Annaler*, **58B**, 28–41.

Palm, R. I. (1976c). *Urban Social Geography from the Perspective of the Real Estate Salesman*. Research Report No. 38, Center for Real Estate and Urban Economics, University of California, Berkeley, California.

Papageorgiou, G. J. (1971). The population density and rent distribution models within a multicentre framework. *Environment and Planning*, **3**, 267–282.

Papageorgiou, G. J. (1976). Urban residential analysis: 1. spatial consumer behaviour. *Environment and Planning*, **A8**, 423–442.

Porter, S. (1975). *Sylvia Porter's Money Book*, Doubleday, Garden City, New York.

Pred, A. R. (1977). The choreography of existence: comments on Hagerstrand's time-geography and its usefulness. *Economic Geography*, **53**, 207–221.

Rapkin, C. and Grigsby, W. G. (1960). *The Demand for Housing in Racially Mixed Areas: A Study of the Nature of Neighborhood Change*, University of California Press, Berkeley, California.

Ridker, R. G. and Henning, J. A. (1967). The determinants of residential property values with special reference to air pollution. *Review of Economics and Statistics*, **49**, 246–257.

Rose-Ackerman, S. (1974). Location, space and urban structure: the Wingo model reconsidered. *Land Economics*, **50**, 281–284.

Rose-Ackerman, S. (1975). Racism and urban structure. *Journal of Urban Economics*, **2**, 85–103.

Rossi, P. H. (1955). *Why Families Move*, The Free Press, Glenocoe, Illinois.

Schnare, A. B. (1976). Racial and ethnic price differentials in an urban housing market. *Urban Studies*, **13**, 107–120.

Schnare, A. B. and Struyk, R. J. (1976). Segmentation in urban housing markets. *Journal of Urban Economics*, **3**, 146–166.

Smith, K., and Deyak, T. A. (1975). Measuring the impact of air pollution on property values *Journal of Regional Science*, **15**, 277–288.

Smith, T. R. (1970). Land value versus real property taxation: a case study comparison. *Land Economics*, **25**, 305–313.

Smith, W. F. (1970). *Housing: The Social and Economic Elements*, University of California Press, Berkeley, California.

Smith, W. F. (1975). Redlining. *Current Urban Land Topics*, Center for Real Estate and Urban Economics, University of California, Berkeley, California, Vol. 1.

Stegman, M. A. (1972). *Housing Investment in the Inner City*, M.I.T. Press, Cambridge, Massachusetts.

Sternlieb, G., Burchell, R., and Listokin, D. (1975). The urban financing dilemma, *Committee on Banking, Housing and Urban Affairs, Hearings on S. 1281*, U.S. Government Printing Office, Washington, D.C., pp. 547–578.

Stone, M. E. (1973). Federal housing policy: a political–economic analysis. In J. Pynoow, R. Schafer, and C. W. Hartman (Eds.), *Housing Urban America*, Aldine, Chicago, pp. 423–433.

Stone, M. E. (1975). The housing crisis, mortgage lending, and class struggle. *Antipode*, **7**, 22–37.

Straszheim, M. (1974). Hedonic estimation of the housing market prices: a further comment. *Review of Economics and Statistics*, **56**, 404–406.

Thoma, L. and Lindemann, E. (1961). Newcomers' problems in a suburban community. *Journal of the American Institute of Planners*, **27**, 185–193.

Vance, J. (1976). The cities by the San Francisco Bay. In J. S. Adams (Ed.), *Contemporary Metropolitan America: Twenty Geographical Vignettes*. Vol. 1, Part 2, Nineteenth Century Ports, Ballinger, Cambridge, Massachusetts, pp. 217–307.

Wall, N. F. (1972). Pollution and real property values. *The Real Estate Appraiser*, **38**, 5–11.

Weinstein, J. I. (1974). Housing subsidies: an overview. *Journal of Urban Law*, **51**, 723–750.

Wendt, P. F. (1963). *Housing Policy—The Search for Solutions*. University of California Press, Berkeley and Los Angeles, California.

Wilkinson, R. K., and Archer, C. A. (1973). Measuring the determinants of relative house prices. *Environment and Planning*, **5**, 357–367.

Wilkinson, R. K., with Archer, C. A. (1976). The quality of housing and the measurement of long-term changes in house prices. *Urban Studies*, **13**, 273–283.

Wingo, Lowdon (1961). *Transportation and Urban Land*, Johns Hopkins Press, Baltimore.

Yeates, M. (1965). Some factors affecting the spatial distribution of Chicago land values, 1910–1960. *Economic Geography*, **41**, 55–70.

Chapter 5

Unemployment in the Inner City: Urban Problem or Structural Imperative? A Review of the British Experience

Nigel Thrift

*A great many so-called urban problems are really conditions that
we either cannot eliminate or do not want to incur the disadvantages of eliminating.*

EDWARD C. BANFIELD (1974)

In July 1977 unemployment in Britain, as so often forecast, finally rose to over $1\frac{1}{2}$ million (5.9 per cent of the labour force). By December of the same year the figure had dropped to just below that baleful number, but the rate of unemployment had increased very slightly to 6 per cent. The cities of Britain were experiencing the brunt of this unemployment, not in terms of rates but rather in terms of absolute numbers unemployed. In December 1977 the Greater Manchester area had a rate of unemployment almost exactly on the national average of 6.1 per cent—that figure represented 72 343 unemployed workers. Where both rate of unemployment and absolute numbers unemployed were high, as in Merseyside with 83 409 workers unemployed and a rate of 11.6 per cent, the seriousness of the situation was compounded. In the inner areas of cities like Manchester or Liverpool rates of unemployment, on past experience, must have been three to five percentage points higher and sometimes more. But, as with the city as a whole, it is the concentration of the unemployed and low paid in the inner city, in terms of absolute numbers rather than relative proportions, which is what sets the inner city off from the outer urban area. This chapter is primarily concerned with explaining the reasons for the inner-city unemployment problem with particular emphasis on the years since the start of the rise in unemployment in 1966.

Unemployment is a very real problem. Although not a view amplified in this chapter, unemployment has many detrimental psychological impacts in terms of enforced idleness (Hill *et al.*, 1973; Marsden and Duff, 1975), for one of the strongest experiences of alienation for man, apart from having to work all day, is not being able to work all day. Unemployment also has considerable costs. According to Field (1977), between 1974 and 1976 the overall cost to the

125

126

community of unemployment through loss in tax revenue, payment of benefit, and loss in national income amounted to some £20 000 million. But perhaps worse than both these factors is that each unemployed person is a hostage to society, given no access to work when work provides 'the sole legitimate standard for the distribution of life-chances', even if 'the factual distribution of life-chances is actually totally at variance with this standard' (Offe, 1976, p. 134).

Figure 5.1 shows the sharp rise in unemployment since 1966. This chapter contends that this national trend is reflected differentially in worse unemployment trends at the inner-city level because of differences in skill structure in inner areas and also because of the large absolute numbers of people in these areas. The argument therefore takes the form outlined in Figure 5.2, proceeding from recent changes in the national economy through current trends in manufacturing industry to the impact of these trends on the inner city. The chapter then examines the various government responses to urban problems, against the backcloth of the various competing or complementary ideologies involved and finally outlines certain policy implications which seem to arise.

Two introductory points remain to be made. First, the inner cities are not homogeneous entities. Inner Liverpool is very different from inner Manchester or inner London. 'The inner city' is a convenient category to sum up a system of problems which exists, in particular, in inner urban locations, but the seriousness of each problem varies with the inner city being examined. However, since so very little research has been carried out on the differences between particular inner cities it is sometimes necessary to generalize. Secondly, the characteristic inner cities' problems of unemployment, bad housing, and so on are hardly new

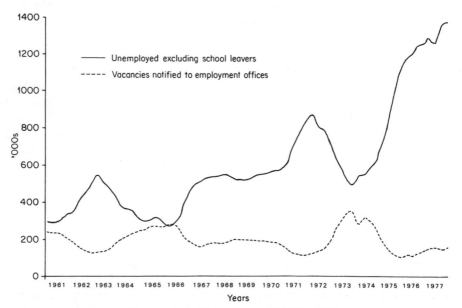

FIGURE 5.1. Unemployment 1961–1977.
(*Source: Department of Employment Gazette*)

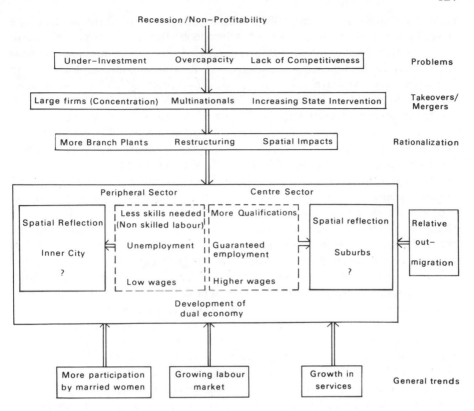

FIGURE 5.2. Some elements of the inner-city situation: the argument in outline

(Engels, 1969; Foster, 1974; Stearns, 1975; Stedman Jones, 1971). The inner cities of today and the problems they contain are the outcome of a long historical process with its base in the Industrial Revolution, but the economic context of the current problems has changed.

THE LOCATION OF THE INNER CITY

Where are the inner cities? This is a deceptively simple question with almost Byzantine ramifications. In most studies of inner-city areas concern with definition has not been a major factor and a pragmatic solution has usually been adopted. This nearly always means annexing the most convenient administrative boundary at whatever scale is being examined.

Clearly, delimitation of severity of deprivation is crucial to the success of policies based on spatial areas. Yet surprisingly little work has been carried out on this aspect. There are formidable difficulties involved. Two examples will suffice. The 1971 census data in use so far have been based on enumeration districts (EDs), with all the consequent problems, although with the release of kilometre-square small area statistics the situation now looks more hopeful

(Rhind, Stanness, and Evans, 1977). Similarly, British employment statistics are based on the employment exchange district which often does not approximate to any satisfactory definition of a labour market. Census indicators are the most often used in documenting the degree of deprivation at any location; in particular, the extensive series of *Census Indicators of Urban Deprivation Working Notes* (Department of the Environment, 1–10, 1974–1976) establish the government's concern with this aspect of the inner-city problem.

All data sources available have some problems associated with them and it has become common practice to supplement the census figures with, for instance, local authority data (Flynn and Mellor, 1972; Webber, 1975). But there are many problems with the social indicator approach as used in measuring the degree and extent of deprivation. Hamnett (1976a) has pointed out that it is rare for direct indicators of deprivation to be available; most tend to be indirect. Then again there are problems with choosing weights for particular indicators, and the reconciliation of different spatial scales also proves difficult. Edwards (1975) has pointed to omissions in areas identified as being of high stress or deprivation because they are not of the type which show deprivation associated with more easily identifiable physical decay (e.g. lack of basic housing amenities) but instead show disadvantage in relation to the market (e.g. areas with transient populations) with which physical decay is not automatically coupled. And census indicator studies of London show areas of high employment stress and areas of high housing stress in completely different locations within the inner area (Lomas, 1975). All these problems are partially skirted by combining a series of indicators into a single measure (for instance, local authorities within EDs in the overlap of the worst 5, 10, or 15 per cent of EDs on a series of measures) but, however sophisticated the cluster analysis, the result is crucially dependent upon the choice of indicators made, which must be arbitrary. Attempts at an objective delimitation are thus hampered in many ways but, worse than this, the results call into question the idea that many areas of really intense deprivation exist, and suggest that 'the degree of spatial concentration of individual aspects of deprivation is really quite low' (Department of the Environment, 1974a, p. 10). In terms of an area policy to deliver extra resources to improve severe overcrowding, priority area treatment would have to be given to 15 per cent of EDs in order to accommodate as many as 61 per cent of households with this kind of deprivation. Thus, although areas of intense deprivation do exist—notably in Clydeside—so much deprivation exists outside the worst areas that an area policy is immediately suspect. This is a theme to which we will return. In Figure 5.3 the results of an indicator study by Holtermann (1975) are used to show the local authorities in Britain that have EDs which score high on deprivation on three indicators, including male unemployment. The map serves as a rough guide to the spatial location of the inner-city problem—as a problem of deprivation—but it must be borne in mind even here that these figures indicate the geographical distribution of EDs with large proportions of their population deprived. They do not show the actual distribution of deprived individuals.

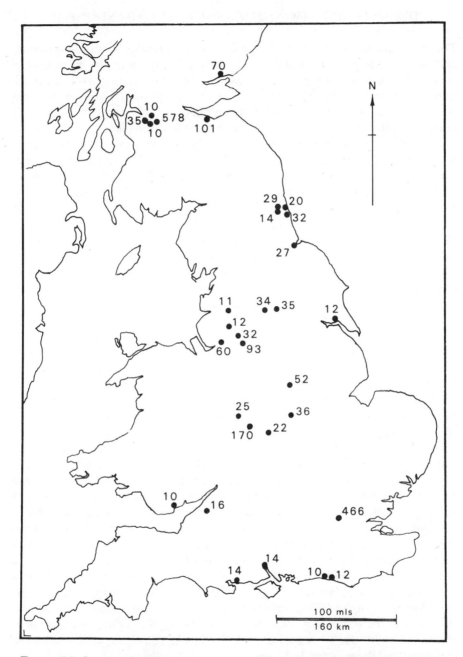

FIGURE 5.3. Local authorities with ten or more EDs in the overlap of the worst 15 per cent on overcrowding, lacking exclusive use of all basic amenities, and male unemployment. (*Source:* Holtermann, 1975.)

DECENTRALIZATION: THE INNER CITY ABANDONED?

The inner city is, to an extent, the product of differential migration effects of employment and population since the Industrial Revolution. The movement of professional and skilled workers to the outer cities or suburbs, it is often argued, leads to an increase in the concentration of the unskilled in the inner areas (absolutely and relatively), with consequent higher rates of unemployment. This movement out of the inner city goes hand in hand with movement out of a city as a whole. Thus from 1966 to 1976 Liverpool lost 22 per cent of its population, Manchester 18 per cent, inner London 16 per cent, Newcastle 12 per cent, and Birmingham and Nottingham 8 per cent each (Department of the Environment, 1977 f). Such population loss is assumed to be of mainly skilled manual workers, plus white-collar and professional and managerial workers. Therefore from 1966 to 1971 only 15 per cent of migrants (net) from Birmingham and 14 per cent from Manchester were unskilled or semiskilled (Department of the Environment, 1977 f). By dint of emigration from the inner city to the outer areas or the suburbs, inner areas are therefore left with an 'unbalanced' population skill distribution. But this sketch proves to have only a limited validity in that the increase in concentration of unskilled, in recent years at least, does not seem to have taken place.

Most of our information on the scale of urban decentralization comes, of course, from the work of Hall *et al.* (1973) and its continuation by Drewett *et al.* (1976a), which shows that whereas from 1951 to 1961 population was decentralizing *relatively* from the 'cores' of British urban areas into the surrounding 'rings' (essentially zones representing employment cores, and rings their commuting hinterlands) from 1961 to 1971 population was decentralizing *absolutely*. By 1971 decentralization, whether absolute or relative, characterized 85 per cent of the British urban system (Coursey, 1977a). Employment, in contrast, was centralizing absolutely from 1951 to 1961 (owing to faster increase in employment in core areas than rings), but from 1961 to 1971 this trend changed to one of absolute decentralization from cores to rings (owing to a decrease in employment in urban areas, an increase in metropolitan rings and a slower increase in outer metropolitan rings). There is some evidence that between 1966 and 1971 British conurbations experienced a faster rate of decrease in employment than the rest of the regions in which they were situated, or the nation as a whole, but there has been no radical change in this rate of employment decline (Stone, 1975; Warnes, 1977). If these population and employment trends have continued in the 1970s, perhaps towards some 'pivotal density' (Coursey, 1977a), then the situation by now may be producing that reinforced process of inner-city decline due to migration of skilled labour sometimes characterized as the 'selective labour hypothesis'.

But metropolitan areas are *not* becoming dominated by unskilled manual workers (Department of Employment, 1977) as a selective labour hypothesis would imply. Dugmore (1975) has analysed recent patterns of moves in Greater London by socio-economic group. He found a greater outflow from London of white-collar than manual workers, and of skilled workers rather than unskilled, but the observed change from 1966 to 1971 in London has proved to be of a relative increase in the population of white-collar workers and a corresponding decrease in manual workers, against a backcloth of overall decline in the London labour force. This contradiction is explained by the joint effects of migration. Whereas migration did account for the decrease in skilled manual workers, it did not account for the decrease in the number of semi-skilled and unskilled workers which was probably due to other internal labour force restructuring effects, for instance socio-economic mobility and the pattern of entries and exits from the labour force (which, as shown by Hamnett (1976b), can be important). This pattern for Greater London 'is broadly repeated in the other conurbations'. It suggests that 'net migration is of relatively little importance compared with other factors as an explanation of the reduction in the number of semi-skilled and unskilled manual workers' and that 'selective migration has certainly not been the only factor, and perhaps not even the major factor in the changing socio-economic structure' (Department of Employment, 1977, p. 26). This, of course, does not mean that migration is not having an effect on the absolute size of the labour force in conurbations. All conurbations are losing economically active males. But, in general, *within* conurbations net outmigration is greatest for non-manual groups and is lowest for unskilled manual workers.

This very gradual population movement out of the city, which has been operating in some inner areas of London, for instance, since before the turn of the century (Morrey, 1973), has a number of determinants. The general lack of information on reasons for movement of labour means that these can only be outlined for the recent period. In all probability the major reason is a desire for better accommodation. Thus, Harris and Clausen (1966) found that 47 per cent of reasons given by their sample of movers were connected with housing, followed by work reasons and marriage. Most moves are short distance, so there are few between conurbations, and most are within conurbation boundaries. Longer moves tend to be more the province of the managerial and professional worker rather than those at the unskilled end of the spectrum, and are usually connected with work reasons (Johnson, Salt, and Wood, 1974).

Decentralization from the inner city is now occurring, both in population and employment terms. On present evidence employment is leading population in the inner areas (Warnes, 1977). Whether the relationship is causal is another matter, however; rather it is a function of many different reasons. The different cycles of housing moves and employment births or relocations mean that adjustment between employment movement and population movement, and population movement and employment movement must be relatively slow and are mediated by other forces. But, in any final analysis, it must be that differential migration effects, allied with internal labour force restructuring effects, have been at the root of many inner-city problems and have led to the particular distribution of skills in inner cities, which in turn mean that unemployment in inner areas will always be high when demand for labour in the economy as a whole is low.

This problem is in its essentials an historical problem, a legacy of the Industrial

132

Revolution, when movement into the inner areas by 'unskilled' labour first took place. As an historical problem it can be suggestively interpreted as due to the uneven nature of development in capitalism (Brenner, 1977; Pilling, 1973). Profitability is constantly boosted in particular capitals by new kinds of rationalization and production processes. But, concurrently, capitals have to cope with problems of worn-out stock of fixed capital and increasing technical obsolescence. British industry, in particular, has tended to under-invest during economic booms, and during economic recession it often does not have the capital to invest in any case (Carney, Lewis, and Hudson, 1977). That proportion of capital which is invested in the firm will be invested in profitable enterprises to the further detriment of particular areas with large proportions of obsolescent plant—like the inner cities. This feedback loop whereby the rich areas get richer while the poor areas get (at least relatively) poorer leads to a two-phase structure at all levels of spatial scale which, by its very nature, creates an opportunity between a developed and underdeveloped area (see Figure 5.4). This process is documented in full by Mellor (1977). At present in Britain there may be an overall swing to the less developed regions which in the years of decline have had their infrastructure regenerated by successive governments and are now a source of cheaper labour, but meanwhile the inner cities remain 'internal colonies' (Mellor, 1977, p. 46). However, characterizing the history of British urbanism as a process of uneven development does not tell us as much as we might hope: 'The fact is that both Marxist and Non-Marxist approaches to analysing the relationships between development and underdevelopment has been inadequate' (Mingione, in Meller, 1975, p. 164). The processes operating in British urbanism and industrialism which have produced the inner city are still only partially understood. They await a concrete and particular historical study of political and

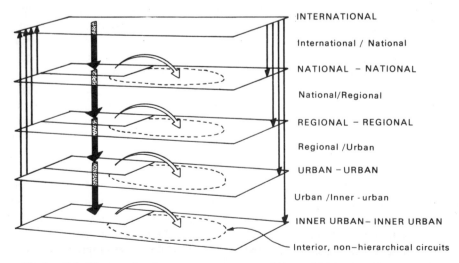

FIGURE 5.4. Uneven development as a process of hierarchical movement of capital (adapted from Santos, 1973)

economic relations reflected in geographical inequality and located in processes of social inequality.

The economic background to the British inner city problem

The backcloth of British economic problems is crucial to any coherent discussion of the present inner city and must be considered in some detail. No apology needs to be made for this since 'any discussion about urban development or planning must begin with an account of the national economy' (Broadbent, 1977, p. 28).

There is at least no difference of opinion concerning the decline of the British economy in the 1970s: indeed a growth industry has built up around predictions of imminent economic collapse. For our purposes it is important to isolate the general economic decline of Britain relative to the world as a whole at the end of, or still perhaps within, the recession of the 1970s. The recent global recession, through the differentially severe impact it has had on inner city areas, has confirmed the inner city in its role of 'urban problem'. But this is as yet relatively short-term, and general decrease in demand should not be allowed to conceal the more specific structural problems of the British economy, the product of many years of subjugation to the uneven character of economic change in an industrial capitalist society.

The early years

From about 1875 Britain has experienced a loss of foreign markets. The very fact of being the birthplace of the Industrial Revolution and the obvious initial competitive advantage this gave over other countries became a serious handicap. Up until the 1930s Britain's rate of growth was closely dependent upon the growth of exports. Yet as other countries industrialized Britain's relative share of available foreign markets was bound to decrease (Kaldor, 1977), especially as the Empire fragmented. Other factors, such as a general failure to keep up with growth of modern technology and poor management, no doubt also played their part in this decline, but were in general subordinate to the overall trend. Thus, Britain's present relatively precarious economic position has its roots in the fact that the conditions for the Industrial Revolution were first met in a West Midlands town. The cities which had mushroomed in the Industrial Revolution, therefore, already contained the seeds of the present inner city problem. The time at which it first actively appeared as a problem in the inner cities depended upon the industrial mix of each inner area.

Many inner-city observers (e.g. Community Development Project, 1977a; Department of the Environment, 1977d) identify a simple three-stage model of the rise and fall of the inner city. Thus, there is a time of *growth* when the area is first settled by firms locating on green field sites, followed, or in some cases preceded by, residential development. Then comes a period of *maturity* in which, due in no small measure to the protected Empire economy, the area remains profitable and which, depending on location, may stretch to the end of the Second World War. Sadly, we are more concerned with the third period, of *decline*. This started in some inner areas following the First World War but usually dates from the end of the Second World War, and has continued ever since.

The inner areas in which decline was evident before the Second World War were usually those with a determinedly traditional industry, like textiles in West Yorkshire and shipbuilding on the Tyne, which was susceptible to increased competition. For these local economies the increased demand of the Second World War was usually only a brief reprieve.

The age of growth

The post-war era was a period of unprecedented and sustained growth in the world economy. As Shonfield (1969, p. 3) puts it, capitalism had been converted 'from the cataclysmic failure which it appeared to be in the 1930s, into the great engine of prosperity of the post-war Western world'. In contrast to the pre-war period, trade *between* the highly industrialized countries increased substantially relative to total domestic production or consumption in terms of both exports and imports of manufactured goods. In most industrialized countries growth of exports in manufactured goods was higher than the rate of growth of total output of these goods; Kaldor (1977) points out that this was true for nine of the eleven countries which accounted for 85 to 90 per cent of total world trade in manufactured goods. The two significant exceptions were the U.S.A. and U.K. In the last twenty years their joint share of world trade has fallen from 40 to 20 per cent, although their overall rate of economic growth has still been quite satisfactory when compared with the pre-war disasters. In Britain 'bastard Keynesian' demand management policies meant that growth of demand for industrial production no longer depended on growth of export demand. The pursuit of full employment led to what Kaldor (1971) has called the substitution of consumption-led growth for export-led growth; the general lack of effective demand of the 1930s was replaced by a tendency for growth of imports to outpace growth of exports, inducing balance of payments crises and stop-go government policies. We must not forget, however, that 'during the very period when Britain was consistently at the bottom of the league table in terms of the rate of economic growth in relation to other advanced countries, she was at the top in terms of her own historical record' (Kaldor, 1977, p. 203). The 'age of growth' (Robinson and Wilkinson, 1977) from 1945 to 1976 saw higher rates of growth in GNP, *per capita* income, outputs per head, and exports than for any previous twenty-five years of British history.

What did this unparalleled period of economic growth promise for employment and unemployment prospects? From 1945 to 1966, with the exception of the winter of 1947, unemployment in Britain never exceeded 2.5 per cent of the labour force and indeed for some years it never exceeded 1 per cent. In absolute terms the unemployed rose above half a million during only three years (Chisholm, 1976). But in 1966 unemployment began to rise, and has continued to do so (in cyclical fashion) ever since. The initial trigger mechanism in Britain was probably the Labour government's fight to maintain the exchange value of sterling which ended in a spectacularly unsuccessful fashion with devaluation of the pound in November 1967. But the general cause was the impact of the world recession.

Recession

In late 1967 or early 1968 the age of growth was terminated. In all the main industrial countries the rise in labour costs per unit of industrial output began to accelerate. Fixed exchange rates were abandoned in 1971 as the dollar was devalued (Tew, 1977). In 1972 and 1973 came the rapid rise in commodity prices, to be followed by the massive rise in the price of oil in the aftermath of the Arab–Israeli War. The consequent inflation in wage settlements produced a general increase in prices, leading to a spiralling inflation in consumer prices in all countries (Eatwell, Llewellyn, and Tarling, 1974). After a brief period of growth from 1971 to 1973, from 1973 to 1975 inflation averaged 26 per cent for all O.E.C.D. countries: for the same period it was 44 per cent in the United Kingdom (Kaldor, 1976).

Such a worldwide inflation has never occurred before in times of peace. I would contend that it produced a worldwide fall-off in demand for industrial goods, and in particular demand for consumer goods. Certainly such a fall-off must have been one cause of the marked recession in world industrial production. In the 1960s world industrial production rose at a steady rate of 6 or 7 per cent a year to a peak of 8 per cent a year in the period 1971–1973. It was stagnant in 1974 and actually fell by 10 per cent in 1975 (Kaldor, 1976).

Thus the autumnal decline in Britain's industrial fortunes, which had been partially concealed by the roman summer of the age of growth, was now transformed by the cold and wintry blast in the outside world. To Britain's own structural misfortunes were added the more general misfortunes of a world in recession. In 1975 GNP fell in nine out of ten European countries, particularly steeply in the four large countries (by 1.2 per cent in France, 1.8 per cent in Britain, 3.2 per cent in West Germany, and 3.7 per cent in Italy).

Following Kaldor (1976), it is possible to say that it is unlikely that there was a single basic cause for this recession, such as universal cost push resulting from collective bargaining, increase in money supply in all countries, or increased trade union militancy. Rather, a whole system of causes has come together under particular historical conditions to produce the present problems. The mini-recovery of 1976 did not continue and although, at the end of 1977, there are some signs of a general worldwide recovery this is reflected more in a lessening of inflation than in a shortening of the dole queue.

The problems for industry

The main effect, in human terms, of this economic recession has been unemployment. The decline in some sectors of British industry and, in particular, in heavy industry, is no new thing. It has been in progress since as early as 1900, punctuated by the demands of wars. The major phase of decline of British manufacturing industry in inner areas started as early as the end of the Second World War in some areas, but as late as the mid-1960s in others. In Canning Town in London and Saltley in Birmingham, for instance, traditional industries maintained a strong presence until the mid-1960s and with it, until then, a relatively stable employment base. The differences in industrial structure at the onset of a sharper rate of change of economic decline are best illustrated by the fact that three-quarters of all industrial jobs in Canning Town and Saltley were still in the traditional sector in 1966, whereas this proportion had already declined to two-fifths in Batley in West Yorkshire and to less than one-fifth in North Shields (Community Development Project, 1977a).

This differential decline in traditional industries must be seen as a prologue to the recent more pronounced rate of decline of manufacturing industry. It is this latter-day industrial decline which is primarily responsible for the severity of the employment problem inner cities now face, but it is conditioned by the inheritance of a long history of decline in the areas where traditional industry has been fading since the turn of the century. However, whether this rate of decline has been any faster or slower in the present economic recession in areas still left with a large traditional sector is debatable. Thus, still-traditional Canning Town and Saltley lost, respectively, 24 and 14 per cent of industrial jobs in the space of five years from 1966 to 1971, but more modern Batley also lost 20 per cent and North Shields 13 per cent of its industrial jobs over the same time (Community Development Project, 1977a).

The point which must be made concerns the general nature of the present economic recession. The cutbacks in demand have been present in almost every industrial sector. They have occurred similarly in most of the industrialized countries in the world. In times of economic recession the markets which industries have to compete in, both at home and abroad, shrink. Industries worldwide are caught with spare capacity invested on the assumption that growth will continue. Competition for the remaining markets becomes stronger and an active search for new markets is initiated. Thus, in recession the problem becomes overcapacity and overcompetition. In this latest recession Japanese industry, due, at least in part, to a need to pay off massive interest on loans, has made particular inroads into traditionally British markets at home and abroad. Similarly, cheap labour products from the Third World and Eastern blocs have made progress at the expense of British products. But 'the real issue is one of specific industries in trouble' (Economist, 1977). Whether the problem arises from a growth in world capacity or a fall in world demand the fact remains that many industries in Britain would still have problems. The world recession has only called them to account earlier than would have been the case if the age of growth had continued.

The problems of British industry are many and the reader is referred to Singh (1977) for a full account. However, in the context of the recession with its lower demand and higher competition we can isolate a number of easily recognizable themes. The first is obsolescence. Much of the plant in British industry is old-fashioned and unable to provide the productivity needed to compete. Steel is an obvious example. The problem here is to find the time that is needed to allow this obsolete plant to be run down at a socially acceptable pace.

The second theme is under-investment. In 1975 investment in new manufacturing plant and equipment was 20 per cent less than in 1974; in 1976 it was even lower (Community Development Project, 1977a). While part of this figure no doubt reflects less need for investment as demand fell, most of it reflects the fact that in Britain alternative sources for investment, in which capital can circulate at much faster rates than in industrial investment, have lured capital away. Since 1953 no European country has ever managed to emulate Japan and devote more than 30 per cent of its GDP to productive investment. And within Europe Britain had from 1955 to 1975 the lowest investment ratio (of GDP) of any country (Economist, 1977). Woodward (cited in Singh, 1977) has shown that this position has worsened. Thus, whereas between 1954 and 1956 and 1963 and 1965 manufacturing investment grew by 39 per cent, in the period between 1972 and 1974 it increased by only 19 per cent. Holland (1976) has shown that during 1970 to 1975 net manufacturing investment (constant prices) ran at only approximately four-fifths of the levels reached in previous years. This dilemma is due to the 'low absolute levels of security issue and investment undertaken in the U.K. compared with other economies' (Thompson, 1977, p. 261); the conservative and short-term nature of British banks' lending policies to industry (now changing owing to competition from American banks), the greater attraction of investment in insurance companies, pension funds, and, recently, the building societies and the short-lived but highly profitable speculative booms like the office boom of the early 1970s (in which the banks played their ignominious part). In Britain any company is judged in terms of its efficiency in the ideology of banking capital, rather than its industrial performance. The seminal paper by Thompson (1977) articulates this contradiction.

The result is that most investment funds have to be internally generated (on average about 75 per cent from 1950 to 1972, compared with 68 per cent in the U.S.A. from 1960 to 1971, 49 per cent in France from 1959 to 1970, and 44 per cent in Japan over the same period: Thompson, 1977). If the company is not doing well there are no funds to reinvest. In addition, there is some evidence that the effectiveness of investment in Britain is lower (Singh, 1977). This has further implications in that there is less money available to be invested in achieving technical progress and product improvements to respond effectively to increased competition.

The third theme is that of productivity. The general lack of investment in British industry has obviously affected productivity—British workers have less efficient machine power. But an exact index of British industrial performance, measured in terms of capital or labour productivity, is hard to ascertain. Many indicators of productivity are physical rather than monetary and therefore 'rely on the internal prices of each country' (Kravis, 1976, p. 40). What figures there are suggest that on a *per capita* basis U.K. labour productivity is much the same as for the rest of Europe; however, when the *per capita* figure is adjusted to take into account hours of work, number of persons in employment and 'quality' of the workforce, Britain slips down the table. There seems little doubt that in the period 1950 to 1973 productivity in Britain saw a relative decline but an absolute increase, mainly due to the fall in the number of persons employed in manufacturing. But from 1973 there were signs of stagnation in productivity growth (Kravis, 1976; Singh, 1977).

The net result is that British industry, in a more competitive world, is less competitive than it was. The quality, design, and general performance of its products have fallen behind and they are less in demand. Partially as a result of this the propensity to import is high (Panić, 1975). As we have seen, overcapacity, under-investment and a relative decline in productivity, apart from other contributory problems such as overmanning, industrial disputes, and so on, are endemic. Furthermore, capacity planned in pre-recession days has come on stream when there is a dearth of demand. The overall result has been a fall in the rate of profit of British manufacturing industry. It is to this fundamental issue that we must now turn.

The fall in the rate of profit—crisis for capitalism or Marxism?

The recent debate on the profitability of British industry is important not only because of its obvious relevance to the problems of inner-city employment but also because it illuminates some of the problems in this kind of economic analysis. Very few economists would now dispute the fact of a profits squeeze in British industry. It was first brought to general attention by Glyn and Sutcliffe (1972), who estimated that the rate of profit of U.K. companies fell from 11 per cent 1964 to 5.8 per cent in 1971. Panić and Close (1973, p. 30) concluded that 'there has been a decline in the rate of profit in the manufacturing sector over the last two decades', but contended that whereas *post-tax* returns fell from 9.5 per cent in 1961 to 7.8 per cent in 1969, *pre-tax* profitability had ceased to fall in the 1960s. King (1975) argued that many of the assumptions and definitions in studies of profitability were loose, but his very careful analysis still confirmed the existence of a profits squeeze. He calculated that there had been a downwards trend in the share of profits before tax from 1950 to 1973, but that tax concessions seemed to have evened out any post-tax fall. Burgess and Webb (1974, p. 18), in another careful study, concluded that:

> All the profit-share or rate-of-return series which we have considered indicate similar trends when allowance is made for cyclical factors. Before tax, both profit shares and rates of return have been in decline since the early 1950's. After tax there is evidence that profit shares have been in decline since at least the mid-1960's, whilst rates of return have been falling from the early 1960's.

Post-tax rate of return was calculated as around 13 per cent in the mid-1950s, falling to less than 10 per cent in the period 1971 to 1972. Glyn (1972) has reviewed the recent evidence on profits in a reply to his critics, with particular regard to stock appreciation. He found that from 1962 to 1970 post-tax share of profits in GDP at factor cost (deducting indirect taxation) fell from 16.8 to 10.7 per cent. He argues that the indices constructed by Paníc and Close and by King have defects, and that the fall in the rate of profit was maintained after 1970, becoming 'critical' in 1974.

Such a general fall in the rate of profit is obviously serious for British industry since it must reduce its ability to reinvest and therefore compete with the general and sustained increase in foreign competition. But, as importantly, the continuous fall in rate of profit is 'the traditional indicator of crisis in a capitalist economy' (Gamble and Walton, 1976, p. 140).

In the Marxist analysis profits are the *raison d'être* of the capitalist structure: 'Without profits the incentive to produce and the means of producing both disappear' (Glyn and Sutcliffe, 1972, p. 230). Classically—given that c = constant capital (the value of machinery inputs, etc.); v = variable capital (the value of goods necessary for reproduction of labour power, i.e. wages, etc.); and s = surplus (the value of the goods produced in surplus labour time)—then if the rate of exploitation s/v is constant the rate of profit r (defined as $s/c + v$) will fall if the organic composition of capital c/v rises. Marx laid special emphasis on the organic composition of capital. He thought it likely that it would rise over time as the result of a constant search by capitalists for new labour-saving methods of production. Hence, if the rate of exploitation were to remain the same the rate of profit would fall since it is only the variable part of capital that yields surplus value, whereas rate of profit is measured on total investments (that is, constant and variable capital). Marx, with a flair for understatement, calls this inbuilt 'tendency' for the rate of profit to fall 'the most important law of modern political economy and the most essential for understanding the most difficult relations. It is most important law from the historical standpoint' (Marx, 1973, p. 748). Contrarily, Joan Robinson argues that if the rate of exploitation is reduced then the rate of profit can still fall even when the organic composition of capital does not rise. This would have to be the interpretation in modern Britain where, although there has perhaps been an increase in the organic composition of capital, it is more likely that the wage push by the unions from the 1960s to the time of the first social contract in 1974 had more to do with the fall in the rate of profit. Howard and King (1975) list five of Marx's main 'counteracting influences' to the law of the falling rate of profit: increasing the intensity of exploitation by, for instance, lengthening the working day; depression of wages below the value of labour power; capital-saving innovations which reduce the organic composition of capital; foreign trade which can bring down the costs of both constant and variable capital; and the formation of an 'industrial reserve army' or relatively surplus population to encourage expansion of industries with a low organic composition of capital and hence slow down the rate of growth of the average organic composition. (This last influence we shall return to in another context.) Marx realized that these counteracting influences acted as checks on his law, reducing it to a 'tendency', albeit an innate tendency.

Their presence meant that 'the fall in the rate of profit is, therefore, not linear but in some periods is only latent coming to the fore more or less strongly in other periods and appearing in the form of crisis cycle' (Yaffe, 1973a, p. 203).

Many factors can precipitate a crisis, and they may appear to be the cause. But the general cause lies in the conditions of capitalist production and accumulation itself. At each of these points of crisis there is an 'absolute overaccumulation' of capital, 'an overproduction of capital with respect to the degree of exploitation' (Yaffe, 1973a, p. 204). Or, put in cruder form, the accumulation process, involving as it does a rise in organic composition of capital, a rise in the productivity of labour, and a *relative* decrease in amount of labour employed, can only increase the mass of profits or surplus value to a certain point, then this 'expansion of production outruns its profitability' (Yaffe, 1973a, p. 203) precluding a further increase in profits and resulting in a crisis. In the crisis the profitability of the capitalist system somehow has to be restored. For this to be achieved some devaluation of constant capital must take place, and there must also be a centralization and restructuring of capital, allowing increasing economies of scale and the abandonment of the least profitable and other absolute constant capital. Also the increased unemployment of the crisis allows wages to be pushed below their former value and new methods of production to be introduced. This allows the whole process of accumulation to begin again, *but* on a higher level.

There are many criticisms of the theory of the falling rate of profit and its reflection in the complex nature of crises, for instance, that the formula for the rate of profit is not general (Howard and King, 1975), or that the theory lacks rigour (Meek, 1973). It presents a number of other unsolved problems. In particular Hodgson (1974), in common with Glyn and Sutcliffe (1972), has attacked the assumption that the organic composition of capital is the main cause of the present profits squeeze; it is due, they claim, to increased worker militancy in the 1960s and increased international competition. Cutler *et al.* (1977) have attacked the whole status of the 'law', arguing that 'there can be no "laws of tendency" at all and therefore no tendency of the rate of profit to decline' (Cutler *et al.*, 1977, p. 158), which develops from Hindess and Hirst's (1977) objectivist critique of Marx's general method and conception of causality. The arguments regarding the law of the tendency of the falling rate of profit are many and have never been fully documented; however, the reader is referred to, among others, Balibar (1970), Yaffe (1973a, b). Hodgson (1974), Gamble and Walton (1976), Howard and King (1975), Kay (1976), Meek (1973), Desai (1974), Koshimura (1975), Morishima (1973), Mandel (1968, 1975), and, of course, Volume 3 of *Capital*.

It seems clear that the law of the tendency of the falling rate of profit has many problems—whether these add up to a 'degenerating problem shift' which invalidates the law (or whether indeed the law can ever be invalidated) is hard to assess among the noise of the arguments and counter-arguments. This essay uses the concept where it seems to illuminate the argument rather than obfuscate it in the full realization that such a pragmatic approach will satisfy neither side. It seems certain that sooner or later the law will have to be replaced or radically modified, and especially items of the theory of crises to which it leads. In this context telling criticisms have been made by Hussain (1977) in a discussion of the work of two firm advocates of the law, namely Gamble and Walton (1976) and Mandel (1975). (It should be made clear here that at least two kinds of correction are made to the notion of crisis in Marxist theory. In the one on which we concentrate here the crises are signs of the impending breakdown of capitalism; in the other, Althusserian, view the impending breakdown of capitalism is not linked to actual economic events.)

The main point that is at issue in the works of Gamble and Walton, Mandel, and others is that there is a *limit* to capitalism which it cannot survive when its inherent contradictions are resolved in a socialist mode of production. Some well-known Marxists like Lefebvre (1976) have despaired of this limit ever being reached. The debate upon the breakdown (or survival) of capitalism, in essence, becomes a matter of whether the theory of the fall in the rate of profit is correct and whether the evidence supports this. Thus the post-war boom could not continue because, by the theory, booms are transitory, but although 'it is regarded as necessary to explain why booms are transitory the question of why crises too may not be temporary is never raised' (Hussain, 1977, p. 441). Yet presumably if the 'crisis' Marxist waits long enough an economic crisis will always occur which can vindicate the theory of the fall of the rate of profit. Thus 'once it is taken for granted that capitalism will one day disappear through its internal contradictions the significance of economic events . . . is, at least in their general outline, given beforehand' (Hussain, 1977, p. 442). In other words 'the claim that capitalism has behaved in accordance with the laws of motion laid down does not rest on any evidence but on the *belief* that that is so' (Hussain, 1977, p. 498, my emphasis). Any reading of Mandel shows how evidence can be preconditioned by belief that 'the contemporary crisis of the bourgeois nation state is indivisible from the crisis of capitalist relations of production' (Mandel, 1975, p. 589). These and other criticisms cast doubt upon the efficacy of a crisis interpretation of capitalism and upon the rate of profit as a seismograph of capitalism, and lead to the need for an objective reworking of Marxist theory such as that proposed by Cutler *et al.* (1977).

EXISTING TRENDS IN BRITISH INDUSTRY

The present economic recession, whether a crisis for capitalism or not, has had a series of marked impacts upon industrial organization in Britain. These are not particular to the recession, but rather are continuations of trends that existed before. The problems of overcapacity, increased competition, and lack of investment are the same, but their degree of severity has much increased. The proposed solutions also tend to be the same.

The reply of British industry to the recession was to reinforce several extant trends. The first of these is simply the growth of the giant corporation with the consequent centralization of capital. In 1950 the top 100 companies accounted for one-fifth of manufacturing net output; by 1970 that proportion was over 40 per cent and the National Institute for Economic and Social Research forecasts that it will have increased to two-thirds by 1985 (Community Development Project, 1977a). There has been a similar growth in their shares of total net assets of the company population. Thus, in 1957 they accounted for 50 per cent of these assets; by 1969 this share had increased to 65 per cent (Meeks and Whittington, 1975). Concentration ratios have obviously increased. A recent E.E.C. study shows that in each market studied, in Britain the share of the top four firms was nearly 80 per cent; in food industries it was 95 per cent. Whereas in 1909 more than 2 000 firms were needed to produce half the total manufacturing output of the U.K., by 1970 this number had fallen to 170 (Prais, 1976). Much of this increased concentration and centralization is, of course, due to merger activity. Although the rash of merger activity of the late 1960s and early 1970s (with 5 000 firms acquired in Britain from 1963 to 1968) is now over it still continues steadily.

The state has been an important influence. One of the biggest forces for industrial concentration in recent years has been the Wilson government's Industrial Reorganization Corporation, which was involved directly in 30 large mergers between 1966 and its demise in 1971, and actively encouraged at least 100 others. And yet, as Meeks and Whittington (1975) have shown, the top 100 firms in Britain had an average rate of profit 2.4 per cent below that of the next 800: perhaps paradoxically, these companies were better able to obtain external finance. From 1964 to 1969 the capital market supplied about 70 per cent of their external finance, compared with 56 per cent of the rest (Meeks and Whittington, 1975). This was because the giants may not have had a greater rate of profit *but* they were more reliable in making a stable profit from year to year and were therefore a better risk.

This brings us to an important point which has its implications both for Marxist theory and for the inner city. Giant firms are not interested in making a profit in the same way as smaller companies are. To their managers profit does not have the same connotations as it has in the perception of, say, the average Tory Member of Parliament. The giant firm is looking for share of the market as well as profit (Hannah and Kay, 1977). With the market for its products in thrall its position is assured. It is a survival-maximizer as well as a profit-maximizer. Thus, nearly half of new share issues by the 100 top companies from 1964 to 1969 were made in exchange for subsidiaries, usually within roughly the same industry but also ensuring expansion into other industrial sectors by 'vertical integration' (i.e. buying up of firms in supply or consumer industries: Meeks and Whittington, 1975, Glyn and Sutcliffe, 1972). This particular intimate involvement of the giant firm with the finance sector also means that its 'profits' become an entirely different affair from that of smaller firms, involving as it does large transfers of capital, tax write-offs, and so on among numbers of subsidiaries (some of which may even be customers for other plants' production within the firm) and sources of finance which it may itself have a connection to or an interest in.

The connotations of the growing economic power of giant firms in employment terms is clear enough. The E.E.C. Commission study showed that the share of manufacturing employment of firms with 40 000 or more employees in all markets studied in Britain averaged out at nearly 35 per cent (Economist, 1977), and 30 per cent of employment is now in firms with over a 90 per cent concentration ratio. Thus, giant firms acting as oligopolistic industries have a singular hold on the employment prospects of many workers in the U.K., more so in fact than in nearly any other country in the world. (In the U.S.A. anti-trust laws have recently restricted the growth of such a concentration of economic power, as have less restrictive laws in Germany and Japan.) The economies of giant firms are now larger than many local inner city economies and in their multinational manifestation giant firms have more power than many smaller countries.

The second trend to be reinforced, in the face of the recession, has been the increasing predominance of multinational or transnational companies in Britain. Of course their pre-eminence is linked with the growth of giant firms; it should be remembered that many multinationals are British-owned. There is some evidence, indeed, that 'relative to large firms elsewhere large British manufacturing firms may be investing more abroad than at home' (Singh, 1977). In 1973 the volume of production abroad by U.K. multinationals was more than twice the value of their exports from the U.K., in comparison with corresponding proportions of 0.38 and 0.37 for Japanese and West German multinationals, respectively (Holland, 1976). From 1962, when it equalled £3 750 million, British direct investment abroad rose to almost £7 000 million by 1970, with a corresponding leap in foreign profits: 30 per cent of the profits of the top thirty U.K. companies are now derived from overseas (Glyn and Sutcliffe, 1972), a new trend attributed to the need to respond to international competition by either purchasing overseas rivals or building production facilities abroad.

But while U.K.-based multinationals have increasingly transferred their money out of the country, foreign-owned multinationals have played an increasing role in the British manufacturing economy. Neither they nor U.K. multinationals are hedged in by the rules of location which apply to indigenous firms. They can indulge in transfer pricing and similar strategies with impunity and have become adept at playing the circuits of capital (Glyn and Sutcliffe, 1972; Rowthorn and Hymer, 1971). By 1973 the total value of U.S. direct investment in the U.K. was £1 115 million, twice the 1966 figure and thirteen times the 1950 figure (Dicken and Lloyd, 1976). Multinationals tend to concentrate in particular industrial categories; by 1974 more than 72 per cent of employment in the leading 100 U.S. enterprises in the U.K. was in the four categories of motor vehicles, electrical engineering, mechanical engineering, and the food, drink, and tobacco industry (Dicken and Lloyd, 1976).

The third major trend in British manufacturing industry has been the increasing role of the state in promoting concentration and internationalization. Until the 1960s the main thrust was the English Industrial Estates Corporation, but since then the whole gamut of regional policy measures (which are essentially measures to combat unemployment) has been brought to bear. In 1966 the Industrial Reorganization Corporation was set up and it was certainly responsible for considerable merger activity (see above). Since then the National Enterprise Board has been set up. The state is increasingly involved in investing in manufacturing industry, and this no longer always means a shoring-up operation for firms about to go under, with consequent socially unacceptable job loss. If actual nationalization is added to this, the state's degree of involvement becomes clear (Jessop, 1977). Following O'Connor (1973), it is possible to see that a considerable portion of this expenditure must have helped directly or indirectly to raise productivity ('social investment') and lower labour costs ('social consumption') and has had the added impact of making much of private industry dependent on government orders. In a sense, for instance, through the provision of infrastructure and paying many of the costs of the reproduction of labour power, the state is now the instrument of capital (Broadbent, 1977).

The effect of the economic recession on British industry

The effect of the recent economic recession upon British industry can be seen mainly in terms of a general slackening of demand. It has accelerated existing processes, although some structural change is evident. But before we can look at these processes we need to consider the effects of the trends in British manufacturing industry examined above in order to make sense of the susceptibility of local inner-city areas to heavy employment loss.

The increase in dependency

Increasing market and aggregate concentration and internationalization have been at least partially responsible for the decrease in the *number* of small firms, as their markets have been snapped up, from 136 000 employing less than 200 workers in 1935 and accounting for about 35 per cent of total net output in manufacturing, to 58 000 in 1968 accounting for only 16 per cent of total net output in manufacturing. The *size* of firms in terms of employment is increasing, and the average number of plants owned by particular corporations has also increased. Thus, while in 1958 the top 100 firms in Great Britain had an average of 27 plants, by 1972 this had increased to 72 (Prais, 1976). The specific implications for inner city employment are brought out below.

Such a change in the size distribution of the typical plant is explained in part by the growth in large firms, including multinationals, and in particular by the common characteristic of such large-scale enterprises—their operation as *multiplant* concerns (see especially Lloyd and Dicken, 1977, Ch. 9; Scherer *et al.*, 1975). Such multi-plant firms are often part of larger multi-product conglomerates. Many factories in inner-city locations have, through the process of merger or expansion, become links in a chain of such plants. In 1972 I.C.I. had 60 plants in Britain employing 142 000 workers in 8 product groups (Rees, 1972). In 1975 Courtaulds employed 110 932 workers in Britain and had control over 487 employing units. The British Steel Corporation employed 225 000 workers in 1974 at 53 plants; in 1976 Rio Tinto Zinc had 46 plants and B.P. Chemicals (part of the much larger B.P. group) employed 24 924 workers in 9 plants in 1975 (Carmichael, 1977b).

The result of such a large multiplant sector is the emergence of what Averitt (1968) has called the dual economy consisting of two sectors—that of 'centre' firms, the large and complex multiplant operations, and 'periphery' firms, the smaller single-plant operations. Of particular concern to this discussion is the question of whether the operating policies of large corporations in this centre sector benefit the inner city. Their headquarters are usually not in inner city locations. For a British company the probability is that the headquarters will be in London or the South-east (Parsons, 1972, 1973). Westaway (1974b) found that in 1972 86 per cent of the largest 100 firms had headquarters' addresses in the London metropolitan labour area, and 53 per cent of the largest 1 000—the next most important centre was Birmingham with 66! The obvious corollary is that most inner-city plants in multiplant organizations are controlled from without, and have 'branch plant economies'. This problem of external control can be exacerbated when the controlling corporation is a multinational, since then its headquarters may not even be in the U.K. (Dicken, 1977). Thus Firn (1975) found that in 1973 14.9 per cent of manufacturing employment in Scotland was in plants owned by North American firms, although such plants accounted for only 4.9 per cent of manufacturing establishments. Hood and Young (1976; 1977) found that this influence was differentially concentrated, having far more impact on, for instance, the Scottish New Towns in terms of number of plants, *but* in employment terms more dependence was exhibited by the older city areas where jobs were concentrated in a few large plants. Dicken and Lloyd (1976, p. 688) show that in 1968 'United States owned enterprises accounted for only 0.8 per cent of all private manufacturing enterprises in the United Kingdom and for only 1.4 per cent of all private manufacturing establishments. Yet this minuscule proportion employed one out of every fourteen workers in United Kingdom manufacturing and produced 10.4 per cent of total net output.'

We can therefore see that multinationals concentrate on large plants in terms of employment size—a trend that the evidence indicates is carried over into entirely U.K.-based multiplant operations. Firn (1975) found that, of the 90 per cent of plants whose ownership was readily identifiable operating in Scotland in 1973, in plants employing over 100 people 50.6 per cent were controlled from outside Scotland. In the same year the Northern Region Strategy Team found that of the 1 778 plants employing over 100 workers surveyed by them nearly 70 per cent were subsidiaries or branches of companies based outside the Northern Region (Northern Region Strategy Team, 1976b). These plants accounted for nearly 77 per cent of employment in the sample. The average size of outside-controlled plants had decreased in terms of employment loss from 1962 to 1973 at a much slower rate than had those plants controlled from the region itself. In the same period the number of outside-controlled plants had increased by over 50 per cent, while the number of regional plants had decreased by nearly 20 per cent. The regional net increase in employment of 33 030 decomposed into an employment loss of 61 750 in regionally controlled plants, as contrasted with a

94 780 employment gain in outside-controlled plants. This shows the increasing share of employment controlled by multi-plant operations in the Northern Region—a trend which there is no reason to suppose is not repeated nationwide. It also indicates the increased dependency of inner-city employment on large multi-plant concerns.

The increasing trend to dependence on externally controlled firms must present considerable reservations. It means that, in the inner city context, a large part of the inner-city economy is reliant on allocated growth. Major decisions affecting employment, investment, sales, and purchasing are made elsewhere. In the case of non-U.K. multinationals, decisions can be made without much reference to government. The inner-city economy thus becomes an 'open economy' (Carmichael, 1977a) subject to the rapid transmission of economic fluctuations from other regions or countries. In addition the increased influence of the branch plant economy means that there are few employment opportunities open to young local professionals within an area. They are forced to migrate to headquarters locations which in the British context almost inevitably means London. The jobs which are provided locally, as described below, tend towards production-line assembly operations employing semi-skilled and female workers. As has been pointed out, however, multiplant operations, being large, tend to be financially more stable and therefore they have greater employment security and permanence. They also provide a relative increase in job opportunities.

The decrease in number and increase in size of plants and the concomitant and highly correlated increase in multi-plant and often multinational operations in the economy have perhaps made the U.K. economy more susceptible to changes in the world economy. Such changes have also meant that the capacity for *restructuring* (in effect the restructuring of restructuring) is much enhanced. This accelerated trend to restructuring by companies to meet the exigencies of the world loss of demand has perhaps been the most noticeable trend in employment terms in recent years in the U.K. economy.

Restructuring

Only three countries in Europe show an actual decrease in manufacturing capability in recent years—Austria, Italy, and Britain. In its efforts to surmount the double crisis at the international and national level British industry has been forced to adopt various strategies, and these are revealed in particular in differing locational and unemployment patterns.

Many strategies can be adopted in order to retain or expand profitability during a lack of demand. Broadly, however, they are threefold. First, the introduction or accelerated diffusion of new technology; secondly, and often tied to the first, reorganization of the methods of production; and thirdly, a direct reduction in wages (Massey, 1976). The latter strategy is rarely an option and most firms have adopted a mix of reorganization of methods of production and new technology, with a consequent shedding of jobs. Production therefore tends to become concentrated in larger and fewer firms.

We have already seen a number of the ways in which the capitalist system is restructuring itself in order to adapt to the market and its consequent problems. Inherent in the system is this contradiction in which all solutions become problems. The problems of British industry—under-investment, overcapacity, and lack of competitiveness—are solved in part by the prevailing trends to large and increasingly multinational firms as promoted and increasingly paid for by the state. But these trends bring their own problems of dependency and profitability. A further need of firms is to retain sufficient profitability, but simultaneously compete at a time when demand is low. Large companies in oligopolistic positions have an advantage here which can be enhanced through various subsidiaries. This diversification—organizational and geographical—can be an insurance against a fall in demand and profitability in any sector, while owning means of distribution like warehouses means that middle-men are increasingly omitted and capital flows more smoothly. The main problem for British industry and state becomes a restructuring which allows a coordinated reduction in capacity rather than one based upon competition (which would simply lead to more firms going out of business). We shall examine two aspects of this problem in particular; changes in production processes and changes in labour processes. Following Massey (1976), we can identify three strategies which allow a coordinated reduction in capacity in the face of lack of demand and increased competition and which allow profitability to be retained (see Figure 5.5).

1. Reduction in the labour force without closure. In the very short term substantial stockpiling will no doubt take place, both financial and physical. However, as the period of fall in demand and increased competition lengthens, the firm will require to cut its labour force. Here we can expect the hoarding of labour through either maintaining hours and decreasing output, decreasing hours and output, introduction of short-time working, or temporary suspension. Non-replacement of labour will also no doubt operate as a policy and will be paralleled by a decrease in recruitment (Carmichael, 1977a).

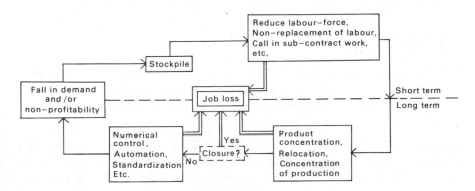

FIGURE 5.5. Multiplant firm strategies under fall of demand and/or non-profitability

Decisions can also influence the level of labour indirectly employed, for instance by the calling in of sub-contract work.

2. Cutting capacity by closure—this can mean the closure of single-plant firms or of branch plants in multi-plant companies. In multi-plant companies such closures are usually due to rationalization.

3. Long-term adjustments—this is restructuring in the true sense. Again following Massey (1976) we can identify three long-term strategies—
   (a) introduction of numerical control;
   (b) partial standardization of components and automation; and
   (c) full standardization and automation.

It is instructive to reflect that nearly all these options, short- or long-term, involve a loss of labour and closure of plants that do not fit into long-term plans. They form an inexorable continuum from possibilities like short-term working through automation to the final knell of closure. There are certainly no absolute gains in jobs to be had from these strategies currently being pursued in British industry.

THE IMPACT OF THESE TRENDS ON THE INNER CITY

The price of these trends in restructuring by industry to meet new levels of demand and competition is measured out in jobs lost. It is often argued that the inner areas contain those plants which are most susceptible to closure, and have, as a consequence, high rates of unemployment. Although this argument is compelling, it is not necessarily borne out by the facts gleaned from a number of components of change analyses. The pattern of closure often seems hard to pin down as specifically 'inner city' in its effects. Rather there seems to have been a general and constant rate of closure nationwide.

Closures and in situ contractions

As is shown by Figure 5.6, there is a general and absolute loss of manufacturing jobs in Britain. This trend could be expected to be reflected in the inner city. Following Massey and Meegan (1976, 1977) we can isolate three kinds of job loss in the inner city:

1. Total closure ('absolute loss' in their terminology).
2. Locational change being a 'shedding' of employment in the move ('in transit loss') and an absolute loss of jobs for the country as a whole.
3. Locational change resulting in losses in the inner city but gains elsewhere ('locational loss').

Massey and Meegan's (1976, 1977) studies are unusual in trying to take a view which examines inner-city areas comparatively by taking note of the problems encountered in the inner areas of London, Birmingham, Manchester, and Liverpool. Looking at the pattern of different kinds of job loss in the electrical engineering and electronics sectors of British manufacturing industry from 1966 to 1971 in the three categories above, they found that 89 per cent of employment loss in the four cities was due to absolute loss as a result of total closure. This absolute loss was composed of an *in situ* loss of 58 per cent and an in transit loss of 31 per cent. Locational loss accounted for only 11 per cent of the total. Thus, well over half the jobs lost to these four inner cities were the result of 'either closure or capacity cuts *in which no locational change was involved*' (Massey and Meegan, 1977, p. 26). Nearly all the employment lost was lost to the economy as a whole. Locational losses which actually generated gains in employment at destinations accounted for only a small proportion of total job loss. Within the four cities the pattern of job loss was much the same as at the national level. Absolute loss accounted for well over 90 per cent of all employment loss except in London, where the figure was 80 per cent: only in London was a significant locational loss reported.

Since London is in many ways a special case we can begin our survey with a closer look at the situation there. London is predominantly a service city with more workers employed in offices than on the shop floor. In 1921 manufacturing accounted for less than 50 per cent of the total male employment in Greater London, and by 1966 this figure was only 29 per cent of male (822 500 workers) and 27 per cent of female employment. But it is this sector which has been differentially much the hardest hit (Weatheritt and Lovett, 1976).

According to a Department of Industry survey, between 1966 and 1974 net manufacturing employment decline in Greater London resulted in a loss of 383 400 jobs (defined on the Census of Employment basis, cited in Keeble, 1976; Weatheritt and Lovett, 1976, and Department of Employment, 1977). As Table 5.1 shows, no less than 73 per cent of these jobs were lost through actual factory closures. This figure comprises 48 per cent of closures which were actual deaths and 25 per cent closures due to transfers. The remaining 27 per cent of employment decline was the result of *in situ* contraction. This evidence is corroborated by the work of Martin and Seaman (1975), who estimated that between 1954 and 1968 the total number of factories in the G.L.C. area employing 100 or more workers fell by 28 per cent (from 1 905 to 1 370). In inner London (taken to be the I.L.E.A. area) the rate was higher at 44 per cent, but in outer London it was 17 per cent.

Lomas (1975) collected data from firms for which redundancies totalled more than twenty at any point from 1966 to 1972 and found that from 1966 to 1971 the number of manufacturing jobs in Greater London fell by 5.5 per cent (239 000) according to Census of Production figures, and by 8.9 per cent (417 490) according to Department of Employment figures. Of total male losses 20 per cent were in service industries and 3 per cent were in construction; the remaining 77 per cent were in manufacturing, with 6.8 per cent of redundancies in textiles, clothing, and footwear, 37 per cent in the metal and electrical industries, and a further 32 per cent in other manufacturing industry. From 1966 to 1972, 107 051 jobs for men in inner London (usually taken as the London 'A' boroughs) were lost at an increasing rate, and accounted for 13.7 per cent of the total jobs available. The loss of jobs for women in manufacturing was even heavier. The expanding areas of employment were broadly those of the national employment trends, particularly the 'non-basic' services like banking, insurance, and finance. Redundancies in manufacturing were hitting those resident and working in London, particularly in the inner city, disproportionately.

Lomas (1975) shows conclusively that the inner areas bore the brunt of the contraction of labour demand, particularly on eastern Thameside. The main reasons for this loss rate were divided between six contenders:

1. closure of the plant (absolute loss);
2. transfer of production to other areas (locational loss);
3. a compulsory purchase order is served;
4. reorganization of production methods;
5. economic difficulties and changes; and
6. takeovers and mergers.

The first three were the predominant reasons for job loss and show the repeated pattern of a *permanent loss* of jobs. Gripaios (1977a, 1977b) has examined this pattern of closures in more detail by taking a closer look at closures in South-east London, where, from 1966 to 1974, 69 per cent of *closures* have been due to deaths (72 per cent of employment loss) and 31 per cent due to relocations. Gripaios's results from the Kompass survey of South-east London from 1968 to 1974 show 61 per cent of *closures* attributable to deaths and 39 per cent to relocations. His examination of Department of Employment data showed that for the six inner South-east London employment areas, from 1970 to 1975 an average of 74 per cent of *closures* were deaths, with a range in the six areas examined from 65 to 90 per cent. From 1970 to 1975 more closures (72 per cent) were found in establishments with less than 50 employees as opposed to those with 10 to 30 employees (53 per cent), but there was *no* evidence to suggest that small firms were more likely to close than large ones. More manufacturing firms closed than service firms, but not by any large difference (48 per cent to 42 per cent) and the industrial structure of the area did not seem to distort the pattern of closure (the minimum closure was 40 per cent). Neither did size of plant. Interestingly, the death rate was higher in services (at 79 per cent) than manufacturing (68 per cent): construction outstripped both of these at 85 per cent. This latter closure rate is not so surprising—construction is always tied to the economic fortunes and has, as well, a notoriously high rate of bankruptcy. However, there was a locational variation in the pattern of inner-area closures such that the dockland areas did not suffer as many closures as 'inland' areas. Again this was not a function of industrial structure, since the dockland areas had more manufacturing industry than the 'inland' areas. Thus the industrial decline in inner London seems to be general rather than specific to any sector.

Further evidence as to the pattern of closure and contraction comes from local studies of the London employment situation. In Canning Town closures accounted for 64 per cent of the gross total of 10 500 manufacturing jobs lost from 1966 to 1972: 36 per cent of gross total job loss was due to *in situ* contraction, while the lower net decline in manufacturing jobs could be attributed to existing firm growth and some births (Canning Town Community Development Project, 1975). The Lambeth Inner Area Study (Department of the Environment, 1977e) attributed 23 per cent of *job loss* to closure, 58 per cent to relocation, and 19 per cent to *in situ* contraction. These last figures almost certainly underestimated job loss due to closure: Jeffrey (1977), using Department of Employment data and a small quota sample, looked at firms in Southwark closing or moving out in the periods 1967 to 1970 and 1970 to 1973. Most closures were attributable to takeover and merger activity, conclusions supported by the Southwark Trades Council and Roberts (1976).

But what of the other inner cities of Britain? Table 5.1 gives some evidence on the components of change in these areas. Strict comparison is difficult because time periods do not match and in the following passages this fact should be borne in mind.

In inner Manchester, Lloyd and Mason (1977) found that 85 per cent of total employment decline during 1966–1972 was due to deaths and transfers, of which the bulk was attributed to actual closures with no gains to the economy at new locations: 15 per cent of the decline was attributed to an *in situ* contraction of 5 984 jobs. By contrast Lloyd's (1977) study of inner Merseyside from 1966 to 1975 shows 65 per cent of total employment contraction as due to deaths and transfers, with a much higher figure for net contraction in *in situ* employment of 35 per cent.

In Manchester the major employment loss by closure from 1966 to 1972 was in single-plant firms. Size of plant in employment terms had a significant impact on ability to survive; the larger the plant the greater its chance of survival. Most of the decline in plant numbers was due to the deaths of small plants in specific industries, *but* most employment decline was due to the closures of plants with more than fifty employees. These accounted for only 13 per cent of plant closures, but 65 per cent of the job loss. Against the background of constant and massive employment decline the situation was surprisingly dynamic. Industries which are by tradition inner-city industries—for instance printing and publishing, and clothing—were still predisposed to favour the inner-city location. Plant deaths were concentrated in some industries, but the general impression was of an overall decline. In inner Liverpool, by contrast, the situation was somewhat different because of a relatively small number of dominant industrial activities compared to the more diverse industrial structure of Manchester. Food, drink, and tobacco accounted for almost 28 per cent of all manual workers employed in inner Merseyside in 1975; shipbuilding with 13.4 per cent and electrical engineering with 12.9 per cent were equally dominant. Merseyside is particularly susceptible to closures, therefore, since it has many workers in a few large plants. Thus, from 1966 to 1975 the heaviest absolute falls in employment concentrated in the industries with highest employment in the area, and the fortunes of the area are now wrapped up in the 12 or so plants employing more than 1 000 workers. While in inner Manchester most employment was in medium-sized plants employing about 500 workers, in inner Liverpool in 1966 nearly 75 per cent of the manual workforce was in 40 plants employing more than 100 workers, including 19 plants with more than 1 000 workers. In 1975 this situation of dependency was retained at the 75 per cent level. Lloyd (1977) found no evidence to support a view that any of the jobs created by the declaration of Merseyside as a Special Development Area had found their way to the inner city.

Further components of change evidence for inner city problems are given by Flagg (1973) for Greater Leicester from 1947 to 1970. Unfortunately, by concentrating on locational change some of this paper's impact is dissipated. However, as is shown in Table 5.1, net employment loss in the inner areas of Leicester was due to closures rather than loss due to transfers or loss due to *in situ* change. This was in contrast to the outer area which showed net employment growth in terms of births, transfers, and some *in situ* growth.

One of the problems with a components of change analysis restricted to inner-city areas is that it throws no real light on the differences between the inner city, outer city, and city region. The analysis may well demonstrate that an excess of closures over openings is responsible for part of the industrial decline of an inner city but 'insofar as the explanation is in terms of plant openings and closures, this result is tautological' (Department of Employment 1977, p. 32). What really needs to be discovered is whether an inner city suffers from a higher rate of closures and/or lower rates of births, relative to other areas, in relation to its existing stock of plant. The policy implications of a higher rate of closures are very different from those of a lower rate of births. In the former case the problem might be the hostility of the inner-city environment to existing industry, but in the latter case it might be the difficulty of setting up in the inner city.

The only study with information of this kind is that by Cameron (1973) which examined industrial change in the Clydeside conurbation from 1958 to 1968 (see Table 5.1). The conurbation was divided into three areas—the 'central city' of Glasgow, 'subcentre' towns, and 'non-urban' quadrants. In 1958, 74 per cent of plants were located in Glasgow, and within Glasgow 25 per cent of plants were located within one kilometre of the city centre. By 1968 the total number of plants had fallen by 6 per cent, of which the heaviest fall was in the city centre. Most startling, this was *not* due to a differential death rate within the city from 1958 to 1968—the average for the central city of 28.2 per cent did not fluctuate to any great degree over the city as a whole; in the 'subcentre' towns the death rate average was markedly higher at 34.5 per cent, while in the non-urban quadrants it was 29.4 per cent. Rather, the variation was due to the pattern of new openings. The central city had a much lower birth rate of 16.8 per cent from 1958 to 1968 compared with 30.3 per cent in the 'subcentre' towns and 21.9 per cent in the non-urban quadrants. The inner city had a particularly low birth rate (which increased towards the edge of the city) *and* a very heavy loss of transferred plants compared with a net inflow of transferred plants in the outer central city. Plant size also militated against the central city since although it still gained more than one out of every two new plants between 1958 and 1968, due to their smaller size this only represented one-quarter of new plant employment.

The net result was a gradual decentralization of employment opportunity

TABLE 5.1. Employment and/or plant loss in some U.K. cities and inner cities: results of components of change analyses

	Greater London 1966–1974	Inner Manchester 1966–1972	Inner Merseyside 1966–1975	S.E. Inner London 1968–1974 Kompass data	S.E. Inner London 1968–1974 Dept. of Industry data
Total employment decline	383 400	30 387	18 291		
1. Deaths	−183 200	−28 260 (1002)	−17 094	(98)	−28 000 (160)
2. Transfers	−97 100	−7 135 (289)		(63)	−11 041 (71)
		Σ(1291)	Σ(766)	Σ(161)	Σ(231)
Net in situ decline	−116 000	−5 984	−9 167	—	—
Total growth	12 900	10 992	7 970		894
1. Births	9 900	6 514 (462)		(31)	338 (11)
2. Transfers	3 000	4 478 (225)		(38)	556 (8)
		Σ (687)	Σ(479)	Σ (69)	Σ (19)
Source:	Dept. of Industry (1974 cited in Weatheritt and Lovitt (1976))	Lloyd and Mason (1977)	Lloyd (1977)	Gripaios (1977a)	

Greater Leicester 1947–1970

	Inner	Outer	Greater
(Entries−exists)	−8 357	6 217	−2 140
Net in situ decline	−4 704	15 212	1 421
Net transfer	−730	4 313	3 583
Source:	Flagg (1973)		

Clydeside

		Central	'Subcentre'	'Non-urban'	Total
(Entries−exists)	1. Deaths	(485)	(139)	(83)	(707)
	2. Transfers	(363)	(22)	(17)	(402)
Net in situ decline		—	—	—	—
Net transfer	1. Births	(289)	(122)	(115)	(526)
	2. Transfers	(289)	(73)	(41)	(402)
Source:		Cameron (1973)			

N.B. Plants italicized (and in parentheses).

over the period studied as new plants tended to locate further out. Evidence by Cameron and Evans (1973) suggests that the amount of decentralization of manufacturing industry in Clydeside is similar to that occurring in other British conurbations, although whether the mechanism is a lower birth rate, as in inner Glasgow, or a lower death rate must remain a moot point.

Births and transfers

As Cameron (1973) has shown, it is lack of births, rather than the death rate, in Glasgow which is the major cause of the inner city being a net exporter instead of a net importer of jobs. However, it is hard to generalize this to other British inner cities. The main detailed evidence on births comes from the work by Lloyd (1977) and Lloyd and Mason (1977). As Table 5.1 shows, the number of births relative to deaths is very small in all British cities studied at a variety of time periods. In Manchester Lloyd and Mason (1977) seem to confirm the traditional 'seed-bed' view of the inner city, with a large number of small firms (with a median employment size of only six) which need access congregating there. Most of these plants probably do not survive very long—few last more than ten years and most close at about five years of age (Sant, 1975). In Liverpool Lloyd (1977) has shown that even in the larger-firm-dominated economy of the inner city most births have been of small firms looking for the traditional 'seed-bed' virtues and perhaps, therefore, finding the inner area attractive because of its very decay. But as a result they have a vested interest in inner city decay! In any case, such births are peripheral to the issue of current inner city employment (although perhaps not to any long-term success of an employment policy).

What of transfers? Within the inner city most transfers tend to be within that area itself (Gripaios, 1977a, b; Lloyd and Mason, 1977; Lloyd, 1977). These transfers tended to be of small firms, with a definite tendency for large firms to move further out. Thus, in Liverpool from 1966 to 1975 the average employment size of plant for internal movers was fifteen, while for movers out it was thirty-six (Lloyd, 1977). Movers out also tended to be larger than average at origin.

There is very little information concerning transfers into the inner city. As has been shown by Lloyd and Mason (1977) and Lloyd (1977), the majority of firms moving in were small 'seed-bed' firms in the traditional inner city sectors like printing and publishing, clothing, and so on. This volatility among small firms in the inner city is traditional, however, and there is nothing to link it, in its essential characteristics, to new developments—rather it is a continuing background noise which is important in terms of long-run economic stability rather than prospects for employment. The provision of advance factories, which has been put forward as one aspect of government inner-city policy, seems unlikely to halt this volatility which is an essential component of the inner city as seed-bed and which ends in successful firms *moving out* in order to expand.

'Emigrant' firms over a certain size are often considered to have two facets which make their loss particularly harmful to the inner city (Lloyd and Mason, 1977). One is that mobile firms are considered more likely to be successful and therefore more likely to grow. Their removal therefore brings severe problems (Keeble, 1968; Townroe, 1971). But Henderson (1974) has cast doubts on this hypothesis in relation to Glasgow, showing that less than half of plants moving from Glasgow to overspill areas were expanding. Similarly, Lloyd and Mason (1977) have shown in relation to Manchester that although just over 50 per cent of employment in all transfers could be assigned to growing industries this figure was little different from the breakdown into growth and decline industries in the city as a whole. The second facet is that industries transferring out of the area are those which have strong local linkages to other inner-city businesses. Their loss therefore causes 'long-run multiplier effects' leading to a cascade of closures (e.g. Gripaios, 1977b). No evidence on inner-city linkages of a detailed enough kind seems to be available to ascertain the efficacy of this hypothesis.

Finally, in this section we can look at the characteristics of survivors, for, perhaps contrary to the tone of some of the foregoing paragraphs, plants do survive over long periods of time. As already pointed out, most closures are of small firms, but in employment terms it is the closure of the larger firms which is more important. Lloyd (1977) shows that in Liverpool the survivors were identified with a small number of large factories. There is some evidence that they survived by some quite drastic shedding of labour.

The decision to relocate or close and multiplant companies

Important relocation decisions—those by large firms to move out of the inner city—are increasingly based upon decisions by multiplant companies, often externally headquartered, to reorganize. These decisions have two characteristics. One involves actual closure of a subsidiary plant with loss of jobs to the inner city and economy as a whole, the other transfer from one location to another involving closure in inner city areas and, in all probability, 'locational loss' (see above) with, once again, loss of jobs to the inner city and the economy as a whole. Increasingly, the only companies which can afford major relocation decisions are multiplant companies which have considerable available finance. They can also avoid a relocation decision by substituting an acquisition for it (North, 1974). Technological change can often require new sites, with a consequent abandonment of large investment in plant and abandonment of existing capital.

What kind of reorganization precipitates the movement of firms from the inner city? In many cases such firms will be only branch plants of a large concern. A parent company has a series of reasons for relocating from the inner city. It may decide that it needs to add to capacity, and in the conditions of cramped access, limited space, and high land values of the inner city it must move if it wishes to do this. Secondly, rationalization may take place as a result of a merger or simply as company policy. Thirdly, a sectoral reorganization may lead to closure of a plant. Endless permutations of these and other reasons can be spun out, but Massey and Meegan (1976, 1977) are able to identify five major types of locational change. Investment in and coordination of growth sectors is the first type, technological change is the second, the public sector–private sector relationship is the third, production economies of scale are the fourth, and loss of capacity resulting from concentration of production is the last. In their study of the electrical engineering and electronics industry, Massey and Meegan (1976, 1977) found that the inner cities' share of localized changes was mainly in the second, third, and fifth sectors. In the light of lack of data to the contrary, the electrical and electronics industry can be taken as at least partially reflecting other industries—a not unreasonable assumption. Massey and Meegan found that investment on growth has not taken place in the inner cities, but instead in the outer South-east, the middle-sized towns of central England, and the Development Areas. They suggest that in the technological category the main movement has been to suburban areas. In the category of public sector–private sector relationships looms the fact of how dependent private industry now is on government orders. As there have been government cutbacks so the need to merge in order to build export strength and shift the balance away from the declining heavy engineering sector has led to many absolute losses and of course 'locational loss' from transfers of production. Similarly, with the fourth and fifth types of change, both of which eliminate duplicated capacity, the fourth predominantly by reorganization, the fifth by concentration and rationalization.

Keeble has pointed out that complete closures are preferred to contraction for at least three reasons. One is the continuing scale economy of 'operating $n - 1$ plants at full capacity, rather than n plants each at reduced capacity' (Keeble, 1976, p. 124). Another reason is the sale value of inner city sites, which can be very substantial. In Southwark, as the City extended into the area, 'finance companies were able to make attractive offers to industrial concerns making it worth their while to sell and re-locate out of London' (Southwark Trades Council and Roberts, 1976, p. 57). The same effect has been noted by Canning Town observers (Canning Town Community Development Project, 1975) and counterparts in most other inner areas (Community Development Project, 1977a). Some manufacturing firms have even gone as far as establishing a special property division to undertake redevelopment of their land holdings, while a valuable part of the process of asset stripping is generally acknowledged to be the resale value of some firms' land. However, such property activity varies in its concentration, depending upon the inner city involved: in London, declining profitability combined with the office boom no doubt helped concentrate a number of manufacturers' minds (Ambrose and Colenutt, 1975). As nationalized industries have contracted they have become entrepreneurs—British Rail and British Gas have vast tracts of unused land in the inner cities. The net result of this selling off of industrial land has been the growth of warehousing—'the real growth industries of (inner) areas today' (Community Development Project, 1977a, p. 12). The industrial estates which are springing up as a result of inner city land sales are mainly for warehousing. But warehouses employ very few workers per unit of land and only the unskilled, so the growth of warehousing has contributed to employment decline in the inner city. A third and final reason is that closure of a plant can avoid the trade union difficulties that a partial run-down brings.

Multiplant firms rationalize by closing the least efficient units. Watts (1974) discusses four rationalization strategies for multiplant firms, all of which are currently relevant: (1) concentrating production of particular products at different sites ('specialization'); (2) concentrating production on fewer sites ('concentration and partial disinvestment'); (3) concentrating all production on a green field site ('complete disinvestment and green field site'); (4) a mix of strategies. As multiplant firms increasingly become multinationals, location is not restricted to the United Kingdom and becomes flexible on a global scale. Holland (1976) has suggested that part of the location change of recent years is due to the multinationals' product cycle. The 'trial and error' period which demands labour skills needs a central location and is restricted to the home market. But in the 'growth' period labour demands fall and skills are not needed, which results in location in a development area to sell abroad. This in turn results in the 'production-line' period. As profitability from the domestic market falls the company goes multinational and further dispersal occurs (Holland, 1976). As restructuring of British capitalism has taken place many firms have entered the 'growth' and 'production-line' periods and since they no longer need skilled labour they go to Development Areas where cheap green-field sites are available and where the expense of rebuilding in already expensive inner city sites, which are honeycombed with power lines and sewers, and zoning (conforming uses) regulations, is foregone.

Furthermore, access to markets is no longer as important as it was. Keeble (1976) has pointed out that transport costs often no longer play an important part in a location choice, especially for manufacturing firms. Transport costs are now only 4 to 5 per cent of all manufacturing costs. The building of the motorway system has emphasized this trend, as has the container revolution. The general switch of British industry to a more export-oriented strategy has only hastened the demise of the locational advantage enjoyed by the inner city. Thus, Hoare (1977) has shown that a port location now has little to do with export generation. All this makes an inner area location much less attractive.

In both inner Manchester and inner Merseyside the employment dominance of multiplant firms has increased considerably—from 45 per cent to 51 per cent in inner Manchester from 1966 to 1972 and from 76 per cent to 80 per cent from 1966 to 1975 in inner Merseyside (however, there was still an absolute decline in employment in multi-plant firms: Lloyd and Mason, 1977; Dicken and Lloyd, 1977). In 1975 in inner Merseyside 63 per cent of employment in multi-plant firms as a percentage of total employment was in firms with headquarters elsewhere in the U.K., and nearly 8 per cent was in firms with headquarters overseas. Only 10 per cent was in locally headquartered multiplants. The percentage change from 1966 to 1975 was – 70 per cent for locally headquartered firms, –5.6 per cent for British-headquartered firms, but a staggering 599 per cent increase for firms with overseas headquarters: most multi-plant industry was concentrated in large plants. Liverpool is dependent to some degree on port-related industry which is notoriously vulnerable to world trade cycles. Its increasing dependency on multiplant firms, with their dependence on the larger economic trends, does not bode well for the future in that it gives Merseyside an added susceptibility and results in a dual vulnerability, not helped by the probability that in any recession inner-city plants with their older, less efficient capacity will be the first to be closed down. Thus, Coursey (1977b) has shown that in five of the seven major conurbations productivity was below the national average, with only Greater London and Merseyside as exceptions.

Are multi-plant firms more stable and therefore more likely to survive? Dicken and Lloyd (1977) found that 46.2 per cent of closure employment was in single-plant firms and 53.8 per cent in multi-plant firms in inner Merseyside from 1966 to 1975. Of this latter figure, 37.9 per cent was headquartered outside Merseyside, compared with 14.9 per cent locally headquartered. Dicken and Lloyd were able to show that most closures have been in single-plant firms with a small number of employees. They also found that most new starts were of local origin, although in employment terms the split between multi-plant and single-plant firms was about 50/50. Allowing for the fact that single-plant firms can become part of a multi-plant organization, a striking fact emerged: 55 per cent of total employment loss in the inner area was due to contraction in a small number of large, externally headquartered multi-plant firms. Most of this loss was due to rationalization in the face of prevailing economic conditions.

Identification of change of ownership of a plant followed by closures in inner Merseyside also suggested that closure *may* have been caused by change of ownership producing a rationalization to account for about 18 per cent of total job loss in closed plants, and that change of ownership contributed to the rate of job loss. In inner Manchester, Lloyd and Mason were able to suggest that multi-plant companies were more likely to have a significant impact on employment loss by decentralizing. However, as Rake (cited in Keeble, 1976) has found, closure decisions by multi-plant firms in the East Midlands are balanced by acquisitions by takeover and establishment of new branch units.

What of the reasons for relocation given by firms moving? It must be remembered that transfers are not the most important part of the present employment decline, and the geographer's obsession with relocation effects, although easy to understand, has been unfortunate in that it has masked the more serious causes of employment decline—closure and *in situ* contraction.

The classic studies of reasons for relocation are by Luttrell (1962) and Howard (1968). These are now somewhat out of date. The first recent survey, in 1973 by the Department of Industry for the House of Commons Expenditure Committee (cited in Department of Employment, 1977 and Sant, 1975), covered *all* firms opening a new manufacturing plant from 1964 to 1967 in an area they had not manufactured in previously. Most firms gave several reasons why they had considered opening a new plant in a new location, but by far the outstanding one was expansion of output (83 per cent gave this as their major reason). This was followed by inadequate existing premises or site (50 per cent) and labour supply (particularly female labour supply) difficulties at the existing location (40 per cent).

A more recent study by Northcott (1977) surveyed 62 manufacturing firms which moved into special development areas. The main reasons given for deciding to move into a new area were shortage of space and labour at their existing location (49 firms cited this as their main reason), followed by labour considerations, in that some firms had experienced skilled labour shortages (41 firms), and government incentives (30 firms). An interesting variant was that for the 24 overseas companies the primary consideration was markets—the new factory was seen as a base for supplying the Western European market. This is a pattern which is accentuated by Forsyth's (1972) study of American companies locating in Scotland.

The results of surveys are always fraught with risks of overinterpretation, but studies of industrial movement in the U.K. do, at least in part, point towards expansion as a major reason for deciding to relocate (North, 1974; Townroe, 1971). They suggest (but no more) that the considerations which cause established employers actually to move away from inner-city areas (as opposed to the decision as to where to move to) are simply that the need for expansion cannot be satisfied by inner-city locations, and indeed that this same factor also acts as a disincentive to many employers to move back in.

Finally, a common factor which is mentioned as having an adverse effect on both the position of resident firms and on firms that might want to move into the inner city is urban renewal—the competition of local authorities with firms for space. This has been expressed in the use of compulsory purchase orders. Although often mentioned there is in fact little concrete evidence on its effects. An exception is provided by the work of Lloyd and Mason (1977) who cite the case of a projection by Manchester Planning Department that by 1981 more than 25 per cent of all industry in the city would have been touched by compulsory purchase orders, with a consequent employment loss of 27 000 jobs. A further 12 per cent of all manufacturing jobs were expected to be affected by road planning; these effects were expected to be felt mainly by lighter industry dependent upon cheap premises in the CBD 'twilight' zone periphery. Smith (1977a) has noted that redevelopment has two main effects—it reduces the available labour supply and it reduces the population of firms, in particular because 'planners have grossly underestimated the number of employing units located in such areas before redevelopment' (Smith, 1977a, p. 20). Redevelopment in inner Birmingham seemed to slow the rate of births of firms rather than increase the rate of departures, probably due to a deterrence effect. It was more likely to affect manufacturing and the use of over-zealous zoning accentuated this problem.

In addition it is generally agreed that, along with Council planning regulations, the use of industrial development certificates to control location of industry has been over-zealous in most inner cities and has resulted in many of the moves out of the inner city. This has been often to the new industrial estates on the outskirts, in part because room to expand has not been granted. The effect of redevelopment and a severe IDC policy has been that in many inner cities there is now a problem of large areas of land being left derelict, particularly in the Black Country (Carter, 1977) and Liverpool. Thus, in one inner area of Liverpool 11 per cent of the land was vacant, much of it industrial; three-quarters of this land was likely to remain vacant for at least five years (Department of the

Environment, 1977c). In Greater London in 1971 4 per cent of the total land area was vacant (Civic Trust, 1977).

Conclusions

We are now in a position to summarize the broad sweep of the evidence. The gradual movement of manufacturing out of the inner city is the result of a number of factors. One is new production processes, in many cases incorporating technological changes. Longer production runs and a high land to output ratio are required, so that space is substituted for labour (Cameron, 1977a). The second factor is market considerations—the growth of multi-plant firms and multinationals, the extension of product markets, and so on. The third is the reduction in the proportion of costs devoted to transport and communications which cuts down the need for access. The growth of communications has also curtailed the need for face-to-face contracts. The fourth factor is employee decentralization, the relative dispersion of the labour market due to the move to the suburbs (Cameron, 1977a), Lastly, the impact of the present economic recession has, at least, accelerated the process. These effects affect each inner city differently. 'Traditional' inner cities like those of Manchester or Birmingham (Smith, 1977c) are less susceptible to world trade fluctuations and retain the attractions of access: Liverpool, on the other hand, is wide open to such fluctuations. The process of decentralization of manufacturing has been set off in different ways in different cities. In Manchester urban renewal has no doubt given a helping hand; in London competitive bidding by other economic activity with a greater demand for centrality, like offices, has added momentum. In Liverpool 'top-heavy' industrial structure, dependent on very few firms for the bulk of employment, has made the area susceptible to decline. In all cases the causes may be different but the result is the same—the general and absolute decline in U.K. manufacturing has been accompanied by a relative drift of firms away from the inner city.

THE DECLINE IN SERVICE EMPLOYMENT

The focus of this paper is upon the decline in manufacturing industry, which is not meant to deny the importance of the services sector. However, the continuing importance of the manufacturing sector for the U.K. balance of payments can hardly be overstated—services have little effect on this and their ability to grow to fill the gap left by the 'deindustrialization' of the U.K. economy seems limited. In addition, manufacturing is a much more dynamic sector than the services sector 'where both the level and the rate of growth of productivity tend to be much lower' (Singh, 1977, p. 122). In other words the general economic importance of manufacturing to Britain and therefore to the inner cities makes it important that its dynamics are studied in detail, but in employment terms the services sector deserves considerable attention.

Figures 5.6 and 5.7 show the recent trends in employment in the services and manufacturing sectors. The recent dramatic upturn in unemployment figures is so pronounced because until at least 1966 the rise in employment in services to some extent compensated for the loss of jobs in manufacturing, both in the country as a whole and in the inner city: there was a move from manufacturing into services by those coming on to the labour market and presumably also some

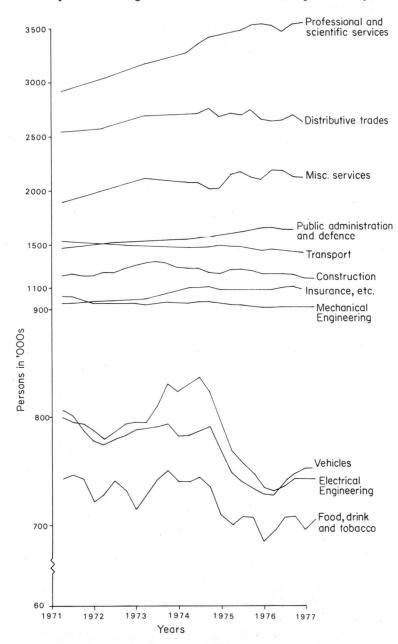

FIGURE 5.6. Employees in Great Britain by industry 1971–1977.
(*Source: Department of Employment Gazette, 1971–1977*)

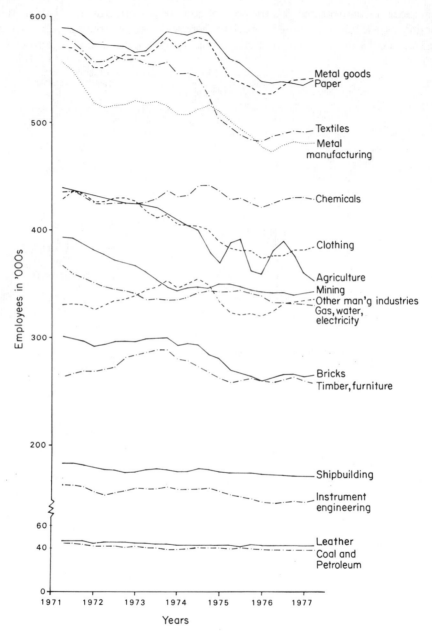

FIGURE 5.7. Employees in Great Britain by Industry (continued).
(*Source: Department of Employment Gazette*)

employment moves across from the declining manufacturing sector into services (Lomas, 1975). However, the general decline of manufacturing employment is no longer counteracted by the growth in service employment, particularly as it is estimated that the labour force will continue to grow in number until about 1983. In any case the inner-city population has not been helped by those overall trends as much as it might because the growth in particular sectors of the service economy has been markedly differential. Thus, from 1966 to 1971 growth in services has mainly occurred in the sectors of insurance, banking, finance, and professional services, scientific services, and public administration and defence, and predominantly the growth in services has been a growth in female and part-time employment. Since the inner-city population consists mainly of unskilled, semi-skilled, and skilled manual workers this growth has affected the inner city less. Furthermore, it seems certain that the inner city has been more affected by the concomitant and pronounced decline in, for instance, the transport and communications sector since at least 1951 and the similar decline since 1961 in the gas, electricity, and water industries, and in the distributive trades and miscellaneous services sector (Harris, 1977). The decline in construction sector employment has also been marked and must have affected the inner-city workforce. Perhaps the only bright cloud on the employment horizon for the inner city has been the rise in female employment (particularly due to increased participation rates by married women) in services which has continued until very recently. But this rise in a sector crucial to the incomes of many inner-city households has probably been partially offset by the growth of part-time employment and a general, if limited, increase in productivity. Thus the trends in service employment of the last twenty-five years paint a grim picture for the inner city for they reveal a workforce there which is often the most vulnerable to the trends in the economy as a whole. This is made no better by the indirect influence of the decline in job replacement—in times of recession fewer jobs are created. The differential trends in service employment have been documented for Leeds by Allen and Campbell (1976), but general or specific studies are in short supply.

Townsend (1977) has considered services employment in inner cities in some detail. Figure 5.8 shows the make-up of employment in some British cities and conurbations by standard industrial classification. In all cases except Sheffield the dependence on services is far greater within the cities than in the conurbations as a whole. Townsend suggests that a characterization of inner-city services as a ring of varied, locationally and organizationally, services around the CBD is in order for most British cities and that these 'blue-collar' services are subject to the same problems as manufacturing industry in the inner city (structural reduction in employment and decentralization from the inner area), as opposed to the traditionally 'white-collar' services based in offices and shops. Such blue-collar services (which Townsend, 1977, divided into 'depot' functions, repair functions, and 'supply' functions) have received almost no academic attention. Townsend also suggests that their decline is, along with manufacturing decline, one of the main reasons for employment decline in the inner city, particularly in Liverpool and perhaps also in Newcastle.

Lomas (1975) showed that in 1973 only 29.8 per cent of the unemployed in Greater London registered as manufacturing unemployed, while 69.8 per cent registered as service industry unemployed—a proportion which reflected almost

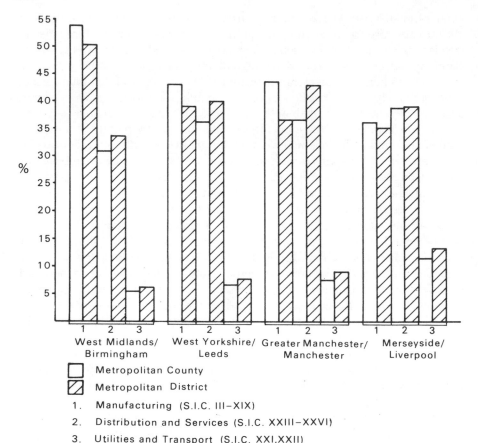

FIGURE 5.8. Metropolitan counties residents in service employment.
(*Source:* Townsend, 1977)

exactly the broad employment structure of Greater London. Almost no work has been carried out on the employment dynamics of the service industries. Yet whereas in 1929 less than 10 per cent of Batley's workforce was employed in services (including construction) by 1971 the figure was 40 per cent (Community Development Project, 1977a). Much the same increase has been evident in other inner areas and the situation in blue-collar services presumably has been made worse by public sector cutbacks. A large and specific comparative study of services employment in British inner cities is called for.

THE CONSEQUENCES OF DECLINE IN MANUFACTURING AND BLUE-COLLAR SERVICES: THE RISE IN INNER-CITY UNEMPLOYMENT

The rise in inner-city unemployment has paralleled the national trends in unemployment. As we shall see there is no conclusive evidence to suggest any particular 'inner city component' at work. Rather the concentration of particular groups of the population, both in terms of skills and age, means that what might be seen as an inherently spatial variation is in fact a differential organization of skill and age reflected in a spatial location.

It will be assumed that *registered* unemployment is a valid measure of total unemployment and that the proportion of registered unemployed does not vary spatially, temporally, or between groups. Recent radical papers by Taylor (1976) and Evans (1977) question all these assumptions and suggest that variation in registered unemployment rates 'between different regions or at different times cannot be used by applied economists to test theories of the labour market or of regional development without qualification, since these variations may represent differences in the proportions registered, and not real differences in the number of employed' (Evans, 1977, p. 193). However, the trends in unemployment still seem to be valid, in which case the registered figures can at least be taken as pointers to labour market processes.

It will be assumed further that unemployment figures are a reliable guide to the number of persons wishing to obtain work, despite arguments over who should and who should not be classed as unemployed, over the inclusion of school-leavers (Wood, 1972), over the inclusion of those unsuitable for full-time work (Brittan, 1975), over who is and who is not 'short-term' unemployed, over who is and who is not 'voluntarily' unemployed (Boulet and Bell, 1972), and over fraudulent claims. The usual criticisms are that the number of unemployed is overestimated, but some think that it is underestimated (Evans, 1977; Field, 1977).

That the problem of inner city unemployment is serious is not a controversial point. Lomas (1975) has shown that 'major' redundancies in inner London (that is from firms with more than twenty employees) accounted for the loss of 118 251 jobs from 1966 to 1973, and if smaller firms are added on (and they may constitute anywhere from a further 30 to 50 per cent of this total) probably 200 000 jobs lost in that time, of which 140 000 were in manufacturing, and nearly all the rest in basic services.

We have noted the trend in employment composition—the move from manufacturing to services—and the general decline in labour demand. We have also noted the general characteristics of economic decline and the effect on the industrial equilibrium of the inner city areas. The result is a level of unemployment in the inner cities far above that found in, for instance, the outer areas of cities (with exceptions that will be noted). Figure 5.1 shows unemployment from 1961 to 1976. The unemployment rates in cities tend to reflect this rate, but also accentuate it. Nationally, between 1966 and 1977 the number registered as unemployed rose from 1.5 per cent of the adult working population to over 6 per cent.

But the problem is not just one of the unemployed, it is also one of low pay. In mid-1977 1½ million people were officially classed as low paid. Fiegehen, Lansley, and Smith, (1977, p. 112) estimated that in 1971 2.6 million individuals lived in households receiving net normal incomes below the current level of supplementary benefits, and they described this as 'the amount of poverty that is unacceptable by contemporary standards'. In 1964 the poorest 10 per cent of male manual workers earned 71.6 per cent of average (medium) earnings: by 1974 that figure was 61.6 per cent (the same percentage as in 1896). There is also the problem of supplementary benefit while unemployed. In 1967 the supplementary benefit scale reached its peak, being equivalent to 20.1 per cent of a male manual worker's average earnings, but by 1975 the figure was at 17.5 per cent (Community Development Project, 1977b).

The 1960s saw a number of large firms going out of business in the inner cities. Thus, in Canning Town from 1966 to 1972 P. & O. ship repair cut 4 000 jobs and Tate & Lyle sugar refining a further 2 400: three-quarters of the total job loss (24 000) was from just six companies. Similarly, in Saltley 8 400 jobs were lost between 1966 and 1974, three-quarters of the loss being in just two firms. Thus the impact of redundancy was always at its most severe in inner cities, particularly in the areas like Canning Town or inner Liverpool which still had a particular dependency on a few firms (Community Development Project, 1977a).

The results of this kind of wastage can be seen by reference to the inner area studies (Department of the Environment, 1977b, 1977c, 1977d, 1977e). In Small Heath, Birmingham since the late 1950s about 40 per cent of jobs seem to have been lost, and this was larger than the population change in the area. In 1961, according to Census figures, the unemployment rate was 1.16 times that of the city; by 1966 it was 1.35 and by 1971 it was 1.53 times the rate of the city (Department of the Environment, 1977d). But from 1974 to 1976 the number of wholly unemployed adult males increased by 1.34 per cent. In fact the rate of unemployment was not particularly high in 1971 at 9 per cent or in 1974 at 8 per cent, but in the present recession it has seen levels of 20 per cent, which is far higher than Birmingham as a whole.

In the Liverpool area the risk of being unemployed is about four times as great if a person lives in the inner city. The rate for the city for male workers was 8 per cent in 1971, for the inner city 11 per cent, and for some areas went as high as 20 per cent. By 1977 the rate for the city was 12 per cent, suggesting an inner-city 'rate' of *at least* 15 per cent. For two streets in Liverpool, Dennehy and Sullivan (1977) observed an unemployment rate of 17.4 per cent in 1976. There was a net loss of manufacturing employment from the Liverpool Exchanges (which is mainly an inner-city area) of 6 300 jobs from 1961 to 1971 compared with a growth of 26 000 jobs in the outer areas. The drop in services was just as pronounced. In total the Liverpool Exchanges are a lost 50 000 jobs. The loss from the city itself was greater still—a net loss of 28 000 workers in transport, construction, and utilities from 1961 to 1971, mainly from the docks and railways. There was a corresponding fall in wholesale and retail distribution of 21 000 jobs, mainly as a consequence of the loss of purchasing power from job loss (Department of Employment, 1977). From 1971 to 1975 the differential decline of jobs in Liverpool was 14 per cent for the inner area, 6 per cent for the outer areas, and 7 per cent for the city as a whole (Hubbard and Attenburrow, 1977).

In Greater London from 1961 to 1971 at least a quarter of a million jobs were lost to the city—10 per cent of all jobs and 25 per cent of manufacturing jobs but, as we have seen, at least 200 000 of these were lost from inner areas. The metropolitan area of Greater London saw a rise in the rate of unemployment from 1.5 per cent in 1971 to over 4 per cent in 1977; in Merseyside the corresponding figures were 4.7 per cent and 12 per cent. Thus, although the rates differ between parts of the country (Merseyside is particularly bad), the rise in the level of unemployment was 'surprisingly uniform' (Lomas, 1975, p. 15). Although, theoretically, rates of unemployment cannot be calculated for inner areas because they do not form labour-market areas (Oakeshott, 1975, was not even able to obtain coherent labour-market areas for Greater London) they are sometimes calculated and do form useful estimates. Thus the London average of 4.7 per cent in 1971 compared with the 5.5 per cent of Lewisham, 6.5 per cent of Newham, 5.7 per cent of Hackney, 7 per cent in Lambeth and Southwark, and 8.6 per cent of Tower Hamlets (Lomas, 1975). In April 1976 the London average for male unemployment was 5.4 per cent (compared with the South-east's 3.8 per cent, and the country's 5.9 per cent): in Canning Town it was 9.2 per cent, in Poplar 15 per cent, and in Stepney 13.4 per cent (Lapping, 1977). The Brixton employment exchange area, along with three others, has had unemployment rates consistently more than double the national average since 1971.

Nevertheless, as Figure 5.9 shows, the employment situation is not necessarily any worse in the inner cities than in other areas of the country, at least in terms of employment rates. Indeed the highest rates tend to be in peripheral areas. The pattern for October 1977 reflects the general evening out in employment rates over the country which has been brought about by improvement in the North, North-east, Scotland and South Wales and the deterioration in the positions of the East of England and the West Midlands (Keeble, 1977; Salt, 1976). The Northern Region Strategy Team (1976a) puts the relative improvement in the North down to an increased demand for labour due to a relative catching up in share of public sector employment, a greater increase in consumer spending power, and a 'relatively smaller decline in manufacturing employment'. We can guess that similar reasons have helped the other improving regions. However, as Campbell (1977b) has pointed out, it is too early as yet to interpret the relatively small figures involved in this trend as a reversal of the classic centre–periphery patterns of manufacturing (employment) growth of the late 1960s. Regional disparities in unemployment are wider in 1977 than at any time since 1947, although rates can be misleading since in some areas with a small labour force a small rise in unemployment can become a large rise in the local rate. Thus, Greater London may have a lower unemployment rate than many areas of Britain, but in terms of absolute numbers it has more unemployed persons than the whole of Scotland (Department of Employment, 1977). Rates indicate the sharp point of the problem, but to gain an idea of extent the absolute numbers employed have to be examined. The situation of Clydeside or Merseyside then becomes truly horrifying. In 1977 Clydeside had a high unemployment rate—usually over 10 per cent—with well over 100 000 workers unemployed.

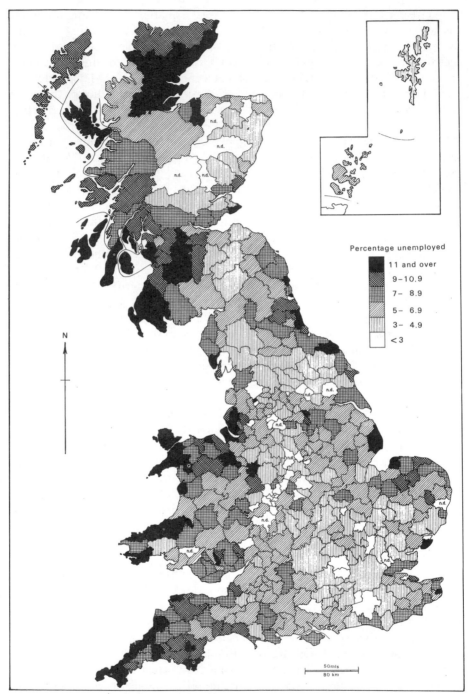

FIGURE 5.9. Local unemployment in Britain, October 1977. (*Source*: Department of Employment figures (unpublished))

The plight of the inner cities is then easy to locate. In April 1976 seven conurbations (Greater London, Central Clydeside, Merseyside, South-east Lancashire, Tyneside, the West Midlands, and West Yorkshire) accounted for 40 per cent of all registered unemployment in Great Britain; Greater London by itself accounted for 12 per cent of all unemployment in Great Britain (Department of Employment, 1977). It is the large absolute numbers of unemployed that characterize the inner cities rather than their rates of unemployment, although when these coincide, as in Tyneside, Clydeside, and Merseyside, the situation becomes extreme. In October 1977 Greater London had 167 130 persons unemployed and a rate of 4.3 per cent; Birmingham 46 066 (6.8 per cent); Leeds 18 978 (6.1 per cent); Sheffield 13 300 (6.7 per cent); Liverpool 77 852 (12.1 per cent); Manchester 45 108 (6.6 per cent); Tyneside 38 619 (9.1 per cent) and Glasgow 52 035 (9.7 per cent). It is to the analysis of these hostage populations that we now turn, realizing that analysis of these populations, while not providing *causes* for the present unemployment (they lie in the pattern of excess demand for labour), does provide a description of the population subgroups particularly at risk when unemployment is high nationally.

Unskilled labour

Most unemployment in the inner cities reflects loss of manufacturing jobs and blue-collar service jobs, most of them unskilled or semi-skilled. As we have seen, the decline of the manufacturing sector has eroded the skill base of the inner city. Many of the workers in inner city manufacturing were 'skilled', but when, in particular, a traditional industry dies or relocates the worker may find himself or herself with a skill which is obsolete. Thus, Massey and Meegan (1976, 1977) found, in their study of electrical engineering and electronics, that most employment loss was of a skilled nature and that the bulk of the loss was craft labour and was absolute. The conventional wisdom is that only the unskilled are going out of work but, as we shall show, that is only partially the case. The reorganization of the manufacturing sector is towards mass production processes and mechanization. It is therefore also a swing towards unskilled labour: from 1961 to 1971 there was a fall in the total number of skilled and semi-skilled workers of 990 000, mainly due to the obsolescence of particular skills, demanding a reclassification by the workers themselves.

This means that the rise in the proportion of unskilled and semi-skilled workers cannot all be laid at the door of relative population effects like the outmigration of skilled workers or the inmigration of unskilled workers. Undoubtedly these have taken place, but so has 'deskilling' of inner city residents. Table 5.2 shows the change in skill structure in five Community Development Project areas from 1966 to 1971. All show a relative rise in the unskilled and some absolute rise. These figures can be compared with those from the inner area studies; in 1971, inner Liverpool, for example, included 19 per cent of workers who were unskilled compared with 10 per cent in the rest of the city.

TABLE 5.2. Change in skills of local residents for five Community Development Project areas. 1966/1971

	Per cent skilled		Per cent semi-skilled		Per cent unskilled		Per cent residents in local workplace in 1966
	1966	1971	1966	1971	1966	1971	
Batley	39.5	38.9	21.9	19.7	9.8	9.3	52.0
Benwell	42.6	42.2	19.6	15.4	14.8	17.1	31.4
Canning Town	34.9	32.4	21.7	18.9	25.0	24.0	48.0
North Shields	40.0	40.2	21.6	18.9	16.0	18.1	58.8
Saltley	44.5	37.4	26.6	28.7	16.0	20.3	(36.0) 1961

Source: Community Development Project (1977a, p. 38).

From 1961 to 1971 the total number of jobs for men in Liverpool fell by 18 per cent, and yet the number of unskilled manual jobs and semi-skilled manual jobs fell by 25 per cent and 24 per cent respectively, while personal services jobs fell by 41 per cent. The inner Liverpool employment exchange in 1976 had more than 60 per cent of its clients classified as unskilled although at least 30 per cent of these would at some time have been called 'skilled'. The reason is, of course, that the skilled new to the register tend to or have to downgrade their classification in order to take advantage of the wider employment opportunities thereby offered (Department of the Environment, 1977c). Small Heath in Birmingham had similar troubles. In 1974 only about 22 per cent of jobs there were skilled, 58 per cent were semi-skilled, and 20 per cent were unskilled. In 1971 the unskilled and semi-skilled constituted 38 per cent of the workforce in Birmingham.

In London Lomas (1975) has looked at the occupational structure of the city in some detail. An inner city is usually understood in the literature to have a large proportion of unskilled workers, but analysis of the 1971 Census data showed the number of less skilled men to be declining in all London boroughs and furthermore, that 'the unskilled and by implication the less-educated and the lower paid have *not* become concentrated in inner London, (Hamnett, 1976b, p. 269). As a percentage of all economically active men their proportion has decreased from 41 per cent in 1961 to 37 per cent in 1971, in Greater London as a whole, while in the inner areas their proportions have decreased from 46 per cent to 44 per cent in the same time period. Only in the 'middle ring' of London are less skilled workers becoming proportionally more important. However, the evidence did 'not point to any evidence of polarisation' (Lomas, 1975, p. 9). Professional and managerial workers were growing in numbers in all areas of London, only the skilled manual workers were decreasing significantly in number. Less skilled workers were increasing in absolute numbers in outer London, but relatively their proportion fell from 38 per cent in 1961 to 31 per cent in 1971. These findings are borne out by Hamnett who shows the existence of 'a clear upward shift in the socio-economic composition of inner London's economically active male population' (Hamnett, 1976b, p. 264), which may be indicative of a structural change in the skill structure of the labour force in inner London, and may be a process which is operating on a smaller scale elsewhere.

There is pressing evidence that it is lack of skills which does provide the foremost factor in 'explaining' unemployment. Since 1959 over half the males unemployed have been registered as general labourers (Burghes, 1977), and the Department of Employment has carried out surveys for a number of years in which the main labouring occupations always account for more than 50 per cent of unemployed whatever level total unemployment has reached. At higher levels of unemployment the percentage of general labourers tends to be relatively less but absolutely more. The 1971 General Household Survey showed 27 per cent of the economically active to be unskilled or semi-skilled (Burghes, 1977). In terms of vacancies the labourer is also disadvantaged; Sinfield (1976) has shown that over the fifteen years from 1959 to 1974 there was one vacancy to every four labourers, while vacancies for other categories often exceeded those out of work. In 1974 the ratio of unskilled men to job vacancies was 13 : 1 (compared with a ratio of 1.5 : 1 for all other categories) and Burghes (1977) has shown that this ratio increased to 56 : 1 by 1976 (a situation that is ten times worse than for any other group).

Spatially we have seen the specific effects. What of the general picture? Gripaios (1977d) looked at seven conurbations, using data from the 1975 Department of the Environment study, and found that semi- and unskilled workers as a percentage of economically active males in the inner areas reached a figure that, on average, was 2.5 percentage points higher than in the outer area, and 4.5 higher than in the rest of the region. Metcalf and Richardson (1976) found that variations in male residential unemployment rates between the thirty-two London boroughs were in the main due to skill, marital status, age, and race, a result corroborated for the seventy-eight county boroughs in England by Metcalf (1975). Another main relationship to emerge was again the 'coincidence of high overall unemployment rates and large percentages of the labour force in the unskilled category' (Department of Employment, 1977, p. 51), particularly in the three worst areas—Tyneside, Merseyside, and central Clydeside. The reasons for this higher propensity to unemployment among the unskilled have been enumerated by the Department of Employment (1977) as the fact that in any recession employers will always tend to hoard skilled labour and lay off unskilled, that the skilled can carry out unskilled jobs but not vice versa, that the unskilled are more likely to be on the register because the level of benefit is higher for them in proportion to anticipated net earnings, and that, due to narrowing pay differentials, the cost of employing an unskilled worker relative to a skilled worker has gone up.

The major reason for the high rate of unemployment in the inner area is almost certainly the number of unskilled or semi-skilled workers there. As a general rule it is true that where there are proportionately more unskilled there will be proportionately more unemployed (Cheshire, 1977). Thus, according to Evans and Russell (1976), in 1971 the natural unemployment rate for the unskilled was

9.4 per cent when the national figure was about 3 per cent. By itself such a figure explains at least part of the 'spatial' variation in urban employment rates.

Age

As a rough guide the older the worker the longer the period out of work and the more inferior the next job found. Older members of the workforce, especially those over 50, are more likely to be unemployed and more likely to remain so for a long duration. This is a trend which has been rising since 1963 (Bowers, 1974, 1977). For men over 60, who comprise 8 per cent of the labour force, unemployment is always twice as high as the national rate, and sometimes reaches 20 per cent (Burghes, 1977). In 1976 the under-20s and over-50s made up 36 per cent of the labour force but 42 per cent of the unemployed.

For the inner cities, however, age does not seem to be as important as skill in producing inner city unemployment. Metcalf and Richardson's (1976) regression analysis of London unemployment suggests that 'ceteris paribus, neither young or old workers are more likely to be unemployed than prime age males' (Metcalf and Richardon, 1976, p. 215). The analysis by Gripaios (1977d) of seven major conurbations bears this out. The percentage of unemployed males aged more than 44 was indeed lower in the inner areas than elsewhere, although the percentage of unemployed males in the 18–24 age group was higher. Youth unemployment is in any case very high at present in Britain as a whole, even allowing for much higher registration rates among 18–24-year-olds (Oakeshott, 1975). In 1976 the ratio of the youth unemployment rate to the adult rate was over 3:1, and was particularly high among the young New Commonwealth population, although the reason for their unemployment is probably because they are largely unskilled relatively to the young population as a whole. Although youth employment is serious (in Liverpool it was already 17 per cent for those under 18 in 1971) it is at least a volatile situation—in 1976 in the 18–24 age group the proportion of unemployed men who had been without a job for a least a year was just over 6 per cent; in the over-55 age group this proportion reached more that one-third. It is perhaps this last age group we should be more concerned about since age discrimination in employment terms is far greater in Britain than in, for instance, the United States, Italy, or Sweden (Sinfield, 1976),

Race

The immigrant community is particularly disadvantaged by the present recession because so many of its workers are unskilled and employed in manufacturing (in London, 40 to 50 per cent in 1971 compared with 29 per cent for the male workforce as a whole). Not all inner-city areas have sizeable immigrant communities of course; Birmingham and London have but Tyneside does not. Precise figures on the problem are hard to come by. There are no reliable estimates on total numbers of blacks economically active, although the Department of Employment does provide quarterly figures on unemployed minority group workers (for a summary see Department of Employment, 1975). The result is that *rates* cannot be estimated. However, an analysis of minority group workers (Keys and Thrift, 1978) shows that the proportional increase in unemployment among minority group workers was very much higher. While total unemployment has increased by over 120 per cent since 1974, the number of coloured workers unemployed has increased by 350 per cent (Manpower Services Commission Review and Plan, 1977). This rapid increase follows a period from 1970 to 1974 when unemployment rates were broadly similar to the population as a whole (Smith, 1976) and suggests that the minority group community is particularly susceptible to the economic recession, functioning as a marginal group of labour. The minority group population also has a much younger age structure and therefore the rise in youth unemployment must also affect this group more.

The effects on the inner-city areas with large minority group populations are that the rate of unemployment will be much higher. Smith (1976) found that 58 per cent of Pakistani men and 32 per cent of West Indians were doing semi-skilled or unskilled jobs compared with only 18 per cent of whites, mainly due to lack of skills. Thus, in May 1976 in Small Heath 28 per cent of the unemployed were immigrants (Department of Employment, 1977). Unemployment is particularly high among black youth and this is without doubt a serious problem (Figuera, 1976): in a survey carried out in the Edge Hill area of Birmingham six out of ten black 18-year-olds were found to be without a job.

Sex

One of the most prominent features of the last 25 years has been the changing role of women in the workforce. This is mainly due to increased participation rates of married women, particularly in the 35–44 age group. But with this increased participation has come increased unemployment. In 1970 women accounted for 38 per cent of employees in employment: in 1976, 41 per cent. But unemployment in the same time period increased from 14 per cent to 25 per cent, and trebled in absolute terms (Burghes, 1977). With this increase in participation has also come an increased tendency to register as unemployed. Thus, while until the end of 1974 men outnumbered women on the register by five to one, this ratio has now decreased to three to one (see Evans, 1977, for the very real problems of analysis this gives). Most of the increase in female labour has been in the clerical and secretarial sectors; the number of women in manual jobs has fallen quite substantially. However, 15 per cent of all women workers were still engaged in engineering and allied trades in 1975 in the Birmingham conurbation. In 1975 in the West Midlands region 862 000 women were in employment, representing nearly 40 per cent of all employees. This rate was similar to those in the conurbation and Britain as a whole. *But* nearly 40 per cent of those women were employed for less than 30 hours per week (Crompton and Penketh, 1977). Much female labour is part-time.

In 1971 about 50 per cent of married women worked in Great Britain as a whole; in Greater London the figure was 56 per cent and in Lambeth/Stockwell in inner London 64 per cent (Department of the Environment, 1977e). The recession hits hardest at immigrant women whose rate of unemployment is often very high compared to that of white women, particularly, as Smith (1976) has shown, because a larger proportion work (except for the case of Moslem Asian women). Between February 1976 and February 1977 black male unemployment remained stable, while, by contrast, black female unemployment increased by 24 per cent, particularly among females in the 18–24 age group. Being young, black, and female is becoming a passport to unemployment.

There are many other subgroups of the hostage population—the disabled, for instance. They function as a marginal labour force, their level of unemployment always following an exaggerated version of the national or local trends: unemployment among the disabled increased from 11.3 per cent in February 1973 to 14.1 per cent in October 1977, although 76 per cent of people registered as disabled are in fact considered as fit for work (Burghes, 1977).

The frequency and duration of unemployment

There is still very little evidence on repeated spells of unemployment in the British workforce, although two Department of Employment surveys (cited in Burghes, 1977), one in 1961 and the second in 1973, suggest that recurring unemployment has declined. In 1961, 43 per cent of men and 40 per cent of women had suffered two or more spells of unemployment in the preceding year; by 1973 the proportion was 28 per cent in both cases. However, whereas in 1961 28 per cent of men had had no job in the previous year, by 1971 this figure had increased to 44 per cent. Thus, while recurring unemployment has declined there are more long-term unemployed; once unemployed, the probability of staying unemployed is now much higher. This is borne out by Department of Employment surveys on characteristics of the unemployed, and Gripaios (1977d) has pointed out that in the seven conurbation inner areas he studied more hard-core unemployed *and* more short-period unemployed are now in evidence.

Cripps and Tarling (1974) looked at unemployment duration from 1932 to 1973. From the 1950s a general trend towards lengthening duration of unemployment can be discerned, with upward variations around the trend during times when the number of unemployed is high, so that during the present recession, if past experience is valid, duration of unemployment will have increased again. Variations in probabilities per day of leaving the register were 'closely associated with personal characteristics such as age, physical and mental condition and occupation' (Cripps and Tarling, 1974 p. 310), a finding also borne out by MacKay and Reid (1972).

Spatial variation in duration of unemployment has been examined recently by MacGregor (1977). He compared intra-urban variation in duration of unemployment in the notorious Ferguslie Park council estate in Paisley, near Glasgow, with Paisley as a whole, and found that 'on average the duration of completed spells of unemployment was almost 50 per cent higher in the Ferguslie Park sample' (MacGregor, 1977, p. 303). From this conclusion it is suggested that actually residing in the Ferguslie Park estate means that workers suffer a reduction in their labour market chances which 'traps' them in the estate, a conclusion also reached about council estates in Liverpool by Webber (1975).

In Small Heath only 26 per cent of the increasingly susceptible 18- and 19-year-old males registered as unemployed in June 1975 had been out of work more than three months. But by July 1976 this proportion had risen to 57 per cent. Their actual numbers had increased by 670 per cent and the ratio of this group to all adult males unemployed over three months from $2\frac{1}{2}$ to 7 per cent: by July 1976 more than 56 per cent of all men registered as unemployed had been without a job for over six months, compared with less than 42 per cent two years earlier (Department of Employment, 1977). But the paucity of data on inner-city employment duration is striking, as is any analysis of *flows* on and off the register (Lancaster, 1976).

Service employment and low pay

Apart from high rates of unemployment it might be reasonably conjectured that inner-city areas also contain a large absolute number of low-paid workers. This situation may have been made worse by the drift of employment from manufacturing to services, and the two are inseparable: indeed we cannot ignore the part of the job market which now often accounts for a major part of the employment in inner areas. Thus manufacturing accounted for 52 per cent of employment (male and female) in Small Heath in 1971, but services accounted for another 36 per cent, while in Lambeth the situation reverses with manufacturing accounting for 17 per cent of employment and services for 75 per cent in 1971 (Department of Employment, 1977). In case the crisis of the inner cities is presented exclusively as a crisis of manufacturing industry it should be remembered that, despite the heavy redundancies in manufacturing in many inner-city areas, the unemployed now arise *mainly* from the service sector: in Greater London 39.8 per cent of the unemployed have registered as manufacturing unemployed and 69.8 per cent as services unemployed (Lomas, 1975), and a Lambeth inner area study report (Department of the Environment, 1974b) found that the industrial structure of that area, particularly the large proportion of men in low-paid service industries, accounted for much of the low pay situation. The lack of manufacturing jobs has undoubtedly led to men having to move to service or construction jobs which are normally less skilled, and often less well paid; thus a man's income falls. And then, in an economic recession such as that of recent years, these jobs are the most swiftly forfeited. A three-stage unemployment process for inner-city male unemployment might be hypothesized. The first step is one in which men are pushed out of work in a manufacturing industry, for instance one of the traditional industries, and due to the decline in the supply of that kind of work and a lack of skill to apply to any other job are forced into the next stage which is to take lower-paid, often unskilled jobs in services from which they are often pushed by the economic decline into unemployment of a more permanent nature.

In some ways low pay, as we shall see, is a more serious problem for the inner city than is unemployment, which can be seen as the final expression in a merciless equation. In Small Heath the average household income, according to a survey carried out in 1974, was £38 per week: the average for the West Midlands at that time was £41 and for the U.K. as a whole £40. Even more importantly there were very few incomes over £38—the distribution grouped tightly around that figure. Such low wages are probably due to a combination of lack of relevant skills mingled with services jobs. The Lambeth labour market study showed that in 1973 the average wage for manual males was £34 per week, £7, or $17\frac{1}{2}$ per cent, below the national average. The non-manual males' average wage was almost exactly the same and was even further below the national average than the manual male's wage. By contrast manual women and non-manual women's rates were on or above the national average, showing the benefit of London wages (Department of the Environment, 1974d).

It must be remembered that a perhaps more realistic figure than wages is the household income of particular groups which takes into account the effect of working wives. Tables in Krishna-Murty (1977) show some indication that inner London borough households earn less on average than those in outer boroughs: further information can be found in O'Cleireacain (1974), Jaroszek (1976), and, in terms of very low-income families, in S.H.A.C. (1976). Recently, however, there seems to have been 'a move towards greater equality of earnings between (inner areas) and the rest of the conurbation with the notable exceptions of the inner areas of London and S.E. Lancashire' (Foreman-Peck and Gripaios, 1977, p. 402).

THE 'TRAPPED' AND 'MISMATCH' HYPOTHESES: SPATIAL REFLECTIONS OR SPATIAL CAUSES?

All three of the inner area studies (Department of the Environment, 1977a, 1977b, 1977c) expound some variant of the 'trapped' hypothesis. Briefly, this suggests that the large numbers of unskilled workers in inner cities have become caught in the inner areas as industry has moved to the suburbs. These are now left stranded without jobs in a vicious circle of unemployment and immobility.

The supportive evidence for this hypothesis is not really forthcoming. Often the high unemployment rates associated with inner city areas are quoted but these, by themselves, do not verify a hypothesis. Evans and Russell (1976) have rejected the 'trapped' hypothesis on at least two grounds by examining the variation in unemployment in parliamentary constituencies in the South-east. First they found almost no more variation in unemployment rates of the unskilled than of other groups of workers, and secondly, after taking into account skill differences in each constituency area, there were systematic differences in unemployment at all skill levels in some areas, especially in inner London, which Evans and Russell suggest are caused by the high rates of inmigration of young people. Metcalf and Richardson (1976) also reject the 'trapped' hypothesis in London, first because they are unable to find an association between the proportion of a borough's labour force (by residence) working in manufacturing in 1966 and unemployment in 1971, as would be expected, and secondly because boroughs experiencing a large number of redundancies from 1966 to 1969 had a relatively low unemployment rate in 1971, which fact is attributable to a diverse range of factors, but not to workers being 'trapped'. Cheshire (1977), looking at the change in unemployment in London from 1966 to 1971, shows that against a background of suburbanization of higher socio-economic groups from 1966 to 1971 relatively more unemployment was suffered by the higher groups in the Greater London area. He suggests that this 'is best explained by a changing pattern of spatial demand for labour' (a suggestion with which this writer concurs) in which 'the most highly skilled suffered relatively worse because the demand for their services in the G. L. C. area was falling relative to the demand for them nationally', even taking into account 'a composition effect' whereby 'the higher the skill level the larger the proportion of the nationally economically active who live in London' and therefore 'the higher will be the London weight in the national rate' (Cheshire, 1977, p. 23). If people are 'trapped' it is because they are trapped in poor housing or in local authority housing where few transfers take place.

The mode of analysis of employment and unemployment described by studies of inner areas of all kinds and frozen in the urban land-use models of Alonso, Muth, and others is part of the continuing highly ideological tradition of spatial fetishism whereby problems of society become problems of space, somehow embedded in the qualities of space itself. But the spatial variation in levels of unemployment is not due to spatial variation acting as a causal agent.

Another aspect of the spatial fetish concerns the supposed 'mismatch' between certain skills and the vacancies for them in particular local labour markets (see for instance, the Lambeth Study, Department of the Environment, 1977f). If such a 'mismatch' does occur it is a symptom and not a cause which could just as well be due to an overall drop in excess demand for labour in the economy, and to associated local differences in excess demand for labour, caused by the skill structure. As we have seen, different skill levels have differential employment rates. Cheshire (1977) has pointed out that from 1965 to 1976 the unemployment rate of the unskilled changed by 2.5 points for every 1 per cent change in aggregate unemployment, while the professional and managerial rate increased only by 0.5 point for every 1 per cent change. By age group a similar pattern can be seen with the unemployment rate of younger and older workers usually rising more rapidly as demand falls than for workers in other age groups. At any time, therefore, during a period of rising unemployment differential spatial mismatches will occur dependent upon the population mix in a particular area. Lack of a particular skill does not 'cause' these, rather the fall in the level of excess demand does (Cheshire, 1977). And it follows that the usual remedy given for a mismatch—to give unskilled workers job skills through vocational training—does not necessarily guarantee a skilled job.

There is very little evidence of a spatial employment effect, although there is indisputable evidence of spatial 'reflects'. This point emerges again and again in the literature. Both Metcalf (1975) and Metcalf and Richardson (1976) reject the idea (although not entirely) of 'the importance of area characteristics in explaining unemployment' (Metcalf and Richardson, 1976, p. 217), as does a report on London unemployment (Oakeshott, 1975). The conclusions of the Department of Employment (1977) report, *Employment in Metropolitan Areas*, are worth quoting at length. The report realizes that

> The geographical differences in residential unemployment rates that exist between different parts of the same metropolitan area are directly attributable to other non-geographical differences. For example, inner areas contain higher proportions of unskilled manual workers among their workforces than do other occupational groups regardless of where they are living. Also it seems clear that differences in unemployment rates within or even between metropolitan areas are less serious than other non-geographical differences. The inequality between unskilled manual workers and the remainder of the population in this respect is significantly greater than any geographical inequality.

The report goes on:

> nor is there much evidence to suggest that geographical differences have been widening over time . . . whether the comparisons are between regions or within regions. There is little evidence that the unemployment rate has been worsening relative to the average unemployed rate for the region in which it is located. What evidence there is does not suggest that unemployment rates have been worsening relative to those in other parts. (Department of Employment, 1977, p. 58).

Here the problem is one of evidence. Residential unemployment rates have only been examined in detail for London. Similarly, most of the evidence on unemployment in this paper (and others) is for London, and there is some evidence that geographical differences are important in areas of Merseyside (Webber, 1976) and in Paisley (MacGregor, 1977). This writer suggests that at very small spatial scales (for instance in particular housing estates) there may be significant locational effects, but at any larger spatial scale some doubt must set in.

The answer to this problem will remain elusive simply because hardly any small-area unemployment information or studies over time exist, although an analysis of the Census one kilometre square data did suggest a bundle of higher intercorrelations associated with deprivation at the SMLA area level (Evans, 1977) and the work of Campbell (1975) and Boon (1974) should be noted.

The social and spatial variance in the unemployment rate, it is suggested, is the result of patterns of excess demand for labour (Cheshire, 1977). The characteristics of the unemployed in a particular area reveal little or nothing about the causes of unemployment there. They are, instead, the outcome of long-term trends in the reorganization of British capitalism and their consequent spatial reflections. The apparently dramatic unemployment rates in particular urban areas are the spatial manifestations of differential effects in particular socio-economic groups as the national or regional labour demand falls. Thus, as demand for labour decreases demand for unskilled labour decreases even more. It is to this pattern of excess demand that we now turn.

CHANGES IN THE SPATIAL PATTERN OF DEMAND

At the level of the national or regional economy it is usual to distinguish three types of unemployment which exist concurrently—frictional unemployment, structural unemployment, and demand-deficient unemployment (Dixon and Thirlwall, 1975; Thirlwall, 1969). Following Hughes (1974), unemployment is caused either by the inadequacy of aggregate demand or as the result of the imperfect operation of the labour market. The former is referred to as demand-deficient unemployment; the latter as non-demand-deficient unemployment, and can be divided into frictional and structural unemployment. *Frictional* unemployment is the amount of unemployment existing at the full-employment level and, whether Keynesian or monetarist, this is roughly when aggregate unemployment is just about equal to aggregate unfilled vacancies. Owing to barriers to perfect mobility and lack of information these two will never exactly correspond. Any unemployment in excess of this amount is *demand-deficient* unemployment. Where actual unemployment falls below this amount there is excess demand. Structural unemployment is, in its essentials, a vacancy concept. There are vacancies of the right type to absorb the unemployed and those of the wrong type. Unemployment is *structural* when a worker does not possess the right qualifications to fill a vacancy and frictional when he or she does. If all vacancies were to be of the right type all non-demand-deficient unemployment would be frictional; if of the wrong type it will be structural. In operation these concepts can prove difficult to use (see Cheshire, 1973).

There is considerable evidence that since 1966 the relationship between output and unemployment enshrined in the Phillips curve no longer holds in Britain. Bowers (1976) has looked at the relationships between output and turnover and turnover and unemployment. He found that turnover (and therefore unemployment) in manufacturing was moving in the opposite direction to turnover in the rest of the economy. Thus, manufacturing *employment* fell continuously from 1969, and the rise in overall employment at that time came entirely from outside the manufacturing sector where employment continued to grow until 1971. Thus 'the fall in manufacturing *unemployment* (and more, since it would otherwise have been rising) was brought about in aggregate by a transfer of workers out of the sector'. The brief expansion of the economy at this time 'involved a substantial structural shift of employment away from manufacturing industry' (Bowers, 1976, p. 126). Corroborative evidence for this is provided by the mean duration of male unemployment for older workers which deteriorated sharply relative to that for younger male workers during 1971 and 1972 (Bowers and

Harkness, 1974) as a consequence of their inability to adjust in a period of structural change; 1972 to 1973 was the period of greatest structural shift from manufacturing. Bowers (1976) investigated from 1963 to 1973, however, when male manufacturing employment was static and the employment decline concentrated outside manufacturing. In 1976 the decline in manufacturing employment halted (National Institute for Economic and Social Research, 1977).

What of these trends in terms of demand-deficient, frictional, and structural unemployment categories? We shall look only at trends since 1965, when the recent exceptional rise in unemployment began (Figure 5.1). Various explanations have been offered for the dramatic nature of the rise from 1966 to 1969, as represented by the shift in unemployment relative to vacancies. Thus the shift was due to a mix of the introduction of selective employment tax in September 1966, regional policy, the rundown of public investment programmes, changes in income policy and related changes in worker expenditures, and so on (Bowers, Cheshire and Webb, 1970; Sleeper, 1970). It was due to introduction of the Redundancy Payments Act in December 1965 and earnings-related benefit (Gujarati, 1972). It was also due to a 'shake out' of labour by employers as labour hoarding was reduced (Brown, 1976; Taylor, 1972) or to an increase in the birth rate in the late 1940s, leading to a concomitant rise in 'unexperienced labour' (Foster, 1974). Accepting for the moment that there actually was a shift and not just something going wrong with recording of unemployment and vacancies (but see Evans, 1977; Taylor, 1976) several attempts have been made to calculate levels of demand-deficient, frictional and structural unemployment at the time of the shift.

First, frictional unemployment. Taylor (1976, p. 65) has suggested that the upward trend in the rate of registered unemployment during the period 1953 to 1973 was 'due entirely to the upward trend in frictional unemployment', which rose from almost zero in the period 1953 to 1959 to 2.3 per cent in 1973. Frictional unemployment fluctuated contra-cyclically from 1953 to 1973, which perhaps meant that workers' search activity increased when labour market conditions were favourable. However, in the early 1970s demand-deficient unemployment seemed to become more important, a rise corroborated by Hughes (1974) and Dixon and Thirlwall (1975), who used a different approach to that of Taylor. Structural unemployment has seen a general upward trend from 1963 to 1972 (Hughes, 1974; Dixon and Thirlwall, 1975) but at each downturn in total unemployment the level of structural unemployment is slightly larger than before, suggesting a gradual build-up in this component over time. It would be dangerous to infer too much from these studies, however, which are few in number and do not take into account more recent time periods. The present explanations of increase in frictional unemployment over time are based on length of job search and income incentive to seek a job and do not seem very convincing. Hannah (1977) has suggested that frictional unemployment is anyway much less in inner cities.

The increase in demand-deficient unemployment and the small increase in structural unemployment, both of which have varying regional patterns, suggest, as does much other evidence, that the change in unemployment levels since 1966 is more than partially a function of a drop in aggregate demand (Hannah, 1977) helped by, firstly, an increase in the working population, especially teenagers since 1970 and female labour since 1975 which is expected to be of the order of 2.8 million from 1966 to 1981, and secondly by variations in registration rates. There may also be a small element of increased technological unemployment. Recent noticeable trends have been increased female unemployment (perhaps due to increased female registration) and increased flow on and off the register. This drop in demand is supported by a N.I.E.S.R. survey in 1976 (National Institute for Economic Research, 1976, cited in Hannah, 1977) which showed that *if demand existed* it would be possible, with existing capital capacity, to increase output in manufacturing industry by 7.5 per cent with the existing labour force and hours of work, by about 12.5 per cent with the existing labour force and longer hours of work, and by 20 per cent with labour readily available. There is an unprecedented degree of spare resources, both labour and capital, in the British economy: depending on assumptions, utilization measures show a degree of spare capacity running at 7 14 per cent (Hannah, 1977). The current spatial variations in excess demand for labour suggest the differential spatial impact of this fall in demand as a major factor, mediated by the effect of long-term periods in the labour force as brought out in the skill, age, and sex structure at particular locations.

To this writer a powerful concept not brought out sufficiently in the literature has been the concept of the dual labour market (Doeringer and Piore, 1971). This assumes that there is not one labour market but at least two. One is the 'core' or 'primary' labour market. Here there are high wages, good working conditions, and job security, in the higher echelons of government service or in firms with rigid occupational hierarchies. Such institutions take on people at the bottom of the ladder and they then work their way up within the organization. The external labour market is not important to these people. The prevailing level of unemployment affects only those at the bottom of the ladder where jobs are still insecure. There is therefore a 'secondary' labour market of low wages, poor working conditions, and very little job security, of a marginal workforce which, in a recession in particular, has a high turnover (Bosanquet and Doeringer, 1973). Such jobs are in firms which are more susceptible to closure in times of economic hardship. Averitt's (1968) concept of the dual economy works in well with the concept of a dual labour market. It suggests the British economy as consisting of a hard centre of firms and institutions with secure labour forces surrounded by a soft periphery of firms and institutions with insecure labour forces exposed to current economic vicissitudes and always susceptible to unemployment.

Government measures against unemployment

Table 5.3 tells the story of the remedies that government has operated to combat unemployment; these schemes are described in detail in Field and

TABLE 5.3. Government remedies

Employment measure	Announced and instigated	Number covered in September 1977
Temporary employment subsidy	1975	187 373
Job release scheme	1977	13 641
Job-creation programme	1975	43 593
Work experience programme	1976	20 683
Community industry	1972	4 212
Youth employment subsidy	1975	12 984
(originally recruitment subsidy for school-leavers)		
Job introduction scheme	1977	38
Small firms employment subsidy	1977	893
Training measures		
Training places supported in industry		28 669
Training services agency special courses for young people		1 536
		313 622

Also: help with job search is sometimes given.
Employment transfer scheme (helps workers move).

Source: *Economist*, 1 October 1977, and Field and Winyard (1977).

Winyard (1977). Some have been particularly successful, particularly the temporary employment subsidy and the job-creation programme, others have not. All are temporary measures, however, and few people are employed as a result of them at any one time. Thus, although the aim of the job-creation programme was to create 90 000 jobs by September 1977, at any particular time a much smaller number of people were actually employed (for instance 7 949 people were employed in 620 projects in January 1977), since the average length of projects was only 31 weeks, only one in eight projects lasted 12 weeks, and the longest period a person could be employed on the programme was 12 months (Field and Winyard, 1977).

Although these government measures operate in some cities many were specifically designed for the assisted areas and are somewhat self-conscious translations of regional policy measures to a national setting. Six options which are discussed specifically with reference to inner cities but about which, except for the first, fourth, and fifth, little has been done, are job training, better public transport, assisted mobility, advance factories, help to small firms, and a change in regional policy.

1. Job training: there is little reason to believe that this will have much effect if the present approach is maintained. Certainly there is a need for training if the unskilled worker problem is to be even partially solved. This problem is exacerbated when apprenticeships are not available for school-leavers, as there are not when the economic cycle is at a low point. Courses for school-leavers and

for those trying to acquire new skills (i.e. retrain) are heavily over-subsidized and can demand high entry qualifications which immediately debar many unskilled workers. That this is a severe problem is shown by Small Heath. There, no one over 45 had passed any school examinations; 8 per cent of men between 45 and 64 and 55 per cent of those over 65 had, however, received a full industrial apprenticeship. But as the age groups get younger this advantage disappears. Thus less than 5 per cent of men between 25 and 44 had an apprenticeship and only 1 per cent of those under 25. On the other hand, 11 per cent and 38 per cent, respectively, of all adults in these age groups possessed some credentials—but these are the most likely to leave the area.

2. Better transport: the dispersal of factories and the move to service jobs has often meant longer journeys to work for inner-city residents, and many do not have access to a car. Thus, in Liverpool in 1971 car ownership in the inner areas (in terms of households, not access to a car) was generally only two-thirds of that in the city (where it was 67 per cent) and dropped to 8 per cent in the Vauxhall Community Development Project area (see Figure 5.10). Much of this low figure can be attributed to the predominance of unskilled workers in the labour force for which car ownership is only one-tenth of that of the population, but since it is generally lower in all groups in inner areas this cannot be the full explanation. Forty-eight per cent of households in Great Britain owned a car in 1971; the inner cities are all consistently 10 to 20 per cent below this figure. Transport problems are acute in the inner city. For example in Small Heath only 24 per cent

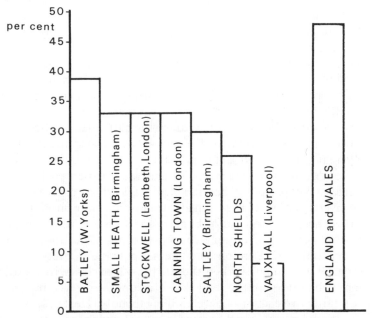

FIGURE 5.10. Per cent of households with a car in selected inner-city areas, 1971. (*Source*: Various Community Development publications)

of the labour force resident in the area actually worked there; 10 per cent worked in the city centre: another 50 per cent worked in other areas of Birmingham, 13 per cent of workers took less than 5 minutes to get to work, 37 per cent took 6–15 minutes, 28 per cent 16–30 minutes, and 19 per cent more than half an hour. Only 15 per cent of workers travelled more than five miles to their workplace, a pattern repeated in Liverpool. In Small Heath 48 per cent of workers travelled by bus to work in 1971, 19 per cent on foot, and 25 per cent by car. Corresponding figures for Liverpool were 50, 23, and 17 per cent. Inner-city workers are crucially dependent upon easy access to their jobs, either on foot or, often more importantly, by public transport. Car usage is strongly connected with income and therefore leaves many people forced to rely on public transport.

And yet the inner areas are not always well served by public transport, which is geared to in–out travel, and public transport is becoming more and more expensive relative to other costs. Thus, an inner-city worker is effectively banned from large parts of the labour market, and many workers have been forced to take jobs further and further from their residence thus explicitly foiling one of the long-standing attractions of the inner city as an area that was at least close to work. Of people asked in Lambeth in 1973 if they wanted to stay there, and if so why, 38 per cent answered in the affirmative on account of 'proximity to work, needs of job' (Department of the Environment, 1977a). In Canning Town a survey of Tate & Lyle workers made redundant in 1968 found that, by 1975, two-thirds were travelling much further to work and a similar proportion were working for less money than sugar workers currently earned (Community Development Project, 1977a). Many of the local manufacturing jobs are now on industrial estates at the edge of the city which cannot easily be reached. Where it had been common to walk to work at no expense, considerable transport costs are now being incurred by these new working-class commuters, although in the present situation of low overall demand for labour, efforts to subsidize the journey to work (Chisholm, 1976) for inner-city residents may well be misconceived.

3. Further dispersal of population: this is a particularly attractive option which has been brought to the fore in the inner-city context by the Lambeth Inner Area Study Team, but is at present opposed by the Greater London Council. In both inner London and Clydeside there is some reason to believe that this option should be at least part of a policy because these areas still suffer severe, sometimes very severe, overcrowding. However, it also means that more unskilled and semi-skilled workers need to move out of London and Glasgow, and at present they cannot do this because of current council housing allocation schemes and monetary constraints. In London chief among potential movers were couples with children. Of the manual workers those in the skilled class were more likely to want to move than those in the semi-skilled or unskilled class, but there were people in the latter two classes who were willing to move (Deakin and Ungerson, 1977). However, whether council housing in outer London, or more particularly the New Towns, would be bought or made more available to unemployed manual workers would be a genuine test of administration courage and is hard to

envisage. Similarly, the setting up of a National Housing Allocations Pool still seems some way off.

4. Advance factories: a regional policy strategy often advanced as a means of reducing unemployment in the inner cities and generally accepted now is to build advance factories for firms to move into, the local authorities acting increasingly in entrepreneurial fashion. In 1974 31 advance factories and units were built; by 1977 the number had risen to 129 (*New Society*, 8 December 1977) but they are not built in sufficient numbers to make much impact on inner-city unemployment, and it is doubtful that they ever could be.

5. Small firms: it seems to be accepted that redevelopment and road-building policies have been rapidly killing off small industry in the inner city and that redeveloped areas attract fewer new firms (Smith, 1976b). Small firms have certainly declined generally faster in Britain than elsewhere and Falk (1978) argues that their high death rate, low growth rate, and low birth rate are at the root of the poor British industrial performance. Small firms are believed to be flexible, innovative, labour intensive, and give a higher return on assets—all things that large firms are unable to do. The government seems convinced—there is now a minister with special responsibility for small firms, a small firms employment subsidy, and various tax measures to help them. In their traditional role, inner cities are seen as seed-beds for new small firms which constantly feed prosperity into the economy from the bottom as they grow. This may be so, but in terms of capability to generate *employment* opportunity in a time of low overall demand in the economy the proposition seems a little ethereal. Small firms, even in aggregate, do not usually employ many people as a proportion of the inner city workforce. Whereas in inner Manchester a small firms' revival might have some employment effects, in inner Liverpool and many other inner areas it would be meaningless in the face of high unemployment and the few large firms with such a large share of employment, who by shedding some small part of the labour force could undo any hard-won increase in small firm employment immediately. In a period of low overall demand how many small firms are being set up? It is unlikely to be many and these would be the small share of the cake which local authorities must now try and attract to their inner city. The successful Greenwich experiment cannot be repeated many times before there are no small firms left to attract.

6. Changes in regional policy: it has been argued that British regional policy is a contributory factor in the decline of the inner city, although Keeble (1977) has argued against this. Certainly some of the inner-city areas are not in the Development Areas, as with London and Birmingham. The West Riding is in an Intermediate Area, Liverpool is in the Merseyside Special Development Area and Glasgow is in the Clydeside Special Development Area. Moore and Rhodes (1973, 1976a) have calculated that the Development Areas have received 250 000 to 300 000 jobs that would not have been received if the regional policy had not been in operation, mainly due to the regional employment premium. These jobs represent an overall gain to the economy because they would have been ineffective in prosperous areas due to labour shortages. Although that figure and

the rationale behind it are still open to doubt (Chisholm, 1976), it is now generally accepted even by critics (e.g. Mackay, 1976). Whether unemployment is a particularly effective measure of the success of regional policy, as opposed to growth or investment, is another matter (Moore and Rhodes, 1976a).

Added to this calculation is the common piece of wisdom that unemployment disparities between regions are decreasing. If this is not due simply to differences in registration rates (Evans, 1977) then in 1975 unemployment in Scotland and Wales and the North was twice that of the South-east, yet in 1965 it had been three times the South-east's figures (Broadbent, 1977). Certainly as population growth has levelled off and perhaps halted (or rather as growth in the labour force halts about 1983–1984) it must mean that very soon gains by one region in working population must be at the expense of another region (Chisholm, 1976). But in recent years narrowing of differentials in unemployment between regions is probably mainly due to a catching-up process (Northern Region Strategy Team, 1976a, see above). Also during the time of the regional policy there have been some significant structural changes in the manufacturing and services sectors which have probably had an effect on the policy's effectiveness (Townsend, 1977).

In many ways regional policy was a first run of the general idea of positive discrimination and it should be possible to learn from it. It has used four main lines of attack. Following Chisholm (1976), the most obvious is subsidies to industry in the shape of capital grants, tax allowances, and so on. The second thrust has been subsidies to labour, for instance as employment premiums. The third is measures to direct industrial employment—industrial development certificates (IDCs), office development permits (ODPs) and so on, and the last has been the use of indirect subsidies in the way of infrastructure development. How effective has each of these thrusts been, and how has success (or lack of it) affected the inner cities, if at all?

If we take negative determinants first, one piece of speculation which has almost reached the level of folk wisdom is that the use of IDCs and ODPs has prevented the establishment of new industry in the inner areas. But there is very little evidence that until 1972, when controls were relaxed, this has had much effect except in directing industry to industrial estates (Lloyd and Mason, 1977). Thus, in Lambeth 'no moves had been explained by refusal of Industrial Development Certificates and only one firm had been refused an Office Development Permit' (Department of the Environment, 1977e, p. 93). In Birmingham as a whole between the mid-1960s and 1972 refusal of IDC applications 'lost' the city fewer than 2 000 jobs (under 3 per cent of the total decrease in manufacturing employment). Job 'loss' through IDC refusals in the West Midlands as a whole was only two to three times higher over the same period (Department of the Environment, 1977d). In the English inner cities it may well be that lack of interest by the English Industrial Estates Corporation in inner-city sites until recently has had just as much if not more effect on new jobs. Of course, one of the problems is that it is not possible to find out how many firms were deterred from inner-city areas by the thought of IDC refusal; it would seem to be very few.

Recent trends in regional balance do not alter the fact that London and the South-east still dominate the scene, but since 1960 there does seem to have been an increasing spatial dispersion of industry. This has led to the decline of various subregions which include most of the inner-city problems of any magnitude. Gains in manufacturing growth in the peripheral regions have also been apparent. According to Chisholm (1976), Keeble (1976), and others, regional policy began to bite in 1966 (a lag of three to four years is obligatory before this kind of policy change begins to be first felt). Moreover, since 1966 Development Areas have greatly increased in number, and in 1970 the establishment of Intermediate Areas (with extensions in 1972) increased the sphere of influence of regional policy measures (Keeble, 1976). Thus, at present 44 per cent of the population is in assisted areas. However, the Intermediate Areas seem to have had little effect on location of firms simply because not enough money has been put into these areas to be effective (Allen and Campbell, 1976): from 1974 to 1976 the Regional Development Grant was £262 million, yet West Yorkshire, as an Intermediate Area, received only 1.1 per cent of this (Wiener, 1976). There is little evidence that the Intermediate Areas have attracted any new firms, so we shall concentrate on the Development Areas.

In the Development Areas our hypothesis is simply that regional policy has had only marginal effects on the regional trends in unemployment or output, and certainly it has not attracted *labour-intensive* industry as it was meant to. The restructuring of manufacturing industry which has been occurring during the same period is often mistaken for the effects of regional policy. The recent restructuring has also led to a series of regional effects, but the locational shift of firms that has taken place is mainly a result of the rationalization that such reorganization entails. Thus, in the inner cities, as we have seen, the tendency has been to *closure* of plants (and, therefore, absolute loss of employment). The amount of relocation has been relatively small and the relocation that has taken place has entailed job loss to the economy as a whole (Massey and Meegan, 1977). The rate of unemployment in the inner cities and the non-development areas (with exceptions like the South-east) has probably been greater than in Development Areas, which has brought some equalization in regional unemployment profiles. Added to this there has been a relative increase in employment in the Development Areas which has helped them converge upon the national rate. Much of this relative increase has been due to receiving more new plants, and receiving the bulk of new investment in the production and growth sectors (Massey, 1976). These latter points *may* be the result of the financial advantages the regions offer, particularly the regional employment premium. But they may also be due to the cheap labour force available in the Development Areas (see, for instance, Northcott, 1977). There is little evidence to point to *initial* location strategies being influenced by regional employment premiums. Thus, in essence, the Development Areas have been less affected by the higher rate of unemployment than the non-development areas and have also sustained an increase in output relative to the non-development areas due in part to a more productive labour force (Massey, 1976). As a result unemployment rates and rates of output have converged. But to interpret this convergence as due *in toto* to regional policy would be to tread dangerous ground.

We have seen how the restructuring of manufacturing industry has affected the inner city. For instance, inner-city subsidiaries, due to reasons of age, access, and so on, have been the first to be closed in any rationalization, especially when their expensive land can produce a good return. And in a recession it seems foolish to operate all plants at a reduced capacity rather than fewer plants at full capacity (Keeble, 1976). But we must remember that the bulk of inner-city jobs lost have been permanently lost and have not relocated. That loss seems to be constant for *all* inner cities, whether in development areas or not. Thus, Liverpool suffered the same employment loss as inner cities in non-development areas. The real issue is the decline in *national* employment opportunities as it is reflected in space (Chisholm and Oeppen, 1973), not the local variations produced.

So where are the jobs to come from? From an expanded services sector? From small firms? From a boom in the British economy? The conclusion of this chapter discusses these propositions in detail. The answer is that there is no answer. But before a discussion of the inevitability of such a contradiction we turn to the urban programme, which was meant to assay and offer solutions to the inner-city problem.

THE PROBLEMS OF THE INNER CITY—THEORIES FOR SALE

A word which has been over-used in recent years is 'ideology'. It is used here in a general sense as a false theory about the world which is used to legitimate the interests of the established order, as a *belief* in a set of rules as the 'real' or 'natural' order of things. Ideology endures because it is not rigidly defined. Its effectiveness lies in its elasticity which makes it seem a product of each man's mind. An ideology has generality, it is never explored in depth. It has a surface appearance of the truth—indeed parts of the theory may be true. Through its legitimation function it enables people to be more easily managed (Habermas, 1976). It is possible, following Hamnett (1976a), to isolate at least five ideologies concerning the explanation of urban problems, or (more generally) why people are poor.

The culture of poverty

In its essentials this is due to the anthropologist Oscar Lewis. To paraphrase F. Scott Fitzgerald, 'the poor are different', they form a distinctive culture in society and they pass this culture on to their sons and daughters (such that the culture is fixed by the age of six or seven) in a never-ending cycle. Poverty becomes something rather romantic in Lewis's eyes; poor people's defence against the class society. But the poor stay poor because the defence they initiate in the face of poverty, of particular values and attitudes, is also a self-perpetuating trap (Wasman, 1977): 'The culture of poverty would consist of those cultural patterns that keep people poor *even when opportunity beckons*' (Gans, 1973a, p. 15).

Recently Banfield (1974) has resurrected this idea. His analysis of the urban problem is without doubt a nice dismemberment of the well-meaning technician and has gained respect for at least articulating what many people think. Because *The Unheavenly City* threatens a good many people's livelihoods, however, little notice has been taken of it in practice.

Gans (1973a, 1973b) has probably been the strongest critic of the culture of poverty. To him, there may be a 'behavioural lower-class culture' which consists of the behaviour people have to adopt in order to adapt to poverty, but there is no such thing as a Lewisian 'aspirational lower-class culture' since most poor people do not want to stay poor and have the same aspirations as the less poor. Thus, one can presume that if poor people were to become rich then this behavioural lower-class culture would soon disappear. The basic difference between Lewis and Gans is that whereas Lewis sees the lower-class culture as a cause of poverty, Gans sees it as an effect. He is, to paraphrase Hemingway's reply to Fitzgerald, saying 'yes, they have less money'. For Gans 'poverty exists because it has so many positive functions for the affluent society' (Gans, 1973a, p. 320), and so we must agree with Rutter and Madge (1976, p. 30) that 'the culture of poverty concept is inadequate for an analysis of British society'.

The cycle of disadvantage

This has been a basic theme in the work of the British urban programme. It allows the legitimation of urban problems in our society by use of a technical model—the social pathology model. In essence, the inner city population is poor because it has caught a disease passed from generation to generation called 'deprivation' or 'disadvantage'. The metaphor of illness has, of course, a long and hallowed history in social science dating from the days of Octavia Hill when the problems of the poor were felt to be 'sanitary'. That it still forms a powerful paradigm can be seen by a reading of Adams (1977); it was probably best articulated by Sir Keith Joseph in his well-known speech of 29 June 1972, in which he addressed the vexing question of why 'deprivation and problems of maladjustment so *conspicuously* persist' (my emphasis) despite the improvement in absolute prosperity since the Second World War which included the onset of the Welfare State and growth of public housing.

The dominant stress is not laid on low income and poor housing *per se*, but instead on the inadequacies of the home background and child-rearing. Deprivation can be found in all levels of society and includes 'poverty', 'emotional impoverishment', 'personality disorder' and 'depression and despair'. Three basic factors cause this rot—economic factors like unemployment and low income, living conditions like bad housing and overcrowding, and personal factors such as lack of paternal love or genetic endowment. These basic factors are transmitted from generation to generation and rely for transmission on the family unit. Children born into the cycle often cannot get out. Thus, efforts to reduce poverty, improve bad housing, and so on, are not enough unless reinforced by what Joseph called 'preparation for parenthood' because 'inadequate people tend to be inadequate parents and . . . inadequate parents tend to rear inadequate children' (speech quoted in Hamnett, 1976a, pp. 20–21). The problem is firmly located in unskilled and semi-skilled working-class households and Joseph went as far as hinting at the need for greater family planning to reduce the number of such people. A seven-year research programme was jointly initiated by the D.H.S.S. and S.S.R.C. to look at the cycle of deprivation (Rutter and Madge, 1976).

We can see that deprivation has two meanings—the first being social disadvantage through the environment, the second the psychological process of children damaged in each generation. Certainly a better and broader word would be 'disadvantage', since at least it does not have the explicitly ideological linking of poverty with maladjustment, bad parenthood, and genetics. Rutter and Madge (1976), in their compendious volume on cycles of disadvantage, point out that measuring disadvantage is often difficult. They find five criteria for measuring disadvantage—a statistical criterion, an administrative criterion, the inability to purchase goods, a self-perception criterion, and a criterion of industrial values.

Perhaps certain forms of disadvantage are more common in the inner city than elsewhere, but Rutter and Madge (1976) isolate at least three 'causal' processes at work:

1. factors which underlie the effect of inequalities;
2. factors which underlie the level of poverty; and
3. factors which determine who is poor.

There seems little doubt that the cycle of disadvantage has now been generally rejected, in favour of a broader theory. Research continually shows the difficulties involved in isolation of psychological and educational factors from low income. Thus, marital disharmony in inner-city families is as often linked to taut budgeting as to parental upbringing, and problems like illegitimacy are no more common in the unskilled and semi-skilled manual groups than in the better-off categories. Certainly disadvantage *is* passed on from generation to generation, but that is because British society is organized to perpetuate unequal wealth, not because of the existence of a disease called 'deprivation' which causes such problems. And almost no attention has been paid to those brought up in a deprived household who are *not* damaged by such circumstances. The problems involved in the cycle of disadvantage as both an ideological and an epistemological entity are best summed up in a condition called 'deprivation dwarfism' which is found in children from grossly disturbed families and is described by Rutter and Madge (1976, p. 11) thus:

The dwarfism is not associated with any disease or illness and at first it was thought that lack of love or emotional privation impaired growth even when the intake of food remained adequate. This now seems not to be so, at least in most cases. The answer is more humdrum—the children have not received enough to eat. To that extent the dwarfism is 'caused' by starvation. However, that leaves open the question of why the children had been inadequately fed and the answer to that question often lies in parental neglect or in the child's depression following chronic stress. Therefore it could be said that parental neglect or lack of love is really the case. But that only put the matter back one stage further. Why did the parents neglect the child? The answer may lie in current social disadvantage (e.g. loss of job and housing) or in adverse childhood experiences which failed to provide the proper basis for parenting. Are these then the causes? Of course in a sense all of them are and appropriate action requires an understanding of the process as a whole.

Poverty as a consequence of administrative failure

Procedures for dealing with urban problems often cut across standard administrative demarcations; different agencies support different problems. Remedial action is rarely coordinated. Certainly, the overadministration of our society by a series of different government departments with different priorities from different ministers, overlooked by the Treasury, cannot help any urban programme that is needed. The duplication of effort between the Home Office and the Department of the Environment has not helped, neither have the recent local government reorganization, the control systems of central government, the problems of opportunistic planning in a planning system which emphasizes negative strategies, nor central government's tight control over financial expenditure (Stewart et al., 1976).

In April 1977 the Lambeth Inner Area Study plotted fifteen different boundary patterns in their small area belonging to different organizations, and these were by no means all the organizational boundaries. Often there are firm rules about which centre must be visited if a person lives in a particular area and these can be complicated—in 1974 the Department of Health and Social Security did not necessarily pay out unemployment benefit or supplementary benefit at the same place as sickness benefit (Department of the Environment, 1977e).

When the cycle of deprivation started to decline as the most popular theory explaining urban poverty it was at least partially replaced by an emphasis on better administrative procedures (Davis, McIntosh, and Williams, 1977). Comprehensive community programmes, urban guideline studies, area management schemes, and other ad hoc bodies were set up to try to coordinate local authority and government activity (Horn et al., 1977; Mason et al., 1977; Stewart, Spencer, and Webster, 1976). There was a general and genuine realization of the need for local authorities to draw up better management schemes, probably touched off by Liverpool City Council's decision to call in management consultants in 1971. But a theoretical model which has at its core institutional malfunctioning seems less than realistic. Certainly the failure of planning, management, or administration have been symptomatic of the urban problems that abound (Simmie, 1974), but they have, with a few exceptions, hardly been failures grand enough to be labelled 'causal'.

The working of the administrative machinery may have led to a more profound alienation (Benington, 1976; Cockburn, 1977): why otherwise are most community groups initially formed to fight local government or government action? The administrative framework is out of touch with ordinary people because it has become a technical enterprise, distanced from reality. The 'elected representatives' of the people often voice opinions that would horrify the electorate (Newton, 1976). Inner-city areas show their alienation by demonstrating the irrelevancy of local government to their lives in election turn-out figures which rarely reach above 30 per cent as working-class politics continues its decline (Hindess, 1973). New practices like corporate management are unlikely to do anything to change this alienation (indeed such innovations can, in practice, allow departments to avoid responsibility for a project because so many are involved). They may reshuffle the management structure of a local authority, but they do nothing to improve the interface between planner and planned. Indeed, would that urban problems were so amply identified with administrative failure and the maldistribution of resources therefrom! Nevertheless from the theoretical constructs of institutional malfunction leading to a maldistribution of resources and the cycle of disadvantage did come the key concept of the disadvantaged or underprivileged person, and from that in turn came the general idea of positive discrimination over space.

Poverty as a consequence of location

Crucially, the British urban programme rests on the supposition that the spatial dimension somehow produces what Donnison (1975a, p. 129) has aptly called 'a third explanation of social problems' in which the area is the base of explanation. This means that the social services' 'fundamental dilemma', whether to 'be universal and go to everyone as with primary education or . . . be selective and go only to those in greatest need as with supplementary benefits' (Hatch and Sherrat, 1973, p. 223) can be solved in favour of selective benefits which are also universal in a small enough area. Put simply, it was felt that since there were areas in which were concentrated people who were 'disadvantaged' or 'underprivileged' then in order to balance the scales extra resources should be placed in these areas. For the 'educational priority area' (see below) the justification was that extra resources could be devoted to supplying an environment for children at school which would compensate for their home life. By the 1970s, when the emphasis on redevelopment transformed into an emphasis on improvement, the idea often seemed to be that if the physical environment could be brought up to the level of a quiet suburban area the area would become suburbia by dint of sympathetic magic.

To achieve such areal effects assumes that it is possible to delineate an area which can serve as a universe, and that there is such a thing as a concentration of deprivations by which it can be identified. Additionally, it also hopes for an ideal population size of about 10 000 (Department of the Environment, 1977d). *But* in fact there is little evidence that even the worst inner areas of cities contain a large number of deprived people. In order to know how many people will be helped by positive discrimination policies it is first necessary to know many 'deprived' people live in such areas. One Department of the Environment (1974a, p. 10) census indicator study, for instance, found that 'the degree of spatial concentration of individual aspects of deprivation is really quite low'. Thus, severe overcrowding was one direct social indicator showing a high level of concentration, yet priority area treatment would have to be given to 15 per cent of all enumeration districts in order to catch as many as 61 per cent of households with this type of deprivation. And areas of multiple deprivation are particularly hard to define. Lomas (1975) has shown that areas of housing stress and employment stress are geographically separate in London—one part of London suffers from restricted job opportunities but has reasonable housing chances, whereas the other part has better job prospects but these are accompanied by housing problems: these two types of stress only combine in the southern quadrant of the inner area. Berthoud (1975) has also shown for London that geographical factors are not important in explaining income differentials and that an area-based poverty programme would only account for a relatively small proportion of the worse-off—a result confirmed by Simon (1977) and the Department of the Environment (1975a). Halsey (1972), too, showed that spatial concentration of deprivation is not as dense as often assumed. Most children in educational priority areas, for instance, were not deprived, and most of the deprived were not in educational priority areas!

If most of the deprived are outside priority areas and a good many of those who are not deprived are in them, then the idea of 'spatial' equity must break down on two counts: one is that it is unfair to the deprived who are left outside the area and the second is that it is unfair to the non-deprived living outside the area. The priority areas seem to lay down a principle of being selective, but only to the part of the disadvantaged group which has the good fortune to live inside an arbitrarily chosen boundary. However, this quandary only comes about if inner areas are defined solely on the criterion of personal deprivation: of the inner area study areas, Small Heath and Lambeth could not be described as severely deprived areas of the country (Cheshire, 1977). If personal deprivation is regarded as only a part of a much greater whole which goes to create the particular inner-area environment, on the other hand, then they do qualify. It seems that if area studies are to be justified and are to have any rationale it must not be on criteria like 'deprivation' or 'disadvantage' but on an altogether broader front as particularly bad examples of the general problems of society, although, more fundamentally, it is hard to see how a focus of services on a few specific areas of need could ever be successful in reversing the maldistribution of resources which lies at the heart of a market economy.

The structural explanation: the industrial reserve army

The structural explanation of inner-city problems explains them as a spatial manifestation of the inherent contradictions of capitalism. The inner city becomes the spatial manifestation of the 'industrial reserve army' or 'relative surplus population' (Braverman, 1974; Community Development Project 1975, 1977a; Holland, 1976; Howard and King, 1975; Marx, 1970; Meek, 1973; Stuckey, 1976).

Capitalism needs an industrial reserve army (what some might now call 'demand pull') to satisfy its needs for extra labour when capital accumulation is successful. In an economic boom the industrial reserve army holds down active labour by providing competition and thus keeping a check on any extravagant demands, while during a slump it weighs down active labour. Marx distinguishes three components of 'relative surplus population':

1. *Floating* labour is essentially urban surplus population which changes jobs continually and can therefore take advantage of different demands from different sectors at different times. It consists in the main of labourers who are not tied to particular sectors by the division of labour, and might now be called frictional unemployment (Holland, 1976).
2. *Latent* labour is that part of the agricultural population displaced by technological change and capitalist reorganization. According to Stuckey (1977) and Braverman (1974) this component also includes housewives who work only when the economy is on the upswing. It might now be called 'disguised unemployment'.
3. *Stagnant* labour is irregular employment 'characterized by a maximum of working time and a minimum of wages'. It included, in Marx's time, domestic industry, the areas where handicrafts were becoming manufacturing industry.

Marx also briefly distinguished two other components of relative surplus population:

4. *Nomad* labour is 'the flying infantry of capital', comprising immigrant labourers.
5. *Pauper* labour includes those who are nearly always out of work although capable of it, like middle-aged workers made redundant as well as those unable to work, like the disabled and victims of industrial accidents.

Quite obviously some of the entries in these categories are no longer applicable; they represent a specific historical conjuncture of capitalism which no longer exists. However, it is often thought possible to rewrite these categories in modern equivalents (see Braverman, 1974; Campbell, 1977a; Stuckey, 1976). Thus floating labour is much the same as in Marx's time—the unskilled (or semi-skilled) labourer. Not so latent labour; the process of rural–urban migration is almost complete now in developed countries, although such a category description might still apply in underdeveloped countries. We might even see latent labour as housewives who would work if jobs were available, but otherwise are supported by the wages of their husbands. Then again pauper labour must include the disabled who are on the unemployment register as available for work.

It also probably includes a large number of men over fifty who, having been made redundant, cannot get another job. Stagnant labour must include a substantial proportion of the immigrant population, while nomad labour is probably still the migrant labour—the 'guest' worker of the economic boom or the omnipresent Irish navvy.

It would be comparatively simple to say that the vast proportion of relative surplus population lived in the inner city—immigrants, unskilled labour, migrant labourers in rooming houses, and so on. But would this process of relabelling be at all helpful analytically? The Community Development Project description of Hillfields in Coventry certainly seems to take this view, equating relative surplus population with the pool of unskilled labour in the inner city (Community Development project, 1975; Harford, 1977). In Coventry the small firms linked to the motor industry go out of business first in any recession, and it is from these firms that the reserve army is recruited in times of economic boom. To cope with the fluctuations in motor industry demand it is necessary for large firms to operate below capacity in slack periods and at full capacity when demand for products runs high. But in large firms there are limits to the amount of unused plant which can be left idle or underproducing in slack times, and this means that in times of economic boom the large firms cannot always meet all the demand. In such a situation small firms flourish since they have a higher marginal return; there is a place for such small firms in a boom, especially since they can use cheap labour like immigrants or women to increase productivity. They are forced out of business in a recession, throwing many people into the labour pool until the next upswing. Thus the profitability of the large firms depends upon maintaining a reserve army of labour which can be siphoned off as the market expands and contracts. The state supports the system by paying benefit in times of recession and gets this money back in times of boom through taxes. Bread and circuses become benefit and colour television. The inner city in this variant is a spatial manifestation of a labour imperative of state capitalism.

The reserve army no longer has much effect on the economic circumstances of the rest of the working population owing to the advent of trade union power, although it may still have a disciplining effect in that the threat of unemployment prevents workers assuming too much control over production (Holland, 1976). But this assumes that such a thing as a reserve army exists. Such a possibility is only present if 'the romance of labour', to use Cutler's (1977) telling phrase, is taken into account. As we have seen, for Marx the accumulation of capital is accompanied by a rise in its organic composition; the relative surplus population is 'a necessary product of accumulation' (Marx, 1970, p. 592) because 'the labouring population . . . produces along with the accumulation of capital produced by it, the means by which it itself is made relatively superfluous, is turned into a relative surplus population; and it does this to an always increasing extent' (Marx, 1970, p. 591). Thus the industrial reserve army is determined by a rise in the organic composition of capital, which leads to a tendency to expand production without any corresponding growth of employment and allows short-term rapid expansion of production without affecting the labour supply of other sectors. This results in a larger and larger reserve army to be exploited in terms of a given working population, although Marx provides no proof that technical progress will have a labour-saving bias sufficiently strong to produce an increasing reserve army (Howard and King, 1975, p. 203). Braverman (1974) and others tend to equate the reserve army with the body of unemployed, but there is no evidence to suggest that Marx meant this, and furthermore the movement from a pre-capitalist to capitalist society is now all but over and with it that source of surplus labour power (Howard and King, 1975). There is, for instance a cavalier tendency to equate women with the reserve army (Braverman, 1974; Campbell, 1977; Stuckey, 1976), yet 'changes in employment of women are not in terms of a given working population but affect the boundaries of the working population, that is allow for the wider entry of a social category into the workforce' (Cutler, 1977, p. 88). Immigrant labour produces this same objection. In addition 'women entering the labour force are clearly not displaced by changes in the organic composition of capital and immigrant labour is obviously not a homogeneous group' (Cutler, 1977, p. 89). Similarly, Cutler (1977) questions the isomorphic use of mode of production and national economy in many Marxist writings, and casts further doubt on the use of the industrial reserve army as an analytical concept. Rather it seems to have become simply a Marxist term for the unemployed, such that 'an increase in the rate of unemployment is taken to signify either the appearance or the enlargement of the reserve army of the unemployed' (Hussain, 1977, p. 443). Its non-ideological status therefore seems doubtful.

THE BRITISH URBAN PROGRAMME

From the late 1960s onwards the British government has shown an awareness of the problem of the cities reflected in a series of projects and reports upon positive discrimination in a number of small inner city areas. Several developments contributed to the genesis of what came to be known as 'the urban programme'. Probably the most influential was a group of four reports—the Ingleby Report (1960) on children and young people, the Milner Holland Report (1965) on housing in Greater London, the Plowden report (1966) on primary education, and the Seebohm Report (1966) on personal social services. Their constant theme was the designation of special areas which would be given extra resources—the ideology of space that has been the backbone of urban aid in Britain (see Table 5.4 and Figure 5.11). Furthermore, at this time there was a rediscovery of poverty as it was realized that the Welfare State was not going to cure all the ills of British society, and the influence of Titmuss, Halsey, and others directly on government evangelized the idea of positive discrimination. Further impetus was provided by the American 'War on Poverty'.

The first positive discrimination initiative probably stemmed from the Plowden Report. The Department of Education and Science set up, in conjunction with the S.S.R.C., *educational priority areas* (EPAs) in four urban areas, Deptford in London, Conisbrough/Denaby in the West Riding, Balsall

Heath/Sparkbrook in inner Birmingham, and inner Liverpool 8—at a cost of £175 000. These pilot projects were followed later by EPAs in other parts of London (e.g. Islington, Greenwich) and in Dundee. Schools in these areas were given priority far beyond the usual resources in order to compensate for the homes and neighbourhoods from which many children came and which provided little support or stimulus to learn (Carney and Taylor, 1974; Community Development Project, 1977b; Halsey, 1972; Hancock, 1976b; Pownall, 1975; Rutter and Madge, 1976).

The next major initiative was the urban programme. This was announced by the then Prime Minister, Harold Wilson, in a speech in Birmingham in May 1968: it is generally agreed that his timing was a response to Enoch Powell's

TABLE 5.4. Urban initiatives in Britain, 1968–77

Type of Project	Date established	Areas	Govt. Dept.
Educational priority area (EPA)	1968	London (Deptford), West Riding (Conisbrough Denaby), Birmingham (Ballsall Heath, Sparkbrook), Liverpool (8), London, Dundee	D.E.S.
Community Development Project (CDP)	1970	West Riding (Batley), Newcastle (Benwell), London (Canning Town), Cumbria (Cleator Moor), West Glamorgan (Clyncorrwg), Coventry (Hillfields), Liverpool (Vauxhall), Tyneside (North Shields), Oldham (Clarksfield), Glasgow (Paisley), Birmingham (Saltley), London (Southwark)	Home Office
Neighbourhood schemes	1971	Liverpool (Brunswick), Teesside (Newport)	Home Office
Urban guidelines studies	1972	Oldham, Rotherham, Sunderland	D.O.E.
Inner area studies	1973	London (Lambeth), Birmingham (Small Heath), Liverpool (8)	D.O.E.
Quality of life studies	1973	Stoke-on-Trent, Sunderland, Clwyd, Dumbarton	D.O.E.
Area management trials	1975/ 1977	Dudley, Haringey, Newcastle, Liverpool, Islington, Middlesbrough Stockport, Kirklees	D.O.E. D.O.E.
G.L.C. deprived areas	1976	Spitalhead, Tower Hamlets, Islington	Home Office
Comprehensive community programme (CCP)	1976/ 1977	Bradford, Gateshead, London (Wandsworth), Wirral, Motherwell	Home Office
Special partnerships	1977	Liverpool, Birmingham, Manchester/ Salford, London (Lambeth), London (Docklands), London (Hackney and Islington), Newcastle/Gateshead	D.O.E.

notorious 'rivers of blood' speech in Birmingham on 20 April 1968, and almost no prior preparation of the programme had been carried out. Proposals for something which was to become the Community Development Project had been taking shape in the Children's Department of the Home Office in response to the White Paper 'Children in trouble' (Specht, 1976), but that was all. So when Harold Wilson wrote in his diary how in May 1968 he 'then announced the Urban Programme which had been worked out interdepartmentally under the direction of the Home Office' (Wilson, 1971, Penguin edition, p. 666) it came as

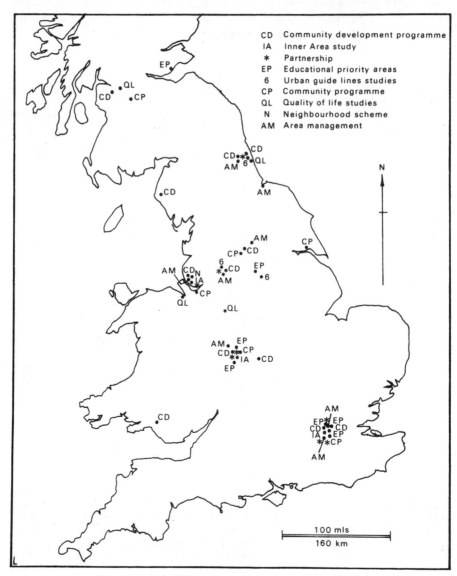

FIGURE 5.11. The urban programme, 1968–1977

little short of a complete surprise to the Home Office (Batley and Edwards, 1978). The Working Party set up to put together an urban programme transformed the vague commitments of the Wilson speech into a positive discrimination project (of which no hint had emerged in the May speech), at first with almost no idea of what money was available. By July 1968 Richard Crossman could record

> at this afternoon's social services committee we had a quite unprecedented paper from the Home Office. Nothing like the normal Civil Service brief . . . but a philosophical paper on a project developed by a man called Derek Morrell. . . . It asks that we should select 12 blackspots where social crisis and tension are at their highest [and] there should be sent into each an inter-service team . . . to assess the problem of how such a community can pull itself up by its own bootstraps. Having made the assessments they must then get down to the job of seeing that the community tackles it itself. (Crossman, 1977, pp. 125–126)

This was the Community Development Project in embryo. Much of its development must be seen as the work of Derek Morrell, an Assistant Under-Secretary of State, whose constant enthusiasm pushed it along, although the Home Secretary, James Callaghan, did not like all the 'bloody religious nonsense' (Crossman, 1977, p. 139) that was the more philosophical part of the project brief. Circulars went out from the Department to local authorities in October 1968, and in January 1969 the Urban Programme Bill received the Royal Assent (Holman and Hamilton, 1973).

The major content of the Bill was to establish twelve local projects called *Community Development Projects* (CDPs), each with a five year life span, to be supported by the Home Office and the Local Authority. The first four were set up in 1970 in Coventry, Southwark, Liverpool, and Glyncorrwg and were followed by another eight (see Table 5.4). The cost would be £5 million. There were two teams in each area—action teams and research teams. The action teams were responsible to a council management committee on which the Home Office was represented and were funded in the ratio 75/25 by the Home Office and relevant local authorities. The research teams were funded 100 per cent by the Home Office and were based in various local universities and polytechnics. They were to provide the diagnosis of local problems, generate policy recommendations, and evaluate the work of the action team. Not all projects were located in inner urban areas; Cleator Moor and Glyncorrwg were in small towns in rural areas.

In retrospect it is easy to see the problems. The deprived were seen as having a lot to do with the causes of urban deprivation, so that the problems were best solved by transferring the apathy of the local people into self-help which would, incidentally, save large amounts of money being expended on social services in particular urban areas. This 'diagnosis' proved generally incorrect, but the action and research teams found no easy way to put this over to government in order to bring about the changes in policy needed to achieve results. In fact, with the death of Derek Morrell in 1970 and movements and general transcience of staff in the

Home Office, the Community Development Projects were left, at one point for over a year, with only relatively junior civil servants to take responsibility for the whole programme. The breakdowns in communication that occurred become more understandable; the early days of the Community Development Projects are reviewed in Mayo (1975), Batley and Edwards (1975), Specht (1976), and Carney and Taylor (1974).

Three distinct phases can be seen in the genesis of CDP thought on urban problems (Community Development Project, 1977b). The first leaned to the pathological view and involved the setting up of numerous information and law centres, playgrounds, traffic management schemes, youth work, and community centres. The second phase turned its attention to putting pressure on local authorities to adjust their policies and management organization. The last phase coincided with the surviving projects deciding to pool their experience by setting up the CDP Information and Intelligence Unit at the Centre for Environmental Studies in London (with the somewhat hesitant support of the Home Office). This latter phase involved a structural explanation of the urban problem and political affiliation with, for instance, the trade union movement. The move to a structural explanation was, unsurprisingly, less than popular with the Home Office and the local authorities and brought inevitable conflict. The action and research teams had already come into conflict with local authorities, for instance in Liverpool in 1972. The Batley project was closed in 1974 and in early 1976 the Cleator Moor project was ended. In November 1976 the Birmingham project was closed, and also in that year, after the publication of 'Cutting the Welfare State (who profits?)' by the Information and Intelligence Unit, the Home Secretary ordered its closure (Community Development Project, 1977b).

Specht (1976) has documented this conflict as an inevitable one between a 'national' strategy focusing on bringing about change in the structure of society, and the original 'local' strategy which emphasized improvement of local service delivery and streamlining local agencies. Although originally it is doubtful that either of these ideologies was particularly clear-cut, as conflict developed so polarization took place. The CDPs suffered other problems apart from direct or indirect conflict; they were not all started at the same time, for example so that the final Coventry report was printed in 1975 but some projects did not complete until 1977.

It is extremely hard (and perhaps too early) to assess the Community Development Project experience and contribution. In particular there has been almost no follow-up work as to the impact of the CDPs (but note Corina, 1977). In addition, writing tends to be polarized; there is, on one side, work which is clearly structural in emphasis (e.g. Benington, 1975b; Coventry Community Development Project, 1975; most Community Development Project Information and Intelligence Units publications; Cockburn, 1977; Harford, 1977), and on the other side literature more easily assimilated into professional journals. But whether putting money into an area for such a short space of time as five years, then withdrawing it when it has had no time to have an effect and indeed when local councils then tend to divert money to other areas which have not been so privileged (Department of the Environment, 1977d), can have a major impact is a moot point.

The Community Development Project has certainly not been the only initiative to emerge. Meanwhile the Community Relations Department of the Home Office had been made responsible for the urban programme. The money which was to be available for 'urban aid' was not, however, an extra slice of the cake—it was taken from the rate support grant (Holman and Hamilton, 1974). Local authorities had to apply for grants for specific projects, which could be for up to five years in duration, on a 75/25 basis.

The range of projects has been great but, in real terms, the money decreased since it stayed at £4 million per year, although in 1974 aid for Uganda was diverted to immigrant projects (at £2.3 million) and in 1971 the programme did release £6 million, as a one-off from a special £160 million government building programme, to assist the building industry in urban areas. By 1976 £4.3 million out of a potential pool of about £60 million had been approved. Apparently five times more applications have been made than have been granted (Community Development Project, 1977b): in 1971 Lambeth applied for £103 500 worth of aid for various projects but it received only £13 650.

In 1971 the Community Programmes Department was set up to administer all Home Office urban programmes. One of the first projects launched (in June 1971) was to set up *neighbourhood schemes* (Batley, 1975). These were meant to complement the Community Development Projects and arose out of a report by Donnison (1975b) for the Department of Health and Social Security. Here the idea was to observe the effects of concentrating a large amount of money—£150 000—in an urban area. The emphasis was on intensive action and all expenditure was to be on capital projects with no money for running costs. There were to be ten schemes, but only two were set up, in Liverpool (Brunswick) and Teesside (Newport). The local authorities were heavily involved, and a small research team was funded to evaluate the schemes. Both projects ended rather haphazardly, mainly because the local authorities tended to use the money for schemes they had always had in mind—the money was just seen as an extra windfall (Batley, 1975). The timetabling of projects also lagged behind what was envisaged.

In 1972 the Department of Environment announced its own 'total approach'—the 'six towns studies'. The first three of these studies covered complete towns—Oldham, Rotherham, and Sunderland—and were subsequently known as the *urban guidelines studies*. They were carried out by private management and economic consultants, who produced their reports in the summer of 1973 (Department of the Environment, 1973a, 1973b, 1973c): their emphasis was very much on local authority coordination. They were seen as brief studies into the management of cities and were meant, as their name implies, to have a guideline function.

The second half of the six towns studies metamorphosed into the *inner area studies*. Again these were undertaken by private consultants but, in contrast to the urban guidelines studies, they were to be action research projects. The local authorities did not pay for research, but again the 75/25 ratio was used for contributions towards the action projects. The three areas chosen were Birmingham (Small Heath), Liverpool 8, and London (Stockwell/Lambeth). In September 1972 consultants were invited to prepare a brief and full studies started in July 1973. They were well supported, costing about £1.3 million in all. The flavour of their brief can be seen by references to the Liverpool Inner Area Study (Department of the Environment 1977c, p. 4):

1. 'to discover by study a better definition of inner areas and their problems';
2. 'to investigate by experiments on the ground the actions affecting the physical environment of these areas which could usefully be undertaken for social and environmental purposes';
3. 'to examine whether the concept of area management can usefully be developed and what the practical implications would be for the local authority'; and
4. 'to provide the base for general conclusions on statutory powers, finance and resource questions, and techniques'.

The final reports were submitted in 1976 and published in 1977, and have proved the most influential of all these programmes (Department of the Environment, 1977b, 1977c, 1977d).

Yet another initiative by the Department of the Environment came in 1973 with the setting up of *quality of life studies*. These projects, located in Stoke-on-Trent, Sunderland, Clwyd, and Dumbarton, were envisaged as part of a larger programme to improve the urban quality of life. They were, essentially, action research projects. In each area a local steering group was set up and aimed to involve, in particular, voluntary organizations. The programme was meant to last two years at a cost of £1 million. The final reports have yet to be published.

By 1973 there was a number of schemes run by various government departments which seemed to run the risk of duplicating each other. Following an initiative by the Treasury an interdepartmental study was undertaken which looked into the possibility of rationalization. This led to the setting up by the Home Office of the 'Urban Deprivation Unit'. And for a short time in 1974 there was a Minister of State (Urban Affairs), who was to appear again in 1977. The Urban Deprivation Unit came up with the idea of the *comprehensive community programme* (CCP). The object was to put money into small areas of urban Britain that could qualify as areas of intense urban deprivation. Four pilot studies were planned, but after some argument over the extent of the areas of deprivation by the Home Office and local authorities, the CCP areas eventually became local authority areas. The emphasis in CCPs is on coordination of services and redirection of existing resources, rather than provision of extra funds. Essentially the CCP would seem to be meant to act as a policy guide in each area. Four areas were initially selected—Gateshead, Bradford, London (Wandsworth), and the Wirral—but 'a trial of a trial' is now under way at Gateshead and will cost £30–40 000 per year. The Scottish Office also set up a CCP, in Motherwell, in 1976.

Apart from these major initiatives there has also been a series of more low-key components to the urban programme. Thus the Urban Deprivation Unit has sponsored G.L.C. *deprived areas projects*, providing funds on the usual 75/25 basis (at £267 000 per annum). So far there are three projects—in Spitalfields, Tower Hamlets, and Hanley Road, Islington. These pilot schemes, which are essentially seen as coordination exercises, will form the base of a 'strategic policy for deprived areas in London'.

Shortly after the announcement of the CCPs, the Department of the Environment introduced *area management trials*. Apparently the idea for this came from the Liverpool Inner Area Study which ran such a scheme. The trials did not involve new staff but acted as a focal point for local groups and as an administrative scheme. Eight schemes have been initiatied on a 75/25 basis with the local authorities. The cost—£25 000 per year—is really meant to cover only overheads. Two schemes, in Stockport and Liverpool, started in 1974, followed by a further four in Kirklees, Newcastle upon Tyne, Dudley, and Haringey in London at various times in 1976 and two in Islington and Middlesbrough in mid-1977 (Stewart, Spencer, and Webster, 1976; Horn *et al.*, 1977; Mason *et al.*, 1977).

The latest source of money is the E.E.C., which is proposing its own 'poverty programme' (Community Development Project, 1977a). It was to last for five years, but has since been cut back to two. In Britain the agency for the E.E.C. is the Department of Health and Social Security which will handle the £850 000 available on a 50/50 basis with the E.E.C. Apparently schemes will include seven family advice centres, area resource centres, an anti-poverty action centre in South Wales, and a scheme for improving advocacy. It should also not be forgotten that various voluntary organizations have often had considerable influence on the course of events. The Child Poverty Action Group is one; another is Shelter, with its Shelter Neighbourhood Action Project (SNAP) in Liverpool which was set up in 1969 and ran for three years, and the Shelter Housing Aid Centres (SHACs). On the urban programme as a whole the reader can consult Hamnett (1976a), Community Development Project (1977b), Batley and Edwards (1974), Holman and Hamilton (1974), Rutter and Madge (1976), Hancock (1976b), and Cockburn (1977).

Following all these positive discrimination area studies came the government inner cities' initiative. On 10 September 1976 the Prime Minister moved responsibility for the urban programme from the Home Office, and the Urban Deprivation Unit to the Department of the Environment and Welsh Office. Apparently responsibility for CCPs is also being transferred to the Department of the Environment, but the Home Office will keep race relations (Department of the Environment, 1977f). The major new thrust has been the declaration of new *partnership* areas.

The White Paper of June 1977 promised to 'recast' the urban programme. Thus it would be extended to cover industrial, environmental, and recreation provision as well as the social aspects and, more importantly, its level of support would increase from less than £30 million per annum to £125 million per annum

(£95 million to England) in 1979/1980 (at 1977/1978 out-turn prices). Precedence was to be given to CCPs and other areas where local authorities have taken action, and to new 'partnership' areas. These partnerships would give special attention to a few areas, and each partnership will be run by a joint committee and will include a small research team. In Scotland it seems certain that Glasgow will receive some similar help, its present £6 million per annum will build up to £20 million by 1980/1981, while for Wales the government will 'announce its decision in due course' (Wales will get £5 million per annum). Other innovations will be that in future inner London and Birmingham will come before New Towns and only after assisted areas in consideration of industrial development certificate applications, and advance factories will be built by the Department of Industry in inner areas: the Location of Offices Bureau will promote location of offices in inner areas and office development permits will be used more forcefully. Housing investment programmes will be introduced.

The Inner Urban Areas Bill was published on the 15 December 1977. Its main purpose was to give increased powers to local authorities. Where 'spatial social need' exists in any inner urban area the Bill provides that the Secretary of State can specify that area as a 'designated district'. Authorities in such a district have the powers to make loans at commercial rates for land purchase and works on land for up to 90 per cent of the value of the land and building whether or not the authority owns the land. They can also establish, as put forward in the White Paper, *industrial improvement areas* where the authorities can give grants or loans to convert buildings or make environmental improvements so as to promote employment opportunities. Parts of the designated districts can, if particularly special social needs exist, be designated as 'special areas' in which additional powers, like giving grants towards rents to assist firms taking leases on premises not owned by the local authority or making interest-free loans to firms, will be available.

Initially, the money for the programme came from resources made available by the Chancellor for assistance to the construction industry and to be spent in inner areas. This amounted to £83 million for the two years 1977/1978 and 1978/1979, of which £57 million was allocated to the five original partnerships, £16 million to other areas and £10 million was held in reserve for the two extra partnerships finally decided upon.

The partnership authorities and their urban aid grants for 1978/1979 have now been decided. In addition to those originally mentioned in the White Paper—Liverpool (£2½ million), Birmingham (£2¼ million), Manchester/Salford (£2½ million), London (Lambeth) (£1 million), and London (Dockland) (£3½ million)—two more were added in November 1977, in Newcastle/Gateshead (£1¾ million) and in London (Hackney/Islington) (£1¾ million) (*New Society*, 10 November 1977). Some are already spending the construction industry money, mainly on projects previously planned (Whitbread, 1977). In addition £25 million from the urban programme has been made available to help a further fifteen local authorities (for instance, Leeds) to draw up inner area programmes, help industry, and start community projects, and the rate support grant is being adjusted to benefit urban areas. No time limit seems to have been set to which the government is committed to give aid. It can therefore be seen that the urban programme in its various forms has changed little in the ten years it has run, except for a gradual change of emphasis from action research in small areas to the wider arena of a local authority. Much of the urban programme will now become the domain of the 'inner city programme' (ICP) and this document, drawn up each year, will decide the annual priorities for 'regeneration'.

By 1974 the government had spent £1 707 213 on 146 different urban aid projects (Community Development Project, 1977b) to no dramatic effect. This highlights the whole problem of urban first-aid, which, put simply, is 'the achievement of *political and administrative commitment* to a sustained and meaningful reduction in the problems of inner cities identified as requiring government action' (Inner City Working Group, 1977, p. 6). There is little evidence of such a commitment. Indeed there is some evidence that the present accent on inner-city problems by the government was very much a 'one-minister' initiative which took the Department of the Environment somewhat by surprise. It is problematic that there is any widespread administrative support for the Inner City initiative, although, due to the recent policy decision by the Conservative party to concentrate political resources in the area, there seems little doubt that the inner city as a political issue will not suddenly fade away.

Then again the economic recession and public expenditure cuts have meant that those inner urban areas *with* urban aid schemes are still marginally worse off than they were before the recession and cuts: 'The contradiction in government policy is apparent in the five Dockland boroughs of London which have cut capital spending by £19 million while the Government has granted them £17 million in urban aid'—from construction money (Short and Williams, 1977, p. 167). Similarly, Lambeth has used most of its £5 million of construction money on housing, the sector where public expenditure cuts were greatest (Whitbread, 1977). And yet areas like the Docklands are favoured and have been almost continuously in receipt of aid—in the same way Liverpool 8 has had an educational priority area, a community development project, a neighbourhood scheme, an inner area study, an area management scheme, and now a partnership. Lambeth, too, has done well. But what of those inner areas which have received no attention? They have borne the full impact of the expenditure cuts and have sometimes seen radical declines in the level of services provided. By not being positively discriminated for they have been discriminated against.

CONCLUSIONS: STRATEGIES FOR REDUCING INNER-CITY UNEMPLOYMENT

The White Paper and the Inner Urban Areas Bill offer nothing new. A few half-hearted measures like industrial improvement areas and allowing local authorities to act in an entrepreneur capacity will not solve the unemployment and employment problems in the inner city, while the current emphases on small firms and advance factories completely miss the point—the scale of problem.

Housing and transport go almost unmentioned and, more surprisingly, race relations are hardly touched upon (Inner City Working Group, 1977). Indeed the racial issue, on which the urban programme was originally founded, has sunk without trace, yet it is certainly far more serious in its proportions now than it was (Paris, 1978).

It is difficult not to be cynical. The action is cosmetic. The purpose is legitimation (Jacobs, 1977; Paris, 1978). The government must be seen to be doing something. Thus the urban programme 'has been a *visible expression* of the concern of successive Governments with the problems of urban deprivation' (Department of the Environment, 1977f, p. 15: my emphasis). It is important that the government is visible, but it is equally certain that it will do as little as it can. Where else but in the White Paper could one read 'sometimes people from particular inner areas experience extra difficulty in getting a job or mortgage'? The government realizes that 'some of the changes which have taken place are due to social and economic forces which could be reversed only with great difficulty or at unacceptable cost' (Department of the Environment, 1977f, p. 5). Therefore it will do nothing about them. Government inner-city policy is, rather ironically, best described by those of free(er) market persuasion. It is 'dull, unimaginative and wholly inadequate' (Michael Heseltine, *Guardian*, 17 April 1977) and the inner-city problem, 'the most serious social problem facing British government', has costs of failure which 'will be paid in lives of misery for many of the inhabitants' (Peter Walker, *Sunday Times*, 31 July 1977).

The basic problems currently facing British inner cities are the result of the many years of the old engrained processes of social inequality. They are not, by any means, confined to the inner city but reach into almost every community in the British Isles. Put simply the basic problem is poverty. The inner-city problem is more acute because more poor people live there in absolute terms, although relatively there is little concrete proof that the proportion of poor is any greater. The poorest people are those who are unemployed or among the low paid. It is these people that need help and yet it is precisely these people who seem to slip through the social services net so often. In the preceding analysis we have seen how the economic recession has exacerbated long-term trends in the economy, and we have seen how the composite forces of these trends and the recession result in job loss, a job loss which, in particular, has had a greater impact on inner cities owing to the absolutely greater number of workers in the susceptible peripheral or secondary labour market living there.

The obvious remedy to inner-city problems is therefore a national policy to tackle the basic question of employment and low pay. But it must be a policy to increase employment which must fly in the face of the prevailing labour market trends outlined above. Where are the jobs to come from? One option which no longer realistically exists is the provision of more jobs by manufacturing industry. Even if there was to be an economic boom the 1977 Manpower Services Commission Report (see above) shows that output can be increased quite substantially by British industry without new labour demands being incurred. Thus, any economic upturn will not have the dramatic effect on employment sometimes foreseen. In addition, rationalization, new production processes, and especially automation are, almost certainly, reducing the demand for manufacturing industry labour by a substantial degree. Certainly productivity is at present rising faster than output.

A second option might be a vastly expanded service sector. Owing to the paucity of research in this field it is almost impossible to say if this is possible to achieve. It seems that government employment policy envisages about 75 per cent of the workforce being employed in the service sector (Lloyd and Mason, 1977) in the next few years. Ignoring Bacon and Eltis' (1976) recent polemic, the implications of such a shift to services are not easy to understand, but one can guess that the secondary or peripheral labour market would become, because so often unskilled, increasingly unemployable.

It is hard to believe, as Chisholm (1976) does, that a redeployment of the workforce by use of a more sophisticated system of accounts coupled with acquisition by the workforce of new skills and more flexibility is another option in an era of constant low demand for labour. Similarly, concern with overmanning in British industry is gradually being answered by natural processes of erosion. The fact is that there is an absolute decrease in demand for labour and yet an increase in the total working population is expected every year until 1983/1984 (or, on other estimates, 1986). Demand for labour does not seem set to increase unless cost of labour falls, and that is unlikely. The change in unemployment rate and numbers is also structural; it is no longer a case of waiting until the end of the next cycle for unemployment to become only frictional, because each trough in the cycle has a higher number of unemployed then the last.

Barring a revolution (which would anyway still have to cope with many of the problems outlined above) two strategies are available at the national level to reflect and deflect jobs to the inner city. One is to increase the supply of jobs. Following Harris (1977), three lines of attack are open here: the first is by labour subsidies like the regional employment premium and the present temporary employment subsidies; the second is to increase public expenditure; the third is a more wide ranging job-creation programme (Alden, 1977). These represent the conventional widsom yet all could hold back productivity, undermine competitiveness, cause overmanning, and produce a situation of local authorities having to compete for what jobs there are. But, worse than this, they are increasingly unrealistic. With unemployment apparently at 1.5 million or thereabouts for some time to come, jobs would have to be created at the rate of about 1 000 a day until 1981 to reach a full employment level then, against the background of an expanding workforce, and with only six employment sectors currently growing, all in services. In employment terms two of these are growing due to part-time job increases, while two others are in the public sector and therefore vulnerable to expenditure cuts. The Manpower Services Commission (1977) estimates that 1 070 000 jobs need to be created by 1981 to have only 1 million unemployed in that year.

The alternative, as suggested by Harris (1977), is a *reduction in the supply of labour* by: (1) a reduction in hours worked by the working population; (2) a reduction of the working life (through raising the school-leaving age, more further education, earlier retirement, and so on); and (3) by encouraging migration to other countries. The reduction in the supply of labour seems the most sensible solution. A cut in the male retirement age to sixty would be comparatively simple and would bring the U.K. into line with most other European countries. Emigration is now falling so that a reduction in hours worked to thirty-five a week, which is supported by the T.U.C., although not necessarily helping with new jobs of the kind needed may well be the only other alternative. This could be coupled with an increase in public expenditure of a moderate proportion, since this has always proved effective. This strategy could generate 750 000 new jobs by a sensible process of productivity bargaining. An even more effective way of redistributing work hours would be to redistribute the 40 million hours of overtime worked every year by manual male workers.

Yet would this help the inner cities? This is *not* certain. Of those who would have to retire many would be in the inner city and retirement still too often equals poverty in this country. More seriously, how many of the jobs created by cutting back labour supply would be in the inner city? Almost certainly in the inner cities it would also be necessary to include a positive policy to create jobs. Massey and Meegan (1976) have suggested using the National Enterprise Board, which would supply money to firms only if they move to the inner city. Others have suggested using the National Enterprise Board to stimulate new employment by direct action to create firms, or by equity investment in existing or new firms (Inner City Working Group, 1977; Minns and Thornley, 1977). However, the Lambeth Inner Area Study (Department of the Environment, 1977e) considers the use of such institutions unlikely to help because labour and space constraints would still operate, although a plan which combined very considerable reduction of labour supply with an aggressive programme to increase labour demand seems at present the only strategy that could possibly succeed in reducing the number of unemployed to a less miserable number, and which might therefore go some way towards solving the inner-city problem.

In a perceptive paper Chisholm (1976, p. 201) has argued that the high levels of unemployment of the last decade 'suggest that something rather permanent has happened'. It is a new high level of unemployment, probably always hovering around 1 million, which I believe will increasingly polarize into a majority of the population who are in a job and reasonably paid and a small part of the population who are always unemployed (and who will, in the main, reside in inner cities). Worryingly, there is some suggestion of a permanent break with the halcyon days (in unemployment terms) of the early 1960s. Owing to the absolute numbers of unemployed, and those susceptible to unemployment, in the inner city this break will spell out a worse problem there than elsewhere. It is time that policies other than some job creation and praying for an economic upturn were developed to deal with the outcast of the space-economy.

ACKNOWLEDGEMENTS

I would like to thank the following for critically reading the draft and/or making valuable points: Keith Bassett, Mike Campbell, Martin Clarke, John Greve, Paul Keys, Ron Johnston, Alan Wilson, and Huw Williams. Of course no blame attaches to them for the outcome.

REFERENCES

Note: includes references not cited in the text.

Aaronovitch, S., and Sawyer, M. C. (1974). The concentration of British manufacturing. *Lloyds Bank Review*, **114** (Oct.), 14–23.

Adams, J. G. U. (1977). The national health. *Environment and Planning*, **9**, 23–24.

Alden, J. (1970). Double jobholding: a regional analysis of Scotland, *Scottish Journal of Political Economy*, **17**, 99–112.

Alden, J. (1977). Economic problems facing urban areas in South Wales, *Regional Studies*, **11**, 285–96.

Allen, J. M., and Campbell, M. (1976). Employment performance and the structure of industry in Leeds, 1948–73. *Leeds Polytechnic School of Accounting and Applied Economics, Discussion Paper 3*.

Ambrose, P., and Colenutt, R. (1975). *The Property Machine*, Penguin, Harmondsworth, Middlesex.

Anderson, J. (1975). *The Political Economy of Urbanism: An Introduction and Bibliography*, Department of Urban and Regional Planning, Architecture Association, London.

Ash, M. (1976). Open letter to the Secretary of State for the Environment. *Town and Country Planning*, **44**(12) (Dec.), 516–519.

Ash, M. (1977). Liverpool revisited. *Town and Country Planning*, **45**(5) (May), 357–359.

Association of Metropolitan Authorities (1976). *Cities in Decline: A Report on the Problems of the Old Industrial Cities of the Metropolitan Areas*, Association of Metropolitan Authorities, London.

Atkins, D. W. W. (1973). Employment change in branch and parent manufacturing plants in the U.K.: 1966–71. *Trade and Industry*, 30 Aug., 437–439.

Averitt, R. T. (1968). *The Dual Economy: The Dynamics of American Industry Structure*, Norton, New York.

Bacon, R., and Eltis, W. (1976). *Britain's Economic Problems: Too Few Producers*, Macmillan, London.

Balibar, E. (1970). The basic concepts of historical materialism. In L. Althusser and R. Balibar (Eds.), *Reading Capital*, New Left Books, London, pp. 199–309.

Banfield, E. C. (1974). *The Unheavenly City Revisited*, Little, Brown, Boston.

Bannock, G. (1976). *The Smaller Business in Britain and Germany*, Wilton House, London.

Barrowclough, R. (1975). *A Social Atlas of Kirklees: Patterns of Social Differentiation in a New Metropolitan District*, Batley CDP/Department of Geography, Huddersfield Polytechnic.

Batley, R. (1975). The neighbourhood scheme: cases of central government intervention in local deprivation. *Centre for Environmental Studies, Research Paper 19*.

Batley, R. and Edwards, J. (1974). The urban programme: a report on some programme funded projects. *British Journal of Social Work*, **4**, 305–332.

Batley, R., and Edwards, J. (1975). C.D.P. and the urban programme. In R. Lees, and G. Smith (Eds.), *Action Research in Community Development*, Routledge and Kegan Paul, London, pp. 174–187.

Beaumont, P. R. (1977). The assisted spatial mobility of unemployed labour in Britain. *Area*, **9**, 9–12.

Begg, H. M., and Lythe, C. M. (1977). Regional policy 1960–1971 and the performance of the Scottish economy. *Regional Studies*, **11**, 373–82.

Begg, H. M., Lythe, C. M., and MacDonald, D. R. (1976a). The impact of regional policy on investment in manufacturing industry, Scotland 1960–71, *Urban Studies*, **13**, 171–179.

Begg, H. M., Lythe, C. M., MacDonald, D. R., and Sorley, R. (1976b). *Special Regional Assistance in Scotland*. Research Monograph 3, Fraser of Allander Institute, Glasgow.

Begg, H. M., Lythe, C. M., Sorley, R., and MacDonald, D. R. (1975). Annual expenditure on special regional assistance to industry in Great Britain. *Economic Journal*. **85**, 884–887.

Benington, J. (1975a). Strategies for change at the local level: some reflections. In D. Jones and M. Mayo (Eds.), *Community Work I*, Routledge and Kegan Paul, London, pp. 260–277.

Benington, J. (1975b) The flaw in the pluralist heaven-changing strategies in the Coventry C.D.P. In R. Lees and G. Smith (Eds.), *Action Research in Community Development*, Routledge and Kegan Paul, London, pp. 174–187.

Benington, J. (1976). *Local Government Becomes Big Business*, 2nd edn., CDP Information and Intelligence Unit, London.

Berthoud, R. (1975). Where are London's poor?, draft paper, Political and Economic Planning, London.

Bishop, K. E., and Simpson, C. E. (1972). Components of change analysis: problems of alternative approaches to industrial structure. *Regional Studies*, **6**, 59–68.

Blackaby, F. (1976). The target rate of unemployment. In G. D. N. Worswick (Ed.), *The Concept and Measurement of Involuntary Unemployment*, Allen and Unwin, London.

Boon, G. T. (1974). A household survey of unemployment. *Regional Studies*, **8** 175–184.

Bosanquet, N., and Doeringer, P. B. (1973). Is there a dual labour market in Great Britain? *Economic Journal*, **83**, 213–232.

Boulet, J., and Bell, A. (1973). *Unemployment and Inflation*, Economic Research Council, London.

Bowers, J. K. (1976). Some notes on current unemployment. In G. D. N. Worswick, (Ed.), *The Concept and Measurement of Involuntary Unemployment*, Allen and Unwin, London, pp. 109–133.

Bowers, J. K., and Harkness, D. (1974). Duration of unemployment by age. *University of Leeds, Department of Economics, Discussion Paper 12*, Leeds.

Bowers, J. K., Cheshire, P. C., and Webb, A. E. (1970). The change in the relationship between unemployment and earnings increases. *National Institute Economic Review*, **54**, 235–260.

Braverman, H. (1974). *Labour and Monopoly Capital: The Degradation of Work in the Twentieth Century*, Monthly Review Press, New York.

Brenner, R. (1977). On Sweezy, Frank and Wallenstein. *New Left Review*, **104**, 25–91.

Brittan, S. (1975). *Second Thoughts on Full Employment Policy*, Centre for Policy Studies, London.

Broadbent, T. A. (1977). *Planning and Profit in the Urban Economy*, Methuen, London.

Brooks, E., Herbert, D. T., and Peach, G. C. K. (1975). Spatial and social constraints in the inner city. *Geographical Journal*, **141**, 355–387. Includes: Brooks, E. Development problems of the inner city; Herbert, D. T. Urban deprivation: definition, measurement and spatial qualities; Peach, G. C. K. Immigrants in the inner city.

Brown, A. J. (1972). *The Framework of Regional Economics in the United Kingdom*, Cambridge University Press, Cambridge.

Brown, A. J., and Burrows, M. (1977). *Regional Economic Problems*, Cambridge University Press, Cambridge.

Buck, T. W., and Atkins, M. H. (1967a). The impact of British regional policies on employment growth. *Oxford Economic Papers*, **28**, 119–132.

Buck, T. W., and Atkins, M. H. (1976b). Capital subsidies and unemployed labour: a regional production function approach. *Regional Studies*, **10**, 215–222.

Burgess, G. J., and Webb, A. J. (1974). The profits of British industry. *Lloyds Bank Review*, **112** (Apr.), 1–18.

Burghes, L. (1977). Who are the unemployed? In F. Field (Ed.), *The Conscript Army*, Routledge and Kegan Paul, London, pp. 13–27.

Cameron, G. C. (1973). Intraurban location and the new plant. *Papers of the Regional Science Association*, **31**, 125–143.

Cameron, G. C. (1977a). The economy of the inner city—some policy dimensions. Paper read at the 4th Annual Conference of the Institute of British Geographers, 4 Jan. 1977, Newcastle upon Tyne.

Cameron, G. C. (1977b). Economic renewal in the inner city: Glasgow. *Architects Journal*, 2 Feb. 1977, 215.

Cameron, G. C., and Evans, A. W. (1973). The British conurbation centres. *Regional Studies*, **7**, 47–55.

Camina, M. N. (1974). Local authorities and the attraction of industry, *Progress in Planning*, 3(2).

Campbell, M. (1975). A spatial and typological disaggregation of unemployment as a guide to regional policy—a case study of northwest England, 1959–72. *Regional Studies*, **9**, 157–168.

Campbell, M. (1977a). The restructuring of capital and the industrial reserve army in contemporary Britain. Paper read at Conference of Socialist Economists Meeting, 2–4 July, Bradford.

Campbell, M. (1977b). Recent studies in the economics of urban and regional development. Leeds Polytechnic (mimeo).

Canning Town Community Development Project (1975). *Canning Town to North Woolwich: The Aims of Industry* (mimeo).

Carmichael, C. L. (1977a). The effect of falling demand on firm location. *London School of Economics, Department of Geography, Working Paper 2.*

Carmichael, C. L. (1977b). The spatial organisation of the national production system. *London School of Economics, Department of Geography, Working Paper 3.*

Carney, J. G., and Taylor, C. (1974). Community development projects: review and comment. *Area*, **6**, 226–231.

Carney, J., Hudson, R., Ive, G., and Lewis, J. (1975). Regional underdevelopment in late capitalism: a study of the north-east of England. In M. Harloe (Ed.), *Proceedings of the Conference on Urban Change and Conflict*, Centre for Environmental Studies, Conference Paper 14. Also in I. Masser (Ed.), *Theory and Practice in Regional Science* (1976), London Papers in Regional Science 6, Pion, London, 11–29.

Carney, J., Lewis, J., and Hudson, R. (1977). Coal combines and interregional uneven development in the U.K. In D. B. Massey and P. W. J. Batey (Eds.), *Alternative Frameworks for Analysis*, London Papers in Regional Science 7, 52–67.

Carter, C. (1977). Changing patterns of industrial land use, 1948–75. In Joyce (1977), pp. 127–147.

Castells, M. (1977). *The Urban Question: A Marxist Approach*, Edward Arnold, London.

Castells, M., and Godard, F. (1974). *Monopolville: L'enterprise, l'etat, l'urbain*, Mouton, Paris.

Central Statistical Office (1977). Employment in the public and private sectors, 1971–75, *Economic Trends*, **14**, 78–81.

Cheshire, P. C. C. (1973). Regional unemployment differences in Great Britain, *N.I.E.S.R. Regional Papers 2*, Cambridge University Press, Cambridge. PP. 1–40.

Cheshire, P. C. (1977). A framework for analysing spatial labour markets: a review of progress and a critique of the inner area studies. Paper read at Urban Studies Conference, Oxford, Sept. 1977.

Chisholm, M. (1974). Regional policies for the 1970's. *Geographical Journal*, **140**, 214–244.

Chisholm, M. (1976). Regional policies in an era of slow population growth and higher unemployment. *Regional Studies*, **10**, 201–215.

Chisholm, M. D. I., and Oeppen, J. (1973). *The Changing Pattern of Employment: Regional Specialisation and Industrial Localisation in Britain*, Croom Helm, London.

City of Newcastle upon Tyne (1975). *Urban Trends: A Report on the Newcastle upon Tyne Household Survey 1975*, Department of Planning, Newcastle.

Civic Trust (1977). *Urban Wasteland*, Civic Trust, London.

Cockburn, C. (1977). *The Local State: Management of Cities and People?* Pluto Press, London.

Community Development Project (1974a). The British national community development project, 1969–1974. *Community Development Journal*, **9**, 162–186.

Community Development Project (1974b). *The National Community Development Project: Inter-project Report*, Centre for Environmental Studies, London.

Community Development Project (1975). *The National Community Development Project Forward Plan 1975–76*, C.D.P. Information and Intelligence Unit, London.

Community Development Project (1977a). *The Costs of Industrial Change*, C.D.P., London.

Community Development Project (1977b). *Gilding the Ghetto: The State and the Poverty Experiments*, C.D.P., London.

Corina, L. (1977). Oldham C.D.P.: an assessment of its impact and influence on the local authority. *University of York, Department of Social Administration, Papers in Community Studies, 9*.

Corkindale, J. (1977). The decline of employment in metropolitan areas. *Department of Employment Gazette*, Nov. 199–202.

Coursey, R. (1977a). *The Debate on Urban Policy: Decentralisation Versus Improvement*, Retailing and Planning Associates, Corbridge, Northumberland.

Coursey, R. (1977b). The mobilisation of resources to improve inner cities, *Town and Country Planning*, **45**, 5(May), 260–263.

Coventry Community Development Project (1975). *C.D.P. Final Report. Part 1: Coventry and Hillfields, Prosperity and the Persistence of Inequality. Part 2: Background Working Papers*, C.D.P. Information and Intelligence Unit, London.

Cripps, T. F., and Tarling, R. J. (1974). An analysis of the duration of male unemployment in Great Britain, 1932–73, *Economic Journal*, **84**, 289–316.

Crompton, P. and Penketh, L. (1977). Industrial and employment change. In Joyce (1977), pp. 111–126.

Crossman, R. H. C.). *Diaries of a Cabinet Minister*, Vol. 3, Jonathan Cape/Hamish Hamilton, London.

Cutler, A. (1977). The romance of 'Labour'. *Economy and Society*, **7**, 74–95.

Cutler, A., Hindess, B., Hirst, P., and Hussain, A. (1977). *Marx's Capital and Capitalism Today*, Vol. 1, Routledge and Kegan Paul, London.

Daniel, W. W. (1972). Whatever happened to the workers in Woolwich?. *P. E. P. Broadsheet 537*, P. E. P., London.

Daniel, W. W. (1974). *A National Survey of the Unemployed*. Political and Economic Planning, London.

Davis, A., McIntosh, N., and Williams, J. (1977). *The Management of Deprivation: Final Report of the Southwark Community Development Project*, Polytechnic of the South Bank, London.

Deakin, N., and Ungerson, C. (1977). *Leaving London: Planned Mobility and the Inner City*, Heinemann Educational, London.

Dennehy, C., and Sullivan, J. (1977). Poverty and unemployment in Liverpool. In F. Field (Ed.), *The Conscript Army*, Routledge and Kegan Paul, London.

Department of Employment (1975). *The Changing Structure of the Labour Force*,

Department of Employment, Unit for Manpower Studies, London.

Department of Employment (1976a). Characteristics of the unemployed: sample survey, June 1976. *Department of Employment Gazette*, **83** (June), 559–574.

Department of Employment (1976b). The changed relationship between unemployment and vacancies. *Department of Employment Gazette*, **83** (Oct.), 1093–1099.

Department of Employment (1976c). The unregistered unemployed in Great Britain. *Department of Employment Gazette*, **83**, (Dec.), 1331–1336.

Department of Employment (1977). *Employment in Metropolitan Areas*, Department of Employment, Unit for Manpower Studies, London.

Department of the Environment (1973a). *Making Towns Better: The Sunderland Study*, Vol. 1: *Tackling Urban Problems: A Basic Handbook;* Vol. 2: *Tackling Urban Problems: A Working Guide*, H.M.S.O., London.

Department of the Environment (1973b). *Making Towns Better: The Rotherham Study*, Vol. 1: *A General Approach to Improving the Environment*; Vol. 2: *Technical Appendices*, H.M.S.O., London.

Department of the Environment (1973c). *Making Towns Better: The Oldham Study: Environmental Planning and Management*, H.M.S.O., London.

Department of the Environment (1974a). Census indicators of urban deprivation—Northwest planning region. *C.I.U.D. Working Note 3*.

Department of the Environment (1974b). Census indicators of urban deprivation—supplementary report. Northwest planning region. *C.I.U.D. Working Note 4*.

Department of the Environment (1974c). Census indicators of urban deprivation—the use of census indicators in the selection of housing action areas. *C.I.U.D. Working Note 5*.

Department of the Environment (1974d). Lambeth inner area study: labour market study. *IAS/LA/4*. H.M.S.O., London.

Department of the Environment (1975a). *Study of the Inner Areas of Conurbations*, Vol. 1: Summary and Conclusion; Vol. 2: Detailed Studies, Department of the Environment, London.

Department of the Environment (1975b). Census indicators of urban deprivation—Great Britain. *C.I.U.D. Working Note 6*.

Department of the Environment (1975c). Census indicators of urban deprivation—the conurbations of Great Britain. *C.I.U.D. Working Note 10*.

Department of the Environment (1975d). Census indicators of urban deprivation—economic activity. *C.I.U.D. Working Note 9*.

Department of the Environment (1976a). Areas with a high proportion of the population of new Commonwealth origin. *C.I.U.D. Working Note 8*.

Department of the Environment (1976b). Census indicators of urban deprivation—Greater London. *C.I.U.D. Working Note 11*.

Department of the Environment (1976c). Census indicators of urban deprivation—areas of housing deprivation. *C.I.U.D. Working Note 13*.

Department of the Environment (1977a). *Inner Area Studies: Liverpool, Birmingham and Lambeth: Summaries of Consultants' Final Reports*, H.M.S.O., London.

Department of the Environment (1977b). Brief for external research on inner city areas, Department of the Environment, London (mimeo).

Department of the Environment/Wilson and Womersley, Tym and Associates and Mackay and Partners (1977c). *Change or Decay. Final Report of the Liverpool Inner Area Study*, H.M.S.O., London.

Department of the Environment/Llewelyn-Davies, Weeks, Forestier-Walker and Bor (1977d). *Unequal City—Final Report of the Birmingham Inner Area Study*, H.M.S.O., London.

Department of the Environment/Shankland, G., Willmott, P., and Jordan, D. (1977e) *Inner London: Policies for Dispersal and Balance. Final Report of the Lambeth Inner*

Area Study, H.M.S.O., London.

Department of the Environment (1977f). *Policy for the Inner Cities. White Paper*, Cmnd. 6845, H.M.S.O., London.

Desai, M. (1974). *Marxian Economic Theory*, Gray-Mills, London.

Dicken, P. (1977). The multiplant business enterprise and geographical space; some issues in the study of external control and regional development. *Regional Studies*, **10**, 401–412.

Dicken, P., and Lloyd, P. (1976). Geographical perspectives on United States investment in the United Kingdom. *Environment and Planning*, **A8**, 685–705.

Dicken, P., and Lloyd, P. E. (1977). Inner Merseyside: components of industrial change in the corporate context, *University of Manchester, School of Geography, Northwest Industry Research Unit, Working Paper 4*.

Doeringer, P. B. and Piore, M. J. (1971). *Internal Labour Markets and Manpower Analysis*, Lexington Books, Lexington, Massachusetts.

Dixon, R. J. (1973). Regional specialisation and trade in the United Kingdom: a test of some hypotheses. *Scottish Journal of Political Economy*, **20**, 159–170.

Dixon, R. J., and Thirlwall, (1975). *Regional Growth and Unemployment in the United Kingdom*, Macmillan, London.

Donnison, D. (1975a). Policies for priority areas. *Journal of Social Policy*, **3**, 127–135.

Donnison, D. (1975b). Policies for social deprivation. In E. Butterworth and R. Holman (Eds.), *Social Welfare in Modern Britain*, Fontana, London, pp. 420–425.

Donnison, P., and Eversley, D.E.C. (Eds.) (1973). *London: Urban Patterns, Problems and Policies,* Heinemann, London.

Drewett, R., Goddard, J., and Spence, N. (1976a). British cities: urban population and employment trends 1951–71. *Department of the Environment Research Report,* **10**.

Drewett, R., Goddard, J., and Spence, N. (1976b). What's happening in British cities. *Town and Country Planning,* **44**, 23–33.

Dressant, J. W., and Smart, R. (1977). Evaluating the effects of regional policy: a critique. *Regional Studies*, **11**, 153–164.

Dugmore, K. (Ed.) (1975). The migration and distribution of socio-economic groups in Greater London. *Greater London Council Research Memorandum 443*.

Dunford, M. F. (1977). The restructuring of industrial space. *International Journal of Urban and Regional Research*, **1**, 510–519.

Dunning, J. (Ed.) (1971). *The Multinational Enterprise*, Allen and Unwin, London.

Dunning, J. (1974). The future of the multinational enterprise. *Lloyds Bank Review*, **113** (July), 15–32.

Eatwell, J., Llewellyn, J., and Tarling, R. J. (1974). Money wage inflation in industrial countries. *Review of Economic Studies*, **53**, 515–523.

Economist (1977). Industries in trouble: from free trade to adjustment. *Economist,* **265** (31 Dec.), 7009.

Edwards, J. (1975). Social indicators, urban deprivation and positive discrimination. *Journal of Social Policy*, **4**, 275–287.

Engels, F. (1969). *The Conditions of the Working Class in England*, Panther, London.

Engelman, S. R. (1977). The labour market effects of housing relocation: a preliminary report, in Papers from the Urban Economics Conference, *Centre for Environmental Studies Conference Papers 17*, **2**, 393–419.

Evans, A. (1977). Notes on the changing relationship between registered unemployment and notified vacancies: 1961–66 and 1966–71. *Economica*, **44**, 179–196.

Evans, A. W., with Russell, L. (1976). A portrait of the London labour market. Paper read at Inner City Employment Conference, York, Sept.

Eversley, D.E.C. (1972a). Old cities, falling populations and rising costs. *G.L.C. Quarterly Bulletin*, No. 18 (Mar.), 5–17.

Eversley, D.E.C. (1972b). Urban problems in Britain today, *G.L.C. Quarterly Bulletin*, No. 19 (June), 43–51.

Eversley, D.E.C. (1972c). Rising costs and static incomes: some economic consequences of regional planning in London, *Urban Studies, 9*, 347–368.

Eversley, D.E.C. (1975). Employment planning and income maintenance, *Town and Country Planning, 43* (4) (Apr.), 206–209.

Falk, N. (1978). *Think Small: Enterprise and the Economy*, Fabian Society, London.

Fiegehen, G. C., Lansley, P.S., and Smith, A. P. (1977). *Poverty and Progress in Britain 1953–73: A Statistical Study of Low Income Households: Their Numbers, Types and Expenditure Patterns*, Cambridge University Press, Cambridge.

Field, F. (1974). *Unequal Britain: A Report on the Cycle of Inequality*, Arrow Books, London.

Field, F. (Ed.) (1977).*The Conscript Army: A Study of Britain's Unemployed*, Routledge and Kegan Paul, London.

Field, F., and Winyard, S. (1977). Government action against unemployment. In F. Field (Ed.), *The Conscript Army*, Routledge and Kegan Paul, London. pp. 125–136.

Figuera, P. M. E. (1976). The employment prospects of West Indian school–leavers in London, England. *Social and Economic Studies, 25*, 110–123.

Firn, J. R. (1975). External control and regional development: the case of West Central Scotland. *Environment and Planning, A7*, 393–419.

Firn, J. R., and Hughes, J. T. (1973a). *Employment Growth and Decentralisation of Manufacturing Industry: Some Intriguing Paradoxes*, Centre for Environmental Studies, London.

Firn, J. R., and Hughes, J. T. (1973b). Employment growth and intra-urban manufacturing decentralisation. *C.E.S. Urban Economics Conference Papers*, Centre for Environmental Studies, London.

Flagg, J. J. (1973). Spatial changes in manufacturing employment in Greater Leicester, 1947–70. *East Midlands Geographer, 5*, 400–415.

Flowerdew, A. D. J., and Rodrigus, F. (1977). A retrospective economic evaluation of physical planning. In Papers from the Urban Economics Conference, *Centre for Environmental Studies Conference Paper 17*, 335–392.

Flyn, M. P., and Mellor, N. (1972). Social malaise research: a study in Liverpool. *Social Trends, 3*, 1–15.

Foreman-Peck, J. S., and Gripaios, P. (1977). Inner city problems and inner city policies. *Regional Studies, 11*, 401–412.

Forsyth, D. J. C. (1972). *U.S. Investment in Scotland*, Praeger, New York.

Foster, C. D., and Richardson, R. (1973). Employment trends in London in the 1970's and their relevance for the future. In D. Donnison and D. Eversley (Eds.), *London—Urban Patterns, Problems and Policies*, Heinemann, London.

Foster, J. (1974). *Class Struggle and the Industrial Revolution: Early Industrial Capitalism in Three English Towns*, Weidenfeld and Nicolson, London.

Fulop, C. (1971). Markets for employment. *Institute of Economic Affairs Research Monograph 26*, London.

Gamble, A., and Walton, P. (1976). *Capitalism in Crisis: Inflation and the State*, Macmillan, London.

Gans, H. J. (1973a). *People and Plans*, Penguin, Harmondsworth.

Gans, H. J. (1973b). Poverty and culture: some basic questions about studying life-styles of the poor. In P. Townsend (Ed.), *The Concept of Poverty*, Allen and Unwin, London, pp. 146–164.

Glennester, H., and Hatch, S. (1974). Positive discrimination and inequality *Fabian Research Series*, 314 (Mar.).

Glyn, A. (1975). Notes on the profit squeeze. *Bulletin of the Conference of Socialist Economists* (Feb.), 1–12.

Glyn, A., and Sutcliffe, R. (1972) *British Workers, Capitalism and the Profits Squeeze*, Penguin, Harmondsworth. Published in the U.S.A. with an introduction by E. J. Nell as *Capitalism in Crisis* (1972), Pantheon Books, New York.

Greater London Council (1977). *London We're Staying Here: Rebirth of the Inner City*, Greater London Council, London.

Greve, J. (1975). Research and the community. In D. Jones, and M. Mayo (Eds.), *Community Work 2*. Routledge and Kegan Paul, London, pp. 163–173.

Gripaios, P. (1977a). The closure of firms in the inner city: the south-east London case 1970–75. *Regional Studies*, **11**, 1–6.

Gripaios, P. (1977b). Industrial decline in London: an examination of its causes. *Urban Studies*, **14**, 181–190.

Gripaios, P. (1977c). Inner city economic decline: some implications for regional planning and policy. *Planning Outlook*, **20**, 15–18.

Gripaios, P. (1977d). Spatial employment in England: an urban and a regional problem?. *Thames Polytechnic Division of Economics, Discussion Paper 76. 8*.

Gripaios, P. (1977e). A new employment policy for London. *National Westminster Bank Quarterly Review*. (Aug).

Gujarati, D. (1972). The behaviour of unemployment and unfilled vacancies: Great Britain 1957–1971. *Economic Journal*, **82**, 195–204.

Habermas, J. (1976). *Legitimation Crisis*, Heinemann Educational, London.

Hall, P. (1977). The inner cities dilemma. *New Society*, **39** (748) 223–225.

Hall, P., Thomas, R., Gracey, H., and Drewett, R. (1973). *The Containment of Urban England*. Vol. 1: *Urban and Metropolitan Growth Processes (or Megalopolis Denied)*, Vol. 2: *The Planning System: Objectives, Operations, Impacts*, P.E.P., Allen and Unwin, London.

Hallett, G., Randall, P., and West, E. G. (1973). *Regional Policy for Ever?* Institute of Economic Affairs, London.

Halsey, A. H. (Ed.) (1972). *Educational Priority Areas*, Vols 1, 2, 3, H.M.S.O., London.

Hamnett, C. (1976a). *Patterns of Inequality: Unit 15—Multiple Deprivation and the Inner City*, Open University Press, Milton Keynes.

Hamnett, C. (1976b). Social change and social segregation in inner London, 1961–1971. *Urban Studies*, **13**, 261–271.

Hancock, T. (1976a). An urban programme. In T. Hancock (Ed.), *Growth and Change in the Future City Region*, Leonard Hill, London, pp. 62–113.

Hancock, T. (1976b). The inner city. In T. Hancock (Ed.), *Growth and Change in the Future City Region*, Leonard Hill, London, pp. 93–101.

Hannah, L. (1976). *The Rise of the Corporate Economy* Methuen, London.

Hannah, L., and Kay, J. A. (1977). *Concentration in Modern Industry*, Macmillan, London.

Hannah, S. (1977). Causes of unemployment. In F. Field (Ed.), *The Conscript Army*, Routledge and Kegan Paul, London, pp. 104–124.

Harford, I. (1977). The inner city—whose urban crisis? *The Planner* (July), 99–101.

Harloe, M. (1973). Inner urban areas—a review article. *Centre for Environmental Studies*, WN 356.

Harloe, M. (Ed.) (1977). *Captive Cities: Studies in the Political Economy of Cities and Regions*, Wiley, London.

Harris, A. I., and Clausen, R. (1967). *Labour Mobility in Great Britain, 1953–1963*, H.M.S.O., London.

Harris, D. F. (1977). The service sector: its changing role as a source of employment. Department of the Environment Regional Office, Leeds (mimeo).

Harvey, D. (1973). *Social Justice and the City*, Edward Arnold, London.

Harvey, D. (1975). The geography of capitalist accumulation: a reconstruction of the Marxian theory. *Antipode*, **7**(2), 9–21.

Hatch, S., and Sherrat, R. (1973). Positive discrimination and the distribution of deprivations. *Policy and Politics*, **1**, 223–240.

Henderson, R. A. (1974). Industrial overspill from Glasgow: 1958–68. *Urban Studies*, **11**, 61–79.

Henry, S. G. B., Sawyer, M. C., and Smith, P. (1976). A model of inflation in the U.K.

National Institute Economic Review (Aug.).

Hill, J. (1978). The psychological impact of unemployment. *New Society,* **43**, (19 Jan. 1978), 798.

Hill, M. G., Harrison, R. M., Sargent, A. V., and Talbot, V. (1973). *Men Out of Work,* Cambridge University Press, Cambridge.

Hill, R. C. (1976). Fiscal crisis and political struggle in the decaying central city. *Kapitalistate,* **4/5**, 31–49.

Hill, R. C. (1977). State capitalism and the urban fiscal crisis in the United States. *International Journal of Urban and Regional Research,* **1**, 76–100.

Hindess, B., (1973). *The Decline of Working Class Politics,* MacGibbon and Kee, London.

Hindess, B., and Hirst, P. Q. (1977). *Mode of Production and Social Formation* Macmillan, London.

Hoare, A. G. (1977). The geography of British exports. *Environment and Planning,* **A9**, 121–136.

Hodgson, G. (1974). The theory of the falling rate of profit. *New Left Review,* **84**, 93–111.

Holland, S. (1976). *Capital Versus the Regions,* Macmillan, London.

Holman, R., and Hamilton, L. (1974). The British urban programme. *Policy and Politics,* **2**, 97–112.

Holtermann, S. (1975). Areas of urban deprivation in Great Britain: an analysis of 1971 census data. *Social Trends,* **6**, 33–47.

Hood, N., and Young, S. (1976). U.S. investment in Scotland: aspects of the branch factory syndrome. *Scottish Journal of Political Economy,* **23**, 385–396.

Hood, N., and Young, S. (1977). The long term impact of multinational enterprise on industrial geography: the Scottish case. *Scottish Geographical Magazine,* **37**, 159–167.

Horn, C. J., Mason, T., Spencer, K. M., Vielba, C. A., and Webster, B. A. (1977). *Area Management: Objectives and Structure (first interim report),* University of Birmingham, Institute of Local Government Studies, Birmingham.

Howard, M. C., and King, J. E. (1975). *The Political Economy of Marx,* Longman, London.

Howard, R. S. (1968). *The Movement of Manufacturing Industry in the United Kingdom, 1945–65,* H.M.S.O., London.

Hubbard, A., and Attenburrow, J. (1977). Employment and housing in conurbations. *B.R.E. News,* No. 40 (Summer), 10–12.

Hughes, J. J. (1974). *Profit Trends and Price Controls,* Spokesman Pamphlet 41, Bertrand Russell Foundation, London.

Hughes, J. J. (1975a). How should we measure unemployment?. *Journal of Industrial Relations,* **13**, 53–78.

Hughes, J. J. (1975b). The use of vacancy statistics in classifying and measuring structural and frictional unemployment in Great Britain, 1958–72. *Bulletin of Economic Research,* **10**, 12–33.

Hussain, A. (1977). Crises and tendencies of capitalism. *Economy and Society,* **6**, 436–460.

Hymer, S. (1975). International politics and international economics: a radical approach. In L. N. Lindberg, R. Alford, C. Crouch, and C. Offe (Eds.), *Stress and Contradiction in Modern Capitalism,* Lexington, Mass: Lexington Books, Lexington, Massachusetts, pp. 355–372.

Inner City Working Group (1977). *Inner Area Studies: A Contribution to the Debate,* University of Birmingham Joint Centre for Regional, Urban and Local Government Studies.

Jacobs, R. (1977). Save our cities. *International Journal of Urban and Regional Research,* **1**, 322–326.

Jaroszek, J. (1976). Earnings in relation to employment changes. *Greater London Council Research Memorandum 500.*

Jeffrey, N. (1977). Recent changes in the relationship between 'urban crisis' and the crisis in British capital. Paper given at R.S.A./C.S.E. Conference, Birkbeck, 5–6 Feb. 1977.

Jencks, C. (1975). *Inequality*, Penguin, Harmondsworth, Middlesex.

Jessop, B. (1977). Recent theories of the capitalist state. *Cambridge Journal of Economics*, **1**, 353–373.

Johnson, J. H., Salt, J., and Wood, P. A. (1974). *Housing and the Migration of Labour in England and Wales*, Saxon House, Farnborough, Hants.

Jones, D., and Mayo, M. (Eds.). *Community Work 1/Community Work 2*, Routledge and Kegan Paul, London.

Joyce, F. (Ed.) (1977) *Metropolitan Development and Change: The West Midlands: A Policy Review*, Saxon House, Farnborough, Hants.

Kaldor, N. (1971). The case for regional policies. *Scottish Journal of Political Economy*, **17**, 337–348.

Kaldor, N. (1971). Conflicts in national economic objectives. *Economic Journal*, **81**, 621–643.

Kaldor, N. (1976). Inflation and recession in the world economy. *Economic Journal*, **86**, 703–714.

Kaldor, N. (1977). Capitalism and industrial development: some lessons from Britain's experience. *Cambridge Journal of Economics*, **1**, 193–204.

Kay, G. (1976). The falling rate of profit, unemployment and the crisis. *Critique*, No. 6, 55–75.

Keeble, D. E. (1968). Industrial decentralisation and the metropolis. *Transactions of the Institute of British Geographers*, **44**, 1–54.

Keeble, D. (1976). *Industrial Location and Planning in the United Kingdom*, Methuen, London.

Keeble, D. (1977). Spatial policy in Britain: regional or urban?. *Area*, **9**, 3–8.

Kennedy, D., and Kennedy, M. (Eds.) (1974). *The Inner City*, Paul Elek, London.

Kennett, S. (1977). Migration and 'million city' labour markets, 1966–71. *London School of Economics, Department of Geography, Urban Change in Britain Working Report, 52*.

Keys, P., and Thrift, N. J. (1978). A portrait of employment and unemployment in Britain 1971–77. *University of Leeds, School of Geography, Working Paper 215*.

King, M. A. (1975). The U.K. profits crisis: myth or reality. *Economic Journal*. **85**, 35–54.

Knight, D. W. R., Tsapatsaris, A., and Jaroszek, J. (1975). The structure of employment in London, 1961–1981. *Greater London Council Research Memorandum 501*.

Knight, G. G., and Wilson, R. A. (1974). Labour hoarding, employment and unemployment in British manufacturing industry. *Applied Economics*, **6**, 303–310.

Koshimura, S. (1975). *Theory of Capital Reproduction and Accumulation*, D.P.G. Publishing Co. Kitchener, Ontario.

Kravis, I. B. (1976). A survey of international comparisons of productivity. *Economic Journal*, **86**, 1–44.

Krishna-Murty, R. (1977). Earnings and income data for Greater London (revised version). *Greater London Council Research Memorandum 504*.

Kurth, J. R. (1975). The international politics of post industrial societies: the role of the multinational corporation. In L. N. Lindberg, R. Alford, C. Crouch, and C. Offe (Eds.), *Stress and Contradiction in Modern Capitalism*, Lexington Books, Lexington Massachusetts, pp. 373–392.

Labour Research (1977). The jobless young. *Labour Research*. (Aug.), 166–168.

Lancaster, T. (1976). Redundancy, unemployment and manpower policy: a comment. *Economic Journal*, **86**, 335–338.

Lapping, A. (1977). London's burning! London's burning! A survey. *The Economist*, **262** (6957) (1 Jan.), 17–38.

Leeds Political Economy Class (1977). *The Need to Change the Way we Live: The Social Base of Leeds*, Workers Educational Association, Leeds.

Lees, A. (1977). Merseyside: revitalising an older urban area. *Town and Country Planning*, **45** 5(May), 253–256.

Lees, R. (1975). Research and community work. In D. Jones and M. Mayo (Eds.), *Community Work 2*, Routledge and Kegan Paul, London, pp. 153–162.

Lees, R., and Smith, G. (Eds.) (1975). *Action Research in Community Development*, Routledge and Kegan Paul, London.

Lefebvre, H. (1976). *The Survival of Capitalism: Reproduction of the Relations of Production*. Allison and Busby, London.

Lewis, O. (1966). *La Vida*, Pantheon Books, New York.

Lindberg, L. N., Alford, R., Crouch, C., and Offe, C. (Eds.) (1975). *Stress and Contradiction in Modern Capitalism*, Lexington Books, Lexington, Massachusetts.

Lloyd, P. E. (1977). Manufacturing industry in the inner city: a case study of Merseyside. *North West Industrial Research Unit Working Paper 2*.

Lloyd, P. E., and Dicken, P. (1977). *Location in Space: A Theoretical Approach to Economic Geography*, 2nd edn., Harper and Row, Chicago.

Lloyd, P. E., and Mason, C. M. (1977). Manufacturing industry in the inner city: a case study of Greater Manchester. *North West Industrial Research Unit Working Paper 1.* (published in different form in *Transactions, Institute of British Geographers*, NS **3**, (1978), 66–90).

Lock, D. (1977). Capitally speaking. *Town and Country Planning*, **45**(5) (May), 247–249.

Lojkine, J. (1977). L'etat et l'urbain: contribution a une analyse matérialiste des politiques urbaines dans les pays capitalistes développés. *International Journal of Urban and Regional Research*, **1**, 256–271.

Lomas, G. (1975). *The Inner City: A Preliminary Investigation of the Dynamics of Current Labour and Housing Markets with Special Reference to Minority Groups in Inner London*, London Council of Social Services, London.

Luttrell, W. F. (1962). *Factory Location and Industrial Movement*, National Institute of Economic and Social Research, London.

Mackay, D. E. and Reid, G. L. (1972). Redundancy, unemployment and manpower policy. *Economic Journal*, **82**, 1256–1272.

McCrone, G. (1972). The location of economic activity in the United Kingdom. *Urban Studies*, **9**, 369–375.

McDermott, P. J. (1977). Overseas investment and industrial geography. *Area*, **9**, 200–207.

McGrath, M. (1976). Batley east and west—a C.D.P. survey. *University of York, Department of Social Administration Papers in Community Studies 6*.

McGregor, A. (1977). Intra-urban variations in unemployment duration: a case study. *Urban Studies*, **14**, 303–313.

Mackay, R. R. (1972). Employment creation in the development areas. *Scottish Journal of Political Economy*, **19**, 287–296.

Mackay, R. R. (1976). The impact of the regional employment premium. In A. Whiting (Ed.) *The Economics of Industrial Subsidies*, HMSO, London, 225–241.

Mackay, R., and Segal, L. (1976). United Kingdom regional policy, the northern region and the E.E.C. *University of Newcastle-upon-Tyne, Department of Economics, Discussion Paper 17*.

Mandel, E. (1968). *Marxist Economic Theory*, Merlin Press, London.

Mandel, E. (1975). *Late Capitalism*, New Left Books, London.

Manners, G. (1976). Reinterpreting the regional problem. *The Three Banks Review*, **11**, 33–55.

Manpower Services Commission (1977). *Review and Plan*, Manpower Services Commission, London.

Marris, P. (1975). Experimenting in social reform. In D. Jones and M. Mayo (Eds.), *Community Work 1*, Routledge and Kegan Paul, London, pp. 245–259.

Marsden, D., and Duff, E. (1975). *Workless*, Penguin, Harmondsworth, Middlesex.

Martin, J. E., and Seaman, J. M. (1975). The fate of the London factory: twenty years of change. *Town and Country Planning*, **43**, 192–194.

Marx, K. (1970). *Capital*, Vol. 1, Lawrence and Wishart, London.

Marx, K. (1973). *Grundrisse, Foundations of the Critique of Political Economy*, Penguin Books, Harmondsworth.

Mason, T., Spencer, K. M., Vielba, C. A., and Webster, B. A. (1977). *Tackling Urban Deprivation: The Contribution of Area Based Management*, University of Birmingham Institute of Local Government Studies.

Massey, D. B. (1976). Restructuring and regionalism: some spatial implications of the crisis in the U.K. *Centre for Environmental Studies Working Note WN-449*, C.E.S., London.

Massey, D. B. (1977). Unit 25: Industrial location theory reconsidered. In Section III, *Values, Relevance and Policy Units 25–26*, Open University Press, Milton Keynes, pp. 5–33.

Massey, D. B., and Meegan, R. A. (1976). The inner city and industrial competitiveness of British industry: the employment implications of the industrial reorganisation corporation, *C.E.S. Working Note 437*: Centre for Environmental Studies, London.

Massey, D. B., and Meegan, R. A. (1977). Industrial restructuring versus the cities, Centre for Environmental Studies, London (mimeo).

Mayntz, R. (1975). Legitimacy and the directive capacity of the political system, in L. N. Lindberg, R. Alford, C. Crouch, and C. Offe (Eds.), *Stress and Contradiction in Modern Capitalism*, Lexington Books, Lexington, Massachusetts, pp. 361–375.

Mayo, M. (1975). The history and early development of C.D.P. In R. Lees and G. Smith (Eds.), *Action Research in Community Development*, Routledge and Kegan Paul, London, pp. 6–18.

Medhurst, D. F., and Parry Lewis, J. (1969). *Urban Decay: An Analysis and a Policy*, Macmillan, London.

Meek, R. C. (1973). *Studies in the Labour Theory of Value*, 2nd edn., Lawrence and Wishart, London.

Meeks, G. (1977). *Disappointing Marriage: A Study of the Gains from Merger*, Cambridge University Press, Cambridge.

Meeks, G., and Whittington, G. (1975). Giant companies in the United Kingdom, 1948–69. *Economic Journal*, **85**, 824–843.

Meller, R. (1975). The British experience: combined and uneven development. In M. Harloe (Ed.), *Proceedings of the Conference on Urban Change and Conflict*, Centre for Environmental Studies Conference Paper 14, pp. 99–135.

Mellor, R. (1973). Structure and process in the twilight areas. *Town Planning Review*, **44**, 54–70.

Mellor, J. R. (1977). *Urban Sociology in an Urbanised Society*, Routledge and Kegan Paul, London.

Metcalf, D. (1975). Urban unemployment in England. *Economic Journal*, **85**, 578–589.

Metcalf, D., and Richardson, R. (1976). The nature and measurement of unemployment in the U.K. *Three Banks Review*, 30–42.

Metcalf, D., and Richardson, R. (1976a). Unemployment in London. In G. D. N. Worswick (Ed.), *The Concept and Measurement of Involuntary Unemployment*, Allen and Unwin, London, pp. 203–220.

Midwinter, E. (1972). *Priority Education: An Account of the Liverpool Project*, Penguin, Harmondsworth, Middlesex.

Millar, J., and Mellon, T. (1970). Manchester: survey of a city's industry. *Journal of the Town Planning Institute*, **56**, 384–388.

Minns, R., and Thornley, J. (1977). State shareholding. Paper given to Regional Studies Association Conference, London.

Moore, B. C., and Rhodes, J. (1973). Evaluating the effects of British regional economic policy. *Economic Journal*, **83**, 87–110.

Moore, B. C., and Rhodes, J. (1974). The effects of regional economic policy in the

United Kingdom. In Sant, M. (Ed.), *Regional Policy and Planning for Europe*, Saxon House, Farnborough, Hants., pp. 43–69.

Moore, B. C., and Rhodes, J. (1976a). A quantitative analysis of the effects of the regional employment premium and other regional policy instruments. *University of Cambridge, Department of Applied Economics, Economic Reprint 4.*

Moore, B. C., and Rhodes, J. (1976b). Regional economic policy and the movement of manufacturing firms to development areas. *Economica*, **43**, 17–31.

Moore, B. C., and Rhodes, J. (1976c). Regional policy and the Scottish economy. *Scottish Journal of Political Economy*, **21**, 215–235.

Moore, B. C., and Rhodes, J., and Tyler, D. (1977). The impact of regional policy in the 1970's. *C.E.S. Review*, **1**, 67–77.

Morishima, M. (1973). *Marx's Economics: A Dual Theory of Value and Growth*, Cambridge University Press, Cambridge.

Morrey, C. R. (1973). The changing population of the London boroughs. *G.L.C. Department of Planning and Transportation Research Memorandum 413.*

National Institute for Economic and Social Research (1977). The economy in 1976. *National Institute Economic Review* (Jan.), **79**, 3–28.

Newton, K. (1976). *Second City Politics: Democratic Processes and Decision-making in Birmingham*, Clarendon Press, London.

North, D. J. (1974). The process of locational change in manufacturing organisations. In F.E.I. Hamilton (Ed.), *Spatial Perspectives on Industrial Organisation*, Wiley, London, pp. 213–244.

Northcott, J. (1977). Industry in the development areas: the experience of firms opening new factories. *Political and Economic Planning Broadsheet 573.*

Northern Region Strategy Team (1975a). Evaluation of the impact of regional policy on manufacturing industry in the Northern Region. *Northern Regional Strategy Team Technical Report 2.*

Northern Region Strategy Team (1975b). Change and efficiency in manufacturing industry in the Northern Region, 1948–73. *Northern Regional Strategy Team Technical Report 3.*

Northern Region Strategy Team (1975c). Growth and structural change in the economy of the Northern Region since 1952. *Northern Regional Strategy Team Technical Report 4.*

Northern Region Strategy Team (1975d). The characteristics of the unemployed in the Northern Region, 1966–74. *Northern Regional Strategy Team Technical Report 6.*

Northern Region Strategy Team (1976a). Movement of manufacturing industries: the Northern Region, 1961–73. *Northern Regional Strategy Team Technical Report 10.*

Northern Region Strategy Team (1976b). Causes of the recent improvement in the rate of unemployment in the Northern England relative to Great Britain. *Northern Regional Strategy Team Technical Report 11.*

North Tyneside Trades Council (1977). *Unemployment and Young Workers in Tyneside*, North Tyneside C.D.P., North Tyneside.

Oakeshott, J. J. (1975). Unemployment in London. *Greater London Council Research Memorandum 499.*

O'Cleireacain, C. C. (1974). Labour market trends in London and the rest of the south-east. *Urban Studies*, **11**, 329–339.

O'Connor, J. (1973). *The Fiscal Crisis of the State*, St. Martin's Press, New York.

O'Dell, A., and parker, J. (1977). The use of census data to identify and describe housing stress. *Building Research Establishment Current Paper 6/77.*

Offe, C. (1976). *Industry and Inequality: The Achievement Principle in Work and Social Status*, Edward Arnold, London.

Organisation for European Cooperation and Development (1977). *Structural Determinants of Employment and Unemployment*, Vols. 1 and 2, Organisation for

222

Economic Cooperation and Development, Paris.

Pahl, R. E. (1971). Poverty and the urban system. In M. Chisholm and G. Manners, (Eds.), *Spatial Policy Problems of the British Economy*, Cambridge University Press, Cambridge, pp. 126–145.

Panic, M. (1975). Why the U.K.'s propensity to import is high. *Lloyds Bank Review*, **115** (Jan.), 1–12.

Panic, M., and Close, R. E. (1973). Profitability of British manufacturing industry, *Lloyds Bank Review*, **109** (July), 30–44.

Paris, C. (1977). Causes and symptoms: as assessment of the inner area studies. *C.E.S. Review*, **1**, 7–8.

Paris, C. (1978). The parallels are striking . . . crisis in the inner city? *International Journal of Urban and Regional Research*, **2**, 160–170.

Parry Lewis, J., White, C. J., Kilsby, D. J. R., and Edwards, D. G. (1975). A central area redevelopment simulation model. *Regional Studies*, **9**, 395–421.

Parsons, G. F. (1972). The giant manufacturing corporations and regional growth in Britain. *Area*, **4**, 99–103.

Parsons, G. F. (1973). Some comments on the structure and spatial distribution of corporate manufacturing industry in the U.K. *University College London, Department of Geography, Occasional Paper 14*.

Penn, R., and Alden, J. (1977). *Upper Afan C.D.P.: Final Report to Sponsors. Joint Report by Action Team and Research Team Directors*, University of Wales Institute of Science and Technology, Cardiff.

Peston, M. (1972). Unemployment: why we need a new measurement. *Lloyds Bank Review*, **104** (Apr.), 1–7.

Pigou, A. C. (1933). *Theory of Unemployment*, Cass, London.

Pilling, G. (1973). Imperialism, trade and unequal exchange: the work of Aghiri Emmanuel. *Economy and Society*, **2**, 164–185.

Poulantzas, N. (1973). *Political Power and Social Classes*. New Left Books, London.

Power, A. (1977). Review of inner area studies. *Roof*, **2**, 58–59.

Pownall, C. E. (1975). Educational priority areas in theory and practice. *University of Leeds, School of Geography, Working Paper 98*.

Prais, S. J. (1975). Giant companies in the United Kingdom, 1948–69. *Economic Journal*, **85**, 824–843.

Prais, S. J. (1976). *The Evolution of Giant Firms in Britain*, Cambridge University Press, Cambridge.

Pratten, C. F. (1972). How higher wages can cause unemployment. *Lloyds Bank Review*, **103** (Jan.), 12–24.

Quince, R. E., and Segal, N. S. (1977). The evolution of assisted area industrial policies and their impact on the Northern Regions—past, present and future. *Planning Outlook*, **20**, 8–14.

Reddaway, W. B. (1972). An analysis of take-overs. *Lloyds Bank Review*, **104** (Apr.), 8–19.

Rees, J. (1972). The industrial corporation and location decision analysis. *Area*, **4**, 199–205.

Regional Policy Research Unit (University of Durham) (1977). Inner city employment situations: production, restructuring, employment change and relative surplus populations in the Tyneside conurbation. Paper read at Institute of British Geographers Conference, Newcastle, 5 Jan. 1977.

Rein, M., and Marriss, P. (1975). Equality, inflation and wage control. In L. N. Lindberg, R. Alford, C. Crouch, and C. Offe (Eds.), *Stress and Contradiction in Modern Capitalism*, Lexington Books, Lexington, Massachusetts, pp. 199–215.

Rex, J. (1968). The sociology of a zone of transition. In R. E. Pahl (Ed.), *Readings in Urban Sociology*, Pergamon, London, pp. 211–231.

Rhind, D. W., Stanness, K., and Evans, I. S. (1977). Population distribution in and around selected British cities. *University of Durham, Department of Geography, Census Research Unit Working Paper 11.*

Righter, R. (1977). *Save Our Cities,* Gulbenkian Foundation, London.

Robinson, J., and Wilkinson, F. (1977). What has become of employment policy?, *Cambridge Journal of Economics,* **1,** 5–14.

Robson, B. T. (1969). *Urban Analysis,* Cambridge University Press, Cambridge.

Rogers, P. B., and Smith, C. R. (1977). The local authority's role in economic development: the Tyne and Wear Act 1976. *Regional Studies,* **11,** 153–164.

Rowthorn, R. (1976). Late capitalism: review article. *New Left Review,* **98,** 59–83.

Rowthorn, R. (1977). Conflict, inflation and money. *Cambridge Journal of Economics,* **1,** 215–240.

Rowthorn, R. and Hymer, S. (1971). *International Big Business 1957–67: A Study of Comparative Growth,* Cambridge University Press, Cambridge.

Royal Institute of Chartered Surveyors (1977). *Inner City Regeneration: A Report on Some Aspects of the Inner City Problem,* Royal Institute of Chartered Surveyors, London.

Rutter, M., and Madge, N. (1976). *Cycles of Disadvantage: A Review of Research,* Heinemann, London.

Salt, J. (1976). Local unemployment in the United Kingdom in the 1970's. Paper read to Regional Studies Association Conference, Birmingham, 1976.

Sant, M. E. C. (1975). *Industrial Movement and Regional Development: The British Case,* Pergamon, Oxford.

Santos, M. (1975). *L'espace Partagé: Les Deux Circuits de L'économie Urbaine des Pays Sous-développés,* éditions M.-th-Génin–Libraries Techniques, Paris.

Save Britain's Heritage (1976). The concrete Jerusalem: the failure of the clean sweep. *New Society,* 23 Dec.

Scherer, F. M., Beckenstein, A., Kaufer, E., and Murphy, R. D. (1975). *The Economics of Multi-plant Operation: An International Comparisons Study,* Harvard Economic Studies 145, Harvard University Press, Cambridge, Massachusetts.

Self, P. (1977). This time, listen! *Town and Country Planning,* **45**(5) (May), 244–247.

S.H.A.C. (1976). *Low Income and Bad Housing: Evidence to the Royal Commission on the Distribution of Income and Wealth,* Shelter, London.

Shankland, G. (1977). The next ten years. *Town Planning Review,* **48,** 269–280.

Shapiro, E. (1976). Cyclical fluctuations in prices and output in the United Kingdom. *Economic Journal,* **86,** 746–758.

Shelter Neighbourhood Housing Project (1972). *Another Change for Cities: S.N.A.P. 69/72,* Shelter, Liverpool.

Shonfield, A. (1969). *Modern Capitalism,* Oxford University Press, Oxford.

Short, J. R., and Williams, P. (1977). Public expenditure cuts. *Area,* **9,** 166–167.

Simmie, J. M. (1974). *Citizens in Conflict: The Sociology of Town Planning,* Hutchinson Educational, London.

Simon, N. W. H. (1977). The relative level and changes in earnings in London and Great Britain. *Regional Studies,* **11,** 87–98.

Sinfield, A. (1976). Unemployment and the social structure. In G. D. N. Worswick (Ed.), *The Concept and Measurement of Involuntary Unemployment,* Allen and Unwin, London, pp. 221–246.

Singh, A. (1971). *Take-overs,* Cambridge University Press, Cambridge.

Singh, A. (1977). U.K. industry and world economy: a case of de-industrialisation. *Cambridge Journal of Economics,* **1,** 113–136.

Sleeper, R. D. (1970). Manpower redeployment and the Selective Employment Tax. *Bulletin of the Oxford University Institute of Economics and Statistics,* **32,** 273–299.

Smart, M. W. (1974). Labour market areas: uses and definition. *Progress in Planning,* **2,** 239–353.

Smith, B. M. D. (1974). Employment opportunities in the inner area study part of Small

224

Heath, Birmingham, in 1974. *University of Birmingham, Centre for Urban and Regional Studies, Research Memorandum 38.*

Smith, B. M. D. (1975). Employment in inner city areas: a case study of the position in Small Heath, Birmingham, in 1974. A paper to the Centre for Environmental Studies Seminar, 17 June 1975, *University of Birmingham, Centre for Urban and Regional Studies Working Paper 34.*

Smith, B. M. D. (1976a). The inner city economic problem: a first attempt at an analytical framework. *University of Birmingham, Centre for Urban and Regional Studies, Working Paper 44.*

Smith, B. M. D. (1976b). What can Birmingham Metropolitan District Council do that will benefit the employment and economic situation in an inner area like Small Heath? A personal assessment to stimulate discussion. *University of Birmingham, Centre for Urban and Regional Studies, Working Paper 45.*

Smith, B. M. D. (1977a). Premises in manufacturing and related uses in the Small Heath planning district, Birmingham, 1958–75. *University of Birmingham, Centre for Urban and Regional Studies, Research Memorandum 59.*

Smith, B. M. D. (1977b). Economic problems in the core of the old Birmingham industrial area. In F. Joyce (Ed.), *Metropolitan Development and Change—the West Midlands: A Policy Review.* Saxon House, Farnborough, Hants., pp. 148–163.

Smith, B. M. D. (1977c). The inner city economic and employment problem: a first attempt at an analytical framework. Paper read to I.B.G. Conference. Newcastle upon Tyne, Jan. 1977.

Smith, D. J. (1976). *Racial Disadvantage in Britain: The P.E.P. Report*, Penguin Books, Harmondsworth.

Smith, G. (1975). Action Research: experimental social administration. In R. Lees and G. Smith (Eds.), *Action Research in Community Development*, Routledge and Kegan Paul, London, pp. 174–187.

Southwark Trades Council and Roberts, J. C. (1976). *Employment in Southwark: A Strategy for the Future*, Southwark Trades Council and Southwark Community Development Projects, London.

Specht, H. (1976). The community development project: national and local strategies for improving the delivery of services. *National Institute for Social Work Paper 2.*

Spence, N. A. (1976). Population and employment trends in Britain 1951–71. Paper read to the Regional Studies Association Conference, London, 1976.

Stearns, P. (1975). *Lives of Labour: Work in a Maturing Industrial Society*, Croom Helm, London.

Stedman Jones, G. (1971). *Outcast London: A Study in the Relationship Between Classes in Victorian Society*, Oxford University Press, London.

Steedman, I. (1971). Marx on the falling rate of profit, *Australian Economic Papers*, **10**, 61–66.

Stewart, J., Spencer, K., and Webster, B. (1976). Local Government: approaches to urban deprivation. *Home Office Urban Deprivation Unit Occasional Paper 1.*

Stilwell, F. J. B. (1972). *Regional Economic Policy*, Macmillan, London.

Stone, P. A. (1975). Balancing the optima. *Built Environment Quarterly* (December), 56.

Strarns, P. N. (1975). *Lives of Labour*, Croom Helm, London.

Strathclyde Regional Council (1976). *Urban Deprivation*, Glasgow: Strathclyde Regional Council, Glasgow.

Stuckey, B. (1977). The spatial distribution of the industrial reserve army. Paper presented at the ZONE Werkkongres, Amsterdam, May 1977.

Sugden, R. (1975). Unskilled and unemployed in West Cumbria: a study of unemployment in relation to economic planning and public transportation policies. *University of York, Department of Social Administration, Papers in Community Studies 3.*

Syson, L., and Young, M. (1974). Poverty in Bethnal Green. In M. Young (Ed.), *Poverty Report 1974*, Maurice Temple Smith, London, pp. 100–132.

Taylor, J. (1972). The behaviour of unemployment and unfilled vacancies: Great Britain 1958–71, an alternative view. *Economic Journal*, **82**, 121–133.

Taylor, J. (1976). The unemployment gap in Britain's production sector, 1953–73. In G. D. N. Worswick (Ed.), *The Concept and Measurement of Involuntary Unemployment*, Allen and Unwin, London, pp. 146–167.

Tew, B. (1977). *The Evolution of the International Monetary System 1945–77*, Hutchinson, London.

Thirlwall, A. P. (1969). Types of unemployment, with special reference to non-demand-deficient unemployment in the U.K. *Scottish Journal of Political Economy*, **16**, 232–243.

Thompson, G. (1977). The relationship between the financial and industrial sector in the United Kingdom economy. *Economy and Society*, **11**, 235–283.

Titmuss, R. (1968). *Commitment to Welfare*, Allen and Unwin, London.

Toppin, P., and Smith, G. (1977). *Government Against Poverty?: Liverpool Community Development Project, 1970–75*, Social Evaluation Unit, Oxford.

Town and Country Planning Association (1977). T.C.P.A. policy statement: inner cities of tomorrow. *Town and Country Planning*, **45**, 5 (May), 265–277.

Townroe, P. M. (1971). Industrial location decisions. *University of Birmingham Centre for Urban and Regional Studies, Occasional Paper 15*, Birmingham.

Townroe, P. M. (1973). The supply of mobile industry: a cross-sectional approach. *Regional and Urban Economics*, **2**, 371–386.

Townsend, A. R. (1977). The relationship of inner city problems to regional policy. *Regional Studies*, **11**, 225–252.

Trevithick, J. A. (1976). Inflation, the natural unemployment rate and the theory of economic policy, *Scottish Journal of Political Economy*, **23**, 83–96.

Turner, A. (1974). The future of inner areas. *The Planner*, **60**, 34–36.

Urban Change Project (1975). Employment change in the urban system. *London School of Economics, Department of Geography, Urban Change in Britain Working Report 15*.

Vereker, C., and Mays, J. B. (1961). *Urban Redevelopment and Social Change: A Study of Social Conditions in Central Liverpool 1955–56*, Liverpool University Press, Liverpool.

Walker, P. (1977). Inner area studies: now time for action. *Roof*, **2**, 150–151.

Warnes, A. M. (1975). Commuting towards city centres: a study of population and employment density gradients in Liverpool and Manchester. *Transactions of the Institute of British Geographers*, **64**, 77–96.

Warnes, A. M. (1977). The decentralisation of employment from the larger English cities, *King's College, London, Department of Geography, Occasional Paper 5*.

Watts, H. D. (1972). Further observations on regional growth and large corporations. *Area*, **4**, 269–273.

Watts, H. D. (1974). Spatial rationalisation in multi-plant enterprises. *Geoforum*, **17**, 69–76.

Waxman, C. (1977). *The Stigma of Poverty: A Critique of Theories of Poverty*, Pergamon, New York.

Weatheritt, L., and Lovitt, L. F. (1976). Manufacturing industry in Greater London. *Greater London Council Research Memorandum 498*.

Webb, A. E. (1974). Unemployment, vacancies and the rate of change of earnings. *N.I.E.S.R. Regional Papers 3*, Cambridge University Press, Cambridge, pp. 1–49.

Webber, R. J. (1975). Liverpool social area study 1971 data: final report. *Planning Research Applications Group Technical Paper 14*, Centre for Environmental Studies, London.

Webber, R. J. (1976). National and Liverpool typologies: implications for employment policy. Paper read at Centre for Environmental Studies, Inner City Seminar, London.

Weeden, R. (1974). Regional rates of growth of employment: an analysis of variance treatment. *N.I.E.S.R. Regional Papers 3*, Cambridge University Press, Cambridge, pp. 53–97.

Westaway, J. (1974a). Contact potential and the occupational structure of the British urban system 1961–1966; an empirical study *Regional Studies* **8**, 57–73.

Westaway, J. (1974b). The spatial hierarchy of business organizations and its implications for the British urban system. *Regional Studies*, **8**, 145–155.

Whitbread, M. (1977). Programmes for inner city regeneration: the search for priorities. Paper read at Urban Studies Conference, Oxford, Sept.

Whitelegg, J. (1976). Births and deaths of firms in the inner city. *Urban Studies*, **13**, 333–338.

Whiting, A. (Ed.) (1976). *The Economics of Industrial Subsidies*, H.M.S.O., London.

Wiener, R. (1976). *The Economic Base of Leeds*, Workers Educational Association, Leeds.

Wilson, H. (1971). *The Labour Government 1964–70; A Personal Record*, Weidenfeld and Nicolson/Michael Joseph, London.

Wood, J. B. (1972). How little unemployment?. *Institute of Economic Affairs Research Monograph 28.*

Wood, J. B. (1975). How much unemployment? *Institute of Economic Affairs Research Monograph 65.*

Worswick, G. D. N. (Ed.) (1976). *The Concept and Measure of Involuntary Unemployment*, Allen and Unwin, London.

Yaffe, D. S. (1973a). The Marxian theory of crisis, capital and the state. *Economy and Society*, **2**, 186–232.

Yaffe, D. S. (1973b). The crisis of profitability. *New Left Review*, **80**, 280–296.

Young, S., and Hood, N. (1976). The geographical expansion of U.S. firms in Western Europe: some survey evidence. *Journal of Common Market Studies*, **14**, 211–221.

Chapter 6

Housing Problems and the State: The Case of Birmingham, England

Chris Paris and John Lambert

INTRODUCTION

The relationships between state policies and the urban problems of advanced capitalist societies have been the subject of growing concern over the last five years. In this chapter we shall specifically address ourselves to the question of the role of the state in the housing question by detailed examination of one major city—Birmingham, England's 'second city' with a population of over 1 million persons.

Birmingham has a long tradition of municipal enterprise which has been well documented and remains an important part of the corporate philosophy of the local authority. Often—as the post-war experience of urban renewal can readily testify—Birmingham has been innovatory in the fields of housing and town planning. Any account which seeks to stress the special features of the Birmingham situation, at the expense of more general elucidation of urban processes at work in all British cities, would, however, be misleading. So, although we shall endeavour to signify those features which are of particular local importance, these have to be located in a theoretical context which allows for examination of fundamental societal processes.

Space does not allow a complete analysis of the theoretical issues which need to be considered. We have explored the *development* of our own theoretical position elsewhere (Lambert, Paris, and Blackaby, 1978), and there is already a considerable literature available on radical perspectives on urban theory, notably recent works by Harvey (1973), Pahl (1976), Pickvance (1976), Castells (1977), and Harloe (1977a).

In the introduction to this essay, therefore, we shall outline some of the critical debates about the state in advanced capitalism, review the development of the housing problem in the British context, and articulate a framework for the analysis of state housing policies and their effects in Birmingham, particularly on residential spatial segregation.

The state in capitalist societies

Miliband has recently outlined the dominant form of theoretical explanation of the state among conventional social scientists who adopt a *pluralist* perspective. They assume (Miliband, 1973, pp. 4–5):

> ... that power in Western societies is competitive, fragmented and diffused. . . . There are, in Western societies, no predominant classes, interests or groups. There are only competing blocks of interests whose competition, which is sanctioned and guaranteed by the State itself, ensures that power is diffused or balanced and that no particular interest is able to weigh too heavily upon the State.

The state is seen as the *arbiter* among competing interests. Miliband, however, argues that despite changes in the nature of capitalism, Western societies remain *capitalist* societies (see also Westergard and Resler, 1976). The state in modern Britain—by this interpretation—is a capitalist state in a capitalist society. It is important, though, to look at specific features of the British state as well as to maintain an awareness of general functions of the state in capitalism, so that the state itself becomes an object of analysis.

What do we mean by 'the state'? First, we are not referring to abstract separate phenomena, rather to related institutions which perform critical tasks on behalf of the general interests of the dominant class. The state includes, obviously, the machinery of government, as well as associated bureaucracies, the military, the judiciary, and also various levels and arrangements of subcentral government. The latter, termed 'the local state' by some writers (Cockburn, 1977), are also viewed by Miliband (1973) who describes them as both 'instruments of central control and obstacles to it'.

Thus, not only is central government—Parliament—the locus of contradictory class interests, but different interests also structure relations between central and local levels of the state, depending on the balance of forces at any one moment in time.

What are the general functions of the capitalist state? In the broadest sense the state performs the task of *domination*, on behalf of the dominant class (Cockburn, 1977, p. 42): 'As such, the state is at the heart of the perennial struggle between the bourgeoisie and those it exploits—the working class. Indeed it exists because of this struggle, because the society has become entangled in an insoluble contradiction with itself and is irreconcilably divided.'

But the concept of domination must, by an examination of the different general components and specific aspects of state activity, be broken down into modes of domination. Domination follows from the state's involvement in the *reproduction* (that is, in the Marxist sense, of *creating* anew). This involves both capital and the social division of labour to reproduce historically the coherence of the social formation. In detail this consists of explicit controls on human behaviour and the *ideological* role of state activity. The 'process of legitimation', whereby the form and content of class domination are presented to the majority as 'natural' and 'inevitable', is crucially important.

Housing problems and the state

Clearly, any discussion of British housing problems in 1978 must be based on the recognition that both the overall quantity and quality of housing have changed fundamentally during the last 100 years (Watson and Niner, 1978). Frequently this is explained in terms of reformist zeal and the gradually increasing levels of state involvement in housing. With others (e.g. Community Development Project, 1976; Dickens, 1976) we are sceptical about the former and believe that the latter requires closer exploration.

First, while it is undoubtedly true that state involvement in housing has grown dramatically in extent, the forms of intervention have varied substantially over time. Furthermore, different state interventions have produced varying distributional effects which have often become the object of subsequent political mobilization, both nationally and at the local level. State policies, influencing not merely the 'public sector' but every level of the housing market, have had the effect of restructuring British towns and cities and of producing distinctive patterns of residential spatial segregation.

Four major forms of state intervention can be distinguished, and will be the subjects of the subsequent sections of this chapter:

1. The production and distribution of state housing.
2. Slum clearance and redevelopment.
3. Rehabilitation policy.
4. Mediation within private markets.

In practice there is considerable overlap among these analytical categories, but we shall focus on them in turn in order to specify the different processes at work. The theoretical issues that we seek to elaborate are, firstly, the effects of state interventions on the structure of housing opportunities, and, consequently, the fragmentation of working-class interests in housing. The principal spatial consideration is the effect of interventions on spatial structure, bearing in mind that intervention during one period frequently results in long-term effects on the physical environment which may take on different meaning and significance at a later stage.

Before examining the different forms of state activity in housing we should examine the reasons *why* the state is involved. First and foremost the state has been concerned with the reproduction of labour and with the vital role of housing in the process of reproduction. State policies have sought to resolve the conflict between the general need for capital to minimize the cost of reproducing labour power and the particular interests of the building industry and landlords' capital in maximizing housing costs (Pickvance, 1977a). Secondly, having recognized the essential dynamic, we must consider the political features of the situation. State housing policy in Britain has always involved a crucial relationship between central and local government. It has also, of course, reflected a critical balance between the oppositional ,forces of ruling-class interest and working-class demands, so that there has been a fluctuating rather than a consistent development of working-class interests. Within the limitations of a 'mixed economy', governments have tended to use expenditure on housing—as they have used other facets of public expenditure—as a partial regulator of the economy.

The main political parties have tended to differ in their overall intentions for state policy. The Conservative party has supported state policy insomuch as it provides housing for 'special' sections of the population and helps private capital to make a reasonable return on investment. The Labour party has traditionally sought to foster a strong publicly owned sector of council housing as a means of ensuring good housing standards for the working class at a cost which offsets, to some extent, inequalities in wages. Both parties have shared a determination to clear areas of unfit housing (mostly in the centres of industrial cities) through permitting compulsory purchase by local authorities and subsidizing building of new dwellings in their place, although the balance between local authority-owned development and building for sale or private renting has been the subject of substantial debate.

Since the First World War there have been numerous switches in state housing policy (see Community Development Project, 1976) but the essentials have remained the same: the encouragement via subsidies and controls by loan sanction of council house building (without controls on the price or acquisition of land and only short-term control on the building industry) while, at the same time, fostering a private sector of housing to build for purchase. Until the last few years there has been little evidence that either main political party has sought to abolish one sector and create a monopoly for the other; the parties have, to a greater or lesser extent, subject always to the condition of the national economy, encouraged or restricted *relative* growth in the private or public sectors of housing. The capital cost of housing construction has been met from the money-market. State-sanctioned building societies provide a funding base for private house purchase (Boddy, 1978). Local authorities themselves have to raise money for capital projects from national and even international money markets.

The capital involved is not, and has never been, 'free'. The housing of workers cannot be profitable because without various benefits (usually means-tested) they simply cannot afford high enough rents. Thus, the state takes on the responsibility of provision, but the capital involved has to be repaid with interest.

The local situation in Birmingham

Birmingham City Council is the largest municipal landlord in England, directly controlling nearly 140 000 dwellings, i.e. more than one-third of the city's housing stock. The city's 50 000th council house was opened in 1939, at which time the city had an ambitious and far-sighted inner city redevelopment plan. The war delayed the beginning of redevelopment and only after 1955 did a major house-building and slum-clearance programme start to take effect. Between 1955 and 1970, 63 000 new homes were built, 45 000 homes were demolished in slum-clearance areas, and the number of families registered with the local authority for housing was reduced from 64 000 to 22 000. During this period, too, many homes were provided by private enterprise in and near the city, and other residents were rehoused in other West Midland towns by various 'overspill' agreements and Town Development Act schemes. In 1970 it appeared that state policies would end the housing problem; land for building was available, the remaining slums were scheduled for clearance, and the numbers on the waiting-list were falling steadily.

By 1974 the situation was very different. The housing waiting-list had risen to nearly 35 000; the rate of slum clearance had faltered; projected new peripheral development had met unanticipated delays in planning and building; and a slump in house-building accompanied by soaring prices for new and recently built homes had hit the young family to an extent that the otherwise 'first-time buyer' had to look more and more towards the already oversubscribed council sector.

Meanwhile the City Council had embarked on an ambitious urban renewal policy which envisaged extensive improvement and rehabilitation of both privately owned and public sector housing.

The City Council's own stock was extensive and comprised houses, flats, and maisonettes of diverse age and quality, extensively distributed throughout the area of the local authority. The extent of involvement in private housing—both through control of the privately rented sector and assisted rehabilitation—was rapidly growing. Finally, those private owners who were buying their houses on mortgages were benefiting from tax relief; state involvement in housing had become extensive and complicated.

Discussion in the remainder of this chapter examines each of the four major forms of state intervention. Under each main heading, a similar form of presentation focusing on the forms and origins of each mode of state involvement, their distributional effects, political movements and relationships, and their effects on the spatial structure, is used throughout in order to allow direct comparisons.

PRODUCTION AND DISTRIBUTION OF COUNCIL HOUSING

Forms and periods

We can distinguish a number of different phases in the production of housing by local authorities. In all these phases central government, by means of various subsidies, enabled local authorities to buy land and contract with developers for the construction of housing which was thereafter managed by the local authority. With rental incomes and subsidies, the capital loans taken by the local authorities were paid off. Put very simply, the form of subsidy made available at the centre determined the quantity and style of housing built locally (Community Development Project, 1976).

In the first phase, from 1919 to about 1933, a subsidy for general needs allowed local authorities to become substantial providers of small houses. Subsidies were also available for private enterprise house-building to rent and buy, but in this period we can see the beginning of council housing as a major new tenure. Between 1919 and 1935 some 760 000 council houses were produced; at the same time about 1 400 000 houses were produced in the private sector. The purpose of the new public sector was clear—to provide houses at rents which were within the reach of the ordinary worker.

It is important to appreciate the antecedents to the 1919 Housing and Planning Act which provided the first direct state intervention in housing production. During the First World War, under pressure and protest from tenants—crucially in Glasgow where landlords had tried to exploit the extreme scarcity of housing and the relative size in workers' wages by hoisting rent levels—the government introduced for the first time a system of rent control. This measure, if it brought some respite, made further intervention at the end of the war inevitable when the shortage was exacerbated by returning soldiers forming new households. So rent control remained and subsidies to hasten new building were introduced.

By 1930, however, it was clear that this new small housing was not sufficiently cheap for the lower-paid worker, and if there were to be any substantial attack on the slums then subsidies would have to be recast. However, it was only with the after-effects of the 1931 slump—from 1933 onwards—that new policies emerged.

From 1933, production of council housing no longer aimed at adding housing to the general stock, but was for the 'special needs' of slum clearance and the alleviation of overcrowding. The style of council housing changed and flats and maisonettes at higher densities, with fewer amenities, became the typical product. Progress was, however, slow and by 1939 only 265 000 'replacement' houses for slum clearance by special needs subsidies had been produced.

The wartime period saw very little new building and considerable bomb damage to existing housing; a build-up of acute shortages had therefore to be faced in the post-war period. The 1945 Labour government chose to go all out for a high target figure of good-quality housing, subsidized to bring it within reach of the ordinary worker. This was a formidable task, given the conditions of the construction and building supplies industries and the state of the national economy. With Aneurin Bevan as Minister responsible for a very high output in the public sector through the local authorities, the targets were within reach, but were cut by the demands of the American government in its Marshall Aid negotiations. From 1947 to 1951 some 870 000 houses were produced.

The 1951 Conservative government cut costs and sizes of council housing to boost production and by 1955 had returned to a subsidy system aimed at the 'special needs' of slum clearance: high-density, low-cost housing again became the dominant style. Throughout the 1950s production never kept pace with demand and few cities entered the 1960s with anything but acute housing shortages (Samuel, Kincaid, and Slater, 1962).

The Labour government of 1964 inherited from the Conservatives a situation of appalling gravity and almost immediately faced an economic crisis to which its response was the now routine cuts on public expenditure. These, if they were less severe in relation to housing than to other services, still prevented a major housing drive until after 1966. Moreover, as part of the Labour government's quest for technological innovation, allied to the demand for high production, subsidies were geared to assist high-rise developments taking advantage of system-built constructional forms (Pickvance, 1977b).

From 1970 there was another marked down-turn in the rate of production. The new basis for subsidy devised by the Labour government had been building-cost yardsticks: approval for loans was only granted to schemes which came within these central government-approved cost guidelines. Effective in promoting a high rate of building of approved styles, these guidelines were also a potent weapon for the control and reduction of council house building. In a period of steadily rising costs, the Conservative government of the early 1970s was committed to a major policy change regarding the public sector. The aim was to stabilize its size, give it a function for special needs rather than ordinary or normal housing, and to introduce a different scheme for rents whereby the national subsidy would be transferred to local authority housing revenue accounts. By the simple expedient of not revising the cost yardsticks inherited from Labour, the Conservative government achieved a steep reduction of public sector building which was only slightly eased in 1972 when, significantly, the political conflict over the Conservatives' main housing policy Act (the 1972 Housing Finance Act) was at its peak.

In Birmingham some special features of this national phasing can be observed. The city was quick to respond to the new subsidy system and by 1924 had more council houses than any other local authority; by 1933, 40 000 council houses had been built in the city (Briggs, 1952).

Although the city had a vast central district of slum housing it was slow to switch from house-building to building for slum clearance. The city appears to have foregone the new subsidies and persisted with house production of the 1920s style, albeit at a reduced rate. Only in 1939 was the first major development of the style favoured by the 'clearance' subsidies completed (Bourneville Village Trust, 1941).

Birmingham's post-war council housing proceeded rapidly after a slow start. But the availability of building land within the city became a major constraint and controls on city boundary expansion and green-belt restrictions were severe. To cater for the growing population and to allow a start on slum clearance, the city had to negotiate with other local authorities under schemes permitted by the Town Development Act, 1952.

Birmingham had special reasons to welcome the change of government in 1964. A review of peripheral planning restrictions allowed a major housing development to be launched just over the city's eastern boundary (at Chelmsley Wood) and another to be planned in North Worcestershire. The former was substantially complete by 1968, the latter by 1975. More importantly the result was that major slum clearance and city centre rebuilding could be accelerated to an extent that it was completed by 1969. In the five years 1965 to 1970, another 40 000 units were added to the housing stock; in the thirteen years 1952 to 1965 the figure had been just short of 37 000.

Distributional effects

The Housing Acts of 1919 and 1924 which provided the impetus for council house production specified a certain size of dwelling which, with subsidy, would allow rentals to be at levels working-class families could afford. However, a major study of inter-war housing (Bowley, 1945, p. 129) concludes that: 'the market for local authority houses was largely confined to a limited number of income groups . . . small clerks, the artisans, the better-off semi-skilled workers with safe jobs'.

If we look at Birmingham we can see why this was so. A 1938 survey (Bourneville Village Trust, 1941) showed that rent levels for the local authority houses were well above those of the older houses: 70 per cent of central ward rentals and 70 per cent of middle ring rentals in 1935 were less than 10s. (50p); 60 per cent of houses in the outer ring (where new housing was concentrated) were at rentals above 12s. (60p). and 40 per cent at 16s. (80p) and over.

Perhaps the clearest evidence of the main distributional effects of this first phase emerges from a consideration of overall living conditions in the city. In 1913 a council survey had found 200 000 persons, nearly a quarter of the city's population of 84 000, housed in 44 000 back-to-back houses in the central wards—housing which lacked separate water supplies, sinks and drains, and with only communal closets in courtyards. Overcrowding and subletting was common. By 1938 the city's overall population had increased to just over a million of whom 18 per cent lived in the central wards; 170 000 working class families were the occupants of 39 000 back-to-back houses whose only improvement in the intervening time was a separate water supply and a reduction of subletting. The effect of the new housing was to generate filtering and a leap-frogging, whereby the better-off workers and middle class moved to the new housing and the less well-off moved into their housing, leaving the poorest still dependent upon the worst housing.

In 1947 Birmingham acquired by compulsory purchase some 35 000 of these slum houses for eventual redevelopment. To manage this stock and to cope with a high demand for relatively few available houses, the City Council had to develop an increasingly elaborate apparatus to manage allocations and to determine priorities (Sutcliffe and Smith, 1973 Ch. VII). The waiting-list in the post-war period grew rapidly and by 1955 it stood at 64 000. A five-year residential qualification had been introduced and points were awarded to each applicant family for elements of their 'housing need' and also for the time they had been waiting. The point score achieved influenced not only when and whether a family was made an offer of a council dwelling, but also *where* that offer was located. It will be apparent that the diversity of locations and styles of Birmingham's council housing had become very great, especially after the 1950s. Until 1965 the number of houses produced never exceeded the total of new families registering for housing and the number of houses demolished. The queues got relentlessly longer. When the rate of building increased in the 1960s and the switch to central area clearance came, the proportion of lettings to waiting-list families was reduced in favour of clearance-area families. For *them* to be moved quickly meant that many needed to be given privileged access to the more desirable council dwellings. Following the mini-boom of housing production in 1968–1970 the waiting-list did decline rapidly, but in the 1970s the queues again lengthened. For many of those waiting—not now in the Victorian slums but typically in the lodging houses and multi-occupied dwellings of the middle ring—the complexity of the managerial apparatus was confusing and demoralizing.

We have described this complexity and its effects elsewhere (Lambert, Paris, and Blackaby, 1978, Ch. 3). The persistent shortage, the competing demands for various groups in housing need, and the variety of housing qualities and styles, locations, and rents were all factors contributing to the complexity.

Since 1935 councils have been allowed to pool all rents and subsidies in a single account rather than maintain separate subsidy and rental accounts for different groups of houses built under different subsidy arrangements. This has allowed councils to reduce the effective rents of their most recent dwellings by charging rents on older properties that are higher than historic economic costs. While facilitating easier letting, it has also meant in practice that part of the subsidy toward council rents is generated *within* the sector. The controversial Housing Finance Act of 1972 introduced higher rents and declining subsidies (helped by curtailment of new council house production) and a system of rent rebates to enable the new high rents to be afforded by lower-income families. It was proposed that over time the cost of these rebates would be borne by housing revenue accounts—that is, the better-off council tenants would subsidize the poorer. The Act was repealed by the incoming Labour government of 1974, but the complexities of rent levels and subsidies persisted and in 1972/1973 net rental income from Birmingham municipal housing was £20.8 million. In the same year interest, debt repayment, and debt management amounted to over £22 million. The introduction of rent rebates (this part of the 1972 Act was preserved) provided another opportunity for managerial distribution effects. If local authorities took care to allocate low-rent houses to low-income families and thus reduce rebates, their subsidy claim would be less than where a council allocates housing not so much on rent-paying ability as on other factors. Thus can the financing and management of council housing greatly influence who goes where and at what cost.

Political movements

What were the effects of the production and distribution of council houses on those concerned? What kind of political movements did it inspire? The first rent-control legislation followed tenants' protests and the real inter-war promotion of housing production came from the 1923 Labour government and hinged on an agreement with the organized building workers for rapid growth for their industry and assurance of long-term stability. It can also be noted that for a few years after 1945 the aims were to produce large numbers of good houses which would not be stigmatized as 'workers' houses. All these facts testify to the party political context within which the shifts in rates and forms of council house production occurred. At the same time it can be noted that at those times at which council housing was geared to a subsidy system which produced lesser-quality dwellings and high densities, local authorities did carry on producing—despite the social consequences—stigmatized estates which in later years were to be the municipally managed dumping grounds for the least powerful sections of the working class. Since 1964 the Labour and Conservative parties have converged in their priorities for housing policy—with council housing representing a second-best tenure category for the special problems of slum clearance, homelessness, and low income.

Political and popular controversy have remained important. Rents and levels of maintenance have in many places promoted forms of collective protest. In 1939 Birmingham saw a group of tenants' associations linked to Labour and Communist parties engaging in a major strike by tenants against high rents and poor facilities. But such moments are rare and when in 1972 there was the prospect of rent increases and a major shift in central government policy, there were few tenants' protests in Birmingham and these were taken over by the Labour-controlled Council which negotiated for favourable terms within the proposed legislation in an acquiescent manner.

One way of looking at this issue is to see those who achieved access to the council house sector as broadly content with the benefits so gained. Those for whom the prize was of dubious value—the tenants of the ageing estate or the inconvenient maisonette—were faced with few opportunities to achieve anything better and found little or no determination in either of the established parties to define that situation other than as something to be solved by management. Those denied access at all, or placed on the waiting-list, were hardly in a position to organize or protest, but could find a councillor or official willing to examine their place in the queue to see whether an offer of some kind might be made. The emergence of an elaborate managerial apparatus, notionally controlled by the ruling party of the Council, effectively withdrew many of the opportunities to make a political movement out of housing need and emphasized the problem in terms of individual needs.

Thus, during the 1960s and 1970s there were no political movements based on council housing issues. There was a burgeoning of advice and aid centres, sometimes part of the managerial apparatus, sometimes independent, trying to explain to tenants and applicants the complex rules of the transfer and allocation games and to explain why the wide-ranging housing opportunities conveyed in theory by forty years of council house endeavours in practice provided few opportunities in a situation of continuing scarcity.

Effects on spatial structure

The significance of distributional effects and the rise of a managerial apparatus which de-politicized the housing issue become more explicable when we consider the spatial effects of council house production. As already indicated, the distribution in Birmingham took the new housing considerable distances from workplaces. The house-building of the 1920s and 1930s was almost entirely suburban; the post-war building largely took up available land spaces at the periphery or in specially negotiated tracts over the city boundary. Figure 6.1 shows the spatial distribution of developments. The compulsory purchase in 1947 of 35 000 properties in five city-centre comprehensive development areas gave the City Council a stake in a very different type of property; this was increased following the Housing Act, 1954, which gave councils purchase powers to acquire and manage until demolition any unfit housing in future redevelopment areas. These were concentrated in areas surrounding the first CDAs. Only in the 1960s and 1970s were these areas being substantially cleared with modern housing, often in multi-storey blocks, as replacements.

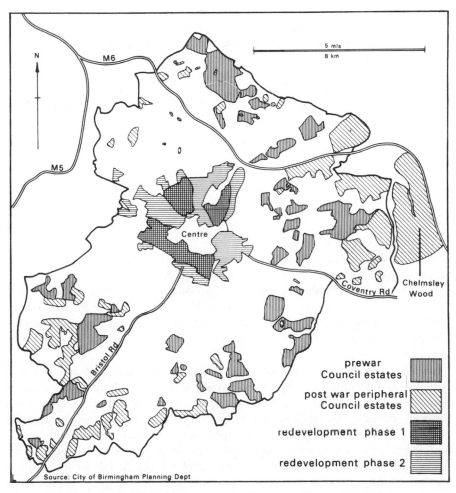

FIGURE 6.1. Birmingham: the development of council housing

This stock of housing, differentiated by location, quality, size, type, rent, and status (and accounting for 40 per cent of Birmingham's population) provided the local authority with powerful influences over the social distribution of the workforce. The real significance of the managerial system of points for housing needs and of grading of prospective tenants' housekeeping standards relates to this historically accumulated housing stock.

During the early 1970s, being a council tenant could could mean any of the following:

1. Being a tenant of a 1930s-built semi-detached house on a tree-lined estate near a main bus route on the city side of the outer ring—within 15–20 minutes of the city centre—at a rental which compared favourably with the cost on mortgage to the purchaser of an identical house in the same zone.
2. Being a tenant of a modern house on one of Birmingham's mixed, low-density, low-rise house and flat developments in a highly accessible position to the city centre and at a relatively high rent.
3. Being the tenant of a 1950s-built suburban estate comprising blocks of deck-access maisonettes lacking gardens, space, or privacy, at moderate rents but inaccessible to locations of employment or other facilities which might render the cost of such a location more reasonable.
4. Being the tenant of a 1950s-built central city tower block in an area stigmatized for its poverty and vandalism.
5. Being the tenant of a modern high-rise block in a city centre or suburban setting.
6. Being the tenant of an old house awaiting demolition at some uncertain date in the future, either among clearance-area housing or among middle-ring property of a very different character being treated by the new urban renewal measures.

The chances of mobility from each of these situations were very different, as were the means of access to them. Each area, each estate, had a different points score threshold for access. So with a mere 150 or 160 points an applicant might be told that all he or she should expect was an offer of situations (3) or (4). The higher the points score, the more favourable the location—degrees of favour deriving from the stability of population—essentially the difference between the number of applicants for such a location and the number of those wishing to move out (e.g. by transfer).

The effect of access and of allocation rules and procedures on urban spatial structure is well illustrated by an examination of the concentration of ethnic minorities in certain areas. At the time of high rates of immigration, there was a five-year 'residential qualification' for eligibility to council housing. During the period 1958–1964, before slum clearance got under way and when house-building rates were very slow, immigrants were forced to devise a quite distinct submarket in housing to cater for their collective needs. Properties in areas awaiting slum clearance whose eventual acquisition was promised but not programmed provided one source; large old properties, probably with short leases, provided another—both types could be purchased with short-term high-interest loans. The latter provided many opportunities for multi-occupation. By and large, Asian immigrants, who have a strong predilection towards owner-occupance, became owners with other Asians, West Indians, and poorer whites as their tenants. These properties were geographically concentrated in the twilight areas of the middle ring adjacent to the areas designated in 1955 for comprehensive redevelopment due to start in 1970–1975 (Rex and Moore, 1967).

Owner-occupiers were not ordinarily eligible for the council waiting-list, but when compulsory purchase occurred, owners were compensated financially for the loss of their home and offered alternative accommodation. Many immigrants were therefore likely to become eligible for rehousing through slum clearance when their areas of settlement became due for redevelopment. However, immigrants who were tenants could register on the waiting-list and after five years take their place with points in the queue (or queues) waiting for decent housing. As they fulfilled the five-year residence qualification, providing they had registered their need, they became eligible for offers of council accommodation. From 1963 to 1968—a period of high rates of house-building, particularly on peripheral estates to the south-west and south-east of the city—many relatively low-pointed, recently qualified council applicants were offered accommodation, but only in certain areas and on certain estates. These were highly unsuitable for many immigrant families whose preference was for central areas which were already in high demand from redevelopment area categories or for high-pointed, long-standing, waiting-list cases—or for tenants of substandard short-life houses.

The high rate of building and the high rate of council offers undoubtedly had a filtering and 'loosening' effect which enabled some immigrant families to move. So it was only gradually that there was any dispersal of immigrants through the 'normal' allocation procedures. Indeed, a further rule was introduced by housing management which critically affected further dispersal. Attempts were made to see that in a row or block or group of houses no more than one in six of lettings would be to a coloured immigrant. The effect of this was to make some areas less accessible to immigrant families and increase their chances of allocation to other areas; but the latter were frequently the less popular, more stigmatized, or distant estates within the range of a low-pointed relatively recent waiting-list case. Moreover, this process was covert, whereas in theory at any rate the normal pointing schemes were public knowledge.

Throughout this period not only were all applicants given a points score which favoured those waiting a long time but they were also given an assessment of housekeeping standards. Moreover, estates and areas had points thresholds and houses were graded by age and area (to tie in with housekeeping standards). From other cities there is clear evidence that typically 'grading' of immigrant families has led to their concentration in poor estates and in older housing (Smith, 1977). From this the complexity of the managerial process of structuring groups of the working population into discrete and spatially distinct areas with very differing amenities and facilities, benefits, and costs, can be appreciated.

SLUM CLEARANCE AND REDEVELOPMENT

Forms and periods

We noted in the previous section that from 1919 to 1935 the main effect of state intervention in house production was to stimulate both private and public sector construction of a large quantity of small houses. The aims of the 1930 Labour government had been to bring new housing within the reach of the low-paid worker. These aims were set aside in the 1931 crisis and during the subsequent Coalition government a new sort of housing policy emerged. The government now reduced local authority construction of 'ordinary' houses and focused its role on the specialist purpose of slum clearance. Five-year slum-clearance programmes were called for and smaller, cheaper housing units for the large families experiencing overcrowding became a feature of house provision. In many cities these new forms of housing were in stark contrast both to earlier council housing and to contemporary private sector development (Community Development Project, 1976).

In Birmingham, distinctive progress was achieved. The council maintained an output of 2 500 houses a year up to 1939, but did *not* switch its style of house construction. Only in 1937 did its first programme for a very modest rate of slum clearance (23 500 back-to-back houses to be cleared over five years) appear. Its reluctance, it seems, stemmed from a recognition that journey-to-work costs from the distant suburbs would deter many slum-clearance families from moving to new housing which even with the special new subsidies would be at rents well above those paid for the existing housing. Furthermore, as a 1946 survey showed (Sutcliffe and Smith, 1973, Ch. VII), overcrowding was now becoming a problem in the small municipal houses which were unsuitable for the typically large families from the central areas. There was, moreover, local opposition to 1938 proposals for flat-building in the middle-ring areas specifically for families from the slums. Indeed, only one major flat development was achieved by the City Council—a 330-unit block on a central area site. More elaborate plans for a 267-acre site at Nechells, just to the north of the central area, indicated how Birmingham City Council was preparing for a major onslaught on its slums.

The war delayed a start on those plans and put an end to slum-clearance programmes, but it also allowed more far-reaching plans to be drawn up and gave a legislative opportunity of great significance. This was the Town and Country Planning Act 1944 which initially was intended to facilitate quick acquisition by local authorities of large areas of bomb damage. But Herbert Manzoni, Birmingham's City Engineer, was able to persuade the new Government Ministry of Planning that the legislation should be widened in scope to include areas of slum housing not just areas of bomb damage (Sutcliffe and Smith, 1973). By this time the city's Estates Department was working on plans for five large areas in the central wards, including Nechells, and shortly after the war it applied—within the terms of the 1944 Act—for the compulsory purchase of 35 000 properties in these five designated Comprehensive Development Areas

(C.D.A.s); the order was confirmed in 1947. Birmingham City Council thus became one of the largest slum landlords in the country with the task of managing this stock until such time as rehousing and clearance could get under way. These properties were the 30 000 back-to-back houses remaining in 1939, together with a variety of shops, workshops, and other properties in the five areas.

Because of the slow return in the post-war period to a high rate of council house production in Birmingham and due also to the priority accorded to special needs in the allocation of the houses built, there was no prospect of swift demolition of these houses. The most basic repairs and modernizations were carried out to keep them habitable. Although work in Nechells started in 1951, the completion of all five areas took until 1967. During this time period, acquired housing was kept in use up to the point of its demolition.

Rebuilding in the CDAs was of a new style. Nechells was the first estate of multi-storey tower blocks; in the other four areas tower blocks grew in number and in height. These provided many one- and two-bedroom units intended to reduce the 'imbalance' in the city's housing stock caused by the predominance of three-bedroom houses in pre-war and early post-war schemes. In the CDAs there were some three-bedroom units in four-storey maisonette blocks and some larger four- and five-bedroom houses of conventional design. Although such production achieved an overall numerical balance, stylistic and spatial imbalances became marked. A managerial assumption is implicit—namely that small families will, irrespective of style and area considerations, go to small units, move to other accommodation as the family grows . . . and move again as family size declines; in other words, adjust to life-cycle changes.

In 1955, as the CDA work was progressing, a second phase of large-scale redevelopment was proposed in fourteen additional areas, affecting 25 000 properties. The 1957 Housing Act, however, removed the powers of swift acquisition and so for these properties a rather different twenty years was in store. Some were acquired and managed by the Council; the majority remained in private ownership until they came piecemeal into municipal ownership through the long processes of compulsory purchase under both housing and planning legislation. These areas became semi-derelict and vandalized, but for some unfortunate families remained their only home. Furthermore, the enthusiasm of the City Council for these large-scale declarations of redevelopment-intent, blighted adjoining areas of similar housing—depressing prices, discouraging landlords to do repairs, and leading to drabness in appearance and demoralization for residents.

In the initial CDAs, progress in building, once begun, was reasonably brisk. In the second-phase areas, everything was slow—acquisition, rehousing, demolition, and redevelopment—for the years of maximum scope for clearance coincided with national economic decline, subsidy shifts, and other measures inimical to a sustained housing drive by the local authority. In the early 1970s, therefore, as policy priorities shifted from redevelopment to improvement, the remaining redevelopment areas were an ugly monument to the vicissitudes of planners, idealists, and reformers who hoped through slum clearance and redevelopment to eradicate the environmental and housing squalor of many working-class areas.

Distributional effects

The distributional effects of Birmingham's slum-clearance and redevelopment policies have to be related to its overall management of acquired slum housing and new council housing. There was no simple transfer of slum-clearance families to special estates or blocks of houses. Such families, the majority already council tenants in their old houses, were merged by the City Council into the overall management of its total housing stock.

The costs of relocation from central areas of slum housing to the new suburban council housing were considerable—a potent deterrent for many families. In 1939 the Estates Department estimated that only 14 per cent of slum dwellers likely to be displaced in the programme then under way would move to the outskirts. Although after 1935 councils could determine rent levels with some flexibility and could introduce rebates, the costs of moving remained a stumbling block for the lower-paid family (Sutcliffe and Smith, 1973).

In the post-war period, the managerial aspects of this problem were reduced. By the time the major task of rehousing slum families was to be tackled, the City Council had a very diverse stock of housing to allocate—central area and suburban flats and houses, post-war maisonettes, and, most important of all, the vast number of central area 'patched' housing units acquired in 1947.

Within this large stock considerable movement could be managed through transfers, many of which did not depend on applications but were offered to tenants when new housing became available. 'Normal' departures from the public sector—by death, emigration, or purchasing in the owner-occupied sector—ensured a steady supply of 're-lets' of existing housing becoming available for letting each year. Between 1966 and 1970, the yearly average number of transactions of all kinds—transfers, re-lets, and new dwellings—was over 19 000. This was an indication of the scope for the filtering redistribution of the population through council housing.

Many of the mechanisms influencing choice of housing and area were critically relevant for redevelopment-area families. Of special significance was the 'grade' of families according to housekeeping standards which determined their access to different types of property. Housing Department evidence shows that three out of ten families from the five CDAs moved to pre-war municipal estates; four out of ten moved to post-war housing developments, and three out of ten moved within the central areas to other old municipally acquired housing (City of Birmingham Housing Dept., c. 1975).

The impact, nationally and in Birmingham, of state-sponsored slum clearance on overall tenure patterns is, of course, considerable. Only in the latter-day redevelopment areas were many owner-occupiers affected. In the first phase (1950–1967) the families living in the CDAs were those who had been unable or unwilling to take part in the massive suburbanization of the population that got under way. In 1938 a survey of the population found above-average percentages of one- and two-person families and of large families in the central areas (Bourneville Village Trust, 1941), and confirmed that poverty remained a permanent problem for the elderly and ageing, especially single persons, and of above-average size families. We cannot know the extent to which the population of the central areas changed between 1938 and the 1950s when redevelopment started, but any movement is unlikely to have altered the basic pattern.

In the second phase of redevelopment, the populations affected were more heterogeneous. In one area studied in detail (Lambert, Paris, and Blackaby, 1978, Ch. 4), 40 per cent of households were small and elderly—these were the long-term residents of the area and most were tenants of private landlords. The more recent arrivals were younger families, immigrants from other towns and cities, and from Commonwealth countries—the latter tended to have remained longer in the area and to have larger families. The younger white families appeared to be 'just passing through', using the area as a temporary phase in their housing history; the Asians in particular appeared settled in the area and were all owners. Seventy per cent of the working population (again including many immigrants) worked within three miles of the area studied and half worked in the immediate vicinity. Many expressed an interest in staying in or near the area. Some of the younger Asians bought houses in non-redevelopment areas with their compensation money and new mortgages: others sought council housing near by. The older residents typically wanted a move to the nearest possible pre-war estate but not to high-rise flats. By and large it seemed that after the long agonizing wait and the appalling demoralization induced by the blight and the process *per se* most residents got what they wanted in the way of alternative accommodation. This evidence shows that, to facilitate clearance, redevelopment families had some priority over available letting.

For some the costs of the process were great. Besides all else, upheaval for the elderly to a new area and new style of housing required fortitude and a helping family. For other families valued features of the old area were its low housing and journey-to-work costs, both of which were greatly altered by redevelopment. For many families, though, redevelopment was a valued opportunity to move to new surroundings, improved facilities, and a better living area.

Political movements

Opposition to particular aspects of redevelopment was a constant, albeit localized and muted, form of protest. In the immediate post-war period the Birmingham Labour party opposed high-rise flats, but the Labour group on the Council retained plans for blocks of flats, and the party consensus within the council chamber on major items of policy relating to redevelopment continued. The plight of those left until last in the clearance areas, the destructive process, the use of substandard housing, the grading of tenants, all attracted attention from the Press and voluntary organizations and were part of localized political debate.

They did not, however, constitute any kind of campaign or threat to policy. An occasional tragedy—death or injury through dangerous play by children in the derelict houses and areas—would provoke angry protests and petitions and receive concerted attention to secure the houses or to fence off hazards. More organized protests sometimes involved a local problem. All these were local criticisms of the manner and process of the policy, not against its promise of a new house in a new area.

If there were any official anxieties they remained out of the public eye. The new estates and tower blocks *were* a visual expression of municipal achievement. The problems—the families in tower blocks, the isolation of the elderly, the disruption of old communities, the impersonality of the new estates, and the drabness and decay of some of the not so new estates—were 'human' stories for the local press, not political issues. Attempts by the more aggressive housing pressure groups like Shelter to dent official complacency achieved nothing. Party agreement was apparent both when high-rise blocks were phased out of council building plans, and during the switch of resources and priorities to improvement.

Spatial aspects

Three important aspects of the influence of redevelopment on the spatial structure of the city up to 1976 need to be noted.

First, as in many other towns (Norman, 1971), Birmingham experienced the creation in a ring around the city's industrial and commercial centre of a 'corporation town', with 12 000 dwellings interspersed with municipally owned shopping precincts, schools, and other buildings. Additional to this were the phase 2 redeveloped areas of similar acreage.

Secondly, the location of this 'corporation town', the history of its growth since 1947, and its anticipated extension had localized blighting effects on its adjacent areas. These took the form of the *relocation* of overcrowding, high densities, multi-occupation, and low amenity, rather than their eradication. Although most of the blighting was within the second-phase areas, there were also important effects in areas of older property near by.

Thirdly, the *complexities* of dispersal—to all the various kinds of housing estates and types of local authority housing, not simply to slum-clearance estates—must be recognized. For the 40 per cent of families relocated to modern post-war housing this meant a move of a very considerable distance to a house with a rental three or four times that paid in the central area and extra travel costs to work of a substantial nature: a move of comfort for an affluent worker but of some discomfort for the unskilled or service sector worker. For the 30 per cent moved to the pre-war estate, a moderate rent, a conventional environment, and shorter distances would be involved. The 30 per cent moved within the central area-acquired housing received a further bout of poor-quality housing and eventually another phase of redevelopment, but longer drawn out and more likely to cause demoralization and uncertainty.

Even these categories imply too simple a categorization of the spatial effects of redevelopment. They need to be related closely to the diffuse fragmentation involved in the process of managing the council's housing stock as a whole and an appreciation of the fact that the private housing sector, too, contains as many spatial and social divides as we have described for the public sector.

IMPROVEMENT POLICY

Forms and periods

The framework for improvement policy, like that for comprehensive redevelopment, is centrally determined but implemented by local authorities; improvement policy, however, was not intended to include extensive state acquisition of privately-owned property. This form of state intervention in Britain has concentrated mainly on the encouragement of *private* improvement promoted initially as a complementary—and later as an alternative—policy to those of redevelopment and council housing.

The main concern of this discussion is the development of improvement policy over the last ten years and the effects of the 1969 and 1974 Housing Acts. Prior to the 1969 Housing Act, improvement grants had been primarily available to encourage the provision of basic amenities (internal w.c., bath, hot water, etc.) in houses which were basically sound but lacking in one or more such amenities. The take-up of grants had been scattered spatially and rarely went to the poorest-quality housing. Many areas of poorer older housing were considered ineligible as local authorities anticipated the probability of redevelopment in the relatively near future.

The 1969 Housing Act sought to concentrate house improvement in 'general improvement areas' (GIAs) within which owners could receive 50 per cent grants towards improvement (originally up to a maximum of £1 000 grant for work costing £2 000 or more, except in development areas where there was a 75 per cent grant). Within GIAs local authorities, assisted by central government grants, would undertake 'environmental improvements' to the neighbourhood as an encouragement to private owners.

It is important to note that GIAs were never intended to be declared in areas of housing stress. There was clear central government guidance to local authorities that GIAs should be declared in areas where the probability of success was greatest (Ministry of Housing and Local Government, 1969). In practice, however, most grants went to local authorities and to owner-occupiers living outside any declared GIAs (Roberts, 1976). Few local authorities undertook more than minimal environmental improvement. Grant take-up was highest in development areas where costs were also lowest (a function of house prices generally) and which had most allowable expenses. Moreover, house conditions surveys indicated that the programme was having very little effect on the rate at which older houses were falling into disrepair.

These problems were acknowledged by the Conservative government of 1970–1974, which stated its intention of embarking on a final drive to abolish slums for all time. Improvement policy was now to concentrate on the elimination of housing *stress*. The Conservatives' Bill was incorporated virtually intact into the incoming Labour government's Housing Act, 1974, which reflected this change of priority and introduced a new form of area management—the 'housing action area' (HAA). While GIAs would still be an important part of local housing policies, local authorities would declare HAAs in areas of housing stress and would seek to ensure an improvement in housing conditions specifically for the benefit of those people actually resident at the time of declaration. There should be less emphasis on environmental work, the idea being that an HAA would probably be declared a GIA once 'stress' had been removed.

So far we have discussed improvement policy as a *technical* element of state housing policy and that, of course, is how it is generally presented. However, it is important to emphasize some political and economic considerations. The major shift towards improvement policy occurred during the middle and late 1960s following the appreciation of the high *cost* of redevelopment and the unpopularity of many new estates. The monetary crisis of the late 1960s was 'midwife' to these concerns—improvement, it was assumed, would be *cheaper*. The Conservative government particularly favoured improvement—which had the additional advantage of reducing public expenditure—as an alternative to new council building (Paris, 1977a). More subtly, the development of improvement policy also provided political legitimation for not rehousing the large concentrations of black workers in inner urban areas (Rex and Moore, 1967).

Before the 1969 Housing Act, the development of improvement policy in Birmingham followed national trends, though unlike many authorities Birmingham City Council vested responsibility in the Public Health rather than Housing Committee (Langstaff, 1972). The City Council used the 1969 Housing Act to declare a ring of GIAs as a 'buffer zone' between better suburban housing and the ring of decaying older dwellings adjacent to its redevelopment areas. Virtually no environmental improvement had been carried out by the mid-1970s, however, and there was little concentration or private grant take-up in these GIAs.

Redevelopment remained the main priority, but increasing local concern was expressed about deteriorating conditions in the 'twilight areas' which had so far received little public attention. Should they be cleared or improved? The incoming Labour Council in 1972 developed a new approach to urban renewal, favouring improvement rather than demolition. A new 'urban renewal policy', announced in January 1973, envisaged intervention at a scale never previously contemplated. The City Council proposed to declare 68 GIAs by 1981, comprising some 60 000 dwellings. In addition, the City Council proposed to declare 26 other areas, containing some 15 000 dwellings, as 'renewal areas'; these had no statutory basis, but contained housing of mixed quality and both clearance and improvement were anticipated.

The outline policy was reorganized in the light of a report from the Council's Performance Review Committee (City of Birmingham, 1975), the provisions of the 1974 Housing Act, and advice from central government. The Council's priority switched from the GIA programme, although the declarations of GIAs continued, to those areas chosen for HAA declaration. Mainly located in the erstwhile renewal areas, the HAAs were expected to be the focus of most active council involvement.

Progress on the ground over the first four years of the urban renewal policy was disappointing (Paris, 1977b). This was partly a result of cutbacks in public expenditure nationally, but there were also bureaucratic delays and unanticipated problems arising from the reaction of residents affected by the policy. Crucially, the implicit assumptions on which improvement policy was based took little account of the organization of the housing market in older areas. The intended effects of improvement and what happened in practice are the subjects of the next section.

Distributional effects

In simplest terms the aim of improvement policy is the reversal of housing decay by means of financial assistance to owners of older housing. This should benefit owners, whose property values are thus enhanced, while tenants of privately-owned dwellings should benefit from better accommodation, albeit at higher rent. Where central resources for improvement constitute a switch from public sector new building, the effect is that those households which remain in *un*improved older housing, have correspondingly *less* chance of being rehoused in the public sector. Private tenants who would have been rehoused automatically as a result of slum clearance, also remain in the private sector, in either improved or unimproved property. For those households with low eligibility for council housing, especially owner-occupiers in poor-quality housing, grant-aided improvement appears to offer an immediate remedy to their housing problems. Immigrants, forced into owner-occupation by virtue of their status in a changing housing market (Karn, 1976), might particularly be expected to welcome the chance to improve their housing at state expense. Frequently, too, it is argued that a benefit of improvement policy is that 'communities' are no longer disrupted as was the case with slum clearance; this, indeed, was a specific objective of Birmingham's urban renewal policy (City of Birmingham, 1973a).

However, in the first twenty-five GIAs, fewer than 1 000 privately owned houses had been improved with grant aid by mid-1976—substantially less than 10 per cent of houses eligible for grant. In the first four HAAs, only 130 out of approximately 1 500 privately-owned dwellings had been improved by the end of the same year. In declared GIAs, housing associations did better: about 73 per cent of the housing association stock has reached the 10-point standard (276 houses out of 375). The local authority itself only achieved this standard in 23 per cent of its houses in such areas (Paris, 1977b).

The City Council had accomplished little improvement in the HAAs and environmental work generally was non-existent. The distributional effect of improvement policy, thus, had been minimal. Moreover, some residents who had improved their houses and then decided to sell reported that surveyors were valuing their improved properties at a lower figure than the original cost plus improvement; this 'valuation gap' clearly undermined assumptions that improvement necessarily made a substantial difference to the market value of older housing (see also Harrison, 1977).

Why was there so little progress? First, there was all the difference in the world between developing the policy in outline during 1972 and articulating detailed proposals for action. One cause of delay was the mixed reception that the new proposals received at local meetings. Councillors and officers were frequently surprised at the suspicion and hostility expressed by residents. For many years the essential features of these areas had been change, decline, decay and uncertainty. Many residents suspected that the shift to improvement policy would be ineffective and were reluctant to invest (or take an extra borrowing) without very positive signs that the policy was working. Moreover, the City Council, in practice, did not provide those signs during the period 1973–1976. Instead there were delays in the classification of houses, little progress on environmental work, and no improvement in older houses that the Council had acquired.

Also crucial was the organization of the housing market as it affected older areas. Building societies rarely if ever gave mortgages on such properties; the usual forms of finance consisting of money from fringe banks or other 'merchant professionals' (Green 1976; Karn, 1976).

The overall context was heavily influenced by the economic climate. Residents of the worst houses, almost by definition, are poorer people, with less secure incomes and more likelihood of unemployment. Cuts in public expenditure contributed to a pessimistic climate; in particular the 'drying up' of local authority mortgage facilities for a nine-month period and the imposition of 'rateable value limits', which made many properties ineligible for grant aid, had deleterious effects. Again, the development of improvement policy was taking place at the same time as the *reduction* in new building. While improvement held out the promise of a better *future*, the present was rather different. The response of building societies to the 'removal of blight' which improvement policy was supposed to achieve was either to *ignore* the new policy, or to suggest that *any* council policy adds to uncertainty! (Lambert, 1976). The collapse of fringe banks and the discrediting of other forms of finance also slowed down property exchange, ensured lower than average increase in property values, and made loans for improvements harder to obtain.

Political movements

The political significance of Birmingham City Council's improvement programme has been diverse and complicated. Indeed, urban renewal policy is still a subject for local action and debate, so we must specify that the period of our concern is up until the end of 1976, when the City Council had changed back to Conservative control and the urban renewal policy announced in January 1973 had been in existence for four years.

The improvement programme had been drawn up in an atmosphere of apparent consensus. Both major political parties supported the idea of improvement, though for different reasons. The Conservatives welcomed the retention of owner-occupation while the Labour party, in public at least, believed that improvement could provide 'what the people wanted'. There was, indeed, more debate within the controlling Labour group than in the Council Chamber; this was rarely made public, but many, especially older members, feared that improvement was a 'second-best' policy which was not likely to succeed.

Voluntary organizations operating in the city's twilight areas had been campaigning for the removal of 'blight' and for the declarations of GIAs. Councillors representing wards in their areas were clearly aware of public opposition to clearance. There was, then, no organized opposition to the policy announced in 1973, though some activists expressed severe reservations on its chances of success (Gibson, 1972). Success was going to depend on the response of residents in the affected areas.

Many other residents were sceptical, however. Their experience of council policies had taught them not to believe any promises about target dates, schedules, or plans. The neighbourhood associations which grew up in response to the City Council's assurance of participation usually comprised older, white owner-occupiers suspicious, not only of the City Council, but also of their new black neighbours, who they neither understood nor liked. They were 'non-political', they were worried about 'problem families' and blacks 'bringing the area down', and their meetings were poorly attended. Councillors, officers of the City Council, and community workers were the driving forces in the development of 'residents' plans'. Blacks frequently became involved, but integration was minimal, though blacks were frequently among the keenest to see improvement working. In general, though, residents were predominantly passive observers of ritual public debates between 'community workers' and 'the Council'. They were distrustful though at times hopeful and optimistic, but rarely put much faith or expectation into any involvement.

The chairmen of the Urban Renewal Committee, however, together with council officials, spent countless evenings meeting residents and preaching the gospel of improvement. They reminded residents that the alternative was a future in a tower block, evacuation to Chelmsley Wood, or the continuing deterioration of their homes and neighbourhood.

The City Council positively encouraged participation at two 'levels': the neighbourhood level and the level of a city-wide residents' representative committee. At the local level participation was organized by the council's neighbourhood-based 'project-teams'. The city-wide level was initiated by voluntary groups responding to a suggestion from the Council's urban renewal chairman that a small group of residents' representatives should meet officers and councillors to discuss general issues and problems. Neighbourhood organizations met and set up the 'Community Forum' where groups affected by the policy could exchange views. The Community Forum in turn elected its 'Liaison Group' which met the councillors and officers.

Such efforts at participation were more frustrating than fruitful: there was debate but little progress on the ground. The idea that participation was 'non-political' was rarely questioned. Attempts to make the Community Forum a more active pressure group got nowhere. The lack of progress failed to become a party political issue as even those councillors who had been the strongest advocates of the new policy began to have their doubts. The inter-party consensus was based on the belief that residents wanted to and would improve their houses voluntarily. For many residents even the lack of an active improvement programme appeared to be preferable to what they had come to expect from the city's redevelopment process.

Effects on spatial structure

Drawing lines on maps and declaring areas GIAs or HAAs has little effect unless action specifically follows. It is worth noting, however, the scale of direct state involvement, albeit passive in many areas, that improvement policy has involved in Birmingham (Figure 6.2). The significance of the programme lies not so much in what had happened between 1972 and the end of 1976 as what did *not* happen. First, the City Council signalled its intention *not* to redevelop in the GIAs and, later, to become more actively involved in the HAAs. The immediate effect was the fossilization of tenures; but unless landlords improved their properties, there is a likelihood of increasing municipal ownership, particularly in the HAAs. At the same time, housing associations are becoming increasingly active in older areas, acquiring property from both private landlords and owner-occupiers (Paris and Blackaby, forthcoming, Chap. 3). As the privately rented sector continues to decline and the public sector in one of its various guises takes it over, then state housing allocation policies crucially determine *who* gets access to *what kind* of housing and *where*. There are also important effects on the spatial distribution of ethnic groups. The perpetuation of cheap owner-occupied housing in GIAs and HAAs ensures, on the one hand, that there is housing for immigrants, but that the opportunities for assimilation through the housing market are limited. On this evidence, therefore, both 'improvement' and 'participating involvement' may in fact constitute a peculiarly British version of 'gilding the ghetto' (Community Development Project, 1977). So much depends on future changes in policy and on the economy as a whole. At the moment older housing is in a strange kind of limbo between council housing and suburban owner-occupation, the dominant forms of tenure in contemporary Britain.

Owner-occupation has continued to grow, both in absolute terms and as a proportion of all housing. Council housing has become an established feature of the housing market, though the future of the sector remains in some doubt, particularly as the Conservative party increasingly favours the sale of council houses (see, for example, Murie, 1977). The privately-rented sector has become a residual form of tenure, though it is critically important for those households excluded from both main sectors. These trends have their roots in the 1920s and 1930s, but are still clearly observable, as Table 6.1 shows.

HOUSING POLICY AND THE HOUSING MARKET

Forms and periods

The three preceding sections have concentrated on specific features of state housing policy. In so doing, however, other features of the relationship between the state and housing, particularly the ways in which state policies have facilitated a process of restructuring the British housing market, have been indicated. State housing policy, then, is concerned with a wide range of interventions which, in combination with ongoing market changes, have revolutionized the system of housing tenure and access in Britain. These changes have had spatial effects and consequences, but these can only make sense with an understanding of the processes involved.

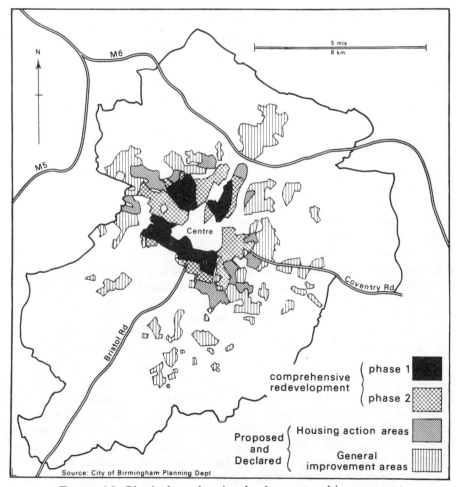

FIGURE 6.2. Birmingham: housing development and improvement

TABLE 6.1. Stock of dwellings^a in the U.K.

	'000s		
	1960	1970	1975
Owner-occupied	6 970	9 570	10 760
	(42)	(49)	(53)
Rented from local authorities	4 400	5 850	6 400
and new town corporations	(27)	(31)	(32)
Rented from private owners	4 310	3 770	3 190
	(26)	(20)	(16)
Other tenures	930		
	(6)		
Total	16 600	19 190	20 250

^{a} Census-based estimates including adjustments for enumeration errors and for reasonably separate dwellings.
Percentages (in parentheses) may not total 100 due to rounding errors.
Source: Social Trends, No. 8, 1977, H.M.S.O., table 9.1, p. 149.

As we have seen, the development of council housing was one response to tenants' struggles and the introduction of rent control during the First World War. With various modifications rent control has been a permanent feature of British housing policy ever since, resulting in the decline of the privately rented sector in housing. Most institutional landlords have got out of the housing market, so that the amount of privately-let accommodation has fallen from some 90 per cent of all housing at the beginning of the First World War to a residual of little more than 15 per cent today.

Of increasing significance since the 1930s has been the state sponsorship of owner-occupation. Originally the subject of political debate, there is today a remarkable consensus between the major Parliamentary parties on this issue. The continued subsidization of owner-occupation by means of tax relief on mortgage interest ensures that those who can afford to buy, usually with a mortgage from a building society, are in a privileged market position. The continued spread of owner-occupied suburban housing is a direct result of state fiscal policies which stimulate demand for this sector of housing.

This is of great importance to the building industry, whose market calculations are based on the predictability of cash flows via income tax relief *and* capital allocation from building societies. While the latter are substantially autonomous, having rapidly become the second most important financial institutions after the banks, they have still relied on government assistance to maintain lending levels at times of their own low liquidity. In other words, when building societies' own fund levels have required a *reduction* in lending for house purchase, the state has 'topped up' their assets to smooth the flow of funds into private house purchase.

Furthermore, Dickens's (1977) examination of the relationship between the state and the building societies during the 1930s amply illustrates the crucial *interdependence* between state housing policy and the development of owner-occupation. State withdrawal from the production of new council housing and its emphasis on slum clearance was accompanied by reliance on the building societies to provide funds for new, privately-owned, house construction. With the rapid growth of owner-occupation and escalating public resentment against both the quality of housing and the 'builder's pool' system of finance, legislation was hurriedly prepared to safeguard the building societies' future (Dickens, 1977).

The state has been a major *customer* of the private house-building industry since the 1920s, particularly in its role as redeveloper of inner areas and developer of new council estates. But as local authorities have had to raise the capital involved themselves, the local state is effectively an entrepreneur like others, but with the crucial difference that predictable flows of work could be relied on. Thus the state provides the conditions for profitable private accumulation of capital, substantially reduces risk, and organizes the allocation of stock and collection of rents, the bulk of which go to pay off interest charges on capital loans.

Other state policies have more directly facilitated the production of housing for private ownership. The 'Chamberlain Act' of 1923 was specifically designed to subsidize the private sector and there were subsequently more subsidized 'private sector' houses built between 1925 and 1930 than subsidized 'public sector' houses (363 000 compared to 359 000 (Dickens, 1977; Bowley, 1945)). The massive growth of unsubsidized private enterprise construction during the later 1930s, funded by the building societies for owner-occupation, thus owes much to state support to the building industry during the earlier period when private investors were switching their funds away from housing.

The thrust of state housing policy has been at one level to reinforce a growing polarization between council housing and owner-occupation. Between these two remains the residual privately-rented sector, which increasingly consists of older, poorer-quality housing, which is overcrowded and multi-occupied.

The recent policy statement of the Labour government (Department of the Environment, 1977)—the *Housing Policy Review*—contains no evidence of any new thinking on housing finance. Instead Harloe (1977b) has suggested that the Green Paper is determined not merely to support and extend owner occupation . . . but to perpetuate the present system whereby the financial burdens of ownership fall heaviest on those who can least afford them.

The dreams of socialist reformers like Aneurin Bevan have been abandoned by the technocrats and apologists in favour of capitalist policies. Current policies seek to maintain the viability of owner-occupation and to reduce council housing to a residual status for those in greatest need. In place of decent council housing for all, the state encourages the development of cooperatives and housing associations outside local political control, to create the appearance of diversity in choice (Swann, 1975).

The development of improvement policy, also, represents state intervention within the private market; but this is a contradictory development. For improvement policies to affect the physical conditions of older housing there would have to be both more resources available and, in many stress areas, substantial public acquisition. Ironically, policies aimed at avoiding increased municipal ownership may necessitate increased state ownership: hence the promotion of housing associations as agencies for area improvement!

Distributional effects

At the macro-level the effect of state policies on the housing market has been to redistribute wealth and privilege in complex and at times contradictory ways. Undoubtedly, owner-occupiers, especially occupiers of substantial properties who pay large amounts of income tax, receive the highest *per capita* benefits. Moreover, under current arrangements they can continually 'trade-up', increasing the ratio of interest to capital repayments, with each new purchase maximizing their tax relief. Many council tenants, too, enjoy a better standard of housing than they could otherwise afford, though it must be emphasized that even the most heavily subsidized council *tenant* never acquires the real assets which accrue to better-off owner-occupiers.

The complex gradations between type and quality of housing and the personal situations of households have suggested to researchers that it is useful to conceptualize a system of 'housing classes'. Rex and Moore (1967) argue that both economic *and* bureaucratic criteria interact to produce a diversity of 'means of access' to housing, and that for those whose only hope of decent housing is through the state, then bureaucratic criteria of eligibility and allocation become crucial.

However, as we have argued more extensively elsewhere, such a formulation has the weakness of treating the state as an autonomous phenomenon, separate from the forces of the market and the structure of social classes (Lambert, Paris, and Blackaby, 1978). Rather, the state has taken over the function of landlord, generalized the conditions for the production and management of housing for the poor, and, in so doing, has transformed economic relations into political/bureaucratic apparatuses. But the state *mediates* an economic relationship, it does not *replace* it. The variety of effects of this mediation are well documented—we have referred to the decline of the privately-rented sector already; another interesting development recently might be termed 'marginal owner-occupation'. The old maxim 'to him that hath shall be given and to him that hath not shall be taken away!' may well apply to low-income immigrant owner-occupiers (Karn, 1977). Immigrants, *forced* into the purchase of poor-quality old housing, pay higher rates of interest than the white purchasers of suburbia.

There can no longer be any doubt that the major financial institutions of house purchase—the building societies—refuse to lend in many inner areas. They have frequently been criticized for 'red-lining' (Weir, 1976) and the recent housing Green Paper urged them to take a more positive approach to older areas. But the extent to which building society refusal to lend in 'twilight areas' *in itself* has affected such areas remains problematic. After all, building societies have rarely, if ever, lent in today's 'inner areas'. During the 1950s and 1960s many of Birmingham's older properties were sold into owner-occupation by their former landlords, either to sitting tenants or at the termination of a tenancy. It is more this low-income/marginal owner-occupation which is innovatory rather than specific disinvestment decisions on the part of building societies; in turn this 'marginal' owner-occupation has come about largely as a result of the combination of the state policies of rent control, sponsorship of owner-occupation generally, and specific blocks on access for certain groups to either council housing or better owner-occupied housing.

The continued diminution of the privately-rented sector during the cutback in new building in Birmingham, at a time of rapid inflation of the cost of house purchase, meant that those who relied on private letting or on the council were in a weaker position than previously. The effect of new rent legislation in 1974 was minimal in areas of housing stress—tenants had more rights in theory but not in practice (Blackaby and Paris, 1976). The queue was daunting and, despite the work of voluntary housing advisers, rents continued to rise without corresponding improvements in living conditions.

In response, the City Council spent much time discussing its new policy on 'multi-occupation'. For many years multi-occupation had been treated like a disease which the City Council sought to control. Planning legislation was utilized to stop the 'change of use' of normal residential properties to multi-occupation and the public health inspectorate (now called environmental health officers) made sporadic checks of multi-occupied premises. The City Council, however, never fully implemented the available legislation in fear that they would end up having to rehouse too many people as a result of their own enforcement action! As Rex and Moore (1967) emphasized ten years ago, the function of multi-occupation has been one of providing accommodation for those households which the City Council could not, or would not rehouse, while also acting as a 'repository for blame' for the existence of bad housing conditions!

Political movements

The restructuring of the British housing market has been the subject of political debate at both national and local levels with, until the last few years, clear party political differences. At the local level, discussion and action concerning state intervention in private markets has tended to be extremely localized and sporadic. Various 'residents' and 'ratepayers' groups occasionally have hit the headlines in the local press with their campaigns against changes in their area, but these groups typically have sought to defend privilege rather than to oppose structural issues.

The debate over municipalization has taken place mainly within the council chamber, but the Labour party, while in power, has never sought to take over the privately-rented sector, so substantial opposition has been unnecessary. Indeed, as in so many areas of local housing policy, party political differences *in effect*, if not in public statement, have been few. Undoubtedly the Conservatives have been less enthusiastic enforcers of improvement policy, but they are not likely to withdraw from public commitments in HAAs and this will almost certainly mean substantial acquisition in some areas.

One campaign of local importance was stimulated by the local community development project. This concerned many properties in Saltley which had very short leases and where the leaseholders, despite the 1967 Leasehold Reform Act, were experiencing great difficulty in acquiring their freeholds (Green, 1975). The existence of short leases prejudiced the occupants' chances of getting improvement grants and also made property exchange very difficult. This unresolved problem has been of great concern to local residents and became the focus of local organization and lobbying of the City Council and MPs. Another issue which became the object of a local campaign was the question of the financing of house purchase in inner areas. Again the local community development project demonstrated the gross inequities of the system of house finance and highlighted some particularly unscrupulous operators (see also Karn, 1977). The City Council has subsequently sought to channel its own mortgage finance into areas of older housing, a policy agreed by both major local parties.

Effects on spatial structure

Continued support, both fiscal and ideological, for owner-occupation, has produced a dominant spatial effect of continued suburbanization both within and outside city boundaries, similar in many ways to that typical of the United States. The population *within* Birmingham's city boundary actually fell between 1961 and 1971, although that of the whole conurbation increased. Much of the out-migration was to adjacent authorities—especially Sutton Coldfield to the north and Solihull to the south-east (although the former subsequently became incorporated into Birmingham with local government reorganization in 1974).

The overall effects on the urban structure were noted in the draft written statement of the City Council's Structure Plan, which remarked on movement of population out of the city, as well as movement within the city (City of Birmingham, 1973b, para. 6.15):

> The social consequences of movement within the City are somewhat similar to the more general effects of migration out of the City . . . That is, those who can afford to move, do so, and groups of the poorly paid tend to become concentrated and isolated in certain districts. This process is accentuated by slum clearance, housing improvements and redevelopment which, while raising the general standard of housing, also reduce the number and diminish the scatter of the cheapest houses.

Thus the polarization of housing tenures within the city, the development of 'twilight areas', and the continued existence of multiple occupation can largely be explained in terms of macro-level fiscal policies which in turn produce these spatial effects. The details are interesting and important at a personal level, but the structure of determination lies outside individual preference or ability. In that sense, it is only useful to think of 'the city of Birmingham' as an administrative unit of the state. The processes of urban restructuring, while influenced by local policies, are not primarily determined by them.

CONCLUSIONS

This chapter has demonstrated how state housing policies over fifty years have influenced every area of the city of Birmingham. Distinctions between private and public sectors of housing are part of the everyday language of those policies but the relationships between the 'private' and 'public' domains are of greater significance. Isolation of housing as a topic for discussion is, of course, an oversimplification. If the impacts of planning and industrial location policies on the rate of building, the style of building, and location of building in 'private' and 'public' sectors are considered, the full complexity becomes apparent.

Arguments which seek to make major distinctions between 'public' and 'private' housing sectors should be regarded with caution. There have been crucial interdependencies between the state and capital, varying over time, which have resulted in different powers and limits on the local state. The apparent polarization of tenures has been accompanied by a much more important fragmentation *within* each of the sectors. The state, in the final analysis, is part of the reproduction of housing, and thus, also, of the reproduction of the housing problem.

REFERENCES

Blackaby, R., and Paris, C. (1976). An act of protection? The Rent Act 1974 and landlordism in the inner ring. *Housing Review*, **24** (6), 153–154.
Boddy, M. (1978). *Building Societies in Britain*, Penguin, London.
Bourneville Village Trust (1941). *When We Build Again*, Bourneville Village Trust, Birmingham.
Bowley, M. (1945). *Housing and the State*, George Allen and Unwin, London.
Briggs, A. (1952). *History of Birmingham*, Vol. II, Oxford University Press, London.
Castells, M. (1977). *The Urban Question*, Arnold, London.
City of Birmingham (1973a). *Urban Renewal Policy*, City of Birmingham Information Publication.
City of Birmingham (1973b). *City of Birmingham Structure Plan: Draft Written Statement*, City of Birmingham.
City of Birmingham (1975). Urban Renewal, *Report of the Performance Review Committee to the City Council*, 7 Jan. 1975.
City of Birmingham Housing Department (1975 approx.). Untitled description of housing policies for visitors to the city, Birmingham.
Community Development Project (1976). *Whatever Happened to Council Housing?* Community Development Project, London.
Community Development Project (1977). *Gilding the Ghetto*, Community Development Project, London.
Cockburn, C. (1977). *The Local State*, Pluto, London.
Department of the Environment (1977). *Housing Policy Review*, H.M.S.O., London.
Dickens, P. (1976) Class conflict and the gift of housing. Paper presented at the International Conference on Sociology of Regional and Urban Development, Messina.
Dickens, P. (1977). Social change, housing and the state, some aspects of class-fragmentation and incorporation: 1915–1946. *C.E.S. Conference on Urban Change and Conflict*, York, Jan. 1977.
Gibson, M. (1972). Urban renewal: some recent developments. *West Midlands Grassroots*, No. 3, Birmingham.
Green, G. (1975). The leasehold problem in Saltley. In R. Lees and G. Smith (Eds.) *Action-research in Community Development*, Routledge and Kegan Paul, London.

258

Green, G. (1976). Property exchange in Saltley. In M. Edwards, F. Gray, S. Merrett, and J. Swann (Eds.), *Housing and Class in Britain*, Political Economy of Housing Workshop, London.

Harloe, M. (1977a). *Captive Cities*, Wiley, London.

Harloe, M. (1977b). Will the Green Paper mean better housing? *Roof*, **2** (5), Sept., 143–148.

Harrison, A. (1977). The valuation gap: a danger signal? *Centre for Environmental Studies Review*, No. 2, 101–102.

Harvey, D. (1973). *Social Justice and the City*, Arnold, London.

Karn, V. (1976). *Priorities for Local Authority Mortgage Lending*, Centre for Urban and Regional Studies, Research Memorandum No. 52.

Karn, V. (1977). The impact of housing finance on low income owner-occupiers. Paper presented at British Association for the Advancement of Science, Aston.

Lambert, C. (1976). *Building Societies, Surveyors and the Older Areas of Birmingham*, Centre for Urban and Regional Studies, Working Paper No. 38.

Lambert, J., Paris, C., and Blackaby, R. (1978). *Housing Policy and the State*, Macmillan, London.

Langstaff, M. (1972). Housing improvement and community action in Birmingham, unpublished M. Soc. Sci. Thesis, Centre for Urban and Regional Studies.

Miliband, R. (1973). *The State in Capitalist Society*, Quartet, London.

Ministry of Housing and Local Government (1969). *Housing Act 1969: Area Improvement*, circular 65/69.

Murie, A. (1977). *The Sale of Council Houses*, Centre for Urban and Regional Studies, Occasional Paper No. 35.

Norman, P. (1971). Corporation Town, *Official Architecture and Planning*, **34** (5), 360–362.

Pahl, R. E. (1976). *Whose City*, Penguin, London.

Paris, C. T. (1977a) Policy change: ideological consensus and conflict, paper given at *C.E.S. Conference on Urban Change and Conflict*, York, Jan. 1977.

Paris, C. T. (1977b). Birmingham: a study in urban renewal. *Centre for Environmental Studies Review*, No. 1, 54–61.

Paris, C. T., and Blackaby, R. (forthcoming). *The Social Context of Urban Renewal*.

Pickvance, C. (1976). *Urban Sociology: Critical Essays*, Tavistock, London.

Pickvance, C. (1977a). Housing: reproduction of capital and reproduction of labour power. In J. Walton and L. H. Masoti (Eds.), *The City in Comparative Perspective*, Sage, New York, pp. 271–290.

Pickvance, C. (1977b). Physical planning and market forces in urban development. *National Westminster Bank Quarterly Review*, Aug. 1977, 41–50.

Rex, J., and Moore, R. (1967). *Race, Community and Conflict*, Oxford University Press, London.

Roberts, J. T. (1976). *General Improvement Areas*, Saxon House, Farnborough.

Samuel, R., Kincaid, J., and Slater, E. (1962). But nothing happens. *New Left Review*, Jan., 38–69.

Smith, D. (1977). *Racial Disadvantage in Britain*, Penguin, Harmondsworth.

Sutcliffe, A. and Smith, R. (1973). *Birmingham 1939–1970*, Oxford University Press, London.

Swann, J. (1975). Housing Associations: a socialist critique. In S. Clarke and G. Ginsburg (Eds.), *Political Economy and the Housing Question*, Political Economy of Housing Workshop, London.

Watson, C. and Niner, P. (1978). Housing in British cities. In D. T. Herbert and R. J. Johnston, (Eds.), *Geography and the Urban Environment*, Vol. 1, Wiley, London, pp. 319–351.

Weir, S. (Ed.) (1976). Red line districts. *Roof*, **1**, (4), July, 109–114.

Westergaard, J., and Resler, H. (1976). *Class in a Capitalist Society*, Heinemann Educational, London.

Chapter 7

The Urbanization Process in South Africa

T. J. D. Fair and J. G. Browett

INTRODUCTION

This study traces the evolution of those processes responsible for the emergence of the present pattern of urbanization in what is now the Republic of South Africa. Prior to the Union in 1910 of the four political entities now comprising the Republic, the area is termed south Africa and, thereafter, as South Africa. In the context of the study, urbanization (Friedmann and Wulff, 1975, p. 4) refers, on the one hand, to the concentration of population and economic activities in towns and to the physical growth of towns—the type referred to here as urbanization$_1$ (Friedmann, 1973, p. 65)—and, on the other hand, to the growth of urbanism as a way of life and to 'urban modes of production, living and thinking originating in these centres and spreading from these to outlying towns and rural populations'—the type referred to here as urbanization$_2$ (Friedmann and Wulff, 1975, p. 4).

Urbanization in South Africa needs to be viewed within a particular spatial context, that is, its position athwart a significant boundary in contemporary world relations. On the one hand, it possesses all the characteristics of a developed country in so far that its white society of 4 million people exhibits the cultural and technological appurtenances of its European origins and its strong economic ties to the Western capitalist system. On the other hand, as the home of more than 18 million indigenous Bantu-speaking peoples (Africans), and a further 3 million Asians and Coloured people of mixed origin, collectively termed blacks, much of its socio-economic and settlement character is identifiable with the underdeveloped countries of black Africa and the Third World generally. Thus, dichotomies have arisen between a highly urbanized rich white group and a less urbanized comparatively poor black group; between economically developed urban agglomerations and a less developed rural periphery, and, most significantly, between a ruling white core élite and politically dependent black counter-élite, which also gives rise to internal divisions within the urban centres themselves. Consequently, the study of urbanization in South Africa, in common with the contemporary world situation 'of "underdevelopment" and "modernization" . . . is concerned at base with a dominance/dependence relationship that is expressed in a great many ways' (Brookfield, 1975, p. 1).

Given this situation, Friedmann's (1973, pp. 67–70) paradigm for the study of urbanization is appropriate as a major frame of reference within which to analyse the process of urbanization in South Africa. Core and periphery comprise the structural components of the spatial system (a territorially organized social system) with which the paradigm is concerned. Its internal dynamics are governed by the autonomy–dependency relation between core and periphery. These relationships are inherently imbalanced and conflicting (Friedmann and Wulff, 1975, p. 12). Thus, 'conflict resolution between core and periphery . . . represents a major turning point in the development process, leading either toward continued deviation-amplification or to the emergence of deviation-counteracting forces within the spatial system' (Soja and Tobin, 1975, p. 206). By 'development' is meant 'the unfolding of the creative possibilities inherent in society. But this can only occur if growth is allowed to pass through a series of successive structural transformations of the system' (Friedmann, 1973, p. 45).

In terms of the paradigm, four major urbanization processes are operative within such a core–periphery system. These are (1) decision-making and control, which generates a spatial distribution of power; (2) capital flows (investment) which promote systems of activity location; (3) innovation diffusion, which yields modernization surfaces; and (4) migration, which gives rise to settlement patterns. 'Urbanization is thus perceived as a complex of spatial processes and their associated patterns, although the spatial relations of power (decision-making and control) are identified as the critical process to which all others are ultimately related' (Friedmann and Wulff, 1975, p. 11). South Africa provides a good example of this contention.

The relationships between these processes and the patterns they produce are applicable to both city-dominant and alternative theses of development. City-dominant protagonists such as Reissman (1964, p. 154) equated urbanization with development as 'social change on a vast scale'. 'Hoselitz thought of cities of heterogenetic transformation as prime movers in developmental change . . . he called them generative cities. . . . The concept also suggested that change processes in rural society could be properly understood only in relation to the cities that engendered them' (Friedmann and Wulff, 1975, p. 35). Alternatively, McGee (1971) discarded the view of the city as the 'prime catalyst of change', regarding it as *parasitical* and, along with Frank (1967), as a centre of international capitalism generating wealth for core élites and contributing to the poverty and underdevelopment of peripheral populations.

Critical to an assessment of whether cities are generative or parasitic in any given situation is an appreciation of the associated processes of spatial diffusion and spatial integration. According to Friedmann (1973, p. 70), the term 'spatial integration' has two meanings (1) in an economic sense, as 'an increase in the volume of transactions among urban places and regions which leads, in turn, to a complex territorial division of labour', and (2) in a socio-political sense, as 'the extension over a given territory of a common basis for social life or, more accurately, a shared frame of socio-cultural expectations, including language, cultural values, political–legal–bureaucratic institutions and a market economy'. Is the city or dominant core the main agent in achieving spatial integration (with its accompanying structural transformation) of the national area in question? Slater (1975) and de Souza and Porter (1974) question the viewpoints that spatial integration, especially centre–periphery integration, is beneficial for both categories; that modernization of peripheral populations means the diffusion of Western values, capital, and technology via major urban growth points; and that development of core areas necessarily promotes the development of peripheral regions.

Three major themes are examined as manifestations of core–periphery interaction and of the city generative–parasitic argument in the course of South Africa's history, since the coming of the whites in 1652. The first is the early conflict between innovative foreign white élites and indigenous, traditionalist black counter-élites. In particular, consideration is given to the way in which power influenced the growth and development of the urban system in the course of this conflict, and the role of the urban system in its eventual outcome and in relation to the degree of spatial integration or disintegration achieved by the time of the great mineral discoveries in the 1860s and 1880s. The second theme is the conflict over these mineral discoveries between the ruling traditional élites, the Afrikaners or Boers, and the entrepreneurial innovative élites, mainly British, in the Transvaal; the subsequent accommodation reached between these groups by the Act of Union in 1910, and the polarization of political and economic power in major urban cores. The third theme is the conflict between white ruling élites and a black subordinate peripheral population, excluded from the accommodation reached in 1910, and the role of each group in the urbanization process to the present day.

Each theme is developed in the light of the four urbanization processes and their associated spatial patterns, already mentioned. The argument running through each theme and through the study as a whole is, first, how the effective distribution of political and economic power has determined the spatial organization of the South African urban system and its evolution (Friedmann and Wulff, 1975, p. 15), and, secondly, how the development of the urban system has or has not contributed to the nation's spatial integration in an economic and a socio-political sense. From the analysis it is clear that there is a high degree of disequilibrium in the South African spatial system arising both from an asymmetry in the behaviour of the urban processes themselves and also from the politically determined discordance between a largely unconstrained white subsystem and a largely constrained black subsystem.

In an essay of this length and scope, justice cannot be done to the nuances, subtleties, details, and manifold interpretations of South African history and of the South African politico-socio-economic situation today. The broad canvas, on which the urbanization process in South Africa is sketched here, must contain the obvious weaknesses of such an approach.

CONFLICT AND CONQUEST

In pre-European tribal south Africa there were found patterns of spatial organization associated with the hunting and gathering groups of the drier west, on the one hand, and with the pastoral–agricultural Bantu-speaking groups of the wetter east, on the other. These groups are broadly similar to Fried's (1967) egalitarian and rank societies, respectively. In the former spatial structures were predominantly of local orientation—a small core area surrounded by an expanse of undefined territory, not in the exclusive possession of one local group, over which tribes wandered in search of food. The rank societies of the Bantu, termed Africans in this study, were the result of higher population densities and a more permanent form of settlement associated with their hybrid pastoral and agricultural economy. In some instances there arose supra-local organizations such as the Zulu under Shaka, the Ndebele under Mzilikazi, and the Basuto under Moshweshwe. In both societies provision was made for a non-permanent core area of activity and an indeterminate outer area purposefully unsettled as buffer zones or reservoirs for future expansion.

Among the Bantu-speaking peoples there were differences in their settlement patterns. For example, the Sotho peoples of the interior plateau lived generally 'in large compact villages' while the Nguni of the eastern coastal areas preferred 'scattered homesteads' (Wilson, 1969, pp. 111–112). However, these were not towns in a commercial sense. They were mainly agricultural villages. Homestead and village were self-sufficient and the pattern was predominantly non-nodal.

The tribal view of the organization of space was based on the regulation of social relations and the juxtaposition of social groups (Bohannan, 1964, pp. 174–176). The European view was influenced more by the concept of property and the subdivision of space into compartments (Soja, 1971, p. 9). Tribal culture considered the use of land more important than ownership, but this did not admit the permanent alienation of their open lands by intruders. The European expansion from Cape Town (de Kaap), established by the Dutch in 1652, was thus the imposition upon the tribal space polity of a partitioning and appropriation of land through a system of defined and defended boundary lines. The first skirmish with the Khoikhoi (Hottentots) in 1653 can be attributed to this conflict of view as, in part, can the subsequent confrontations from the late 1700s onwards between Europeans and Bantu-speaking tribes along the advancing frontier.

The European diffusion in south Africa involved a territorial advance fanning out progressively from a number of coastal beachheads. With this advance went the subjugation of the indigenous peoples and the progressive substitution of white for black political space. The first landing point was Van Riebeeck's settlement at the Cape. The Dutch East India Company (V.O.C.), however, regarded the Cape as no more than a refreshment station and had no pretensions towards economic expansion and large-scale colonization. Indeed, attempts were made to prohibit contact between Khoikhoi and whites through the demarcation of boundary lines. Nevertheless, the settlement grew, first, by the arrival of Dutch free burghers, French Huguenots and Germans, by the importation of slaves, and by the growth of the Cape Coloureds through miscegenation; and, secondly, by the expansion of the activities of the settlers into the hinterland.

However, only near Cape Town in the well-watered valleys of the south-west Cape did the frontier expand by a systematic process of agricultural settlement. Frontier expansion into the drier lands beyond was accomplished by semi-subsistent pastoralists (the *trekboers*). They moved into the lands of the Khoikhoi and San (Bushmen) either incorporating them in the new multi-racial society as servile dependants and servants or exterminating them (Katzen, 1969, p. 184). Conquest of, and defence against, these natives was mainly accomplished by the commando system comprising local inhabitants and by the establishment of frontier posts manned by a few regulars (Katzen, 1969, pp. 226–227). Graaff Reinet (Figure 7.1), established in 1785 and 400 miles from Cape Town, was the only outlying district and hamlet created 'to cope with the eastward dispersal of the *trekboers*' (Katzen, 1969, p. 223).

Thus, the line of European diffusion from Cape Town had not been associated with the establishment of urban centres through which contacts would be maintained with their original points of dispersal. Accessibility to, or interaction with, the older coastal settlements was not critical, or even considered desirable,

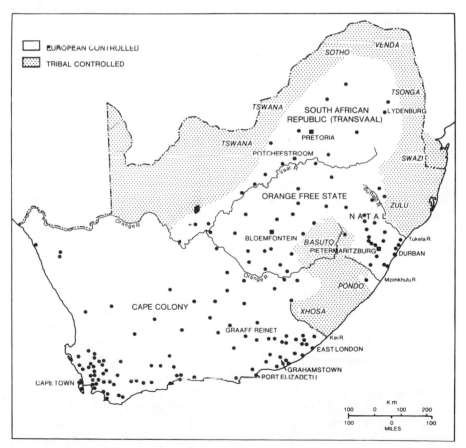

FIGURE 7.1. Urban centres and political organization, 1870 (after Davies, 1972)

once the *trekboers* had proceeded beyond the south-west Cape. Moreover, urban centres had not been founded to serve as the bases from which to take occupation of the land and hence did not precede the agricultural frontier. Consequently, in 1780 life was essentially rural. The free population of the Cape, including free persons of mixed European and Afro-Asian descent, numbered 10 500. Of this, one-fifth were resident in Cape Town. District centres were mere hamlets. For example, Swellendam, founded in 1747, comprised four houses thirty years later (Guelke, 1976, pp. 32, 37). When the British took over the Cape in 1806, only fourteen urban places had been established, ten of them within 50 miles of Cape Town.

The remainder of the Colony was remote periphery. The lack of spatial integration in the sense of the extension of 'a common basis for social life' merely enhanced the differentiation between core and periphery. The Council of Policy at the Cape 'legislated for all who participated in the Cape polity, V.O.C. servants, burghers (including a few "free blacks", liberated slaves, and their descendants), and slaves' (Katzen, 1969, p. 215) and, despite corruption and inefficiency in government, some degree of racial integration in Cape Town urban society was evident. In the periphery, by contrast, a new Afrikaner *volk* had been created, independent, isolationist, and largely self-sufficient. It was strengthened by a Calvinist religion which 'was peculiarly suited to the taste of the White community . . . struggling to survive in a stern environment and accustomed from birth to treating non-White people as slaves, or serfs, or enemies' (Katzen, 1969, p. 229).

Expansion of the frontier 500 miles east of Cape Town brought the *trekboers* face to face in the 1770s with the Bantu-speaking Nguni peoples and the Xhosa in particular who were migrating westward. For the next 100 years, despite attempts at delimiting buffer zones and boundary lines in order to achieve territorial segregation, numerous wars were fought between whites and Xhosa. The latter were a politically fragmented people fighting bitterly to hold on to 'their land and their independence' (Wilson, 1969, p. 252), while the Dutch East India Company and later the British government, reluctant to be involved, sought their defeat, the stabilization of the frontier, and the employment of the local natives as labourers on the growing number of European farms.

British strategy included the close settlement in the eastern Cape around Grahamstown of some 4 000 British immigrants in 1820, and of almost 3 000 German legionnaires in 1856 in British Kaffraria to the east around King William's Town and the port of East London. Associated with these schemes was the establishment of numerous forts, villages and towns, all of which were not only consolidation points of European settlement, but rallying and control points for the subjugation of the Xhosa and other tribes. By 1870 there were some thirty such centres in the eastern frontier districts.

Subsequent to the loss of their land the African social system in the Ciskei disintegrated for its economic base—the provision of land by the chief for his followers—had been subverted (Robertson, 1934, p. 417). The Xhosa were progressively 'hemmed in by fixed boundaries, debarred from movement by an inflexible frontier, effectively controlled by headmen and police posts in subdivided locations (reserves) watched over by vigilant magistrates (and) pauperized by (an) epidemic amongst their cattle' (Pollock and Agnew, 1963, p. 92) and their power finally broken militarily by 1877. Thus, in the eastern Cape, there was imposed a nodally-based, space-organizing system, deep in the periphery, by an imperial government skilled in the art of 'urban rule' (Friedman and Wulff, 1975, p. 8); in this case a hierarchy which embraced London, Cape Town (the capital of the Colony), provincial centres (Grahamstown), and local and district centres and outposts.

> the arrival of the 1820 settlers resulted in at least a doubling of the English-speaking population at the Cape, and the establishment of a bridgehead in the east to balance that which was growing in the capital (Cape Town) itself, from which British culture, and more particularly the characteristics of British urban civilization ... would radiate into the villages of the interior. (Davenport, 1969, p. 280).

Ordinance 49 of 1828 permitted Africans to seek work on farms and in towns in the colony, and according to Breytenbach (1972, p. 7) this may be regarded 'as the start of the process of the Bantu's economic integration into the Western labour system', some believing that this 'experience would contribute to the general civilization of the natives'. This process of diffusion Sir George Grey later attempted to hasten by a policy of 'civilization by mingling' (as Governor Cole had done earlier for the Khoikhoi) through the establishment for the Africans of schools, some of which were mixed white and black, missions, hospitals, and settled farming operations (Wilson, 1969, pp. 260–263). Thus, the centre of (African) activity shifted away from the traditional chiefs' homesteads 'to the trading and administrative centres established by whites, and the mission schools and churches' (Wilson, 1969, p. 265). The mainly British missionaries attempted to westernize the natives in thought, habit, and custom and to encourage them 'to settle in a village round the church and school rather than in scattered homesteads' (Wilson, 1969, p. 266). These policies and trends met with no universal success and many British settlers came to adopt the conservative attitudes to blacks of the *trekboers*.

The outcome of the conflict as it affected ruling whites and subordinate blacks in the Cape Colony as a whole under British rule in the nineteenth century was still one of 'suppression', in which 'counter-élites were prevented from gaining access to positions of authority' (Friedmann, 1973, pp. 49–50). In part, however, it was also one of 'cooptation', a small number of Africans and Coloureds being 'pacified by being allowed to share to a limited extent in the exercise of established authority' for 'the political institutions of an authoritarian trading company gradually gave way to new ones operating on the principle of government by consent, under a franchise based on reasonably low qualifications, which conveyed political power to men of all races on equal terms but, because it was a racially stratified society, not in equal proportions'

(Davenport, 1969, p. 273). Only a small degree of spatial integation, extending 'a common basis for social life', had been achieved in the Cape Colony and only then under the external influence of British rule in the nineteenth century. More evident was the growth of spatial integration in an economic sense through the development of the urban system and an associated network of roads and communications.

Over the period of British rule, the number of urban places in the Cape Colony increased from 14 in 1806 to 103 in 1870. This growth is attributed first to the establishment of service and administrative centres in the areas annexed to the Colony on its northern and especially on its eastern frontiers, and to the addition of new centres to the existing mesh in the longer established parts of the Colony; and, secondly, to the greater pace of economic development witnessed after 1856 in agricultural and pastoral activities and the associated growth of banking and other commercial facilities in the towns (Davies, 1972, p. 26). The South-west Cape accounted for 33 of the centres with Cape Town displaying the high primacy levels of 78 per cent within this subsystem and 65 per cent within the Colony as a whole (Davies, 1972, p. 33). In 1865 the total population of Cape Town and its immediate environs was 37 756 (whites 20 422) followed by Port Elizabeth 8 700 (6 886), Grahamstown 5 949 (5 265) and Paarl 4 929 (1 978). The total population of the Colony was 496 381, of whom 181 592 were white (Cape of Good Hope, 1865). Only 22.1 per cent of the white population (40 068) lived in the eight towns having over 1 000 whites, and half of this number was accounted for by Cape Town. 'The forces conducive to a high rate of urbanization remained weak' (Davies, 1972, p. 27). On the one hand, an agricultural export economy favoured only the coastal ports and, on the other, the population was too small to stimulate the development of widespread urban services on any significant scale.

While the primacy of Cape Town, politically and economically, attracted more and more people to it, it was a large section of the Colony's peripheral population, the descendants of the *trekboers*, who chose to move still more deeply into the periphery and away from the influence of British rule. The Dutch Voortrekkers, as they came to be called, became disenchanted with the liberal policies of the British colonial government, notably with the emancipation of slaves in 1834. Their society still rested on the principles that they had inherited from their early contact with black peoples at the Cape, namely, 'that whites should be allowed to deal with slaves and other non-white dependants more or less as they saw fit, without government interference, and that all whites were entitled to as much land as they wanted without paying for it' (Katzen, 1969, p. 232). Consequently, some 14 000 Voortrekkers, along with their Coloured servants, left the eastern Cape in the 1830s and 1840s, not to create a new society but to preserve an existing rurally-based one where land would be freely available, the natives less populous, and government less demanding. They moved across the Orange and Vaal rivers, penetrated Natal in 1838, and established in time a number of republics, some only short-lived. The fire-power of these Boers was the main cause for the defeat of the tribal groups they encountered. They appropriated large areas of tribal land, much of it sparsely populated, on the grassland plateau, but certainly did not dispose of the Africans who, on the one hand, filtered back to the former lands as dependants of the whites or who, on the other, engulfed the Boers in a vast horseshoe of tribal territory too mountainous, too arid, or too malarial for easy white occupation (Figure 7.1).

However, no centralized system of government was established at first in the conquered territory by the Boers. Instead, while they were largely free and independent of British rule, they were politically disunited and scattered. They initially established a number of small republics, those north of the Vaal River to be amalgamated into the South African Republic (the Transvaal) in 1860, while between the Orange and the Vaal rivers the Orange Free State was finally established in 1854. No union of these two republics emerged, however.

While political power thus became centralized in the two republics, spatial organization of the society and its economy remained locally rather than hierarchically arranged through a network of administrative and commercial centres. The early republics established their capitals of Winburg, Potchefstroom, Lydenburg, Soutpansberg, and Utrecht; Bloemfontein and Pretoria became the capitals of the two consolidated political units, respectively. But numbers remained small. The European population of the Transvaal, for instance, living in towns and villages and hardly an urban population, numbered only 5 000 in the late 1860s, out of a total of some 20 000. Pretoria and Potchefstroom were equivalent in size to only third-order centres in the Cape Colony (Silver, 1876, p. 457). Many administrative centres contained no more than half a dozen houses. These scattered hamlets arose as rallying points for defence and attack by the farmers and many were established around Dutch Reformed churches.

This was not an urban society. In the way that the British in the Cape Colony had a predilection for urban life, so the Boers sought mainly a rural existence. Britishers, in fact, constituted the majority group in the larger towns of the republics (Becker, 1878, p. 36). The Boers retained their character as semi-subsistent pastoralists. Very little was produced for exchange (Thompson, 1969a, pp. 425–426); there was little money available for elementary services for the scattered community, distances to towns in the Cape and Natal were great, and communications were poor.

This was at best a weakly nodal system assisting the consolidation of an alien society in its new environmental setting but doing little to promote the diffusion of an urban culture among the vast majority of whites, let alone the subordinate native peoples. The constitution of the Transvaal Republic (1860) did not permit equality of white and black in church or state and it had earlier been decreed that Africans were not allowed to settle near towns without official permission, so giving rise to the notion that they were white preserves (Welsh, 1971, p. 186). Labour was made available by permitting Africans to live as tenants on white farms or by confining them to scattered 'locations' from which their labour could be drawn as required, but no effective large-scale African land policy was adopted in the Transvaal until 1877 (South Africa, 1946, p. 5). Moreover, by

1870 Africans 'in the Transvaal were indirectly being compelled by legislation to sell their services to Whites' (Breytenbach, 1972, p. 7), but few permanent economic relations developed between Boers and Africans (Frankel, 1960, p. 4). In the area over which white rule predominated, African land tenure was on sufferance (Thompson, 1969a, p. 436).

A fourth salient of white power was created in Natal. Although some English traders established a settlement at Port Natal (Durban) in 1824 and made contact with the powerful Zulu kingdom, north of the Tukela River, under Shaka, it was the Voortrekkers who defeated the Zulu in 1838. Their republic of Natalia, between the Buffalo-Tukela and Mzimkhulu rivers, was short-lived and the British annexed Natal as a colony in 1843. Thereafter most of the Boers moved to the Transvaal. The British wished to secure their control over Port Natal and the southern Indian Ocean and feared the repercussions along the eastern Cape frontier of Boer policies towards Africans in Natal.

As in the eastern Cape, the British established a nodally-based space polity in order to assist in the execution of the administrative, defence, and commercial functions of the new colony. Although the sites of Pietermaritzburg, the capital, and Weenen had been selected by the Voortrekkers, and Durban by the earlier traders, their subsequent growth to a large extent awaited the arrival of the Byrne settlers of 1849–1851 in Natal. Numbering some 4 000, these English settlers were directed to specific villages (e.g. Pinetown, Verulam, Howick, Richmond) associated with the close agricultural settlement planned for them. Moreover, with settlers hemmed in by Zulu, Basuto, and Pondo domains, subject to attacks by San (Bushmen) from the Drakensberg foothills and with some 100 000 Africans scattered in fragmented reserves, established by the British between 1848 and 1852, many villages were established not only as magisterial centres for administrative purposes and as rallying points in case of attack, but specifically as military posts as well (e.g. Estcourt, Ladysmith).

Although, on annexation of the Colony, the British government had insisted upon freedom before the law of all its inhabitants and the rejection of any form of slavery, and was well intentioned towards promoting the development of the Africans, 'many of the Natal (British) settlers very quickly acquired a racialistic attitude to the Colonial situation' . . . 'borne out of a consciousness of their (the African's) difference, a fear of their numbers and a disappointment at their instrumental deficiencies' (Thompson, 1969b, p. 383)—but 'Africans performed the manual work for most of the white people at very low wages—on their farms, in their towns and villages, and in their homes' (Thompson, 1969b, p. 387). There was little being done in Natal, as was attempted in the eastern Cape, of 'civilization by mingling'. For example, tribal law was made applicable to all Africans, whereas in the Cape Colony all people were subject to Roman Dutch law. Moreover, the African reserves were regarded as labour reservoirs and the imposition of a hut tax in 1849 was aimed at coercing Africans to seek wage employment on farms and in towns. It was not an effective measure, however, as the need to import Indian labourers for work on sugar plantations in the 1860s testified. In any case,

Britain was virtually doing nothing to promote economic development in the locations (reserves), or even in the white areas; nor was she sustaining the non-racial principles set out in the annexation Proclamation. But by keeping ultimate control over the executive government she was still sheltering the African (1 250 000) and Asian (6 000) communities from complete domination by the white community. (Thompson, 1969b, p. 390)

For the same reason Basutoland was annexed by the British in 1871.

By 1870 there were twenty-two towns, villages, and hamlets in Natal. Durban, third in size after Cape Town and Port Elizabeth, had a white population of some 3 300 (Silver, 1876, p. 400) which, with that of Pietermaritzburg, constituted 45 per cent of the Colony's white population. The forces of urbanization, owing mainly to the presence of British rule in Natal, were, for political and social reasons alone, more powerful than in the Boer republics. However, it is doubtful whether the urban system established in Natal by 1870 provided a vehicle for the spread of British culture and of modernization among the indigenous peoples of any consequence; certainly, not so long as blacks were regarded as of subordinate and inferior status.

Conclusion

Decision-making and control in southern Africa had by 1870 produced a spatial distribution of power comprising four disparate political systems in each of which dominance–dependency relationships between ruling white élites and a subordinate black majority was well established and articulated in varying degrees through four almost autonomous urban subsystems. The Boers had no wish to increase the level of political integration with the British colonies and even the eastern Cape generated a short-lived separatist movement between 1830 and 1880 over dissatisfaction with the government in Cape Town. In the two British colonies this politically autonomous pattern was strengthened by growing regional economies, each focused on a port and tied directly in a dependency relationship with the metropolitan power. However, the urban system as a whole represented the fact rather that 'the essentials of a modern administration had been established' (Hobart Houghton, 1971, p. 1) than that the market economy had established a viable presence. By contrast, 'the difficulties of creating a modern administrative machine without trained staff or adequate finance proved almost insuperable in both the Orange Free State and the Transvaal' (Hobart Houghton, 1971, p. 8).

In the absence of a single territorial entity there was no national core region at this time. Instead, there was one major regional core (Cape Town), two minor regional political cores (Bloemfontein and Pretoria) and three sets of dual nodes in which commercial and administrative functions respectively were divided, namely, Port Elizabeth and Grahamstown, East London and King William's Town, Durban and Pietermaritzburg. These nodes, 'lingering in a provincial pre-growth atmosphere' (Friedmann, 1966, p. 68) exerted limited influence upon the spatial organization of the regional economic structure.

While European territorial aggrandizement had drastically reduced the areas of independent African occupation (Hobart Houghton, 1971, p. 8) and blacks generally had been drawn into the political sphere of influence and the settlement structure of whites, there was no accompanying integration of them into the new polity and the new society established by the élites. Other than the limited political cooptation in the Cape Colony, and the limited social integration in a multi-racial Cape Town and on scattered mission reserves and stations, blacks were an excluded group—rejected in a political and social sense and wanted only for their labour, without which the new economy could not survive. The pattern of power and exchange relations which had emerged in the south African urban system by 1870 was an asymmetrical/non-reciprocal one in which coercive power (on the part of the ruling white élites) predominated and the passive periphery (the blacks and their 'regional protectorates') is integrated on a basis of submissive dependency (Friedmann, 1975, p. 268).

Migration produced settlement patterns of two types; first, the dispersion of *trekboers*, Voortrekkers, and English and other settlers superimposed upon a tribal settlement structure a pattern of white occupance comprising districts, towns, hamlets, and farms; and secondly, a polarization in the two British colonies caused by a reverse migration of rural people to the larger towns and the concentration in those towns of limited flows of overseas immigrants. To English-speaking whites a preference for urban living and the growth of commercial opportunities prompted this reverse flow. For Africans the flow to towns was mainly a temporary migration generated by a demand for their labour and the associated use of coercive measures to prise them loose from their rural domains. Although the degree of African labour migration before 1870 was small compared with that which was to follow the mineral discoveries and the growth of industrialization, the beginnings of an increasing dependence of the African upon the European for his means of existence had emerged (Slater, 1974, p. 339).

Modernization by the diffusion of European political influence and power over what is now the Republic of South Africa has followed the typical process, described by Friedmann and Wulff (1975, p. 8) of expansion 'outwards from a number of spatially dispersed central points of dominance' and, by conquest and exploitation of land and people, the establishment of a 'coercive authority' over the indigenous peoples. One manifestation of this pattern of innovation diffusion is illustrated in Figure 7.2 showing the dominant direction in which urban centre development proceeded from Cape Town, Port Elizabeth, and Durban. The fourth source of advance, the towns and farms of the eastern Cape, from which the Voortrekkers moved inland, represent springboards from which a classic example of relocation diffusion (Gould, 1969, pp. 3–5) took place.

The rate of this penetration and the accompanying establishment of towns is largely related to the culture and the political strategies of the powers concerned. But the towns were generally small. In 1855 only fifty towns in south Africa housed more than 100 Europeans each and these accounted for possibly a third of the total white population of some 141 000. Forty-five of these towns were in the Cape Colony; the remainder being in Natal (two), the Orange Free State (two), and the Transvaal (one) (Christopher, 1976, p.94). The black population might have numbered 3 million, but the number living in towns is unknown. That the innovations of a European urban culture diffused more slowly to the populations of the two Boer republics is evidenced also by the fact that by 1870 twenty-one towns published daily or weekly newspapers in the Cape Colony (nineteen) and in Natal (two) compared with only four in the republics (Browett, 1975, p. 55). The Boers had in fact migrated into the interior not to extend the forces of modernization derived from a world core region in Europe but to escape interaction with and dominance by these forces of change (Schmidt, 1973, p. 61).

The political decisions of the ruling élite regarding blacks, certainly in Natal and in the Boer republics, as previously outlined, make questionable the view that white urban rule extended and would extend 'substantial benefits to the population it controlled' and so acquire a 'moral authority' (Friedmann and Wulff, 1975, p. 8). Bundy (1972, pp. 370–371) has argued that African agricultur-alists in the nineteenth century, especially in the eastern Cape, Natal, and the Orange Free State, responded positively to the market opportunities that contact

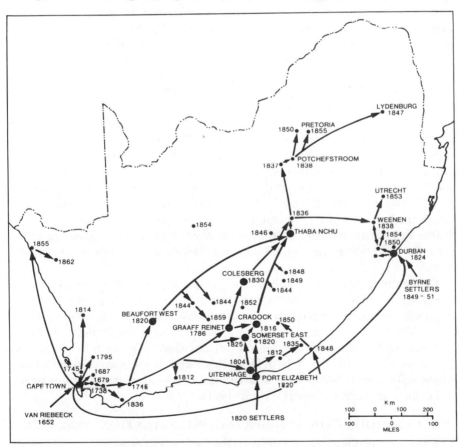

FIGURE 7.2. Diffusion of urban centres to 1870

with whites offered; that some farmers 'made considerable adaptations . . . and competed most effectively with white farmers'. That the response subsequently failed he attributes to 'discriminatory and coercive means' used against the African peasantry to force them into wage labour on white farms and in white towns.

For blacks, and Africans in particular, there was no sign, in this pre-industrial period of over 200 years of European penetration and control, that the city-dominant view—'cities, as centres of influence over regional and national hinterlands, are catalysts to *development*'—had shown any real effects (de Souza and Porter, 1974, p. 8). The imported urban system which was established throughout south Africa could rather be viewed as a vehicle for conquest and control, and as an innovation supportive to the spread of a European-oriented economy and society, into which blacks were drawn only in a subservient capacity. The establishment of towns and farms between and among tribally cohesive areas for the purpose of 'divide and rule' had a disintegrative effect upon the indigenous spatial system. Moreover, with the African 'reserves' delimited largely as labour reservoirs and, in Natal, described as 'generally the most barren, wild and broken parts of the country' (Russell, 1891, p. 189), the imposed spatial system contributed ultimately rather to the underdevelopment of the Africans than to their development. In sum, the extent to which black people were 'exposed to and transformed by the processes of change' (Friedmann and Wulff, 1975, p. 23) were those accompanying 200 years of forceful European aggrandizement rather than modernization.

Consequently, there was no single modernization surface indicative of the areal variations of development at this time, 1870. Rather were there two spatial subsystems. The first, a white spatial subsystem, comprised three cores with their immediate environs as mobilized peripheries. These areas, Cape Town and the south-west Cape, Port Elizabeth/Grahamstown and parts of the eastern Cape and Durban/Pietermaritzburg and the Natal coastal belt and midlands, possessed the highest white population density, the greatest extent of commercial arable and livestock farming, and the most articulated urban structure at this time. Beyond lay the unmobilized periphery largely semi-subsistent and weakly nodal.

The second, the black, subsystem comprised two parts—one partially integrated with the white subsystem through political subservience, labour migration, and some minor commercial activity, and the other still beyond its reach. The time, 1870, is too soon to ascribe the term 'modernization' to the first—either in a 'Eurocentric' sense of blacks absorbing 'western culture' (de Souza and Porter, 1974, p. 9) or in Deutsch's sense (Brookfield, 1973, p. 3) of the processes of 'social mobilization' and 'cultural assimilation' transforming society to create a 'modern nation' (Deutsch, 1961).

ACCOMMODATION AND SPATIAL POLARIZATION (1910–1970)

The discovery of diamonds in 1867 near Kimberley, and especially of gold on the Witwatersrand in the Transvaal in 1886, gave new direction and pace to political, social, and economic development in south Africa. The gold mining industry became one of 'the great capitalist enterprises of the late nineteenth century' (Marais, 1961, p. 3). The introduction of institutional and technological innovations which large-scale mining necessitated were epochal innovations for south Africa in that they changed the course of history and initiated and accelerated industrialization and urbanization. New urban centres arose where previously there had been only sparse pastoral settlement. By 1871 the white population of Kimberley exceeded the number of whites who had participated in the Great Trek (de Kiewiet, 1941, p. 81).

The economic rewards and the large number of problems encountered which were 'resistant to solution by traditional means' (Friedmann, 1973, p. 46) attracted creative and innovative personalities to these enclaves of accelerated change (Friedmann, 1973, p. 45). They were 'men of quite exceptional financial and administrative genius' (Hobart Houghton, 1971, pp. 12–13) committed to setting up the vast technical and organizational infrastructure necessary to promote the mineral fields as a viable proposition. Johannesburg became their chief administrative and financial centre. Its white population in 1896 was 50 907, of whom only 6 205 were local Transvaalers. The newcomers came mainly from Britain and the Cape Colony (31 427). Conditions especially favourable to innovation (Friedmann, 1973, pp. 46–48) were generally present in the Witwatersrand urban region, but conditions necessary for innovation diffusion to, and absorption by, a predominantly rural periphery were not (Schmidt, 1973, pp. 45–47).

The new immigrants came to that part of south Africa where they were 'least assimilable to the existing population' (Marais, 1961, p. 4). The Boers were mainly cattle graziers. 'They had lived further from civilizing influences than the rest of south Africa', whereas 'the new immigrants were largely urban in their outlook and habits' (Marais, 1961, p. 4). This 'sudden irruption' (Welsh, 1971, p. 172) of a mining and urban community immediately generated conflict between the traditional governing élites of the Transvaal Republic, the Boers, and the culturally distinct *uitlander* group of innovative entrepreneurial counter-élites. The former were determined to retain political power and survival as a nation, while the latter were impatient with a social system incapable of absorbing the innovations and with a political system which denied their gaining full access to authority. This confrontation, discussed in some detail by Schmidt (1973), between a governing rural periphery and an urban economic core, yielded a highly unstable situation which resulted in 'open conflict' (Friedmann and Wulff, 1975, p. 15) and the Anglo-Boer War of 1899–1902. The intervention of Great Britain represented the act of a world core region, in an age of colonial expansion, bent upon organizing the peripheral region of southern Africa to its political and economic advantage. The Boers were seen as challenging the core region's authority to do this (Schmidt, 1973, p. 81). The immediate outcome of the conflict in the Transvaal was one of 'replacement—counter-élites are successful in replacing the established authorities and substituting their own authority for them' (Friedmann, 1973, p. 50).

After the defeat of the Boers and the extension of control over tribal land that had been going on since 1870, British political and economic influence was established over all of south Africa. However, after 1905 a Liberal government in Great Britain sought a reconciliation with the Boers, granted the two republics responsible government in 1907, and paved the way for the Union of the four colonies in 1910. In this 'accommodation' (Friedmann and Wulff, 1975, p. 15), reached between predominantly urban British and rural Afrikaners (Boers), the territories occupied by white people were united (Thompson, 1971, p. 363). At the same time, by South Africa's becoming a self-governing Dominion within the British Empire, a new commercial–industrial–military élite emerged which, while safeguarding both white and British political and economic interests in South Africa, excluded blacks from the 'accommodation' and denied them access to positions of power in the new state. They continued to be suppressed.

Power remained strongly centralized in a unitary system of government and the provinces, the former colonies, were given only limited responsibilities. Thus the focus of the spatial distribution of power changed from being regional to national. Three capital cities were designated; Pretoria the administrative capital, Cape Town the legislative, and Bloemfontein the judicial. Moreover, one of the strongest arguments for Union had been the need to end the vicious competition between the Cape and Natal ports and the port of Delagoa Bay (now Maputo) in Portuguese Mozambique for the trade of the Transvaal and of the Witwatersrand in particular. Thus, after 1910, by combining the centres of both political decision-making and economic power, the Pretoria–Witwatersrand region immediately became the first-order urban core in the new national spatial system. Cape Town and Durban, the latter strongly linked economically to Johannesburg and the Witwatersrand, became major second-order cores, and Port Elizabeth, East London, Pietermaritzburg, Bloemfontein, and Kimberley third-order minor metropolitan centres.

However, although all of South Africa had now been brought within a single unified space polity, economic development and the settlement pattern remained highly uneven. Immediately after the Anglo-Boer War, a condition of organized dependency, on the one hand, and a British-dominated colonial spatial system, on the other, were superimposed upon the pre-war disjunction that had already arisen between urban and rural development. Between 1870 and 1910 British investment in south Africa amounted to $351 million, of which $125 million was in mining alone and much of the rest in developing ports and railways to link the mines with Great Britain (Franklin, 1948, p. 41). But the injection of this capital and the foreign enclaves of new economic development so created, initially tended to bring about a greater differentiation in the spatial organization of economic activities. Skilled labour, investment and development capital, and equipment were all imported, while dividends, profits, diamonds, and gold all flowed largely in the opposite direction.

Urban-generated surpluses, as Friedmann (1975, p. 287) has noted in such circumstances, were not used for developing the rural sector. Only two main areas of established arable commercial agriculture, i.e. the south-west Cape and coastal Natal, already tied to the capitalist system (Friedmann and Wulff, 1975, p. 20) and which were accessible by the new rail network to the mining centres, were stimulated by the growth of new internal markets, as later were the cereal-growing areas of the Orange Free State and the Transvaal (Goodfellow, 1931, p. 20). Up to 1910, railways had not been constructed to perform the space-organizing function of connecting market centre and agricultural hinterland, but rather the space-bridging function of connecting only the centres of modernizing development, locally and overseas.

According to Marais (1961, p. 4) 'only a small proportion of the wealth produced on the Rand before the Anglo-Boer War found its way into the pockets of the Boers'. Much of the demand for pastoral and agricultural produce 'was actually supplied from outside the republic' (Transvaal) and 'market gardening and dairy farming . . . in the vicinity of Johannesburg was mostly in the hands of foreigners'. This lack of stimulus is in part attributable to the traditional, economic, social, and cultural way of life of the Boer farmers who, having existed for so long without markets or commerce, were either unwilling or unable to respond instantly to these demands (Goodfellow, 1931, p. 133). In fact, in 1904 only 40 000 (6.3 per cent) out of a total of 630 000 Afrikaners lived in the nine major towns of south Africa. In skills they were little equipped for urban life and regarded the towns as 'foreign' enclaves and as 'the original agent of the destruction of the Boer way of life' (Welsh, 1971, pp. 202–204).

The main impact of the mines and associated towns upon the African population was to draw their able-bodied men as migrant labourers to these new centres of activity, and so to integrate the tribal pre-capitalist economy into the international capitalist system, with deleterious effects upon the former (A. G. Frank, explained by Slater, 1974, p. 333). It was in these terms that Bundy (1972, p. 372) noted the beginnings of a decline in the peasant economy, an 'increasing reliance by peasants upon migrant labour for a cash income', and thus a disruption of African rural society. 'Henceforth, the native problem was urban and industrial as well and no longer simply rural. The first step was taken towards the later detribalized and landless urban proletariat of South African industrial towns' (de Kiewiet, 1941, p. 91).

Outside the main urban centres, most of the country was unmobilized periphery. Consequently, the few inter-regional linkages which did develop were not sufficient either to occasion a subsequent spread effect from the centres, to generate a social transformation in much of the periphery, or to create an integrated core-organized market economy. The rural economy being hardly 'isomorphic with that of the city', most of it was not 'capable of being organized along commercial, capitalistic lines' (Friedmann and Wulff, 1975, p. 20).

Major economic and population growth was concentrated in the new mining centres, at the ports and at intermediate centres located on the major railway links. By 1911, Johannesburg's population numbered 238 273, the city surpassing Cape Town (163 172) as South Africa's primary centre. Most of this growth was attributable to large-scale European immigration, with no less than 114 000 persons entering south Africa in the two years following the Anglo-Boer War

(Hobart Houghton, 1964, p. 15). The economic centre of gravity had shifted to the Transvaal. It increased its share of south Africa's white population from 13 per cent in 1870 to 33 per cent in 1911, while the Cape Colony's share declined from 71 per cent to 46 per cent. Pretoria and the Witwatersrand, the forerunner of the future Pretoria–Witwatersrand–Vereeniging (PWV) urban region, had a population of 516 411 or 34.7 per cent of the total South African urban population. Durban, growing very slowly during the sixty years preceding 1886, grew rapidly to a population of 94 226 in 1911 as its communications relationship with the Witwatersrand was exploited. Along with Kimberley, Port Elizabeth, Pietermaritzburg, Bloemfontein, and East London, these eight towns and urban regions contained 62.9 per cent (937 158) of South Africa's total urban population (1 489 881) in 1911.

In the 'accommodation' of 1910, the power base of the former traditional governing élite, the Afrikaners, remained essentially in the rural areas while that of the entrepreneurial élite, mainly British, was ensconced in the larger urban areas, 'as an enclave . . . related more to the international economy (i.e. the international urban system) than to the rural areas within the country' (Friedmann, 1975, p. 289). Over the ensuing fifty years, as the former came to establish their political and economic power base in the urban areas, as well as retaining it in the rural areas, and as the entrepreneurial élites themselves became more South African in outlook, a more spatially integrated distribution of power was achieved with the former governing élites first regaining a substantial measure of autonomy with respect to foreign entrepreneurial élites (Friedmann, 1975, p. 25) and then political, but not economic, ascendancy over them. In the process, the increasing political power of Pretoria, only 35 miles away, was added to the economic power of the Witwatersrand with its additional advantage of accessibility of management (Friedmann, 1975, p. 272). The overwhelming primacy of the Pretoria–Witwatersrand region in the national spatial system was inevitable in these circumstances—not a primacy measured solely by population but, of greater significance, a 'developmental primacy' measured by the degree of political and economic domination of the spatial system (Soja and Tobin, 1975, p. 212; Rogerson, 1974; Johnston, 1977).

It was the development of mining that first set South Africa firmly on a course towards industrialization. But unlike the growth of industrialization out of a firm agricultural base as in Western Europe, the large-scale development of commercial agriculture in South Africa is mainly attributable to the markets created by the initial stimulus of mining and the accompanying urbanization (Mallows, 1968, p. 8). The mobilization of capital for investment was critical in making these activities possible and in generating associated economic and urban growth (Friedmann and Wulff, 1957, p. 16). The major source of capital after 1870 was initially 'transfers from abroad'—$520 million between 1870 and 1936, or 43 per cent of the total foreign investment in Africa (Hobart Houghton, 1964, p. 39). However, so much went into mining that manufacturing industry did not develop on a large scale until the 1920s, although the metal and engineering and chemical and explosives industries were established on the Witwatersrand at a very early date as a direct response to the needs of mining. Further substantial inflows of capital followed after the rise in the price of gold in 1933, after the stimulus to local manufacture provided by the Second World War, and the development of the Orange Free State and western Transvaal goldfields, and again after 1965, although, more recently, political factors have seriously influenced the attitudes of foreign investors to the country's disadvantage.

In the meantime, national economic development has greatly stimulated the growth of domestic saving (Hobart Houghton, 1964, pp. 39–40). By 1958 it constituted 23 per cent of net national income and 32 per cent by 1973, indicative of a mature economy capable of generating much of its own capital requirements.

It was in the 1920s that government, with revenue derived largely from gold mining taxation, embarked upon a policy of protecting, promoting, and establishing industry. Most of the industries so established were producers of final products and came to be located in the major core areas, especially the PWV, since here not only did they enjoy tariff protection but also the natural protection of an interior location afforded by high transport costs on overseas imports. Moreover, these centres gained from the advantages of their initial locations at a critical stage of change as the national economy moved from a primary to a secondary industrial base. By 1935, 71.5 per cent of gross output in secondary industry was located in the PWV (42.8 per cent), Cape Town (17.0 per cent) and Durban (11.7 per cent). As the metropolitan economy assumed an increasingly tertiary character (Table 7.1), polarization intensified. By 1968, the PWV accounted for 46.9 per cent of the country's gross geographic product (GGP) generated in the secondary and tertiary sectors, and the PWV, Cape Town, and Durban for 70 per cent. In 1973, of the 131 major private and public companies in South Africa, the headquarter offices of 66 per cent were located in the PWV, 13 per cent in Durban, and 11 per cent in Cape Town (Rogerson, 1974)—90 per cent in all in these three centres which, through their strong horizontal linkages, constitute South Africa's non-contiguous core region (Board, Davies, and Fair, 1970, pp. 378–382).

TABLE 7.1. South Africa: sectoral distribution of the gross domestic product, 1911–1970

Year	Total GDP (millions of Rand)	Per cent of total				
		Agriculture	Mining	Manufacturing, electricity, gas, water	Transport, commerce, finance	Other services
1911	299.2	20.8	28.0	5.4	25.1	20.7
1936	759.6	14.1	18.7	15.6	28.0	23.6
1960	4965.0	12.1	13.8	26.1	35.2	12.8
1975	24285.0	7.9	13.1	31.1	34.5	13.4

Source: Department of Statistics, various releases.

Thus, despite the growth of some 300 new urban centres in the 100 years to 1970, it was the main metropolitan areas which captured the greater part of the major generators of economic growth and organized the South African space economy into its major core–periphery subsystems. As a result, in the 1960s, long after the onset of the industrial period in South Africa, a polarization of the space economy persisted (Fair, 1976), and the levels of economic inequality between the cores and especially the African homelands increased. In 1968, 59 per cent of South Africa's total GGP was generated in its three major cores, 38.8 per cent in the rest of white South Africa (the mobilized periphery), and only 2 per cent in the African homelands (the unmobilized periphery). GGP per capita in these three regions was R899, R416, and R38 per capita, respectively.

The unmobilized African periphery, by contrast, suffered a relative, and sometimes an absolute, loss of production factors, and hence potential economic growth, to the core areas. Moreover, it suffered from hindrances, both enforced and voluntary, to the reception of innovative forces. Its institutional structure was largely non-adaptive to radical change, and until recently government policy had been largely one of neglect. The outmigration of its able-bodied workers has been both a voluntary response to higher wages in white mining and urban areas and an involuntary one to relatively poor economic conditions and over-population in the homelands, together with the need to pay hut and poll taxes from the earnings of wage employment. Consequently, although 43.3 per cent of Africans live in homelands (Table 7.2) 86.8 per cent of the African labour force in non-agricultural, i.e. mainly urban, employment is found in white South Africa (1970), and 40 per cent in the three major metropolitan areas alone. Of the African population living in towns, 93 per cent is found in white areas and in those portions of the homelands forming integral parts of white metropolitan centres. The three core areas account for 51 per cent of the urban African population.

After the publication of the Tomlinson Commission report (South Africa, 1955), however, government perceived a greater urgency to pursue more vigorously African homeland development as part of its overall policy of *apartheid* or 'separate development'. This has entailed a policy of dispersal with the establishment of new industry and new urban centres both within and on the borders of homelands. Moreover, Tomlinson had warned that unless the concentration of economic activity in the core areas be reduced 'no other result can be expected than that the relative share of the Bantu in the composition of urban population will increase'.

Attempts to stimulate dispersal of economic activity in the mobilized white periphery had commenced considerably earlier with rural assistance pro-grammes, the construction of branch railway lines, and proposals for greater industrial development. Capital was injected into resource and infrastructural development on a large scale, but much of this was to support the growing metropolitan economies rather than the periphery itself, e.g. power stations and water supply schemes. Legislation to promote this development was embodied in the Natural Resources Development Act of 1947 and in the Physical Planning

TABLE 7.2. South Africa: indices of urbanization, 1970—whites and Africans

Region and ethnic group	Urbanization$_1$						Urbanization$_2$			
	Population		Living in towns		Non-agricultural employment		Standard 8 education and over[a]		White-collar occupations[b]	
	Number	%	Number	%	Number	%	Number	%	Number	%
Core areas[c]	6 024 117	28.1	5 761 386	56.0	2 432 055	48.1	1 267 169	57.2	778 185	60.1
Whites	2 087 276	9.7	2 045 723	19.9	862 453	17.1	1 035 780	46.8	568 874	43.9
Africans	2 762 104	12.9	2 549 101	24.8	1 192 822	23.6	124 457	5.6	110 628	8.6
Asians and Coloureds	1 174 737	5.5	1 166 562	11.3	376 780	7.4	106 932	4.8	98 682	7.6
Mobilized periphery (rest of white South Africa)	8 859 740	41.3	4 152 318	40.4	2 214 137	43.8	830 777	37.5	433 502	33.5
Whites	1 643 802	7.7	1 201 637	11.7	485 770	9.6	687 236	31.0	297 268	22.9
Africans	5 766 985	26.9	2 089 675	20.3	1 425 028	28.2	85 518	3.9	81 162	6.3
Asians and Coloureds	1 448 953	6.7	861 006	8.4	303 339	6.0	58 023	2.6	55 072	4.3
Unmobilized periphery (homelands)[d]	6 564 312	30.6	366 498	3.6	411 028	8.1	117 032	5.3	83 601	6.5
Whites	20 250	0.1	10 445	0.1	8 407	0.2	9 614	0.4	5 677	0.4
Africans	6 528 863	30.4	350 595	3.4	399 552	7.9	106 539	4.8	76 810	5.9
Asians and Coloureds	15 199	0.1	5 458	0.1	3 069	0.1	879	0.1	1 114	0.1
South Africa	21 448 169	100.0	10 280 202	100.0	5 057 220	100.0	2 214 978	100.0	1 295 288	100.0
Whites	3 751 328	17.5	3 257 805	31.7	1 356 630	26.8	1 732 630	78.2	871 819	67.3
Africans	15 057 952	70.2	4 989 371	48.5	3 017 402	59.7	316 514	14.3	268 800	20.8
Asians and Coloureds	2 638 889	12.3	2 033 026	19.8	683 188	13.5	165 834	7.5	154 869	11.9

[a] Std. 10 = matriculation.
[b] Professional, administrative, clerical, sales.
[c] PWV, south-west Cape, Durban-Pinetown including those urban portions of homelands forming integral parts of the metropolitan areas of Pretoria and Durban-Pinetown.
[d] Homelands less urban portions adjacent to Pretoria and Durban-Pinetown.
Source: Population Census, 1970.

and Utilization of Resources Act of 1967. The proposals for development are contained in the National Physical Development Plan published in 1975 (Fair, 1975) which, in addition to the existing metropolitan areas, designates three planned metropolitan areas, nine growth poles and nineteen principal towns in the mobilized periphery and a number of growth points in and near the African homelands.

The extent of the economic spread effects generally, and the diffusion of modernization to African tribal areas in particular, that these entrepreneurial innovations, both growth-supporting and growth-inducing (Friedmann and Wulff, 1975, p. 22), will generate has yet to be assessed over the long term. Two aspects seem clear, however. First, it is unlikely that development of the homelands can alone absorb their growing numbers of job-seekers. During 1973–1975 the annual average of new work-seekers from the homelands numbered 100 100. Of these 28.4 per cent found employment inside the homelands; 36.8 per cent in white areas, including metropolitan centres, bordering on homelands; and 34.8 per cent were migrant workers in towns, mines, and on farms or remained unemployed (B.E.N.B.O., 1976, p. 105). Secondly, assuming the continuation of existing population growth rates in the major metropolitan areas but enhanced growth rates in the planned growth centres, the former's share of the total South African population will be reduced only from 34.5 per cent to 32.6 per cent over the period 1970–2000.

The flow of African labour to the white areas in general, and to the metropolitan cores in particular, seems destined to continue to have a more advantageous impact on the generation of capital and economic development in these centres than the reverse flow of capital in the form of government and private investment, on the one hand, and the wages of African migrant workers and commuters, on the other, will have upon the socio-economic development of the homelands. But an inability to generate sufficient work opportunities within the homelands to contain their growing populations does not imply government acquiescence in an unfettered flow of Africans to white cities and to white centres of work generally. The obverse of the *apartheid* coin—urban containment—arises directly from established economic trends and is dealt with in the next section.

SUPPRESSION AND CONTAINMENT

The mineral discoveries and the devastation of the Anglo-Boer War had profound effects upon Afrikaner society. One of them was that for many rural dwellers 'the closing of the frontiers of white settlement and the growth of the market economy' meant their relegation to landless rural squatters or unskilled urban workers (Thompson, 1971, p. 339). The 'capitalist penetration' of their semi-subsistent economy, along the lines described by McGee (Friedmann and Wulff, 1975, p. 37) in South-east Asia (McGee, 1971) was accompanied by a failure to respond to the demands for new skills and methods required by the new economic system. By 1931, aggravated by economic depression, there were some

200 000–300 000 'poor whites' in South Africa 'flocking to the towns without any training to fit them for employment in an urban environment, where they found they had to compete as unskilled labourers with Coloured and African workers' (Hobart Houghton, 1971, p. 25). Government response entailed the institution of 'civilized labour' policies and industrial colour-bar legislation which resulted in employment opportunities and relatively high wage rates for whites being more certain in the urban than in the rural areas. Consequently, the 1920s and 1930s witnessed the growth of the white population of South Africa's larger cities less by natural increase than by rural–urban migration, the 'drift to the towns' (Shannon, 1937, p. 165), a process of little significance today, however.

These conditions and the humiliation of defeat in war had generated a powerful nationalist political movement in the early 1900s dedicated to rehabilitating the Afrikaner economically and to regaining major control of the decision-making process. This reassertion of Afrikaner authority was greatly assisted by agreement in 1910 that urban constituencies should have 15 per cent more voters and rural 15 per cent less than average, and the coming into power in 1948 of an Afrikaner nationalist government, undiluted by the coalitions with English-oriented parties that had marked previous governments. Afrikaners, determined to recognize themselves, set out to 'conquer the towns' (Welsh, 1971, p. 207), to eliminate the 'poor white' problem and to develop their own urban entrepreneurial élite. By 1960 the Civil Service was overwhelmingly run by Afrikaners, they had become a predominantly urban people comprising 51 per cent of white males working in towns, and Afrikaans business houses claimed to control 10 per cent of invested capital (Welsh, 1971, p. 208). Moreover, between 1948 and 1974, the nationalist government raised the number of constituencies they controlled in urban areas from 12 to 43, i.e. out of a total at the later date of 82 urban seats in the House of Assembly (Williams, 1976). That Afrikaners no longer eschewed the urban life was contained in a resolution of the Dutch Reformed Churches in 1947 that

> urbanization is a desirable and necessary extension of Afrikaner national life; it is a process which all other civilized nations had to undergo to reach maturity. The Afrikaner must therefore abandon his former negative and hostile attitude to town life . . . he should establish himself in the towns and maintain his own nature and traditions. (Welsh, 1971, p. 208)

Having drastically transformed his own social and economic life, modernized his institutions by migration to the cities and by the diffusion of urban values to rural areas, the Afrikaner, and many of his English-speaking compatriots in earlier governments and opposition parties, nevertheless saw a comparable urbanization of the black man, and the African in particular, largely in uncompromising terms. Before 1870, relations between whites and Africans had been governed mainly by conflict over the ownership and use of land. Industrialization and urbanization on a large scale created entirely new conflicts arising out of physical proximity and competition for jobs (Randall, 1972, p. 53).

Moreover, in withdrawing from South Africa (in 1910) and in failing to resolve the political future of the blacks, 'Great Britain left behind a caste-like society, dominated by its white minority. The price of unity and conciliation was the institutionalization of white supremacy' (Thompson, 1971, p. 364). Thereafter, racial segregation in industrial employment, urban residence, and land owner-ship became the leading principle of government policy (de Kiewiet, 1941, p. 234). Even earlier, i.e. by the turn of the century, it had been 'officially held in most parts of south Africa that urban Africans were not permanent members of urban communities but migrants whose domiciles were in the rural areas' (Welsh, 1971, p. 185). These views were expressly embodied in government and provincial reports in 1921 and 1922, respectively, and the Native (Urban Areas) Act of 1923 affirmed that entry to 'white' towns for the majority of Africans was for employment purposes only (Legassick, 1974, p. 7). As one result, little attempt was made to prepare African migrants for life in a comparatively hostile urban environment. Consequently, not only was there widespread material deprivation, malnutrition, general poverty, and social disorder among Africans in the major urban centres (Jones, 1934; Phillips, 1938); but also there occurred a rapid internal social and economic disorganization of tribal life in the homelands (Schapera, 1934).

After the Second World War, however, the then coalition government of English and Afrikaner parties had, through a growing liberal ideology on the part of some influential leaders and the report of the Native Laws Commission of 1946–1948, come to accept that African urban migration was irreversible, as it had been for whites, and that the reality of a permanent African urban population had to be accepted (quoted in Welsh, 1971, p. 190) and the system of employment control mollified (not abolished).

The report was almost immediately a dead letter for in 1948 the present Afrikaner nationalist government came to power on the *apartheid* issue, a policy committed to the dismemberment of South Africa into a white state and nine politically independent African states or homelands, delimited on ethnic grounds. Total political separation decreed that in the homelands the white ruling élite would be 'replaced' by African counter-élites, and in white areas that Africans would be denied all access to positions of power and so 'suppressed'. But at the census of 1951, 58 per cent of the African population was enumerated in white areas, and of these 48 per cent were in urban areas. The problem remained of how to meet the labour requirements of an expanding national and urban economy and yet to regulate the flow of African workers such that they became neither competitors with whites nor, in urban areas, an overwhelming and potentially dangerous permanent resident majority. In 1951 Africans comprised 44 per cent of South Africa's urban population (whites 38 per cent) and by 1970, 49 per cent (whites 32 per cent). By 1960, whites were in a minority in every South African city (Sabbagh, 1968, p. 16).

As government sees it, there is no problem in those metropolitan areas such as Pretoria, Durban, and East London, and other work areas ('border' industrial areas) which immediately abut upon homelands. Africans travel daily to work as 'international' commuters from homeland residential areas which are economically, but not politically, integral parts of the adjacent work area. In 1975, 557 000 African workers commuted in this way (Smit, 1976). For cities such as Johannesburg, Port Elizabeth, and Cape Town, more distant from homelands, the problem is of another order and calls for strong employment-control measures, i.e. 'influx control' and the reference book ('pass') system, through the Act of 1923 and its amendments and other later legislation (Fair and Davies, 1976).

Thus, only those Africans with comparatively long residence and employment records, and their dependants, are permitted some degree of permanence in urban areas and are entitled to rent, and now to own, family houses in designated 'townships', such as Soweto in Johannesburg. All others who migrate to towns, mainly men, are now employed on one-year contracts, are housed in single-quarter hostels or compounds, and are not permitted to bring their families with them. Instead, the dependants are being housed in homeland towns, many of which are, in fact, dormitory areas with little economic base. African contract workers numbered 1 007 255 in 1970 (B.E.N.B.O., 1976, p. 40), and another 500 000 came from neighbouring countries.

Official policy increasingly encourages the 'migratization' of African labour so that the ideal 'labour unit' is the single, male contract worker 'shuttling back and forth, for one year at a time, between his homeland and his place of work in a white city' (Randall, 1973, p. 36). Wilson (1972, p. 40) estimates that one-half of the African males working in Johannesburg do so on a migratory basis. Consequently, African *population* growth rates in a city such as Johannesburg have declined from 3.3 per cent per year between 1951 and 1960 to 2 per cent between 1960 and 1970 in response to government control measures, whereas *employment* rates of Africans have increased from 0.4 per cent to 3.4 per cent over this twenty-year period. As Wilson (1972, p. 152) has shown, despite 'almost a century of spectacular economic growth' which on normal grounds should have led to a reduction in the amplitude of migrant oscillations, political factors have determined that this does not hold true.

Influx-control measures are aimed at going beyond an attempt merely to contain the *flow* of Africans to cities. Implicitly and explicitly they are also aimed, on the one hand, at reducing the perception of permanence of Africans in urban areas, at engendering insecurity, and at inhibiting urbanization as a modernizing process, and, on the other hand, at encouraging permanent domicile in the developing homelands. This applies to the wide range of urban-dwelling Africans from the more modernized town-rooted (urbanized) to the more traditionally country-rooted (Welsh, 1971, p. 210).

Ideologically, this situation presents no problems to the South African government for all Africans in white urban areas are officially 'temporary sojourners' or guest-workers. Thus, both on a national scale (separate white and African homelands),

policy-governing relationships between the races in South Africa have become increasingly framed within a conflict ideology that postulates that physical, social and cultural differences between peoples of different races are incompatible and that harmonious relations . . . can be secured only by reducing points of contact to a minimum. It follows that the racialized society can be maintained only through coercive organization. (Fair and Davies, 1976, p. 165).

To those who reject this form of social organization the problem is one of 'marginality' and a 'crisis of inclusion' (Friedmann, 1973, p. 106); the challenge to white urban society is one of drawing into the orbit of the established and privileged power structure the excluded sector, particularly the detribalized and landless African no longer able to accept inclusion in the traditional and mainly rural tribal system and yet denied an authoritative place in the white urban system.

If African urbanization—of types 1 and 2—is being constrained in white urban areas, to what extent is it being encouraged in homelands for, as Lombard and van der Merwe (1972, p. 27) indicate, '. . . it seems clear that the major strategies for reversing the economic degeneration threatening many, if not most of the homeland communities, revolve in one way or another around the planning of their urbanisation'? The African tribal areas have no urban tradition yet the urban homeland population has grown from 33 486 (0.8 per cent of the total population) in 1960 to 593 380 (8.3 per cent) in 1970. This has been mainly due to deliberate and substantial government development of towns—seventy-four new towns alone since 1960—and the transference of thousands of Africans from white towns to these new homeland towns, most of which are in fact residential settlements with little or no economic base of their own. But the majority, and certainly the largest of these settlements, are those that have been established in the vicinity of metropolitan areas such as Pretoria, East London, Pietermaritzburg, and Durban, and near industrial towns in adjacent white areas. A third category includes the new administrative capitals (Best and Young, 1972) of the homelands, but, other than these, few urban settlements have been established deep within the homelands. Consequently, there has been a considerable shift in the population of the homelands towards their borders and the growth of settlements that are in effect no more than satellites or dormitory areas of the white towns and cities upon which they are economically dependent (Smit, 1976). Moreover, these settlements in turn have attracted a large squatter population which has exacerbated the population shift to the margins of the homelands. Town-building, concludes Smit, has thus far occurred mainly in order to house Africans who are employed in white areas. Few towns, if any, have a 'natural origin'. Rather are they the result of the implementation of the policy of separate development. Consequently, few of the urban settlements in themselves enjoy a secure economic base. There are large leakages of purchasing power to the adjacent white towns and the development of industries in white 'border' areas has seriously disadvantaged the growth of industry within the homelands themselves (Smit, 1976). Perhaps the main advantage of such urban settlements has been to turn what otherwise would have been migrant workers separated from their families into daily commuters living with their families.

The 'urbanization' of the homelands, however, merely underlines the economic dependence of these areas upon the economy of white South Africa and the role of these 'dormitory satellites' as labour reservoirs for white urban/ industrial South Africa. But the long-term implications of such developments are profound. There are in some ways similarities with the urbanization in the Third World countries in the rich associational life of people with tribal affiliations, the 'ruralization' of these settlements, the growth of the squatter problem, and the informal sector. The present relationship between the African and the European town is, economically at least, colonial. In a coercive social organization, as at present, there is little scope for dynamic change. In an integrative, longer-term organization the possibilities for change are considerable.

CONCLUSION

The analysis thus far has indicated that the development of urbanization$_{1+2}$ in South Africa cannot be divorced from the development of the national spatial system as a whole and that the four major urban processes and patterns apply to core and periphery in a single interacting spatial system. In examining the nature of the interaction, Friedmann (1973, p. 83) has hypothesized that the roles of the urbanization process are such that:

1. In the political organization of space, 'the evolution of spatial structure proceeds from a highly centralized to a polycentric system of decision-making . . .'.
2. In the economic organization of space, 'the evolution of spatial structure proceeds from a highly concentrated pattern in the location of modern economic activities to one that is spatially more deconcentrated'.
3. In the socio-cultural organization of space, 'the evolution of spatial structure proceeds from relatively isolated 'islands of innovation' via major communication corridors to a continuously urbanized$_2$ surface'.
4. In the physical organization of space, 'the evolution of spatial structure proceeds from primacy in urban settlements to a log-normal pattern in the hierarchy of cities'.

In short, it is necessary to ask whether 'emergent innovations' originating in South African cities as 'communication fields' with a high level of 'information exchange', diffuse to the periphery in such a way that the core is a major generator of change, a centre of modernization, and a catalyst of economic growth (McGee, 1971, p. 13). Is there a rough isomorphism of the four patterns giving 'a tent-like urbanization$_{1+2}$ surface falling off at various gradients from major peaks in the system' (Friedmann, 1973, p. 84) such that it represents 'the integration (as defined earlier) of the entire social space at a given point in time'? Does economic (and political and social) development take place within a matrix of urban regions (Friedmann, 1966, p. 28)?

Or, instead, has the history of urbanization in South Africa been one of spatial disintegration? Have its cities been vehicles, first, of external colonization and, after Union in 1910, of internal colonization subjecting regional and national hinterlands and subordinate peoples to political dependence, social backwardness, and economic exploitation? Have, in fact, the urban processes operated such that the organization of space has proceeded from centralized to more balanced structures or has it remained polarized, thus displaying little *development* of the spatial system as a whole?

In a society in which whites constitute 17.5 per cent of the total population yet earn 74 per cent of the income, occupy the upper part of the social and economic pyramid, and wield virtually unrestricted political power, it is unrealistic to assume the existence of a single integrated urbanization$_{1+2}$ surface. Rather, it is necessary to assume two surfaces—an unconstrained white surface and a constrained African, and more generally black, surface. Then, by comparing them, can the disequilibria in the South African spatial system be appreciated

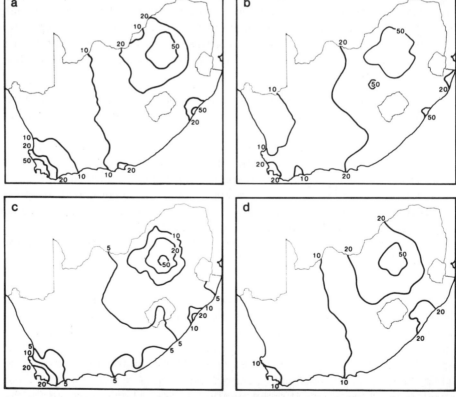

FIGURE 7.3. Urbanization$_1$ surfaces (population potentials for 1970 in thousands of persons per mile): (a) whites: population living in towns; (b) Africans: population living in towns; (c) whites: employees in non-agricultural employment; (d) Africans: employees in non-agricultural employment

and the role of cities be assessed as agents of development, i.e. in reducing unemployment, poverty, and inequality (Seers, 1972, p. 24), and thus reducing underdevelopment.

Table 7.2 and Figures 7.3 and 7.4 attempt a simplified quantitative overview of the essential realities of the South African urbanization$_{1+2}$ surfaces, viewed in terms of its race–class structure and its spatial structure comprising core, mobilized and unmobilized periphery. Comparing only the white (the least constrained) and the African (the most constrained) components of the system, the urbanization$_1$ patterns for the two groups are reasonably isomorphic, i.e. whites and Africans constitute similar proportions of the total numbers living in towns and occupied in non-agricultural employment in both the cores and the periphery, although the African percentage is larger (they constitute 59.7 per cent of South Africa's non-agricultural workforce) and would be larger still in the absence of influx control. However, the isomorphism is more apparent than real since the political and economic power system channels the largely migrant

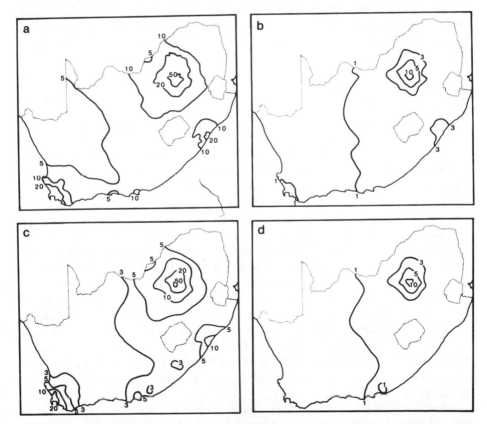

FIGURE 7.4. Urbanization$_2$ surfaces (population potentials for 1970 in thousands of persons per mile): (a) whites: population with Standard 8 education and over; (b) Africans: population with Standard 8 education and over; (c) whites: employees in white-collar occupations; (d) Africans: employees in white-collar occupations

African labour force to those areas where it is required. The observed isomorphism is therefore not one relating to spatial integration in a system where labour is freely mobile, but rather that which results from the regulation of the labour of a subdominant group by a dominant core élite (Fair and Schmidt, 1974, p. 164).

In examining the urbanization$_2$ surface, i.e. the modernization surface, level of education, and employment in white-collar occupations are taken as representative of socio-cultural innovations—education considered as a major instrument of modernization and development, and white-collar employment as a measure of social and economic status actually achieved. For the respective proportion of whites and Africans living in towns, the disparities in level on both these variables are considerable in both the cores and mobilized periphery. The effects upon Africans of the containment of urbanization$_2$ is clearly revealed.

Further disparities emerge. First, internal contradictions exist within the core areas themselves as postulated by McGee for Third World cities (referred to by Slater, 1974, p. 335). Africans are clearly admitted to core areas for the labour they are able to supply (urbanization$_1$), but discouraged from reaching a level of skills commensurate with urbanized$_2$ people. Consequently, the difference in levels of urbanization$_2$ between whites and Africans confirms the dichotomy, typical of colonial and Third World cities, of an élite core and a poor subordinate population 'marginal to the dominant society . . . acted upon but not acting' (Friedmann, 1973, p. 148).

Secondly, the *spatial* disparities in urbanization$_1$ and urbanization$_2$ between core and unmobilized periphery, as illustrated in Figures 7.3 and 7.4, point up the high levels of development in white core areas and low levels in African homelands. In addition to the evidence presented in Table 7.2, the ratio of African to white employment in the predominantly metropolitan and relatively better-paid manufacturing and commercial sectors is 1.8 to 1 and 0.8 to 1 respectively, compared with 9.6 to 1 and 20.0 to 1, respectively, in the predominantly non-metropolitan, rural and relatively less-paid mining and agricultural sectors. This disparity is promoted by government policy so that white social space is becoming increasingly core-oriented and African social space is increasingly periphery-oriented (Fair and Schmidt, 1974, p. 164).

Furthermore, the figures point up that for all the explicit containment of African urbanization$_2$ in core areas, it is in the cores that African modernization is mainly taking place. Thirty-nine per cent and 41 per cent of Africans with high levels of education and in white-collar jobs, respectively, are found in core areas, compared with 33 per cent and 29 per cent of the total in homelands (Table 7.2), despite direct encouragement by government of African advancement in the latter areas.

These disparities or disequilibria indicate that the structure of the South African spatial system is still an unbalanced one as Friedmann and Wulff (1973) hypothesize, and that it cannot be considered integrated in the sense of 'the extension over a given territory of a common basis for social life . . .' (Friedmann, 1973, p. 70). However, a degree of integration as measured by 'the volume of transactions among urban places and regions which leads, in turn, to a complex territorial division of labour' (p. 70) and to 'the assimilation of the periphery into the centre-based market economy' (Slater, 1974, p. 350) is present (1) between core and mobilized periphery by virtue of their organization 'along commercial, capitalistic lines' (Friedmann and Wulff, 1975, p. 20), and (2) between capitalist core and unmobilized periphery, on the other, by virtue of a regulated migrant labour system operating between homelands and white areas.

But socio-political disintegration and economic integration of the type described are really manifestations of a racialization of society affecting practically every facet of South African political, social, and economic life (Fair and Davies, 1976, p. 165). Its explanation lies in Rozman's (Friedmann and Wulff, 1975, p. 15) contention that 'for even pre-industrial societies, it is the distribution of effective political and economic power which, in the end, determines the spatial organization of an urban system and its evolution'. Thus, South Africa's 'race–class-like' society has been maintained by a coercive centralized organization and governed by endless conflict between authoritative ruling élites and dependent counter-élites. The outcomes of this conflict have varied over the past 320 years from neutralization and suppression of Africans (and blacks generally) in the white core areas to peaceful replacement of white power in peripheral homelands. The crucial point in the development process, however, is the resolution of conflict between core and periphery leading to the emergence of deviation-counteracting forces within the spatial system and to peaceful structural transformation (Soja and Weaver, 1976, p. 206). It is clear that in recent years white groups, responding to internal pressures from the black periphery and external pressures from the world core region, have appreciated 'that the point [has been reached] at which transformation of authority-dependency relations in spatial systems [is] imperative for continued development' (Soja and Tobin, 1975, p. 206). How the transformation is to be achieved remains the major point of difference, not only between the main contenders but also between the white élite groups themselves.

Apartheid ideology, linked to the politics of white survival, postulates that 'physical, and social and cultural differences between peoples of different races are incompatible and that harmonious relations between racial groups can be secured only by reducing points of contact to a minimum' (Fair and Davies, 1976, p. 165). The supporting philosophy, it is contended, is one of racial differentiation not discrimination; one of multi-nationalism and separate states and not one of an integrated plural society. But inconsistencies in the approach and the strategy relate, first, to the uncertain political future of Africans in the cores and mobilized periphery, constituting 87 per cent of the land area of South Africa, and which by their labour they have helped develop. Secondly, the creation of viable economic cores in the unmobilized periphery and upon which the welfare and development of homeland Africans depends, is questionable (Schmidt, 1975, p. 490). Nevertheless, Adam (1971, p. 15) asks 'what, apart from naked coercion, enables a society ridden with such deep-seated conflicts to continue to function?' when 'at first sight it displays the classical Marxian prerequisites of a pre-revolutionary situation'. Rather than viewing the *apartheid* system as 'the most outdated relic of a dying colonialism', he sees the key concept in understanding the system and its continuing operation as 'pragmatic oligarchy' (Adam, 1971, p. 16–17), a resolution of conflict largely through a mixture of neutralization and peaceful replacement. The fact that certain African leaders have supported the system, as a means to achieving independence for their homelands, lends some support to this hypothesis.

Alternative strategies of current white opposition groups include the race-federation solutions of the United Party and an accommodation between whites and blacks in a shared society as proposed by the Progressive Reform Party. The latter has developed out of a liberal-reformist ideology, the 'conventional wisdom', propounded since the 1930s by mainly English-speaking groups in and out of Parliament. The belief was that ongoing industrialization would destroy *apartheid* and liberalize race relations, 'that the logical imperatives of industrialization . . . must eventually transcend the irrationality of race discrimination and subject it to the logic of impersonal labour markets, of competition between workers on a basis of industrial aptitude and not of colour' (Yudelman, 1975, p. 82)—in short, that economics will triumph over politics, that the present rigidity and lack of mobility of the class structure will give way to the flexibility and looseness demanded by modern industrial-urbanization (Sjoberg, 1960, p. 110).

Recently these views have been challenged through a critical questioning of conventional interpretations of South African history and the workings of society (Wright, 1977). In essence, the approach (Kallaway, 1975) takes cognizance of the evolution of a political economy and an external and internal colonial relationship in which capitalist core and pre-capitalist periphery are clearly linked through the extraction of cheap labour from the periphery by the core and its appropriation of surplus value. Industrialization is thus seen as an 'illiberal factor causing race discrimination or reinforcing it' and 'as evidence of capitalistic collusion in the South African system' (Yudelman, 1975, p. 82). Moreover, *apartheid* has not developed as a threat to economic growth as the liberal reformists saw it but rather the policy has been designed 'for the specific purpose of perpetuating and indeed promoting the *status quo*' (Kallaway, 1975), i.e. promoting capitalist development, on the one hand, through capital accumulation in core areas and, through influx control, displacing blacks 'to the low-welfare-cost reserves', on the other (Legassick, 1974, p. 21). Moreover, migrant labour has both ensured a cheap, unorganized, and powerless labour force and the undermining of the stability and productive capacity of tribal society. The process is regarded as having commenced in pre-industrial south Africa with the demands made upon African labour by white farmers and intensified with the rise of the mining industry, large-scale commercial farming, and industrial-urbanization producing an 'uneasy union of gold and maize' (Trapido, 1971, p. 311). The outcome of the conflict, it is assumed, is 'open hostility' (Friedmann, 1975, p. 289) as a means towards creating 'a more equitable distribution of the "goods and burdens" of the society' (Kallaway,

1975). Dualistic theories are abandoned and the integrated metropolis–satellite approach of Frank (1967) and internal colonialism are substituted as explanatory frameworks.

The analysis presented in this study supports these more recent approaches to development. In particular it is contended that the processes of urbanization and their spatial manifestations in South Africa may best be viewed in terms of Soja and Weaver's (1976, p. 259) statement, pertaining to East Africa, that 'the process of underdevelopment provides the most comprehensive and persuasive framework for explaining both the present pattern of urbanization . . . and the dynamics of urban change. Underdevelopment is construed as a process not a condition (de Souza and Porter, 1974, p. 40). The evolution of urbanization in South Africa over the past 320 years has in fact been the history of the development of some (not necessarily only whites) and the underdevelopment of others (not necessarily only blacks). For some, development has involved the 'unfolding of the creative possibilities inherent in society' (Friedmann, 1973, p. 45), or 'the movement upward of the entire social system' (Myrdal, 1975, p. 84), most graphically represented in the rehabilitation of Afrikaner society after the Anglo-Boer War. For others, underdevelopment has involved their immiseration in poverty, unemployment (including underemployment), and unequal opportunity (Seers, 1972, p. 24) and the perpetuation of this condition. For some, cities in South Africa have thus been generative, i.e. 'prime movers in developmental change' (Friedmann and Wulff, 1975, p. 35); for others they have been parasitic.

If the developmental role of South African cities has been limited, their potential role is considerable, assuming always that the 'critical urbanization process to which all others are ultimately related' (Friedmann and Wulff, 1975, p. 11), i.e. decision-making and control, can itself be directed towards creative change. Decisions determining the kind and degree of change are, however, not the sole prerogative of the core élite. The relentless pressures from external and internal sources over the past thirty years and the recent unrest in South African cities have prompted some relaxation in the rigidities of the urban system and are indicative of the urban periphery's unwillingness to continue to accept a wholly dependent and submissive role.

REFERENCES

Adam, H. (1971). *Modernizing Racial Domination*, University of California Press, Berkeley and Los Angeles.

Becker, C. J. (1878). *Guide to the Transvaal*, Dollard, Dublin.

BENBO (1976). *Black Development in South Africa*, Bureau for Economic Researcher. Bantu Development (Buro vir Ekonomiese Navorsing insake Bantoe—Ontwikkeling), Pretoria

Best, A. C. G., and Young, B. S. (1972). Capitals of the homelands, *Journal for Geography*, **3**, 1043–1055.

Board, C., Davies, R. J., and Fair, T. J. D. (1970). The South African space economy: an integrated approach. *Regional Studies*, **4**, 367–392.

Bohannan, P. (1964). *Africa and Africans*, Natural History Press, Garden City, New York.

292

Breytenbach, W. J. (1972). *Migratory Labour Arrangements in South Africa*, Africa Institute of South Africa, Pretoria.

Brookfield, H. (1973). On one geography and a third world. *Transactions, Institute of British Geographers*, **58**, 1–20.

Brookfield, H. (1975). *Interdependent Development*, Methuen, London.

Browett, J. G. (1975). The evolution of the South African space economy, unpublished Ph.D. thesis, University of the Witwatersrand.

Bundy, C. (1972). The emergence and decline of a South African peasantry. *African Affairs*, **71**, 369–388.

Cape of Good Hope, (1865). *Census of the Colony*, Solomon.

Christopher, A. J. (1976). *Southern Africa*, Dawson, Folkestone.

Davenport, T. R. H. (1969). The consolidation of a new society: the Cape Colony. In M. Wilson and L. M. Thompson, (Eds.), *The Oxford History of South Africa*, Vol. 1, Claredon Press, Oxford, pp. 272–333.

Davies, R. J. (1972). *The Urban Geography of South Africa*, Institute for Social Research, University of Natal.

Deutsch, K. W. (1961). Social mobilization and political development, *American Political Science Review*, **55**, 493–514.

de Kiewiet, C. W. (1941). *A History of South Africa: Social and Economic*, Clarendon Press, Oxford.

de Souza, A. R., and Porter, P. W. (1974). *The Underdevelopment and Modernization of the Third World*, Association of American Geographers. Washington, D.C.

Fair, T. J. D. (1975). The National Physical Development Plan: a summary and a review. *South African Geographical Journal*, **57**, 126–134.

Fair, T. J. D. (1976). Polarisation, dispersion and decentralisation in the South African space economy. *South African Geographical Journal*, **58**, 40–56.

Fair, T. J. D., and Davies, R. J. (1976). Constrained urbanization: white South Africa and black Africa compared. In B. J. L. Berry (Ed.), *Urbanization and Counterurbanization*, Sage, Beverly Hills and London.

Fair, T. J. D., and Schmidt, C. F. (1974). Contained urbanization: a case study. *South African Geographical Journal*, **56**, 155–166.

Frank, A. G. (1967). *Capitalism and Underdevelopment in Latin America*, Monthly Review Press, New York and London.

Frankel, S. H. (1960). The tyranny of economic paternalism in Africa. *Optima*, **10**, Supplement.

Franklin, N. N. (1948). *Economics in South Africa*, Oxford, Cape Town.

Fried, M. H. (1967). *The Evolution of Political Society: An Essay in Political Anthropology*, Random House, New York.

Friedmann, J. (1966). *Regional Development Policy*, M.I.T. Cambridge, Mass.

Friedmann, J. (1973). *Urbanization, Planning, and National Development*, Sage, Beverly Hills and London.

Friedmann, J. (1975). The spatial organization of power in the development of urban systems. In J. Friedmann and W. Alonso, (Eds.), *Regional Policy*, M.I.T, Cambridge, Mass., pp. 266–304.

Friedmann, J. and Wulff, R. (1975). *The Urban Transition*, Arnold, London.

Goodfellow, D. M. (1931). *A Modern Economic History of South Africa*, Routledge, London.

Gould, P. (1969). *Spatial Diffusion*, Association of American Geographers, Washington, D.C.

Guelke, L. (1976). Frontier settlement in early Dutch South Africa. *Annals of the Association of American Geographers*, **66**, 25–42.

Hobart Houghton, D. (1964). *This South African Economy*, Oxford, Cape Town.

Hobart Houghton, D. (1971). Economic development, 1865–1965. In M. Wilson and L. M. Thompson (Eds.), *The Oxford History of South Africa*, Vol. 2, Clarendon Press, Oxford.

Johnston, R. J. (1977). Regarding urban origins, urbanization and urban patterns. *Geography*, **62**, 1–8.

Jones, J. D. R. (1934). Social and economic conditions of the urban native. In I. Schapera, (Ed.), *Western Civilization and the Natives of South Africa*, Routledge, London, pp. 159–192.

Kallaway, P. (1975). What happened in South African history. *Concept*, **6** (unnumbered), University of Natal.

Katzen, M. F. (1969). White settlers and the origin of a new society, 1652–1778. In M. Wilson and L. M. Thompson (Eds.), *The Oxford History of South Africa*, Vol. 1, Clarendon Press, Oxford, pp. 183–232.

Legassick, M. (1974). Legislation, ideology and economy in post-1948 South Africa. *Journal of Southern African Studies*, **1**, 5–35.

Lombard, J. A., and van der Merwe, P. J. (1972). Central problems of the economic development of Bantu homelands. *Finance and Trade Review*, **10**, 1–46.

McGee, T. G. (1971). *The Urbanization Process in the Third World*, Bell, London.

Mallows, E. W. N. (1968). Some comments on urbanisation in southern Africa. *South African Geographical Journal*, **50**, 3–14.

Marais, J. S. (1961). *The Fall of Kruger's Republic*, Clarendon Press, Oxford.

Myrdal, G. (1975). What is development? *Ekistics*, **237**, 84–87.

Phillips, R. E. (1938). *The Bantu in the City*, Lovedale, Cape Province.

Pollock, N. C., and Agnew, S. (1963). *An Historical Geography of South Africa*, Longman, London.

Randall, P. (1972). *Power, Privilege and Poverty*, SPRO-CAS (The Study Project on Christianity in Apartheid Society), Johannesburg.

Randall, P. (1973). *South Africa's Political Alternatives*, SPRO-CAS (The Study Project on Christianity in Apartheid Society), Johannesburg.

Reissman, L. (1964). *The Urban Process: Cities in Industrial Society*, The Free Press, New York.

Robertson, H. M. (1934). One hundred and fifty years of economic contact between black and white. *South African Journal of Economics*, **2**, 403–425.

Rogerson, C. M. (1974). The geography of business management in South Africa. *South African Geographical Journal*, **56**, 87–93.

Russell, R. (1891). *Natal*, Davis, Pietermaritzburg.

Sabbagh, M. E. (1968). Some geographical characteristics of a plural society: apartheid in South Africa. *Geographical Review*, **58**, 1–28.

Schapera, I. (Ed.) (1934). *Western Civilization and the Natives of South Africa*, Routledge, London.

Schmidt, C. F. (1973). The South African regional system: political independence in an interacting space economy, unpublished Ph.D. thesis, University of South Africa.

Schmidt, C. F. (1975). A spatial model of authority–dependency relations in South Africa. *Journal of Modern African Studies*, **13**, 483–490.

Seers, D. (1972). What are we trying to measure? *Journal of Development Studies*, **8**, 21–36.

Shannon, H. A. (1937). Urbanization, 1904–1936. *South African Journal of Economics*, **5**, 164–242.

Silver, S. W. and Co. (1876). *Handbook to South Africa*, Silver, London.

Sjoberg, G. (1960). *The Pre-Industrial City*, Collier-Macmillan, London.

Slater, D. (1974). Contribution to a critique of development geography, *Canadian Journal of African Studies*, **8**, 325–354.

Slater, D. (1975). Underdevelopment and spatial inequality. *Progress in Planning*, **4**, 97–167.

Smit, P. (1976). Mobiliteit en verstedeliking in die tuislande: unieke beplanningsuitdagings. *Beplanning*, **10**, 41–66.

Soja, E. W. (1971). *The Political Organization of Space*, Association of American Geographers, Washington, D.C.

294

Soja, E. W., and Tobin, R. J. (1975). The geography of modernization: paths, patterns and processes of spatial change in developing countries. In G. D. Brewer and R. D. Brunner (Eds.), *Political Development and Change: A Policy Approach*, The Free Press, New York.

Soja, E. W. and Weaver, C. E. (1976). Urbanization and underdevelopment in East Africa. In B. J. L. Berry, (Ed.), *Urbanization and Counterurbanization*, Sage, London, pp. 197–243.

South Africa (1946). *The Native Reserves and their Place in the Economy of the Union of South Africa*, Report No. 9, Social and Economic Planning Council, U.G. 32.

South Africa (1955). *Report of the Commission for the Socio-economic Development of the Bantu Areas within the Union of South Africa* (Tomlinson Commission), Government Printer, Cape Town and Pretoria.

Thompson, L. M. (1969a). Co-operation and conflict: the high veld. In M. Wilson and L. M. Thompson (Eds.), *The Oxford History of South Africa*, Vol. 1, Clarendon Press, Oxford, pp. 391–446

Thompson, L. M. (1969b). Co-operation and conflict: the Zulu kingdom and Natal. In M. Wilson and L. M. Thompson (Eds.), *The Oxford History of South Africa*, Vol. 1, Clarendon Press, Oxford, pp. 334–390.

Thompson, L. M. (1971). The compromise of Union. In M. Wilson and L. M. Thompson (Eds.), *The Oxford History of South Africa*, Vol. 2, Clarendon Press, Oxford, pp. 323–364.

Trapido, S. (1971). South Africa in a comparative study of industrialization. *Journal of Development Studies*, **7**, 309–319.

Welsh, D. (1971). The growth of towns. In M. Wilson and L. M. Thompson (Eds.), *The Oxford History of South Africa*, Vol. 2, Clarendon Press, Oxford, pp. 172–243.

Williams, O. (1976). Political attitudes and voting behaviour. In A. Lemon (Ed.), *Apartheid: A Geography of Separation*, Saxon House, Farnborough.

Wilson, F. (1972). *Migrant Labour in South Africa*, S.A. Council of Churches and SPRO-CAS., Johannesburg.

Wilson, M. (1969). The Nguni people. In M. Wilson and L. M. Thompson (Eds.), *The Oxford History of South Africa*, Vol. 1, Clarendon Press, Oxford, pp. 75–130.

Wright, H. M. (1977). *The Burden of the Present*, David Philip, Claremont, Cape Province.

Yudelman, D. (1975). Industrialization, race relations and change in South Africa. *African Affairs*, **74**, 82–96.

Index

Page numbers in italics refer to maps and diagrams.